Imperial Educación

New World Studies
Marlene L. Daut, Editor

Imperial Educación

RACE AND REPUBLICAN
MOTHERHOOD IN THE
NINETEENTH-CENTURY AMERICAS

Thomas Genova

University of Virginia Press
Charlottesville and London

University of Virginia Press
© 2021 by the Rector and Visitors of the University of Virginia
All rights reserved
Printed in the United States of America on acid-free paper

First published 2021

9 8 7 6 5 4 3 2 1

Library of Congress Cataloging-in-Publication Data
Names: Genova, Thomas, author.
Title: Imperial educación : race and republican motherhood in the nineteenth-century Americas / Thomas Genova.
Description: Charlottesville : University of Virginia Press, 2021 | Series: New World studies | Includes bibliographical references and index.
Identifiers: LCCN 2021001158 (print) | LCCN 2021001159 (ebook) | ISBN 9780813946238 (hardcover) | ISBN 9780813946245 (paperback) | ISBN 9780813946252 (epub)
Subjects: LCSH: Motherhood—America—History—19th century. | Racially mixed people—America—History—19th century. | Education—America—History—19th century.
Classification: LCC HQ759 .G463 2021 (print) | LCC HQ759 (ebook) | DDC 306.874/309709034—dc23
LC record available at https://lccn.loc.gov/2021001158
LC ebook record available at https://lccn.loc.gov/2021001159

Cover art: Spaniard and Return Backwards, Hold Yourself Suspended in Mid Air (De español y torna atrás, tente en el aire), Juan Patricio X. Morlete Ruiz, circa 1760. Oil on canvas, 41 5/16 × 49 5/8. (Digital image © 2021 Museum Associates/Los Angeles County Museum of Art; licensed by Art Resource, NY)

Contents

	Preface	vii
	Introduction	1
1.	Republican Motherhood and Citizen Educación	25
2.	Mothers, Moors, Mohicans, and Mulattas in Mansilla's *Miranda*	48
3.	Una Maestra Norteamericana in the "South"	88
4.	Foundational Frustrations in Cirilo Villaverde, Mary Mann, and Martín Morúa Delgado	122
5.	"La Dignidad de la Mujer Cubana": Racialized Gender Allegory and the *Intervención Americana*	174
	Conclusion	207
	Notes	223
	Bibliography	273
	Index	317

Preface

THOMAS JEFFERSON'S October 28, 1813, letter to John Adams on "natural aristocracy" often is regarded as a foundational articulation of US republican values.[1] Though generations of schoolchildren have studied Jefferson's juxtaposition of the "natural aristocracy among men" grounded in "virtue and talents" with the "artificial aristocracy founded on wealth and birth," fewer have read the document in its entirety. Mundanely enough, these lofty democratic ideals first appear as part of a discussion on animal husbandry and the best means of breeding a superior stock. The letter begins with a comment on a passage from Theognis, the ancient Greek defender of hereditary aristocracy, which "seems to be a reproof to man, who, while in his domestic animals he is curious to improve the race by employing always the finest male, pays no attention to the improvement of his own race, but intermarries with the vicious, the ugly, or the old, for considerations of wealth and ambition." Jefferson laments that, in Europe, "the commerce of love" has been "made subservient . . . to wealth and ambition by marriages without regard to the beauty, the healthiness, the understanding, or the virtue of the subject from which we are to breed." Instead of marriages of convenience, Jefferson advocates "the selecting of the best male for a Haram of well chosen females . . . , which Theognis seems to recommend from the example of our sheep and asses." This "would doubtless improve the human, as it does the brute animal, and produce a race of veritable aristoi. For experience proves that the moral and physical qualities of man, whether good or evil, are transmissible in a certain degree from father to son." Seeking to forge a "race of veritable aristoi," Jefferson paradoxically rejects the principle of lineage while retaining that of heredity.

Jefferson's egalitarian devaluation of rank based on birth, then, responds (somewhat counterintuitively) to the author's preoccupation with the breeding of a new elite, the best "race" to govern the republic. The word "race," of course, was much more polysemic in Jefferson's time than it is in our own. In the various western European languages in which the Virginian was fluent, it encompassed everything from the socially meaningful biological fiction of geographically determined differences in human heredity to nationality to feudal caste to family lines, to breeds of animals.[2] From the context, it seems that Jefferson is referring to the British titled aristocracy (which he sees as morally debased), yet the polysemous term inevitably invokes all its interrelated meanings, which were not entirely differentiated from one another in the early nineteenth century. Whatever the exact nuance that "race" held in the polyglot Jefferson's mind, his comments on selection and intergenerational transfer of inherited traits in the breeding of republican rulers demonstrate that the third president conceived of the national body in limited hereditary terms, rerouting family bloodlines—the constitutive metaphor of the monarchical system that the United States had just overthrown—through the republican national project.

For a contemporary audience, it is difficult to read of the Virginian's racialized concern for the "subject from which we are to breed" and not think wincingly of his now-notorious sexual relationship with Sally Hemings. An enslaved woman of mixed race, Hemmings would serve as nursemaid to Jefferson's children by his deceased wife, Martha Wayles Jefferson (who was also her half sister), while giving birth to six of the statesman's children. How did "race" affect the breeding of a republican citizenry in that situation? How did Jefferson feel about his enslaved Afro-descended mistress raising the race of natural aristocrats that he and his white wife had produced? Could his children by Hemings join the ranks of this republican aristocracy?[3]

Though uncomfortable, the question is valid. Reformers throughout the nineteenth-century Americas voiced concerns regarding the negative influence that lower-class servants might exert over the moral development of bourgeois children, a discourse that New World thinkers racialized.[4] Jefferson, for his part, believed that the proper formation of children's minds was necessary for the creation of his republican natural aristocracy. Later in the letter from which I have been quoting, he comments on a failed bill in the Virginia legislature that would have "laid the axe to the root of Psuedaristocracy":

> This [law] proposed to divide every county into wards . . . ; to establish in each ward a free school for reading, writing, and common arithmetic; to provide for

the annual selection of the best subjects from these schools who might receive at the public expense a higher education at the district school; and from these district schools to select a certain number of the most promising subjects to be compleated at an University, where all the useful sciences should be taught. Worth and genius would thus have been sought out from every condition of life, and compleately prepared by education for defeating the competition of wealth and birth for public trusts.[5]

For Jefferson, then, not only must republican citizens be produced by "selecting the best male for a Haram of well chosen females"; they must be carefully educated to assume the responsibilities conferred upon them by the new political form.

Imperial Educación explores the place of mixed-race mothers such as Sally Hemings—painfully present through her egregious absence in Jefferson's foundational text—in the national projects of the nineteenth-century Americas. What does it mean that republican citizenship as articulated in Jefferson's notion of natural aristocracy—a foundational formulation with which thinkers across the Americas would have to dialogue as the United States rose to imperial prominence—is predicated on the exclusion of Afro-descended mothers? Why does Jefferson discuss racially selective breeding and public education in the same letter, as though the subjects were related? How does the Jefferson-Wayles-Hemings family drama reflect deeper tensions over race, gender, child-rearing, and citizenship in national families throughout the early New World republics?

I have accrued so many debts in the process of writing this book that I neither know where to begin nor where to end. I am also terrified at the inevitable prospect of leaving someone out, for which I apologize beforehand. What follows is an inadequate list of people and institutions to whom I offer inadequate thanks.

I will begin with material conditions of possibility. I would like to thank the Graduate Division at the University of California, Santa Cruz, for funding my early explorations into inter-American studies. The University of Minnesota system enjoys a privileged research infrastructure at a time when such resources are, unfortunately, becoming a privilege. My trinational project has been funded by several grants from the University of Minnesota Imagine Fund and Grant-in-Aid of Research, Artistry, and Scholarship program, as well as the Faculty Research Enhancement Fund on the Morris campus. I am grateful to the grant reviewers not only for believing in this project when it was in a much more inchoate form but for the valuable feedback that they provided. Equally crucial have been the current and former staff of our campus Grants Development Office: John Hamerlinck, Alisande Allaben, and Roger Wareham, who have always been available for consultations great and small. A travel grant from the Upper Midwest Latin American Studies Initiative at the University of Wisconsin–Madison Latin American, Caribbean, and Iberian Studies Program rescued me and made attendance at a particularly important meeting of the Latin American Studies Association possible when I managed to exhaust my university travel budget.

Librarians, too, have proven instrumental to completing this project. At the University of Minnesota Morris Rodney A. Briggs Library, LeAnn Dean and Peter Bremer have aided me in the search for sources and information while the indefatigable interlibrary loan manager Sandy Kill has tracked down obscure texts from remote corners of the world with a speed that often has left me speechless. Beyond Minnesota, Morgan Gwenwald, head of special collections at the Sojourner Truth Library at the State University of New York at New Paltz kindly sent me PDFs of archival materials. The Cuban Heritage Collection at the University of Miami is a treasure for both researchers and the community, and its sponsors and staff are to be commended for the work that they do.

I would like to express particular gratitude to the archivists and librarians who supported me in Argentina and Cuba. In Buenos Aires, I would like to thank Adriana DuMuro, archivist at the Museo Histórico Sarmiento, who patiently helped me to navigate the museum's extensive documentary holdings and even taught me how to use a microfilm reader. The librarians at the Biblioteca Nacional de Maestros were as warm as they were helpful. In Havana, I enjoyed the support of the staff of the Biblioteca Nacional José Martí. In particular, I would like to offer thanks to the specialists in the Sala Cubana (too numerous to name) for helping me to find materials over my winter breaks, when they really should have been celebrating the new year. Downstairs, my *tocayo* Tomás was able to point me directly to sources I didn't know I needed at a moment when time was crucial. With equal generosity, the staff at the Instituto de Literatura y Lingüística José Antonio Portuondo Valdor facilitated my access to rare periodicals one unfathomably warm December.

As a student, I had the privilege of studying with the forward-thinking faculty of the Graduate Division of the University of California, Santa Cruz, whose transnational, transdisciplinary approach to humanistic and social-scientific knowledge should be a model for us all. Norma Klahn is a paragon of scholarly depth and breadth that few of us can hope to emulate. As an adviser, she went beyond all reasonable expectations—and surpassed many unreasonable ones as well. Along with her husband, Guillermo, she continues to provide mentorship long after I should probably be able to handle things on my own. Readers Lourdes Martínez-Echazábal and Susan Gillman were always available to talk and to challenge me when I was too complacent in my thinking. Graduate seminars offered by Kirsten Silva Gruesz, Juan Poblete, and Vilashini Coopan in Literature and Catherine Ramírez (Latin American and Latino Studies) and Megan Thomas (Politics) proved important for developing the theoretical and methodological frameworks of this book. Eve Zyzik and María Victoria González Pagani, meanwhile, are not only innovative and involved teachers, but generous individuals. Vicqui and her husband George were kind enough to house me during a research stay in Buenos Aires, an act of generosity that will not soon be forgotten.

I could not ask for more supportive colleagues than the ones I have at the University of Minnesota Morris. Spanish Discipline members Stacey Parker Aronson; Adam Coon; Windy González-Roberts; Mary Thrond; James Wojtaszek; and, formerly, Ana Cecilia Iraheta, have created a dynamic and collaborative community in which it is a joy to work. I will always be grateful to the late Vicente Cabrera Funes for chairing the committee that hired me for my first academic position. To these names I add those of Arne Kildegaard, Benjamín Narváez, and Cristina Ortiz, my colleagues in Latin American Area Studies and endless sources of intriguing conversation.

Former and current deans Bart Finzel and Janet Schrunk Ericksen have proven tireless supporters of their faculty's professional goals. The same can be said of former and current Humanities Division chairs Pieranna Garavaso and Stacey Parker Aronson. One could not ask for a stronger advocate for faculty research than Pieranna, while Stacey deserves special commendation for helping a recent graduate and coastal transplant adjust to a new institutional and regional culture. I would like to thank Bradley Deane for his efforts in the faculty mentoring program and former assistant division chairs Julie Eckerle and Julia Dabbs for their support of a new faculty member. Tammy Berberi and Argie Manolis have done much for my sanity during our participation in the Morris Intercultural Education Initiative. Jayne Hacker, Makiko Legate, and Cindy Poppe of the Humanities Division staff are always ready to assist with any request, no matter how burdensome—most recently, in helping me to print my manuscript in the middle of a pandemic-prompted closure. I had the good fortune to be in residence at the University of Minnesota Institute for Advanced Study as I began revising this book, and Jennifer Gunn, Susannah Smith, and my cohort of fellow residents provided intellectual stimulation and moral encouragement at a time that might otherwise have proven unduly stressful. To my students, who have never once complained about being a captive audience to my ravings about race in the Americas—and treated the subject with substantially more maturity than many figures in the public sphere—I express endless gratitude.

Stacey Aronson, Adam Coon, and Cristina Ortiz of Minnesota Morris generously read earlier drafts of sections of this book and offered invaluable feedback. In the broader field, Anne Fountain, Leslie Bary, and William Katra, knowledgeable and encouraging interlocuters, have provided more support over the years than I know how to explain. An earlier draft of the *Cecilia Valdés* section in chapter 4 appeared in *Decimonónica*.

I hope that the University of Virginia Press will allow me to express my appreciation for their patient and professional handling of my manuscript. In particular, I would like to extend my thanks to editor in chief Eric Brandt and acquisitions assistant Helen Chandler for their efforts in bringing this project to fruition. Current series editor Marlene Daut provided encouragement at a time when it was needed, as did the previous editor, the late J. Michael Dash, whose work has been an inspiration to many of us. I also wish humbly to thank my anonymous peer reviewers, who saved me from myself in more than one instance. All remaining errors are, of course, my own.

Finally, let me thank friends, academics and nonacademics alike, in the United States and abroad, for putting up with me and for their ability to talk about things other than my research. Inexpressible gratitude is owed to members of the Genova, Paucar Espinoza, and Genova-Paucar families, living and deceased, for emotional support, as well as food and shelter over the years. Particular thanks to Lupe, who has lived with this project at least as intensely as I have, and to our infant daughter, who will remember none of this when she is older.

Imperial Educación

Introduction

IMPERIAL EDUCACIÓN: Race and Republican Motherhood in the Nineteenth-Century Americas asks how the allegory of the national family—omnipresent in the nationalist discourses of the Americas—reconciles itself to the race hierarchies upon which New World slave and postslavery societies are built. The book analyzes representations of Afro-descended mothers in the United States, Argentina, and Cuba during an era in which governing elites were invested in reproducing bourgeois-republican values—culturally coded as white—in their countries' citizens. Throughout the long nineteenth century, literary texts from these three countries would question the capacity of Afro-descended women to raise good republican citizens for the New World nation-states. Absorbing that discourse and concerned about the fate of their nations' future citizens in the hands of mothers of color, Latin American reformers would invite white women from the United States to train teachers as replacements for their countries' supposedly unfit mothers. Over the course of the nineteenth century, these transnational entanglements of US imperialism and creole neocolonialism through the figure of the republican teacher-mother would contribute to the development of the balance of power in the Western Hemisphere.

Public education represents a rich though underexplored field for considering the interrelationships among race, gender, and ideological soft imperialism in the Americas. Mobilized en masse in the Reconstruction-era United States, maternal white teachers soon were deployed to disseminate northern values among the children of racialized "southern" populations in other areas of the Americas. This helped to create a hemispheric regime of race and gender serving the political-economic interests of the northeastern United States. Yet, far from an outright imposition, the northeastern bourgeoisie collaborated with local elites in Argentina and Cuba. How and why the Argentine and Cuban ruling classes engaged US imperial processes through the figure of the white teacher-mother will be the subject of this book.

Educación

From the writings of the hemisphere's earliest republican thinkers on, public schools in the Americas have been recognized as a form of institutionalized child-rearing, a technology for manufacturing national citizens out of colonial subjects. Venezuelan philosopher Simón Rodríguez—who, at one point, served as tutor to South American Liberator Simón Bolívar—advocated for the Spanish American republics to "colonize the country with its own inhabitants and, in order to have decent colonists, instruct them during childhood" (*Luces y virtudes sociales* 186).[1] This instruction is necessary because "ignorance of social principles is the cause of all the evils that man does to himself and to others" ("Extracto sucinto de mi obra sobre la educación republicana" 281).[2] For Rodríguez, "teaching is a profession that replaces parents [and] fulfills the functions of a common parent," not only providing basic instruction, but also guiding children in their moral development into virtuous republican citizens ("Consejos de amigo dados al Colegio Nacional de Latacunga" 260).[3] Cuban reformer Domingo del Monte displays a similar understanding of the social functions of education in his "Informe sobre el estado actual de la enseñanza en la Isla de Cuba en 1836, su costo y mejoras de que es susceptible" (Report on the current state of education on the island of Cuba in 1836, its costs, and the improvements to which it is susceptible), which seeks to determine "the level of enlightenment and morality" in Havana, not questioning what one would have to do with the other ("Informe" pt. 2, 267).[4]

The slippage between parents and teachers found in Rodríguez's text, and that between upbringing and instruction in del Monte's comments, is made possible by the polysemic nature of the Spanish word *educación*. Derived from the Latin verb *educere,* "to lead forth," educación refers to both formal instruction (the Platonic leading of the mind out of darkness through the bringing out of hidden truth) and the raising of children (the leading of youth into maturity). The *Diccionario de la Real Academia Española* defines "educación" as

1. Acción y efecto de educar.
2. f. Crianza, enseñanza y doctrina que se da a los niños y a los jóvenes.

3. f. Instrucción por medio de la acción docente.
4. f. Cortesía, urbanidad.

(1. The act and effect of educating.
2. The raising or breeding, teaching, and doctrine given to children and young people.
3. Instruction given through teaching.
4. Courtesy, etiquette.)[5]

Significantly, the Royal Academy of the Spanish Language lists "raising" before "instruction" when defining "educación," indicating the greater importance of the former to the word's meaning.

Operating within this Hispanic linguistic and cultural framework, late-nineteenth-century Cuban pedagogue Luis A. Baralt draws a distinction between "educación" and the not-quite-synonymous term "instrucción":

> Instruction, that is, the acquisition of knowledge, is no more than half of Educación. The other half is culture, I mean, the cultivation caused by the unleashing of our full faculties. This and nothing else is meant by the word *educación,* which, derived from Latin, most clearly says that the point is not to impart ideas or to inculcate knowledge, but to bring out what is within the student, developing through exercise the seeds that lay dormant in his mind, changing into fact that which before only existed as possibility and potential. (Baralt 89)[6]

For Baralt, the republican project demands that children be "cultivated"—that is, grown or raised—in virtue. An 1875 Havana newspaper article by Julián López Condeal voices similar opinions, explaining that "education prepares the individual for perfection, it develops and strengthens his faculties, smooths his instincts, directs his passions, moderates his disordered impulses towards self-sacrifice as a gift to his fellow man."[7] Instruction, meanwhile, "teaches man certain things, it gives him ability and talents. It opens his eyes to the great book of nature, penetrating its secrets and disseminating them in science, art, professions, and jobs. It transforms the raw materials that the earth provides into useful objects."[8] He summarizes:

> Educación prepares man for the fulfillment of his duties and instruction shows him what these might be. Educación inspires in him the desire to be useful to his fellow man and instruction provides the means of attaining this desire. Educación gives birth in the soul to thoughts of the love of God and instruction

clears the path by which this Supreme Being is to arrive, providing man with resources to honor Him and revere Him as He deserves, putting into practice that love that was made to be born in his soul by the first spark of educación.[9]

This understanding of "educación" in ethical terms prevailed throughout the nineteenth-century Americas. Argentine intellectual and *salonnière* Mariquita Sánchez de Thompson, for example, felt that "instruction superior to one's means of existence or social class could be dangerous if it is not accompanied by educación," postulating educación as the moral guarantor of democratic instruction (qtd. in Batticuore 95).[10] Later, in 1884, minister of justice, religion, and public instruction Eduardo Wilde would echo the Cubans López Condeal and Baralt when he specified that "instruction refers to intellectual culture; education, to the molding of character" (Wilde, *Memoria 1884* 1:178).[11] Similarly, John Stearns, a North American educator working at Argentina's Escuela Normal de Tucumán, would insist on the school's role in forming a student's character and instilling "the principles of righteous living into the student's soul," which he held to be at least as important as "intellectual culture" (613).[12] The prioritization of "righteous living" and "a proper life" over "intellectual culture" practiced by Stearns reflects an understanding of educación as an ideological state apparatus for inculcating bourgeois-republican values.

This emphasis on values as fundamental to educación, in turn, would lead to the rise of the ideology of "republican motherhood," or the raising of children for bourgeois-republican citizenship, in the nineteenth-century Americas. As feminist scholar V. Spike Peterson explains, "under heteropatriarchal conditions," women hold the "primary responsibility for inculcating beliefs, behaviors, and loyalties that are culturally appropriate and ensure inter-generational continuity. This cultural transmission includes learning the 'mother' tongue—the codified meaning system—as well as the group's identity, symbols, rituals, divisions of labor, and worldviews" (66). Recognizing the primordial role of maternity in nation building, policy makers across the hemisphere began to promote a vision of the patriarchal family supported by "the mother-child relationship, featuring a mother-housewife with moral power over her husband and child, a child that would acquire capital importance for society, the State, and the 'race,' and to whose care and upbringing the mother's life was dedicated" (Nari 63).[13]

Influenced by the dual meaning of "educación" and the republican motherhood construct, nineteenth-century liberal reformers would resituate the traditionally patriarchal role of teacher within the feminine maternal sphere, reconceiving teaching "as a form of reproductive labor essential to a republic" (Leroux, "Money" 191).[14] An 1830 article in the Cuban magazine *La moda, o, recreo semanal del bello sexo* (Fashion, or the weekly recreation of the fair sex), for example, offers "gratitude and recognition from the children of the grandchildren of those women whose instruction is owed to the tireless labors" ("Exámen de niñas" 406) of the headmistress of a Havana girls' school, casting the female schoolteacher as the matriarch of an accomplished family.[15] Similarly, working as an educational administrator in Cuba during the 1898–1902 US occupation, Esteban Borrero Echeverría would ask prospective teachers to explain the popular saying "Lo que con la leche no se mama, en la mortaja se derrama" (What doesn't get drunk in with the milk gets dribbled out on the burial shroud), stressing the new maternal vision of teaching through the metaphor of lactation ("Cuestionario pedagógico" 72). This discourse thus transfigures the female schoolteacher into mother of the nation.

In the United States, meanwhile, pedagogue Horace Mann drew on the ideas of his compatriot Catherine Beecher to discursively collapse the figures of teacher and mother, writing "that woman should be the educator of children [is] as much a requirement of nature as that she should be the mother of children" (*Report* 82). He cites "the greater intensity of the parental instinct in the female sex, their natural love of the society of children, and the superior gentleness and forbearance of their dispositions,—all of which lend them to mildness rather than severity, to the use of hope rather than of fear as a motive of action, and to the various arts of encouragement rather than to annoyances and compulsion, in their management of the young" as evidence for this belief (173). Arguing the potential usefulness of women's supposedly innate maternal qualities in the classroom, Mann transforms the female teacher into the metaphorical mother of her students. As a result of this engagement with the "cult of domesticity" by Mann and like-minded US pedagogues, teaching came to be seen as the "'true' profession of unmarried women" and was "converted from a stopgap choice for men to a profession for well-educated women" (Chevigny 142).[16]

Unlike the United States, where Beecher and the Manns worked to feminize the teaching force, in Argentina, education was "born" as a feminine profession (Morgade, "El determinante" 35) meant to take advantage of a supposedly "privileged sensibility" that rendered women "particularly apt for educational tasks" (Lojo, Introduction 27).[17] Bernardino Rivadavia, for example, would justify his plan for a girls' boarding school run by upper-class matrons by citing "women's civilizing influence" (Batticuore

184).[18] Enjoying few opportunities for remunerated labor, "women were gaining a claim to the role of children's educator, which indeed did not contradict the ideal of the home-bound woman, since the primary school was viewed as an extension of the home and the teacher as a kind of super-mother" (Frederick, *Wily Modesty* 49).[19] Minister of public instruction Onésimo Leguizamón carries the idea further in his October 14, 1875, "Circular a los Gobernadores de Provincias sobre el establecimiento de Escuelas Normales para maestras en la capital de cada Provincia que lo solicite" (Circular to the Governors of the Provinces on the establishment of Normal Schools for female teachers in the capital of any Province that should ask for one), in which he claims that "by giving the guidance of children to educated [*educada*] and moral women, the Argentine pueblo can rightly [say] that it has entrusted mothers with the most august of labors, that of forming the heart and understanding of the coming generations" (208).[20] Not content simply to note the maternal aspects of teaching, Leguizamón claims that, as supposedly feminine vocations, motherhood and teaching are one and the same. Principal of the Colegio Nacional de Uruguay J. B. Zubiar would crystalize this logic a few years later, writing that "no institution prepares . . . mothers better than the Normal School, which seeks to train teachers, because every mother should be a teacher, just like every woman should have a mother's skills, as she is the axis of the home" (Zubiar 61).[21]

Though, at first glance, it may seem a mere tropological trick, the discourse of the teacher as republican mother would have a lasting impact on Argentine educational culture. In 1934, former student Raquel Camaña, praising her teacher at the Escuela Normal de San Juan, would exclaim that "there she trained us to be teachers, there she trained us to be mothers, there she trained us to be women" (qtd. in Chavarria 374).[22] In the same year, director of the Instituto Nacional del Profesorado Secundario (director of the National Institute of Secondary-School Teachers) Roberto Escobar would speak naturally of the "mother school" (Escobar 195) and as late as 1947, Juan Manuel Chavarria in his *La escuela normal y la cultura argentina* would refer to the decree creating the normal schools as the "the mother law of Argentine culture" (353).[23] Tellingly, Sara Figueroa's 1934 *Escuela Normal de Paraná* opens with a poem by former student Guillermo Saraví:

> Si volviese a tus claustros bien amados un día,
> —Aunque al fin nos hubiéramos transformado los dos—
> Tu corazón de madre me reconocería

Y por mi labio un hondo cariño te diría:
Creo en ti, madre mía; creo en ti como creo en Dios!

(If I were to return one day to your beloved cloisters,
—Even if we both finally were changed—
Your mother's heart would recognize me
And from my lips a deep love would say to you:
I believe in you, mother of mine; I believe in you as I believe in God!)

Dedicated to "my former teacher[,] Srta. Sara Figueroa," the poem postulates the teacher as the "madre mía" in whom the speaker so fervently believes.[24]

Yet, much as, as I discussed in the preface, mixed-race mother Sally Hemings haunts Jefferson's discussion of the education of a natural aristocracy, reformers throughout the Americas would define the maternal teacher construct racially. Cuban policy makers, for example, insisted that only white women—preferably those trained in the United States—teach the country's mixed-race popular classes. In the US South, meanwhile, the freedmen's schools supposedly organized by Euro-American New England women after the Civil War would serve a similar function. Argentina would prove the most extreme example of the triad, importing Anglo-Saxon teachers (thought to be whiter than Latin whites, also known as "creoles") from the United States to educate the country's mestizo masses.

Argentina, Cuba, and Imperial Entanglements of Educación

Imperial Educación examines how literary and educational discourses on race and maternity worked together to establish the balance of power among the United States, Argentina, and Cuba during the nineteenth century. The book considers how the two Latin American countries became entangled with the United States—and, through the United States, with one another—specifically in the field of public educación. In Argentina, the traditional narrative of national generation through educational reform centers largely on the labors of statesman and pedagogue Domingo Faustino Sarmiento. Said to be the "author of a nation," Sarmiento sought to replace the feudal legacy of Hispanic dynasticism with capitalist economics and republican rule of law (Halperín Donghi et al.). Though widely held to be a "Europeanizer," Sarmiento looked to mirror the political and pecuniary success of the Jacksonian United States that he saw reflected in the national-allegorical family romances of writer James Fenimore Cooper. This meant adopting the northern country's peculiar mixture of racially exclusive settler-colonialist nationalism and economically inclusive public education. Inspired in part by the Reconstruction-era migration of New England women to the US South in order to teach the freedmen, Sarmiento and other liberal reformers would use racialized familial language as they encouraged North American female schoolteachers to immigrate to their country in an effort to whiten the population by "raising" the nation's children according to Anglo-Saxon paradigms of bourgeois modernity.

These inter-American cultural dynamics, in turn, would have an impact on the developing balance of power in the hemisphere during the late nineteenth and early twentieth centuries. A few years after the *maestras de Sarmiento* began arriving in Argentina, Cuban writers such as the creole Cirilo Villaverde and the Afro-Cuban Martín Morúa Delgado, through the figure of the mixed-race *mulata* mother, also were using familial language in their efforts to break free of Spanish colonialism and found a multiracial republic. This movement was complicated by the military intervention of the United States, which was rising to imperial power in the decades following its experiments in the Southern Cone (Argentina, Chile, Paraguay, and Uruguay). During the 1898–1902 US occupation of Cuba, the imperial government attempted to leverage the experience in cultural influence over Latin America gained through the Argentine teachers' project in a more direct fashion. This included sending a group of northern educators who previously had worked in Argentina to New York to open a special normal school designed to impart proper republican values to a cohort of racialized Cuban women, former Spanish subjects imagined as future teachers and mothers of the neocolonial Caribbean nation.[25]

In tracing this entangled history of the republican teacher-mother construct as it circulates through the hemisphere, *Imperial Educación* explores how two very different Latin American countries—the modernizing, sovereign Argentina and the colonial Cuba—use the racialized allegory of the national family to negotiate their positions on the world stage in light of deepening North American hegemony in the region.[26] The result of a steady increase in the northern power's economic and political influence over the course of the nineteenth century, fin-de-siècle Cuba's colonial relationship with the United States, historians contend, would have a far-reaching impact on the island's revolution two generations later. Argentina, on the other hand, would leverage the United States' cultural and ideological influence critically against the wreckage of its mid-nineteenth-century civil wars to achieve, for a time, the world's highest per capita gross domestic product (Bolt et al.). With multiple actors moving in divergent directions, this entangled history reveals the Americas not as an imperial monolith, but as a heterogeneous space of crisscrossing and conflicting cultural, economic, and geopolitical interests.

This multilayered reality, in turn, begs a reconsideration of the commonly held belief that nineteenth-century republicanism in the Americas represented an uncritical importation of European political thought by creole elites disinterested in the region's racial heterogeneity.[27] Without excusing the neocolonial attitudes of the early national oligarchies, a reconstruction of the hemispheric routes traveled by the racialized republican teacher-mother construct demonstrates that nineteenth-century thinkers in the Americas were keenly aware of how the legacy of colonial race hierarchies complicated paradigms of bourgeois-republican government. Creole elites would seek sometimes to ameliorate and sometimes to exploit this situation. Thus, even though—as Jefferson's letter on "natural aristocracy" makes clear—they were excluded from public life to varying degrees throughout the hemisphere, through the racialized constructions of republican motherhood and educación, Afro-descended women such as Sally Hemings were central to nineteenth-century lettered dialogues and political debates concerning the identity not only of discrete nation-states but of the Americas as a geopolitical system marked by the intersections of creole neocolonialism and US imperialism.[28]

Disciplinary Entanglements: Neocolonial and Imperial Mappings of the "South"

In following the uneven movement of New England–style education to the former Confederate States of America to Argentina to Cuba and the ways in which that system dialogues with local conditions and traditions, I focus on the space that literary scholar Martyn Bone has called the "extended South."[29] This transnational geographic unit resituates the US South in the context of the Global South nations of Latin America and the Caribbean—in this case, Argentina and Cuba—in order to consider the regions' shared histories of conquest, colonialism, and underdevelopment.[30]

Both familiar and unusual, my project's national foci require explanation. While comparative and transnational work on Cuba and the United States is a staple of inter-American studies, Argentina historically has not represented a locus of nineteenth-century hemispheric research, perhaps due to widespread beliefs regarding the Río de la Plata region's closer ties to Europe.[31] More recent studies by scholars such as Gilbert Joseph, Ricardo

Salvatore, Greg Grandin, Juliet Hooker, and Evan C. Rothera however, have questioned this assumption, reconstructing the place of Argentina in the development of US empire, particularly through commercial ties and soft diplomacy.[32] As John Carlos Rowe points out, though military incursions such as the Mexican-American and Spanish-Cuban-American Wars clearly represent important historical moments, nineteenth-century US imperialism was often more cultural than territorial. "The United States developed *non-territorial* forms of colonial domination, ultimately synthetized in an 'imperial' system that in the nineteenth century complemented American nationalism" and later "grew to encompass 'spheres of influence'" such as the Western Hemisphere (11). Through this soft imperialism, the United States was able to create and control markets for its goods. Grandin, for example, notes that, even during the late colonial period, the *porteño* bourgeoisie of Buenos Aires illegally collaborated with New England merchants to import enslaved Africans into the region (27). Just as importantly, the waters off the coasts of the Southern Cone would play a key role in the early-nineteenth-century New England trade in seal furs. This little-known history is registered in Latin American literature in the "Más Afuera" chapter of Sarmiento's 1847 *Viajes por Europa, África y América* (Travels through Europe, Africa, and América), in which the writer encounters a North American mariner living on an island off the Chilean coast. While solitary sailors like the one described by Sarmiento joined together to write a constitution governing their activities on the island, a "council of American sea captains" sought to rule the area less "like republican emissaries than like rival emperors divvying up a continent: they signed treaties defining boundaries, commanded expeditions that fought one another over resources and wealth, came together to enforce common rules governing property and debt, and even issued their own currency" (Grandin 156–57). This history clearly problematizes received ideas regarding the geographic and temporal limits of US imperialism in South America.[33]

The fact that stories like these have generated relatively little interest among students of the national literatures of both Latin America and the United States points to the methodological limits of the scholarly focus on national-linguistic canons through which one qualifies for a PhD in "Spanish" or "English." Intrinsically interested, by virtue of their focus on textuality, in language, literary studies long have been linked to nation-building projects, as scholars from Benedict Anderson to Eugene Weber to Doris Sommer to Homi Bhabha have noted. Indeed, even in the self-consciously cosmopolitan field of comparative literature, most North

American doctoral programs require students to prepare qualifying reading lists drawn from two or three "separate" national-linguistic traditions.

In the case of Spanish America, though country-based literary histories certainly exist, the "nation" often takes on a transnational, area-wide dimension. Foundational studies such as Pedro Henríquez Ureña's canon-building *Corrientes literarias en la América hispánica* (1945) attempt to fashion a panregional literary "nationalism" out of texts thought to be particularly representative of the distinctiveness of the Spanish-speaking Americas, an area that the Global North long has regarded erroneously as a cultural backwater. This inevitably Hispanist project locates the region's artistic wellspring in the Spanish colonial legacy of *mestizaje,* considering the allegedly harmonious coming together of different peoples in Spain and its empire as the source of Hispanic literary genius. Important though their interpellation of an Iberoamerican high culture as a counter-discourse to Euro- and US-centrism is, in pursuing their goal of building a broad Latin American identity out of many component parts, studies such as Carlos Fuentes's *Espejo enterrado* (published in 1992 to commemorate the quincentennial) have tended to plaster over any fissures of race, class, and gender that might split apart the monolithic model of a regionwide mestizo identity based in the Spanish language and Hispanic cultural paradigms. The weight of this Hispanist tradition is sustained by the vastness of literary production in Spanish, the official language of approximately 10 percent of the world's countries. Thus, while, as a result of structural inequalities, scholars of the Global South can never be unaware of the North, specialists in Hispanic literatures have had ample material with which to conduct transnational research without turning to the explicitly interlingual concerns that traditionally have defined comparative literature.[34]

As its name indicates, the field of (US) American studies, too, is marked by a national orientation. From its inception in Cold War–era texts such as Henry Nash Smith's *Virgin Land* (1950), American studies have sought to identify, articulate, and analyze distinctly US cultural values and institutions. The last two generations of scholars have problematized the more triumphal aspects of this project, enriching American studies in important ways through their explorations of the histories and literatures of people of color, women, and members of the LGBTQ+ community. Yet, as Rowe points out, these critiques of internal colonialism rarely engage extraterritorial empire, instead accepting the borders of the US nation-state as natural limits to their scope (6).[35] Much as the traditional organization of scholarly specializations situates Spanish American literature in dialogue with that of Spain, the institutional affiliations often existing between American studies and "the English department" produces a situation in which US literature is studied more frequently in conjunction with that of the British Isles or India than with texts produced by geographically closer neighbors. Thus, as Sandhya Shukla and Heidi Tinsman explain in their introduction to *Imagining Our Americas,* Latin American studies and US American studies as traditionally construed have taken divergent paths to the same state of relative insularity: if Latin American studies historically have felt the need to construct the nation in the face of constant assault by imperial forces, US American studies rarely have been compelled to question the centrality of the imperial United States nation (6–16).

Of course, there is nothing wrong with nation- and language-based literary study per se and both Latin American and US American literary studies have generated generations of venerable and innovative scholars, to whom *Imperial Educación* is very indebted. Like most of the people reading this book, I have studied, loved, and loved to study the Hispanic and Anglo-American literary "traditions" and cannot imagine my world without them. At the same time, however, I cannot imagine this book's project within their confines. The interactions among Argentina, Cuba, and the United States that I will explore here necessarily draw the focus to questions of Anglo-American imperialism in Latin America and comparative racial issues—subjects that more strictly Spanish American and US American scholarly approaches tend to preclude in favor of an (equally valid) emphasis on text-based national(ist) myths and realities. While the national frame does much to enrich our knowledge of particular authors and movements, it is not sufficient for inherently transnational topics such as imperialism and the aftershocks of African chattel slavery and abolition. In some ways, the methodological differences that I am describing cannot be reconciled; transnational approaches to literature, after all, were developed largely as a scholarly counterdiscourse to the traditional disciplinary focus on the "great literature" of national-linguistic canons. The categories of analysis used by the two methodologies—the national and the imperial, canonicity and marginality—exist in inherent tension with one another. As a scholar, one often feels forced to pick a side.

Yet, while national and transnational literary studies probably never will see eye to eye, this book hopes to make them talk by exploring how imperialism intervenes in the construction of the nation. In its effort to identify the intersections of US empire and Latin American nation-building, *Imperial Educación* stresses direct contacts and exchanges among the United States, Argentina, and Cuba over thematic parallels among texts.[36] As

Wilifried Raussert has observed, "While . . . comparative aspects open up venues to shed light upon similarities and differences within and between the two continents, they tend to fall short when it comes to the analysis of relations and processes" (8). In order to analyze these transcultural dynamics, hemispheric studies scholars recently have been turning to the historiographic paradigm of "entanglement."[37] Part of the movement toward global historical studies that has "elevated mobility to the throne" (Conrad 64), entanglement

> is much less interested in similarities and differences between, let us say, Europe and the Arab world, but rather in the process of mutual influencing, of reciprocal or asymmetrical perceptions, in entangled processes of constituting one another. In a way, the history of both sides is taken as one instead of being considered as two units for comparison. One speaks of entanglements; is interested in travelling ideas, migrating people, and transnational commerce; mutually holds images of 'the other;' and one talks about mental mapping, including aspects of power, subordination, and dominance. Cultural dimensions are usually central to such an approach. (Kocka 42–43)

Common in contemporary New World historiography, entanglement slowly is incorporating itself into inter-American literary and cultural studies as a way to "tie together *area*-connected competencies with transdisciplinary research practices" (Ette, *TransArea* 52).[38]

While hemispheric literary studies are themselves nothing new, by incorporating transnational historical methodologies into comparative literature, the entanglement paradigm helps to shift the field's focus from parallels between the New World nations to material points of encounter, influence, and exchange among them.[39] In contrast to traditional comparative studies, which "compare, and, in a manner of speaking, place into static opposition the policies, societies, economies, and symbolic production of different countries," explorations of transareal entanglements "are directed towards movement, exchange, and mutually transforming processes. Transarea studies are interested less in spaces than in paths, less in the location of borders than in the dislocation of borders, less in territories than in relations and communications" (Ette, "Pensar").[40] Focused on the movement of both people and ideas across borders, entanglement allows for a critical engagement with the nation-state—an ideological construct with physical frontiers that has bedeviled comparative and world literary and cultural studies in recent decades—by taking the paradoxically transnational construction of the nation as its object of study.

Race and Language

The multilingual exploration into the construction of both discrete nations and transnational empires that I have just described is bound to create some cultural and linguistic confusion in terms of the categories of analysis used. Indeed, that was the case even for the participants in the events that I will consider in this book. In dialoguing with educational paradigms from the apparently successful United States in order to prepare their own nations' largely Afro-descended mixed-race masses for republican government and capitalist economics while staving off northern imperialism, Argentine and Cuban creoles discovered that the operational racial categories of their transnational projects were defined in different ways across the hemisphere. Thus, even as Latin American creoles, viewing themselves as white, turned to the United States for aid in colonizing their nations' popular classes, Anglo-Americans saw the "Latin" creoles as racially contaminated ("off-white," in cultural studies scholar María de Guzmán's formulation) and fixed their own imperial gaze firmly on creoles, the indigenous, mestizos, and Afro descendants alike. On the one hand, in both English and Spanish, "race" and its cognate "raza" were "used to refer to both human groupings identified in terms of phenotype (such as blacks, whites, etc.) and to refer to distinctions between 'Latins' and 'Saxons'" (Hooker 7). On the other, clearly belonging to the "Latin" category, Spanish American elites would find that they were not always accepted as the racial equals of "Saxon" US whites. Rather, during the nineteenth century, "Anglo-American observers became more concerned with Spain's large Celtic and Jewish populations, its history of Muslim rule, and its frequent commerce with Africa. US Americans began to view this population as only ambivalently white and racially inferior despite its European origins. They moreover became increasingly appalled by perceived creole intermixture with the Native American and African inhabitants of the Americas" (Havard, *Hispanicism* 5–6).

Though racist, North American misgivings regarding the whiteness of Latin American creoles had their basis in a cultural misunderstanding. While US thinkers categorically dismissed the possibility of race mixture as a central element of national life, racial categorization and national belonging proved more complex affairs in Latin America. On a linguistic level, this difference is palpable in the divergent paths taken by the words "miscegenation" and "mestizaje" in English and Spanish. Though both have the Latin verb *miscere* (to mix) as a root, the English word, coined during the Reconstruction period following the US Civil War (though clearly existing as a concept before the term appeared), refers to the then-illegal marriage between persons of different racial adscriptions. The children produced by such unions were considered particularly threatening, as they necessarily problematized the binary division upon which segregated North American society was constructed. On the other hand, far from illegal, mestizaje in Spanish America was acceptable and sometimes encouraged in certain social classes. The offspring of such relations always had a place in the multitiered Latin American social pyramid, though their exact location has varied over history. Mestizaje—and the intercultural exchange that it implies—has been regarded by thinkers from the Argentine Domingo Faustino Sarmiento to the Cuban José Martí to twentieth-century Mexican philosopher Leopoldo Zea as a defining characteristic of Latin American society (though evaluations of that legacy have shifted over time). Thinkers such as the Brazilian João Batista de Lacerda and the Mexican José Vasconcelos have gone so far as to propose mestizaje as a means of whitening national populations through intermarriage. These ideas point to an underlying premise of mestizaje: that it is possible for nonwhites to whiten.

This bleaching away of populations of color is made possible by the conception of "whiteness" prevailing in Latin America, which is clearly broader than the United States' "one drop" binary system of hypodescent. In nineteenth-century Latin America, even as whiteness served as a phenotypical descriptor, the category also encompassed cultural traits not accessible to the lower classes, regardless of phenotype: education, manners, class, adherence to bourgeois or aristocratic values, and (as this book will show) particular forms of mothering. This "spiritual" whiteness is crystallized in works such as the *modernista* poetry of Nicaraguan Rubén Darío and Uruguayan essayist José Enrique Rodó's 1900 *Ariel*. The popular expression *negro con alma blanca* (a black man with a white soul), which is intended as a (backhanded) compliment, encapsulates the slippage between these physical and cultural senses of *blanquedad* (whiteness).

Yet, at the same time that they operated with a definition of *blanco* that blurred—but did not erase—the distinction between race and class, Latin American intellectuals were (perhaps painfully) aware that Europeans and North Americans did not share their nuanced understanding of whiteness. These tensions can be seen, for example, when nineteenth-century Argentine elites, while officially disavowing race mixture, established public schools to whiten the mestizo masses by assimilating them into a system of values sanctioned by the Global North. Cuban thinkers, too, would turn to education as they fretted over the capacity of women of color to raise a citizen body capable of resisting US imperialism.

In a study such as the one undertaken here, then, racial categories of analysis are necessarily problematic. On the one hand, the constitutive differences between US and Latin American racial taxonomies demand that local vocabularies for discussing race be respected so as to avoid the reinscription of imperial assimilation and consequent epistemic violence of false equivalence that, for example, an Anglicization of Spanish-language racial terminologies would entail. On the other, all analyses require categories of analysis, and comparative transnational analysis is predicated on the existence of transnational or comparable categories. In the case of this book, it seems fair to say that "white" people and "black" people existed in the nineteenth-century United States, Argentina, and Cuba in structurally similar (but by no means identical) locations of power and prestige to one another, at the same time that who counts as "white" or "black" varied considerably from location to location. What follows is an explanation of my (admittedly inelegant) efforts to elaborate terminology with which to discuss this situation in English.

In this book, I use the term "creole" to refer to people in the Western Hemisphere (particularly Latin Americans) regarded by their societies of origin as being white/blanco, regardless of what their actual genealogies may be.[41] Meanwhile, depending on the degree of specificity required, I use the terms "black," "Afro-descendant," "Afro–North American" or "African American," "Afro Argentine," and "Afro Cuban" to refer to people in the Americas recognized by their societies of origin as being of mixed or unmixed African descent.

Socially acceptable terms in Spanish, *mulato* and *mulata* (with one *t*), in this book refer to Latin Americans of mixed European and African ancestry who are regarded as nonwhite by their societies of origin, members of a Latin American "third" racial category. Neither black nor white, yet sometimes able to "become" one or the other, Latin American mulatos do not fit neatly into the United States' binary racial logic. I have chosen to leave the word in Spanish partially because I consider it to be untranslatable and partially because of the offensive connotations that its English cognate, *mulatto,* holds in the contemporary United States. That said, I will use the English archaism *mulatta* (with two *t*s) when speaking in the US context and in literary references to the "tragic mulatta," a tropological figure that, though found to varying degrees throughout the hemisphere, has been named and analyzed chiefly by the Anglo-American academy.

For the most part, I have chosen to capitalize the first letters of terms referring to national, continental, and "ethnic" origins (i.e., "Argentine," "Afro-Cuban," and "Guaraní"). Words referring to transareal "racial" categories, on the other hand (i.e., "white," "black," and "indigenous") appear with their first letters lowercase. After an embarrassing amount of deliberation, I have chosen to write "creole" with a lowercase "c." Current debates about whether "Latino/a/x" is a racial or ethnic category and how social diversity within Latin America impacts that question aside, it is clear that, as the nineteenth century progressed, the differences between whites in the United States and whites in Latin America increasingly were understood as racial in nature (to the extent that nineteenth-century thinkers understood "race" and "ethnicity" as distinct from one another). Many of the transnational exchanges mapped in this book are grounded in that (mis)understanding.

What all of this means is that a given character or author could be described using any of the slightly overlapping terms defined above depending on where they are located geographically, who is speaking, and in what language. In the rest of this book, I will analyze how the ways in which individuals negotiated the ambiguities and tensions between and among these categories would give rise to the imperial and neocolonial order of the nineteenth-century Americas.

Summary

More interested in narrating a transnational story than in presenting discrete nation-based case studies, *Imperial Educación* follows the racialized discourse of republican motherhood through the nineteenth-century Americas. The monograph explains how (1) in the nineteenth century, creole writers from the United States, Argentina, and Cuba would consider the potential for republican motherhood of racially and culturally hybrid women as they attempted to make sense of the tensions between republican notions of equality and the economic exigencies of their racialized (neo)colonial economies; (2) how, doubtful of the ability of their nations' nonwhite mothers to (re)produce the national body required by a republic, policy makers from these three countries turned to public education in order to prepare the Afro-descended masses for the challenges of modern citizenship; and (3) how the hemispheric circulation of the racialized

18   *Introduction*

family allegory in the educational sphere would become implicated in the turn-of-the-century balance of power among the New World states.

Theoretical in scope, the first chapter is dedicated to the limits and possibilities of the nation-as-a-family metaphorical construct in the heavily racialized context of the nineteenth-century Americas. If women were to act as "republican mothers" and raise their children to become virtuous citizens, what role would mothers of color—held to be lacking in republican virtues—play in the nation? What would become of their children in a republican system that offered them nominal political inclusion? I will explore these questions through an analysis of Haitian writer Émeric Bergeaud's 1859 novel *Stella*, which situates the future citizens of Haiti between black and white republican mothers. The text ultimately offers a Eurocentric vision of republican motherhood and citizen virtue, despite its purportedly anticolonial message and the supposed radical otherness of Haiti's official antiracism in the nineteenth-century Americas. The chapter concludes by explaining how public education initiatives in the nineteenth-century United States, Argentina, and Cuba were leveraged to contain the perceived threat of Afro-descendant citizenship in the New World postcolonies, attempting to assimilate formerly enslaved citizens to the values of those who would rather exclude them.

The rest of the monograph can be divided into two sections: two chapters are dedicated to Argentine hemispheric entanglements and two to Cuba's transnational place in the Americas. The first chapters of each section are literary in focus and discuss the entanglements among North American, Argentine, and Cuban foundational novels written by a diverse group of creoles, Afro-descendants, men, and women with an eye toward the question of republican motherhood for women of mixed race. The second chapters of each section consider how this literary conversation intersected with educational policy and—examining government documents, memoirs, and newspaper articles—explore how, in dialogue with the United States, the figure of the racialized national mother is grafted onto that of the female schoolteacher in nineteenth-century Argentine and Cuban modernization programs. Read from beginning to end, the chapters explain how the teacher-as-racialized-republican-mother constellation becomes implicated in turn-of-the-century Latin American neocolonial and US imperial designs.

Moving away from the traditional geographic orientation of nineteenth-century hemispheric studies, *Imperial Educación* takes South America's Southern Cone as its point of departure. Chapter 2, "Mothers, Moors, Mohicans, and Mulattas in Mansilla's *Miranda*" discusses how Argentine liberal writer and statesman Domingo Faustino Sarmiento, a literary disciple of North American novelist James Fenimore Cooper, dialogued with Jacksonian US views on miscegenation in his own formulation of race and republican citizenship. Noting how, in his archcanonical 1845 *Facundo,* Sarmiento points to Cooper's foundational 1826 *Last of the Mohicans* as a model for New World republican culture, the chapter explores the reception of the exclusionary racial and gender paradigms presented in Cooper's novel by a mid-nineteenth-century Argentina pursuing economic prosperity and political stability in the aftermath of a decades-long civil war.

I then turn my attention to *Lucía Miranda,* an 1860 Argentine reconsideration of Cooper's classic text written by the little-known writer Eduarda Mansilla de García. The chapter argues that Mansilla's historical captivity novel functions as a counterdiscourse to the official whitening policies of mid-nineteenth-century Argentina. In her counterdiscourse to *The Last of the Mohicans,* Mansilla rejects the racial hierarchy embodied by Cooper's text and embraced by Argentine liberal elites in favor of the colonial social order by casting the Moorish-descended Lucía Miranda (an emblem, I argue, for typically Hispanic notions of cultural hybridity with particular reference to Afro-descendency) as mother of the nation. In this way, she rewrites the racial dynamics of Cooper's classic novel, in which the mixed-race character famously is expelled from the nation before she can produce nonwhite future citizens.

Chapter 3, "Una Maestra Norteamericana in the 'South'" continues to focus on Sarmiento as it probes Argentina's racially fraught modernization through US-inspired population interventions, this time in the educational sphere. Expanding on the previous section's interest in republican motherhood, this chapter turns to child-rearing as it explores North American influence (and lack thereof) on educational reform in Argentina during the second half of the nineteenth century. Hoping to educate his nation's children in the modern ways of capitalism and democracy in the latter half of the nineteenth century, Sarmiento—inspired by the Reconstruction-era migration of northern women to the US South in order to establish schools for the freedmen—worked with the New England reformer Mary Mann, widow of the educationalist Horace Mann, to recruit North American teachers for Argentine normal schools. The chapter examines the internal documents of the late-nineteenth-century Argentine Ministry of Justice, Religion, and Public Instruction, paying attention to the ministry's critical adaptation of North American pedagogical paradigms to ends that were at once both neocolonial and anti-imperialist.

The chapter also analyzes *In Distant Climes and Other Years* (1931), North American teacher Jennie E. Howard's severely understudied memoir of her time in the Argentine schools. I argue that, through her position as teacher, Howard stakes a claim for herself as mother of the Argentine nation. In a curious reversal of the foundational schemas presented by *The Last of the Mohicans* and, to a certain extent, *Lucía Miranda,* in *In Distant Climes,* the culturally hybrid maternal figure is presented as white while the Hispanic children that she Anglicizes are, through their discursive equation with US freedmen, scripted as black. Importantly, however, a close reading of the text shows that, even as Howard brings Anglo-Saxon modernity to Argentina, her Argentine pupils Hispanicize their North American teacher, suggesting that, as in Mansilla's *Lucía Miranda,* here, too, the liberal Argentine government's strategy of US-style whitening through family allegory was not uncontested. Serving the political interests of both the United States and Argentina, the transnational racial readings and misreadings enacted by Howard's narrative point to the ways in which, by the late nineteenth century, the racialized trans-American allegory of the national family had turned into a meeting ground of local histories and global designs.[42]

Simultaneously relying on and resisting the racial politics of North American modernity, Argentina would emerge in the early twentieth century as one of the strongest nation-states in Latin America. Cuba, on the other hand, had the opposite experience, entering into an imperial relationship with the United States in the years surrounding the Spanish-Cuban-American War of 1898. The island's uneasy transfer from Spanish to North American tutelage would find expression in a series of late-nineteenth-century novels on mixed-race families. Chapter 4, "Foundational Frustrations in Cirilo Villaverde, Mary Mann, and Martín Morúa Delgado," discusses how procreation is deployed as a metaphor for Cuba's future in three novels concerning incestuous interracial relationships on the island written in the years leading up to the interimperial 1898 war: Cuban creole Cirilo Villaverde's 1882 *Cecilia Valdés,* North American Mary Mann's 1887 *Juanita,* and Afro-Cuban Martín Morúa Delgado's 1891 *Sofía.* The contrasting fates of the children born of hybrid mothers in the creole, North American, and Afro-Cuban novels indicate the differences among the various postcolonial identities that were being imagined for Cuba at the turn of the nineteenth century: a creole republic, a US colony, or a sovereign racial democracy. The incommensurability of the three views would mark public life in the postcolonial state from the war's conclusion to the present day.

In keeping with the monograph's inter-American nature, this choice of novels has something new to offer to scholars of both Latin America and the United States. While Villaverde's *Cecilia Valdés* is a staple of hemispheric scholarship and the work's genealogical links to Morúa Delgado's *Sofía* long have been known to Latin Americanists—who consider the later novel an Afro-Cuban response to the racially exclusive biases of the canonical 1882 text—few Americanists have studied *Sofía* (which has yet to be translated into English, despite the author's years in the United States), meaning that much of the inter-American literary scholarship on the Spanish-Cuban-American War period is based on creole readings of the conflict. Meanwhile, newly rediscovered by scholars of nineteenth-century US literature, Mann's *Juanita* (which has never been translated into Spanish, despite the writer's prolonged stay in Cuba and later collaboration with Sarmiento) is almost entirely unknown to Latin Americanists. This oversight is unfortunate, given that the uncanny parallels between Mann's novel of semi-incestuous interracial love and canonical Cuban antislavery texts such as *Cecilia Valdés* represent a rich field for comparative analysis. An examination of the three works in conjunction with one another ultimately sheds light on the seldom-considered transnational dimensions of Morúa's thought, demonstrating how the Afro-Cuban author rescripts Villaverde's and Mann's family allegories in order to reject the racism implicit in both creole nationalist and North American imperialist discourses.

The final chapter, "'La Dignidad de la Mujer Cubana': Racialized Gender Allegory and the *Intervención Americana*," triangulates the relationships among Cuba, the United States, and Argentina discussed in the rest of the book. Telling the story of how, after the 1898 war, several of the US schoolteachers originally invited to Argentina by Sarmiento were asked by First Lady Ida McKinley to go to New Paltz, New York, and establish a normal school for girls from US-occupied Cuba, the chapter reveals the little-known link between Sarmiento's racialized modernization-through-education initiative and US imperialism in the Caribbean. Participating in a new "School City" program that shared many goals with the Argentine educational reforms of the previous generation, the former maestras de Sarmiento would instruct their Cuban students in republican mores so that they could return to the island as teachers and raise their compatriots' children in democratic values. This situation, in which North American mothers of the Argentine nation prepare racialized Cuban women in New York for republican motherhood, demonstrates how the three national-familial discourses discussed in this monograph become entangled as

Latin American states brokered with US empire in the late nineteenth and early twentieth centuries.

The chapter explores how the Cuban teachers at New Paltz engaged the racialized and gendered imperial metaphors that underlay their stay in the United States and, metonymically, Cuba's new place in the US imperial orbit. Through a rhetorical analysis of the "Sección cubana" that the Cuban teachers published from 1901 to 1902 in the normal school's periodical, *The Normal Review,* I show that, emphasizing their personal dignity, the Cubans sought to represent themselves as independent (perhaps sovereign) bourgeoise white women. This depiction acts as a counterdiscourse to US imperialist rhetoric of the war period, which tended to depict Cuba in terms of feminized passivity. Obviating any racial difference with Anglo-Americans by scripting themselves as white and insisting on their dignity as female professionals, the Cuban teachers inscribe themselves within the "New Woman" paradigm current in the turn-of-the-nineteenth-century northeastern United States. This reformulation of the Cubans' racial and gender identities distances the writers of the "Sección cubana" from the racialized maternal discourse of the other texts discussed in my monograph—an orientation to which the Cuban nationalists who sent them, the North American imperialists who hosted them, and the former maestras de Sarmiento who taught them all had subscribed. Yet, at the same time that it looks forward to the gendered political allegories that would mark hemispheric relations during the twentieth century, the maestras' efforts to seize an untenable ideology of whiteness encapsulates the paradoxes that characterized nineteenth-century creole thought.

Imperial Educación's transnational narrative points to a hemisphere-wide interest in the biopolitical control of Afro-descended populations and populations perceived to be Afro-descended through the selective reproduction and rearing of children. The literary conversations and educational exchanges to which this concern gives rise indicate the particularly New World nature of racialized republican institutions: Argentines and Cubans engaged North American strategies in literary and educational discourses because they realized that European republican philosophy had not considered how racial heterogeneity would impact the formation of citizen bodies. Though, at first glance, it may sound like a vindication of Americanity, the story that *Imperial Educación* tells is anything but triumphal.[43] Creole elites in both Americas would use their shared racialized national-familial discourse to bolster the causes of neocolonialism and imperialism, as the cases of Cooper, Sarmiento, Howard, Villaverde, and Mann demonstrate. Even then, however, detractors from these projects such as Mansilla de García, Morúa Delgado, and the Cuban teachers at New Paltz would voice their opposition through the very same racialized republican-maternal discourse that they criticized, pointing to the centrality of racialized readings of republican motherhood—and the racialized republican mothers themselves—to the intersection of nation building and imperialism in the nineteenth-century Americas.

1 Republican Motherhood and Citizen Educación

THIS CHAPTER traces the history of the allegory of the national family in nineteenth-century New World literary and educational texts and probes the ways in which that discourse is complicated by the racial heterogeneity of the Americas. I will focus on the construction of the "republican mother" who raises virtuous future citizens for the nation in several nineteenth-century texts from the United States, Argentina, Cuba, and—by way of comparison—Haiti. Looking at the historical, journalistic, and novelistic records, I will consider how women of color often were scripted by nineteenth-century thinkers as beyond the limits of republican motherhood. The chapter concludes with an explanation of the ways in which creole elites deployed public educación against what they saw as the depravation of mothers of color in an effort to preserve their republics from the depredations of the supposedly unvirtuous popular classes.

Family Allegory and Foundational Romance

Family allegory has had a long history in Western political discourse. Paternalist metaphor, in which the monarch is figured as a father to his people, served to justify and maintain feudal-dynastic political systems in Europe and its New World territories throughout the ancien régime (Rey 50). Francisco Suárez, for example, would argue in a 1612 treatise that "one could say that, in the beginning of creation, Adam, by nature, had primacy and thus *imperium* over all men, which derived from him, either originating naturally in first-born sons or through the will of Adam himself. Thus . . . all men have been formed and procreated from Adam to be subordinate to a prince" (22).[1] By postulating royal sovereignty as a "natural" extension of the biblical Adam's *patria potestas* over his descendants, Hispanic Enlightenment thinkers considered that, "in accordance with natural law, . . . authority passed from God to the *paterfamilias*, who would reproduce 'the ties of nature itself' and give origin to peoples and kingdoms. . . . Royal power [was] transferred by God to the first man, from the first man to the *paterfamilias* and from the *paterfamilias* to peoples" (Rojas 81–82).[2] Eighteenth-century Bourbon monarchs would expand on this notion and conceive of the far-flung Spanish empire as "a large family with the king as father and multiple children, different but sharing a common duty to aid and defend him," a metaphor that united Mexico and Montevideo under the paternalistic care of the monarch in Madrid (F. Guerra 21).[3]

Later, enlightened advocates of republican government in the Americas would mobilize this "family formula" against the peninsular dynast during the creole independence movements of the early nineteenth century (Felstiner 167). In the Spanish colonies, "family imagery succeeded in impressing feelings of depravation upon fairly comfortable Spanish Americans, stirred the desire to liberate family patrimony from imperial control while binding citizens into a kindred nation, confirmed hierarchies inherent in the Creole family model, and legitimized the ways families gained a controlling interest in the state" (180).[4] In British North America, meanwhile, J. Hector St. John de Crèvecoeur, the French-born author of the foundational *Letters from an American Farmer* (1782), would critique George III of Britain for failing to protect his "children" on the American frontier:

> I am informed that the king has the most numerous, as well as the fairest, progeny of children, of any potentate now in the world: he may be a great king, but he must feel as we common mortals do, in the good wishes he forms for their lives and prosperity. His mind, no doubt, often springs forward on the wings of anticipation, and contemplates us as happily settled in the world. If a poor frontier-inhabitant may be allowed to suppose this great personage, the first in our system, to be exposed, but for one hour, to the exquisite pangs we so often feel, would not the preservation of so numerous a family engross all his thoughts; would not the ideas of dominion, and other felicities attendant on royalty, all vanish in the hour of danger? The regal character, however sacred, would be superseded by the stronger, because more natural, one of man and father. (194)

In this passage, Crèvecoeur attacks the kingship-as-paternity metaphor from within itself, accepting that George III is a benevolent father with "good wishes" for the "lives and prosperity" of his colonial children but unfortunately is unable to know the "exquisite pangs" that afflict them due to the great distance at which they have "settled" from their monarch.⁵ With their father so far away, the American children might as well be independent, Crèvecoeur seems to say.

The unique geopolitical situation of the Americas, then, would exhaust the metaphorical paternity of the Bourbon and Hanoverian monarchs. The paternalist trope would be rendered completely unviable by independence and the rise of the republican order, yielding to other forms of family thinking. In *Democracy in America* (1835), Alexis de Tocqueville observed that while "amongst aristocratic nations, social institutions recognize, in truth, no one in the family but the father . . . [,] in democracies, where the government picks out every individual singly from the masses, . . . a father is there, in the eye of the law, only as a member of the community, older and richer than his sons" (727–28). In this context, the vertical metaphor of monarchical rule as paternity necessarily came to be replaced by the horizontal metaphor of republican society as fraternity, another variation on the larger gestalt of the nation-as-family tropological construct.⁶

"Race" would mediate the tensions between paternal hierarchy and fraternal egalitarianism inherent in this change. For French neo-Marxist Étienne Balibar, the metaphor of national genealogy represents "the symbolic kernel of the idea of race" through "the idea that the filiation of individuals transmits from generation to generation a substance both biological and spiritual," which "inscribes" members of the national family "in a temporal community known as 'kinship.'" Mobilizing blood as a metaphor to mark the limits of republican fraternity, "race" emerges as a technology to temper the egalitarian excesses unleashed by the political upheavals of the long nineteenth century.

> This idea [of the national family] is correlative with the tendency for "private" genealogies, as (still) codified by traditional systems of preferential marriages and lineage, to disappear. The idea of a racial community makes its appearance when the frontiers of kinship dissolve at the level of the clan, the neighbourhood community, and, theoretically at least, the social class, to be imaginarily transferred to the threshold of nationality: that is to say, when nothing prevents marriage with any of one's "fellow citizens" whatever, and when, on the contrary, such a marriage seems the only one that is "normal" or "natural." The racial community has a tendency to represent itself as one big family or as the common envelope of family relations (the community of "French," "American" or "Algerian" families). (Balibar 100)

Paradoxically, this metaphorical notion of national kinship, or "race," surfaces at the same moment in which the rise of republican government—which, in the Americas, would set abolition in motion—invalidates the feudal-dynastic emphasis on the legitimacy of sovereign bloodlines. Crèvecoeur exemplifies this sort of republican interracial prohibition. Upon fleeing with his family to native territory in order to escape the violence of the War for Independence, Crèvecoeur notes that, "however I respect the simple, the inoffensive, society of these people in their villages, the strongest prejudices would make me abhor any alliance with them in blood: disagreeable, no doubt, to nature's intentions, which have strongly divided us by so many indelible characters" (211). Here, the birth of the new political order is accompanied by the prohibition of interracial marriage as racial exclusion is deployed to contain republican inclusivity. Thus, by using "the structure of the family . . . as the conceptual model for the nation's reproduction as an intact political entity over time, and sexual reproduction [as] the physical mechanism of national history," the metaphor of the national family "naturalizes linear history and the cohesion of white Americans of the past, present, and future" by using the analogy of family belonging to justify racial exclusion from the theoretically inclusive republican body politic (H. Jackson 50).

Both US and Latin American intellectuals drew their nations' boundaries of the blood on the pages of nineteenth-century national novels. Literary theorist Doris Sommer has argued that foundational narratives served to establish social hierarchies in the newly formed New World republics by allegorically modeling the relationships among the heterogeneous elements comprising the nation.[7] This is achieved not through tropes of paternity or brotherhood but through "an erotics of politics" that shows "how a variety of novel national ideals are all ostensibly grounded in 'natural' heterosexual love and in the marriages that provided a figure for apparently nonviolent consolidation during internecine conflicts" that plagued the various nations of the Americas during the mid-1800s (Sommer, *Foundational Fictions* 6). "Once they project that ideal as an image that looks like a wedding portrait, their union . . . becomes the mediating principle that urges the narrative forward" toward its logical conclusion—marriage and the "promise" of future citizens in the form of the foundational couple's progeny (18). Often set in the past, foundational literature thus attempts to conceive proleptically what Argentine critic Noé Jitrik calls "la línea de generación" of the past from the vantage point of the present in order to "orient" the nation toward a future "reasonable state."[8] In the nineteenth-century Americas—simultaneously postcolonial, neocolonial, and imperial—this entailed carefully pruning the nation's family tree to include some members while excluding racialized others, as novels such as James Fenimore Cooper's *Last of the Mohicans* (1826), Eduarda Mansilla de García's *Lucía Miranda* (1860), and Cuban Cirilo Villaverde's *Cecilia Valdés* (1882) attest.

Republican Motherhood

Given the nineteenth-century literary emphasis on racially restrictive marriage and the production of a particular citizen body, it was only natural that, in addition to the paternal and fraternal metaphors of state discussed above, the "'natural' and inalienable mother-child binomial" should rise to discursive prominence (Nari 70).[9] In the "deeply gendered" political economy of the nineteenth-century Americas (Dore 15), a new tropological cornerstone—that of the "domestic woman"—was forged to hold together the ideological structuring of the republican national family (Nari 70).[10] This new discourse mobilized the figure of the virtuous mother to "discipline the social practices of women and families, [bringing] the hope of *regeneration* of the 'race,' society, the nation" (70).[11] "Bourgeois women" such as Mrs. March in Louisa May Alcott's *Little Women* (1868) "were to act as both nurturant moral models to their children and as nurturant supporters and moral guides for husbands on their return from an immoral, corruptive world of work" (Chodorow 5). Imbued with this ideology, Alcott's matriarch regards it as her "duty" to encourage her husband to fight for the Union during the Civil War and raise her four daughters on her own until his return, an attitude that transfigures homemaking into an act of patriotism. "I gave my best to the country I love, and kept my tears till he was gone," Alcott's character explains (96).

Cultural studies scholars, especially in the United States, have used the term "republican motherhood" to refer to this deployment of moral mothers to rear "and continue to rear future generations of citizens" for the nation (Apple and Golden xv). "Focusing attention on their sons and encouraging industry, frugality, temperance, and self-control, republican mothers would nurture virtuous citizens who served their communities; by educating their daughters, mothers would ensure the virtue of future generations" (Blackwell 31). In her work on the United States during the 1700s and 1800s, Linda K. Kerber theorizes republican motherhood as a means of political influence for women, who had been denied suffrage by the early republican governments. "The new republic leaned on the law for structure. In turn, an educated citizenry was expected to maintain the spirit of the law; righteous mothers were asked to raise the virtuous male citizens on whom the health of the republic depended" (10).[12]

In the Spanish-speaking Americas, meanwhile, moral motherhood originally was tied more closely to the Catholic ideals of femininity found, for example, in works such as Fray Luis de León's 1583 *La perfecta casada* than to bourgeois-republican notions of citizenship. In an 1860 article appearing in the *Álbum cubano de lo bello y lo bueno* (Cuban album of the beautiful and the good) entitled "Las mujeres y los niños" (Women and children), Antonio de Trueba appeals to the Catholic Marianist tradition of maternity, stating that "God has given children a mother in every woman" (216).[13] In this way, he frames motherly love in terms of the Christian virtue of charity. A few lines later, he writes, "Let us ask the most vulgar of women why she loves children, and she will tell us, if she succeeds in translating her feelings, 'I love children because I look for angels on the earth and I find them only in children'" (216–17), words that transfigure maternity into a divine calling.[14]

A more modern discourse relating motherhood to the rearing of a bourgeois-republican citizen body was emerging, however, from the pages of Latin America's flourishing periodicals (Provencio Garrigós 43). The liberal press in Buenos Aires and Montevideo, in particular, "display[ed] a sustained interest in the dignification of women as mothers and companions to men" (Garrels, "Sarmiento ante la cuestión").[15] An anonymous 1830 article in *La Aljaba: Dedicada al bello sêxo Argentino* (The quiver: Dedicated to the Argentine fair sex), considered the first Argentine women's magazine (Lojo, Introduction 20), describes Ancient Greek and Roman mothers heroically raising and sacrificing soldiers for the nation. Tellingly entitled "Amor a la patria," the article presents the raising of future citizens as women's civic—not moral or religious—duty.[16] Another anonymous article, entitled "Educacion de las hijas" (Education of daughters), speaks of "the scepter" that women have "in their hands symbolizing morality and religion," an image that evokes republican motherhood and the notion of women's virtuous domestic rule (2).[17] Through the trope of the scepter, a metonymy for government, the author reframes Christian values ("morality and religion") in order to tie educación to national reproduction.

The need for mothers to raise virtuous republican citizens would lead to a renewed emphasis on women's education in nineteenth-century liberal circles as motherhood ceased to be regarded as a natural condition equally available to all women and came to be understood as a function of bourgeois-republican society whose proper fulfillment required special preparation (Provencio Garrigós 62).[18] The subject of women's education has a long history in Hispanic letters, appearing as early as Padre Feijoo's 1676 *Defensa de las mujeres* (Defense of women) on the peninsula and Sor Juana Inés de la Cruz's 1691 *Respuesta de la poetisa a la muy ilustre sor Filotea de la Cruz* (*The Poet's Answer to the Most Illustrious Sor Filotea de la Cruz*) in colonial New Spain. In the nineteenth century, Mexican liberal Joaquín Fernández de Lizardi's 1819 *La Quijotita y su prima* (sometimes called "Little Miss Quixote and Her Cousin" in English) had argued for the importance to the nation of enlightened, bourgeoise mothers during his country's war for independence, transforming the earlier religious understanding of enlightened maternity into a bulwark of republican nation building.

Women's education for motherhood would become a subject of conversation in colonial Cuba, too. Perhaps inspired by the novels of British writer Samuel Richardson, the Cuban women's magazine *La moda, o, recreo semanal del bello sexo* (Fashion, or the weekly recreation of the fair sex) (1829–31) initially advocated that young women be educated in order to protect themselves from seduction.[19] Later issues would begin to reflect the liberal values taking hold in the nineteenth century, insisting upon "the need to free the fair sex . . . by fixing good ideas in their imaginations, before they go out into the world. Their own happiness, the happiness of those upon whom they will exercise immediate influence, and, to an extent, the moral character of society depend upon women's educación" ("De la influencia" 328).[20] In an 1845 article in *La ilustración: Álbum de las damas* (Enlightenment: Ladies' album), a Madrid-based women's magazine with a heavily Cuban editorial staff, the Spanish liberal Ramón de la Sagra would go so far as to argue that "women's education is more important than men's, as that of the latter is the work of the former" (2–3).[21]

In Argentina, too, the notion of "civic motherhood," or "an educated mother who passes on her enlightened values and knowledge to her children, thus improving the national character," would gain traction over the course of the nineteenth century (Frederick, *Wily Modesty* 93). The author of "Educacion de las hijas," for example, urges mothers to oversee their daughters' "educacion moral" (1). Another piece in the same magazine, called simply "Educacion," includes a letter to the editor thanking her for her efforts at promoting women's education, stating that "we wish for there to be not one ignorant woman; in this way the republic would see itself transformed into an earthly paradise" (3).[22] With child-rearing in the hands of "wise and religious mothers," "our feelings will be more orderly, more docile to reason; and we all would know from habit to be less ambitious, less exalted, and more generous in order to make mutual concessions to one another, and we would march to the beat of reason and concord."[23] As a result of this general increase in public morality, "we would all love our patria, we would not outrage her by making her the subject of our hatred, of our vengeance, of our resentment, and of our abominable ambition; we all would respect her" (3).[24] An investment in the education of the republican mother, then, is an investment in the *educación de la república*.[25]

Similar ideas would surface in the United States. In *A Few Thoughts on the Powers and Duties of Woman* (1853), educational reformer Horace Mann claims that "it may truly be said that, if by some inexorable fate, we were prohibited from educating but one of the two sexes, that one should be the female; because a community of intelligent mothers with ignorant fathers would advance the race more rapidly and surely than one of intelligent fathers with ignorant mothers" (75). This is because mothers "determine, to a great extent, the very capacity of the rulers' minds to acquire knowledge and apply it" (65).[26] In this way, Mann collapses the categories of teacher and mother into one another by highlighting what he sees as mothers' primordial place as molders of their children's minds. In a world in which monarchical rule recently had given way to more egalitarian forms of government by citizens, educated republican mothers "guaranteed the steady infusion of virtue into the Republic. Political 'virtue' . . . could be safely domesticated in eighteenth-century America; the mother, and not the masses, came to be seen as the custodian of civic morality" (Kerber 11).[27]

Mothers of Color

Yet what of mothers from those masses? Could they "domesticate" "political virtue" and "civic morality" in the same way in which elite women were expected to? Or "were they to be feared as a source of social and biological 'contagion' for their own and others' children, and best treated only as an ongoing source of domestic labor?" (Cowling 152). Tellingly, even though Alcott's paragonic *Little Women* is set against the backdrop of the US Civil War, all of the book's republican mothers are white Anglo-Saxon Protestants; even the March family's loving maid is a working-class New England Yankee. A few passing references to morally dubious French and Italian maternal figures provide all the alterity that the North American national family seemingly can handle. This counterfactual construction of women of color as beyond the limits of maternity would impact the lived experiences of Afro-descendants, as well as public policy, throughout the hemisphere.

Theorist Angela Davis notes that, even as "women began to be ideologically redefined as guardians of a devalued domestic life[,] there were other women—millions of women—who toiled away from home as the unwilling producers of the slave economy in the South" (228). Importantly, Afro-descended women frequently understood their labor to be a function of their role as "guardians" of their families. Especially in Latin America, where manumission was more common than in the United States, once freed, black women often sought remunerated employment in order to purchase the freedom of enslaved relatives with their earnings (Cowling 176–82). Nineteenth-century ideologues, however, "established the housewife and the mother as universal models of womanhood" when the construction was, in fact, demographically limited, "a symbol of the economic prosperity enjoyed by the emerging middle classes" (A. Davis 228–29). Even after abolition, "harsh economic realities prevented many Blacks from attaining [the] ideals" of republican motherhood (Yee 40–41). Often occupied as racialized labor, denied formal education, and possessing limited rights, women of color generally were considered unable to instill their children with bourgeois-republican values.[28] Instead, "mainstream magazines and literature . . . stereotyped women of African descent as the antithesis of modern femininity." Black women were portrayed by these texts as "sexually immoral *mulatas* . . . and uncivilized *brujas* . . . among other caricatures" (Brunson 180). As a character in Cuban Cirilo Villaverde's 1882 *Cecilia Valdés* says of the novel's mulata protagonist, "As she is of hybrid race, one mustn't trust too much in her virtue," much less expect her to behave as an enlightened national mother (594).[29]

Barred from entry into the cult of domesticity by their participation in the public sphere through (frequently un- or under-remunerated) labor outside the home and commonly held beliefs concerning their sexual availability—and the widespread abuses that accompanied these stereotypes—black women were viewed as racially incapable of reproducing the bourgeois-republican national family "both literally (birth) and figuratively (national values and traditions)" (Moreno 131).[30] These ideas would be codified into law by the 1812 Constitución de Cádiz, which refused citizenship in the Spanish empire to any Afro-descendant who could not meet rigorous criteria for demonstrating "virtue." Legally unable to give birth to full citizens in much of Spanish America and—especially after the 1857 Dred Scott decision denying legal protections to African

Americans—the United States, women of color could not participate fully in the New World republican motherhood construct.

Thus "ideological exaltation of motherhood—as popular as it was during the nineteenth century—did not extend to slaves." Rather, as "slave women were classified as 'breeders' as opposed to 'mothers,' their infant children could be sold away from them like calves from cows" (A. Davis 7). African American freedwoman and abolitionist Sojourner Truth states that, even after abolition, "the Marylanders tormented [the freedmen] by coming over, seizing, and carrying away their children. If the mothers made a 'fuss,' as these heartless wretches called those natural expressions of grief in which bereaved mothers are apt to indulge, they were thrust into the guard-house"—an act that shows the incompatibility of blackness with virtuous motherhood in the popular imaginary of the time (Gilbert 182).[31]

In the United States, centuries of myths regarding "unvirtuous" black families would be canonized in Daniel Patrick Moynihan's now infamous 1965 report *The Negro Family*, which blames the alleged "deterioration of the fabric of Negro society" on the supposed retention of African patterns of matriarchy thought to be emasculating (5). In her classic critique of Moynihan's misogyny and cultural blind spots, literary theorist Hortense Spillers observes that the Atlantic slave trade sought to erase African kinship structures. In their place, enslaved captives were fictively inserted into the slaveholder's patriarchal system, "the dominant symbolic order, pledged to maintain the supremacy of race. . . . It is this rhetorical and symbolic move that declares primacy over any other human and social claim, and in that political order of things, 'kin,' . . . has no decisive legal or social efficacy" (73–74). After all, "if 'kinship' were possible" for Afro-descendants, the "property relations" upon which slavery rested "would be undermined, since the offspring would then 'belong' to a mother and father" (75). In 1808, South Carolina courts would codify this state of affairs by ruling that "female slaves had no legal claims whatever on their children" (A. Davis 7). As African American abolitionist Frances Watkins Harper would lament of an enslaved mother witnessing her son sold at an auction:

> He is not hers, although she bore
> For him a mother's pains;
> He is not hers, although her blood
> Is coursing through his veins!

> He is not hers, for cruel hands
> May rudely tear apart
> The only wreath of household love
> That binds her breaking heart. ("The Slave Mother," xx–xxviii)

In a world in which "cruel hands/may rudely tear apart" enslaved families, Afro-descended women would not occupy the role of republican matriarch demanded by the bourgeois state.[32] After all, the stability of motherhood and domestic life "is at odds with the very definition of a slave; the bought-and-sold person comes and goes by way of the transactions of the market. The slave is always the stranger who resides in one place and belongs to another. The slave is always the one missing from home. Being an outsider permits the slave's uprooting" (Hartman 87).[33] Designed to alienate black labor and subjectivity, the slave system is structurally dependent on the alienation of black maternity and the affiliations and affections that it implies.

Historian Teresa Prados-Torreira writes that, as in the United States, in Cuba, this "disregard for ties between mother and child, as well for the bond between husbands and wives" rendered it difficult for the enslaved to "conform to the standards and expectations of the middle class" in terms of family structure (30). The predicament is embodied in the character of María de Regla in creole writer Cirilo Villaverde's 1882 novel *Cecilia Valdés*. Obligated to work as a wet nurse, she continues to nurse her own daughter in secret and, when discovered, is "banished to the sugar plantation" for violating "the slaveholder's notion of what constitutes an appropriate model of maternity for the slave" (L. Williams 164). In one of the few moments in nineteenth-century literature in which an enslaved woman is allowed to voice her own feelings, Villaverde has the character explain how the slave system strips Afro-descended women of their domestic roles of wife and mother: "She isn't allowed to marry the man she likes or loves. The masters give her a husband, and they take him away. Nor is it certain that she will always live with him, nor that they will raise their children together. When she least expects it, the masters divorce her, sell her husband away on her, and her children, too, and they separate the family so that they are never together again in this world" (507–8).[34] As the ways in which Harper's "slave mother" and Villaverde's María de Regla have not been allowed to fulfill the maternal duties demanded by the bourgeois order of their time show, ideologies of republican motherhood were "not just gendered, but racialized" (Glenn 7).

This racialization means that slave family structures often have proven invisible to white, middle-class observers (Barcia Zequiera 12). The sensationalism surrounding the 1856 trial of escaped slave Margaret Garner, who killed her infant daughter rather than see her returned to bondage, exemplifies white bourgeois consternation when faced with the fact of black familial relations that were simultaneously similar to and different from hegemonic norms. Dubbed *The Modern Medea* in the title of an 1867 painting of the incident by Thomas Satterwhite Nobel, Garner and her motivations seem to have been lost in the Victorian sea of middle-class sentimentality and Gothic horror in which white abolitionist discourse frequently floated. Whatever Garner may have been, she was not an antebellum variation on the Greek Medea.[35]

As might be suspected, the historical record provides ample evidence for strong affective bonds among enslaved families. Herbert G. Gutman notes that, while "no slave family was protected in the law, . . . upon their emancipation most Virginia ex-slave families had two parents, and most older couples had lived together in long-lasting unions" (9). As extralegal institutions, these families existed under constant threat of separation by owners who were either ignorant of or insensitive to the family ties of the people whom they enslaved. Sojourner Truth offers a particularly heartbreaking critique of the impact that these attitudes had on African American families in her *Narrative:* "Of the two [siblings] that immediately preceded her in age, a boy of five years, and a girl of three, who were sold when she was an infant, she heard much; and she wishes that all who would fain believe that slave parents have not natural affection for their offspring could have listened as *she* did, while [her mother and father]—their dark cellar lighted by a blazing pine-knot,—would sit for hours, recalling and recounting every endearing, as well as harrowing circumstance that taxed memory could supply, from the histories of those dear departed ones, of whom they had been robbed, and for whom their hearts still bled" (16). Here, the belief that black families, subject to constant separation, "have not natural affection" is what justifies their constant separation.

At the same time, however, governments and planters did take steps to promote family life among enslaved persons, largely out of economic self-interest. Five years after sugar cultivation was introduced into Cuba, the colonial government passed the 1768 Reglamento de Artillería, proclaiming that married enslaved couples with twelve or more live children were to be granted their liberty in exchange for their services in reproducing the workforce (Barcia Zequiera 64). As part of the same effort, in 1804, legislation was introduced to increase the number of enslaved women imported into Cuba (Ferrer, *Freedom's* 188). Evidence also suggests that some enslaved women sued to prevent the breakup of their families due to sales or to protect their children from abusive masters, a phenomenon that points to both the legal protections for enslaved families in nineteenth-century Cuba and the frequency with which they were disregarded (Castañeda Fuertes 223–25).[36] Indeed, despite official support, marriage rates among the enslaved in Cuba actually dropped over the course of the nineteenth century, as planters may have been disinclined to respect the legal rights of enslaved persons (Meriño Fuentes and Perera Díaz 28–29). It is evident, then, that the bourgeois family headed by a virtuous republican mother was an ideal thought out of the sociocultural logic of the white middle class and really only attainable by members of that group.[37]

Race and Child-Rearing

This fundamentally white and bourgeois nature of the republican motherhood construct can be seen in the liberal campaign against the entrusting of white children to the care of servants of color that arose in early-nineteenth-century Latin America. Writing as his country battled Spain for independence, Mexican liberal Jose Joaquín Fernández de Lizardi in his 1816 *Periquillo sarniento* (*The Mangy Parrot*) argued against the common practice of engaging wet nurses for middle- and upper-class creole children. The concern expressed in this foundational work—considered the first Latin American novel—by one of the region's early nationalist thinkers points to the importance of particular racialized and classed forms of maternity for the establishment of the bourgeois-republican order in the Americas.

Though present in European texts such as Jean-Jacques Rousseau's 1762 *Émile,* this preoccupation with allowing servants to raise children was particularly prevalent in the New World, where domestic labor often was relegated to enslaved Afro-descendants such as La Negra Hipólita, the black Venezuelan woman who famously served as wet nurse to Simón Bolívar, raising him after his parents' death. Reputed to be of partial African descent himself, the Liberator is said to have referred to her as the only parent he had ever known. While Bolívar seems to have survived the experience with his civic virtue intact, nineteenth-century Latin American thinkers "worried because the white children of the elites were being raised by black servants, women who were both uneducated and always suspected of lacking sufficient devotion to the best interests of their master" (Fraunhar 71). The black wet nurse, in particular, was considered to be "plunged by her race into a permanent 'state of ignorance.' This created serious physical dangers for the child, as her lack of education made her susceptible to every sort of excess detrimental to health" (Provencio Garrigós 67).[38]

Black wet nurses were thought to endanger children's moral well-being, too. In 1836, Cuban creole reformer Domingo del Monte noted that "in addition to the great inconveniences that communication between children and servants generally brings . . . we must add, when the servants are slaves, a thousand others" that will put an end to children's wholesome innocence ("Informe," pt. 2 2:42–43).[39] These comments suggest that, for enlightened creoles, contact between children and the enslaved undermined the moral purpose of educación. In an 1846 article for *La ilustración: Álbum de las damas,* Sisto Sáenz de la Cámara similarly would fret about the "abject race that . . . monopolizes the loyal trade in lactation, and to which mothers with too much abandon assign the custodianship of their children." He worries about the fate of the child, who, "when at the age of indelible impressions, finds himself abandoned to the mercantile custody of a wet nurse with no model but her uncouth and unruly manners, without hearing any language but her intemperate tongue." He asks, "What hope for the future can this inspire? What form will a substance poured into such a coarse mold take?" (23).[40] As if in answer to these questions, the tragic plot of Villaverde's *Cecilia Valdés* is put into motion when a black wet nurse defies orders and makes contact with her husband while caring for a slavocrat's children (516). In the postbellum United States, meanwhile, fear of moral contagion led to a decline in the use of black wet nurses in the 1880s (Olds 186), attitudes reflected in Mary Mann's *Juanita* (1888).[41]

An anonymous December 21, 1830, article in the Argentine *Aljaba* goes even further in racializing child-rearing:

> Familiar dealings with slaves is the most dangerous hazard that you place before your children under the domestic roof. The example of bad habits and vices possessed by those beings who have been degraded by their state of servitude has a powerful influence and brings about the downfall of innumerable children of virtuous families, whom trust placed in a state of deplorable blindness against their dearest interest. May mothers take heed, as it is their duty as responsible guardians to their children to be vigilant. ("Educacion" 2)[42]

Even in Argentina, where, until recently, it was thought that slavery and blackness had not played significant roles in the shaping of the national imaginary, it seems that the liberal intelligentsia was concerned with how enslaved servants might "disgrace" the children of the nation's "virtuous families." Significantly, by appealing to "mothers" to protect their children from the corrupting "influence" of "slaves," the writer defines the two categories as mutually exclusive, as though enslaved women could not also be mothers. In this way, the figure of the debased black nanny caring for the children of a supposedly better able white mother serves to create two divergent images of maternity, one degraded and the other domestic (Wade 47–48).[43] Possessing "bad habits and vices," the enslaved were unable to *educar* "the race of veritable aristoi" of which Jefferson and other republican ideologues throughout the Americas dreamed. This understanding of Afro-descended women as something other than republican mothers and the consequent concerns regarding their ability to raise a morally virtuous bourgeois-republican national family would spur the development of public educación in the hemisphere.

A Brief Excursion to Haiti

The case of Haiti complicates but in some ways ultimately confirms the deployment of black maternal figures to racialize republican motherhood as white that I am describing here. The second independent state in the Western Hemisphere and the first black republic on Earth, Haiti represents the only example of a successful revolution by the enslaved in all of New World history. Historian Laurent Dubois has argued that, inherently unassimilable to Enlightenment notions of race and governance, Haiti represented an epistemological threat to the hemisphere's other creole-dominated states, which conserved the racialized labor relations of the colony as the basis of their republican political economies. As a result, for much of the nineteenth century, the legacy of the Haitian Revolution and the black state that it created was "silenced" by the other nations of the hemisphere, even as it impacted everything from the expansion of the sugar industry to the strengthening of slave codes in other areas of the Americas.[44] "Disavowed" in hegemonic discourse, as Sibylle Fischer has shown, the Haitian Revolution haunted the hemispheric racial republican order from its inception.

Because of the centrality of Haitian ex-centricity to racial regimes throughout the Americas, I want to explore briefly the racialized republican motherhood construct in a Haitian foundational text as the exception that proves the rule. Considered the first Haitian novel, Émeric Bergeaud's posthumously published *Stella* (1859) simultaneously upholds and undermines the republican maternity of enslaved African mothers in the Americas.[45] One of the first texts to present a positive vision of the Haitian Revolution (Curtis and Mucher xxiv), the novel centers on two Haitian half brothers, one black and one *mulâtre* (mixed-race), named (of all things) Romulus and Rémus. The brothers vow to avenge their mother's death when she is killed by the family's owner, who is also Rémus's father (17–18), and the fictional struggle that ensues in the novel becomes discursively imbricated with the historical Haitian Revolution. The brothers' final victory over the French ushers in the birth of the Haitian nation-state.

Marlene Daut has studied how, in a fraternal variation on the "erotics of politics" described by Sommer (*Foundational Fictions,* 6), *Stella*'s foundational function lies in the union of the white and mulâtre brothers. This represents a literary expression of the conflict between the descendants of colonial-era *gens de couleur libres* (free people of color), who frequently were mixed race and related to the plantocracy, and the darker-skinned masses consisting of people freed during the revolution. "Bergeaud's description of Haitian revolutionary history as a fraternal romance [thus] projects not only an altogether *idealist* future for Haiti, but an almost entirely *raceless* one" (Daut 418). In this "raceless" world, the division between blacks and mulâtres is no longer socially significant, and Haitian blackness is not regarded as abject by the countries of the Global North. While this interracial fraternal union certainly is a main theme in the text, I want to draw attention to the racialized vision of republican motherhood also present in the novel. As with the republican-maternal discourses from the United States, Argentina, and Cuba that I discuss above—which appeal to canons of femininity available only to bourgeoise white women—here, too, the "racelessness" of the national mother is presented as white.

Importantly, however, *Stella* does not negate the existence of black republican mothers, as do many of the nineteenth-century New World texts discussed above. Rather, Romulus and Rémus are inspired in their battle against colonialism by the ghost of their African-born mother, Marie (often referred to simply as "l'Africaine"), who points them to the mountains from which they are to carry the revolution to the cane fields. She also encourages them when they begin to have doubts. After a nightmare about the horrors that await them in their struggle, the brothers were "called back to themselves by a friendly voice, the voice of their mother, who, from the depths of the tomb, still watched over their days. She was indignant at their guilty weakness, and showed them her torn and bloody body. A noble cry from the heart responded to this new call to vengeance" (30).[46] Here the enslaved African woman appears as the republican mother figure interpellated by texts such as "Amor a la patria," urging her sons toward noble sacrifice for their people. In a departure from the racial politics of many works written in other countries of the Americas during the same period, *Stella*'s foundational framework combines a black republican mother with open depiction of slave revolt.

At the same time, even as he wrote ostensibly to remind Haiti's Francophile mulâtre elite of their nation's glorious past (Hoffman 159), as a member of that elite with close family ties to the Boyer government, Bergeaud was open in his cultural bias against blacks and their role in Haitian national life (Curtis and Mucher xi). Written (like many nineteenth-century Haitian literary texts) in French about a country that communicates primarily in Kreyòl and "stylistically very much embedded in and indebted to a French neoclassical tradition," *Stella* at times presents a remarkably Eurocentric vision of republican virtue (Duchesne 113). The protagonists, after all, are named after the mythical founders of Rome, origin point for the Western Latinity of which, by the 1800s, France would be regarded as the most advanced expression. Invested, as Daut has noted, in legitimizing the world's first black republic to the Global North, *Stella* hardly participates in the tradition of Haiti as radical alterity that scholars such as Dubois and Fischer have identified in other representations of the revolution.

Rather, the author tempers Marie's black maternal agency by offering the brothers another republican mother. In the novel, Romulus and Rémus are guided in their revolutionary endeavors not only by the ghost of the deceased "Africaine" but by a spirit-like white woman from France named Stella, who obviously is intended to represent "la *Liberté*, étoile des nations" (*Liberty*, the star of nations), as the author writes, punning on the etymology of his character's name (308).[47] As critic Dafne Duchesne points out, "No matter her allegorical attributes, Stella is a white French woman. Her trip [from France to Haiti] follows the one-sided flow from the Old World to the New World. The fact that her trip is one-sided marks France as a place of origin" (112). The seemingly anticolonial text thus paradoxically reinforces Eurocentric views, postulating the French tradition as the source of Haitian struggles for *liberté*.

In the novel, Romulus and Rémus adopt Stella as their North(ern) Star, following her white glow as she fulfills the same republican-maternal function as their African mother, offering to support the brothers in their cause (61). The structure of the text makes this clear by placing the brothers' dream of their mother immediately after the chapter in which Stella explains her origins, drawing a maternal parallel by juxtaposing the novel's only two female characters. The relationship between the two maternal figures becomes obvious when the Frenchwoman tells the orphaned brothers that she will "in the future replace your mother's love entirely" (43).[48] In this way, the white Stella effectively becomes the republican mother of the foundational brothers Romulus and Rémus when their African mother is incapacitated.[49]

The novel thus presents a nuanced variation on the racially restrictive view of citizenship and republican motherhood that I have been outlining in this chapter. Bergeaud's decision to allegorize the republican virtue of "liberté" through a white woman cannot be seen as coincidental in the highly racialized context of the Haitian Revolution. Some scholars have suggested that Stella's whiteness serves to present the Haitian Revolution as universal, as indicated by the fact that, in the novel, her republican virtue is clearly available to Afro-descendants such as Romulus, Rémus, and Marie (Hoffman 162). Yet, if the African mother seems to possess republican virtue innately, her sons need to be guided by Stella's star if they are to deliver liberté to the enslaved masses.[50] For Duchesne, this "contradictory discourse" represents "the early crafting of a distinctly Caribbean subjectivity in literature" (110). Indeed, there is something inescapably New World about the racial republicanism imagined by *Stella*. Like the Cádiz Constitution, the novel acknowledges that blacks are capable of republican virtue but paints that virtue as tending toward whiteness. Blacks such as Romulus and Rémus are most likely to be redeemed for the republic if they allow themselves to be instructed by white maternal figures, the novel seems to say.[51] As I will explain, this attitude would guide liberal education reforms throughout the postslavery Americas.

From Mothers to Maestras: Race and Public Educación

Public schools would be mobilized throughout the Americas to provide the sort of bourgeois-republican educación in which the hemisphere's mothers of color were thought to be lacking. Cuban pedagogue Manuel Rodríguez Valdés would write in 1891:

> There is no doubt that, among well-organized peoples, the family's actions can be felt at school. This influence can be justified, from the first moment that it is felt, by the positive effect that it produces. Any solid education, rather than divorced from the home, should be a continuation of and a cooperation with

family life. But the same cannot be said of a society lacking this organization, in which it is necessary, before anything else, to begin by combatting the prejudices of the domestic hearth. Well could we prove our assertion with a multitude of examples, daughters of the lack of *maternal science* among us, along with the errors of the father, which produce disagreement and an almost permanent state of collision between the school and the family. (*Problema* 9)[52]

While "among well-organized peoples," family life supports the education imparted at school, in new-born nations such as Cuba, schools must "combat the prejudices of the domestic hearth," placing public education on a "collision" course with the private family as *maestras* came to replace *madres* as the *educadoras* of the nation's racialized masses.

This concern for the socialization of the popular classes dominated pedagogical thinking in the nineteenth-century Americas. As early as 1823, Bernardino Rivadavia, liberal president of the United Provinces of Río de la Plata (present-day Argentina), "enlisted thirteen socially prominent women to administer a girls' public elementary school," an act that framed public educación as a system for bringing bourgeois-republican maternity to the masses (Chevigny 142; see also Frederic, *Wily Modesty* 175). In 1849, Rivadavia's compatriot Domingo Faustino Sarmiento would explain that the broad enfranchisement ecumenically granted by the republic created a government "obligation to educate [*educar*] the people."[53] Notably, this educación was to be extended to all citizens, including those from the social groups who would not be raised by bourgeois-republican mothers, "without making distinctions between men and women, nor between the chino or the mulato and those who call themselves noble, nor between legitimate and illegitimate children" ("El siglo" 76).[54] While theoretical in 1849, these concerns would become more pressing in 1853, when the new constitution "granted equality to all men living in the Argentinean territory," meaning that "every male, including Afro-descendants and 'civilized' Indians, regardless of their status or possessions, was granted the right to vote" (Rodríguez and Geler 2). It is important to keep in mind, then, that, though twentieth-century US opinion often associates public education with democratic advancement, Sarmiento was interested in using schools to contain the excesses of democracy.

This question of race and educación would seem particularly dire to creoles living in the plantation zone in the years leading up to and following abolition. Writing in 1860, Mariano Cardero would stress the need to educate the racialized popular classes in Cuba:

With the new social order the ties that impeded the movement and development of the masses were destroyed, leaving them slaves to ignorance and subjugated to the empire of their passions. "Be free, and take possession of your rights," all were told and no one thought to teach them the true meaning of liberty, nor to prepare them to make good use of the power deposited in their hands. Be free, they were told, as one might say be rich or be happy without instructing them as to the legitimate means of attaining those goals, and without giving them a clear and exact idea what was being offered them. Empty words, devoid of meaning, more to excite spirits than to honor and exalt the classes whose emancipation was sought. (291–92)[55]

Perhaps in a discreet reference to the racial origins of many of Cuba's poor—a group heavily composed of manumitted slaves and their descendants—Cardero writes that the popular classes are still "enslaved by their ignorance" and unprepared for the "freedom" afforded by liberal forms of government. Like Sarmiento, Cardero believes that the solution to this "problem" is that the popular classes be given an "educación convenient to their state and needs."[56] This, he feels, is "the remedy for the ills that threaten us" (290).[57] Similarly, during the same period in the United States, South Carolinian segregationist James Shepard Pike pessimistically demanded that public education "undo the habits and practices and modes of thought and want of thought engendered by centuries of slavery" and procure "the moral enlightenment and regeneration of a whole people debauched and imbruted for ages" (63).

Pike's bigoted suggestion forms part of a US tradition of mobilizing public schools for the purpose of "absorbing those people and ideologies that stood in the path of the republic's millennial destiny," such as Native Americans, freedmen, and immigrants into the national project (Adams 18). As early as 1804, Congress had created the Civilization Fund to instruct native children in Western ways (6).[58] Washington would redouble these efforts to assimilate indigenous youth through schooling as the nineteenth century progressed, making the conferral of citizen rights contingent upon completion of bourgeois-republican educación. Much as the Cádiz Constitution in Spain demanded that Afro-descendants prove their "virtue" as a prerequisite for citizenship, the 1887 Dawes Act required Native Americans to adopt "the habits of civilized life" in order to gain "the rights, privileges, and immunities of . . . citizens" (sec. 6). A 1917 law would tie schooling explicitly to citizenship, stating that "all students twenty-one years or older and receiving diplomas for completion of the full course of study" at a native boarding school "were eligible to receive . . . a 'certificate of competency'" granting them the right to manage their own affairs as citizens (Adams 146).[59] Well into the twentieth century, "federal Indian policy" called for "the removal of children from their families and in many cases enrollment in a government run boarding school" (Marr). In this state intervention into the raising of nonwhite children, "young people would be immersed in the values and practical knowledge of the dominant American society while also being kept away from any influences imparted by their traditionally-minded relatives."

The Civil War and Reconstruction periods would see public education similarly deployed to negotiate the place of formerly enslaved subjects into the US nation. Northern Freedmen's Aid Societies began sending teachers South in 1862 (Du Bois 642). Later, as the Civil War drew to a close, the newly formed Department of Negro Affairs would open schools for liberated slaves with "women teachers from the North" (Du Bois 71) in what historian of education Adriana Puiggrós has called a "political-pedagogical crusade" (*Imperialismo* 91) that mobilized public education in order to achieve "economic, institutional, and ideological transformations" as Reconstruction incorporated the South into the reunited nation's liberal project (92).[60] These efforts would continue under the direction of the Freedmen's Bureau, leading to the establishment of the first public school systems in the region (Du Bois 654–64). In total, the Freedmen's Bureau spent $5.25 million on the education of formerly enslaved people, while northern freedmen's aid societies contributed another $8 million (Butchart 6–7). By the time the Union army withdrew from the South in 1877, "some 247,000 pupils were attending 4,329 schools" (A. Davis 108–9).

It is not well known that many of the teachers at these freedmen's schools were themselves black, inspired, like the African American Lucy Craft Laney, by the belief that "Negro women of culture, as kindergartners and primary teachers . . . may instill lessons of cleanliness, truthfulness, loving kindness, love for nature, and love for Nature's God" (889). Even before the war had ended, a group of 280 black teachers was busy founding the first freedmen's schools (Butchart 4). The center that eventually evolved into the Hampton Institute, for example, originally was established in 1861 by the mixed-race Mary Peake as the first day school for black children in Virginia (Du Bois 642). Similarly, in 1865, more than half of the teachers in Charleston, South Carolina, were black (643).[61] These Reconstruction-era teachers labored under conditions that would shock even the most mistreated of today's educators, sometimes teaching classes of over one hundred students (Butchart 3).

In fiction, the African American schoolteachers of the Reconstruction period are registered in the figure of Frances Watkins Harper's Iola Leroy, who "was not satisfied to teach her students only the rudiments of knowledge" but "tried to lay the foundation of good character" (147). As a Sunday-school teacher, "she planned meetings for the especial benefit of mothers and children" in order to instill citizen virtue in the children of freedmen and "her doors [were] freely opened for the instruction of the children before their feet have wandered and gone far astray" (278–79). These activities are articulated in explicit relation to republican motherhood; Harper goes out of her way to have Iola read a paper entitled "Education of Mothers" to a Reconstruction-era reform group (253).[62] The phenomenon that Iola embodies was not limited to the United States; as I discuss in chapter 5, throughout the nineteenth century, the few public schools available for children of any race in Cuba were staffed largely by women of color.

Yet, while "between 1861 and 1876, black teachers outnumbered northern white teachers four to three" (Butchart 19), the image of the Reconstruction-era domestic teacher-mother that has endured in the popular imaginary is that of a northern white woman selflessly ministering to freedmen. This image has diverted attention away from "dangerous" examples of black agency and reaffirmed the regime of white supremacy that continued to consolidate even after abolition. Though the Hampton Institute was founded by the mixed-race Mary Peake, in his autobiographical *Up from Slavery* (1901), Booker T. Washington would attribute much of his success to a white teacher, Miss Mackie, "a member of one of the oldest and most cultured families of the North." The writer expresses his admiration at "how a woman of her education and social standing could take such delight in performing such service, in order to assist in the elevation of an unfortunate race." He details how, for the two weeks before the beginning of each school year, "she worked by my side cleaning windows, dusting rooms, putting beds in order, and what not," in this way instilling Washington with the bourgeois regard for "the dignity of labor" that would serve him in his future career, in which he attempted to replicate Mackie's efforts with other black students by founding the Tuskegee Institute for African American education (51–52).

These images of northern white women taking charge of southern African American students would reflect transnationally; in his comments on the freedmen's schools in the United States, Sarmiento fails to mention the large number of African Americans such as Peake employed at the institutions. Instead, like Washington, he represents his ideal teacher as a white woman (Rothera, "South American Cousin"). Indeed, while "the efforts of [the] Northern teachers lasted no more than a decade" and most black schools during the Reconstruction and segregation periods were staffed by black educators, the migration of northern white female teachers to the South to teach the freedmen fit into a model for disciplining racialized masses into a citizen body that was common throughout the hemisphere (Novak 204). In Latin American literature, beliefs regarding the need for bourgeois-republican educación of the nonwhite popular classes by white teacher-mothers would find their canonical embodiment in Peruvian Clorinda Matto de Turner's 1889 *Aves sin nido* (*Birds without a Nest*), which suggests that a "righteous, motherly influence will unite a nation deeply divided by ethnic and class differences" (Paulk, "Beyond" 189). The foundational novel advocates for the assimilation of Andean indigenous peoples to the Hispanic culture of Peru's costal bourgeoisie through educación, presented in the book through the maternal figure of the creole Lucía. Derived from the term for "light" in neo-Latin languages, the character's name references both the whiteness of her skin and enlightenment from instruction. In the novel, Lucía endeavors to teach bourgeois virtues to a pair of orphaned indigenous sisters before sending them to Lima to complete their education. In this way, like Washington's Miss Mackie, the white woman and public educación discursively reproduce the bourgeois republic under the banner of white hegemony, a task structurally impossible for mothers of color.

The mobilization of public educación as a corrective for the supposed moral shortcomings of mothers of color, then, is a phenomenon that exists in many nineteenth-century New World societies. As I will show, the similarities in racial and gender ideologies among educational systems from across the Americas are not coincidences but the result of dynamic interactions between US imperialism and creole neocolonialism. The following chapters will explore how, in the nineteenth century, the discourse of the white maternal teacher mother developed and circulated transnationally as it was transculturated in countries throughout the hemisphere and how it became imbricated with the rise of a tripartite system of coloniality that structured relations between US whites, Latin American creoles, and people of color.

2 Mothers, Moors, Mohicans, and Mulattas in Mansilla's *Miranda*

THIS CHAPTER places North American author James Fenimore Cooper's well-known 1826 *Last of the Mohicans* into dialogue with the work of Argentine writer Eduarda Mansilla de García in order to discuss the uneasy relations between US imperialism and Argentine creole neocolonialism in the nineteenth century. By racially rescripting the trope of republican motherhood found in Cooper's frontier romance, Mansilla de García's 1860 novel *Lucía Miranda* functions as an intervention into the official whitening paradigms of mid-nineteenth-century Argentina. Espoused by liberal reformer Doming Faustino Sarmiento, Argentina's whitening policies were inspired in part by the expansion of Anglo-Saxon culture into the North American West described in Cooper's novel. Thus, Mansilla de García's rewriting of Cooper in many ways represents a critique of the racial-maternal politics governing efforts under way at the time to transform Argentina into a "United States of South America."

Both *The Last of the Mohicans* and *Lucía Miranda* address the racial realignments brought about by the transition from colony to nation-state and the subsequent incorporation of the hinterland into the national project in the United States and Argentina, respectively. While both authors ultimately imagine a community led by creole patricians, they differ in their views as to the place of their countries' nonwhite populations in the national family, as can be seen in the divergent ways in which they deploy the trope of the ethno-racially hybrid maternal figure. If Cooper in his novel sacrifices the mulatta Cora in order to ensure the continuance of the white national-familial line in the face of North American imperial expansion and the potential incorporation of marginalized Afro-descended populations into the bourgeois-republican body politic, Mansilla de García deliberately breaks with the North American writer by presenting the mother of the nation as a hybrid figure.[1] In so doing, she offers an elite challenge to northern-inspired readings of Argentina's racial realities, one that is simultaneously anti-imperial and neocolonial.

Where in the Capitalist World System Is Argentina? Civil Wars, Regional Politics, and National Identity

Argentine politics for much of the early- to mid-nineteenth century were dominated by Eduarda Mansilla de García's maternal uncle, Juan Manuel de Rosas, who rejected the paradigms of European bourgeois modernity embraced by his processor, Bernardino Rivadavia, who had been backed by the Buenos Aires mercantile bourgeoisie. This conflict between the Federales, who supported regional autonomy, and Rosas's opponents, the Unitarios, who favored political and economic centralization in Buenos Aires, resulted in a series of bloody civil conflicts that would occupy a defining place in nineteenth-century Argentine history. While Argentina eventually organized itself into states along a federal system, by the late nineteenth century, government services, wealth, power, and cultural institutions would become concentrated in the capital. The generation following national consolidation would see the fruition of a modernizing project aimed at restructuring the cultural, economic, and racial institutions that had been associated with the Rosas dictatorship, which many viewed as a sequel to Spanish colonialism.[2] This entailed a retrenching of the genocidal wars against Argentina's indigenous population (already begun by Rosas), a Europeanization of the country's culture, and a whitening of the population.

Considered an underdeveloped, peripheral outpost of the Spanish empire for most of the colonial period, modern Argentina's political ancestor, the Viceroyalty of Río de la Plata, was only created in 1776—244 years after the conquest the Incan empire and the initiation of Spanish colonialism in South America and 24 years before the Revolución de Mayo that eventually would lead to Argentine independence. The region previously had belonged to the Viceroyalty of Peru, which, until the late eighteenth century, spanned all of Spanish South America. The creation of Río de la Plata was motivated by a variety of factors: the ungovernability of a viceroyalty as large as colonial Peru, the threat of further Portuguese expansion into the Sothern Cone, and the need to open another port on the South Atlantic. Yet, as Juan Álvarez points out in his classic economic history of the region, "No great care was taken to make the new entity a harmonious whole: Indians of diverse races and languages, agricultural fields, mining regions, mountains and plains, rainforest and glaciers, all the natural differences and all the climates found below 45 degrees latitude were wrapped up by the new border and subject to decisions by the government in Buenos Aires, which was not in the center, but on the edge of the territory" (21).[3]

Chaotic as it was for traditional lifeways in the South American interior, the change proved a boon to agricultural and commercial interests on the Spanish South Atlantic, which benefitted from having direct access to the ocean through the port of Buenos Aires and which would rise to political as well as economic prominence during the nineteenth century. This represented an improvement over the old, impractical system of shipping goods over the Andes to Peru's Pacific port of Callao, from which they would be sent to Panama by water, to be carried over the isthmus by land before being embarked on ships for cities along the Spanish American Atlantic and Seville. Products then would be sent to other points on the peninsula and in Europe (Álvarez 20). After the viceregal reorganization, goods could be shipped directly from Buenos Aires to other areas of the Atlantic World. This proved particularly beneficial to the cattle ranchers of Buenos Aires province, who would rise to political as well as economic prominence during the nineteenth century.

The city of Buenos Aires, for its part, was chosen as the new viceregal capital not for any demographic, cultural, or economic significance—all of which it lacked at the time—but rather for its coastal location. Much less populated or wealthy than the region's interior at the dawn of the eighteenth century, the city would grow in size and importance as a result of the establishment of the viceroyalty (Álvarez 21). The British invasion of 1806, meanwhile, would expose the Argentine littoral to an increasing array of foreign goods and ideas. This rapid transformation from colonial backwater to cosmopolitan trading hub was further propelled by a lively contraband economy, which, among other activities, included the illegal purchase of enslaved Africans from New England suppliers (Grandin 27). However, the capital was by no means dominant in the region during the early 1800s and, with the collapse of the Hispanic monarchy following Napoleon's 1808 invasion of Spain, the viceroyalty splintered into several smaller states as sovereignty reverted to regional governments headed by provincial landowners. This fracturing marked the beginning of what would become the *caudillo* era of government by local strongmen (F. Guerra).

Perhaps not surprisingly, the mercantile city of Buenos Aires entered into conflict with rural agricultural areas and the provinces. The colonial system of land tenure practiced in the interior assigned vast, sparsely populated terrains to particular families, who often dedicated it to cattle ranching and the raising of sheep—industries that required uninhabited, undeveloped land for grazing—and was viewed by the modernizing elites of the port of Buenos Aires as an impediment to social and economic growth. There could be no schools or civic institutions in territories in which families lived miles apart from one another in order to make room for livestock, they felt.

Another, related conflict emerged over economic policy. The capital, which controlled the country's customs revenue, supported free trade with the Atlantic World. The interior, on the other hand, engaged chiefly in interprovincial commerce, sometimes along routes that antedated the creation of Río de la Plata (Álvarez 22). The establishment of the viceroyalty had "produced a fracturing of the pueblos in what is today Northeastern Argentina, as well as the economic and cultural unity that they had enjoyed for more than three centuries" by rerouting interior trade away from its traditional center in Lima and toward Buenos Aires (Puiggrós, *Qué pasó* 17).[4] Many in the provinces would attempt to safeguard regional economies in the face of this economic realignment by advocating for a tariff to protect local products from less expensive European imports (Álvarez 22). Importantly, much of this internal trade was in goods produced by slaves, the "motor" that created much of what was "traded *among* the colonies," as opposed to exported to Europe. "Enslaved Africans and African Americans slaughtered cattle and sheared wool on the pampas," activities that explain the somewhat unexpected presence of an Afro-descended population in the Southern Cone country, an area where scholars traditionally have assumed that blacks and slavery were demographically and economically unimportant (Grandin 27–28). This racial dynamic would surface in literary representations of political divisions in nineteenth-century Argentine society, which tended to figure the popular classes in terms of blackness, as I will discuss below.

The debates over the ideals of free trade, centralization, openness to Europe, and development on the one hand and those of protectionism, local autonomy, and traditional modes of social and economic organization on the other would give rise to the Unitario and Federal parties, respectively. Yet, even as they professed interest in national development, the Unitarios insisted that Buenos Aires retain exclusive control over the country's customs duties. For this reason, the party never found popular support, instead concentrating its membership chiefly in the mercantile and banking bourgeoisies of Buenos Aires and a few other cities. Their cosmopolitan liberalism often seemed at odds with traditional Argentine values; Unitario president Bernardino Rivadavia, for example moved to limit the power of the Catholic Church, a pillar of Hispanic culture in the New World. The Federales, meanwhile, though clearly dominated by the oligarchic *estanciero* elite of the cattle ranches, enjoyed the favor of the urban and rural popular classes, who may have felt drawn by their rhetoric of local control over politics, economics, and culture. The party represented a broad "alliance of classes and ethnicities: gauchos, Afro-Argentines (slaves and freedmen), and 'friendly' natives; small rural landowners and large creole landowners, and also English merchants and hacendados all supported [it], either because they saw a guarantee of order and prosperity in the regime, or because they considered it to be a place to make symbolic and material claims" (Lojo, Introduction 13).[5] These groups may have resented "the forced connection with the port of Buenos Aires, associated with foreign trade and contraband, cradle of a political and financial capital that refused to take care of its own hinterland," which had been plunged into economic instability by the reforms of the late colonial and early republican periods (Puiggrós, *Qué pasó* 17).[6]

Contemporary literary scholars associate the Federales largely with Rosas, whose 1835–52 rule "expressed first and foremost the ascension to power of the new ranching interests, developing since 1810, and the displacement of the mercantile clique that had sustained Rivadavia," as well as the landholders outside of Buenos Aires province who were not dedicated to the raising of livestock. A member of the estanciero elite, Rosas "shifted spending from the city to the countryside for such purposes as frontier expeditions, fortifications, and Indian subsidies" (Rock 105). These measures opened formerly indigenous lands for cattle raising, an industry that was further favored by an 1836 tariff (108). For the liberals of his day, Rosas's "great sin was that he kept the country in a barbarous pastoral state instead of encouraging its incorporation into the era of industry and progress" (J. Franco, *Literary History* 38). For his supporters, however, Rosas represented a "firm defender of national sovereignty" and welcome break with Rivadavia's Europeanizing zeal and heavy reliance on northern capital (Lojo, Introduction 13).[7]

In histories and anthologies of Latin American literature, the conflict between Unitarios and Federales typically is represented through the opposition between the anti-Rosas writers of the *Generación del 37* such as Sarmiento and *gauchesco* poets such as José Hernández, author of the 1872 *Gaucho Martín Fierro*.[8] While the Generation of 1837 favored "libertarianism, the overthrow of tyranny, and Enlightenment ideals" (Lindstrom 89), gauchesque literature was more interested in celebrating the rural laboring classes. Texts from the period articulate this conflict by metonymyzing the debate over the free importation of foreign goods versus the protection of local products as a battle between the North Atlantic modernity entering the country via the port of Buenos Aires and Argentine tradition, a force that the isolation experienced by the countryside as a result of economic centralization had rendered only stronger (Puiggrós, *Qué pasó* 17).[9] Sarmiento, for example, would be outraged to inform his readers that, in the Federal city of San Juan, "there are not three young men who know English, nor four who speak French," projecting the provincial population's economic isolation from Europe onto the cultural sphere (*Facundo*, 40).[10] The author registers his indignation at this nativism and support of political-economic cosmopolitanism by tossing French bons mots around his text in a way that more than one commentator has found gauche. Gauchesque poetry, on the other hand, often is written in a literary form of the regional dialects spoken in the Argentine interior, signaling the region's economic, political, and cultural difference from the standards of the Buenos Aires bourgeoisie.

The debate slowly would take on racial inflections, as Sarmiento and other like-minded thinkers sought to import not only Northern Hemispheric products and culture but also people into Argentina. Though the liberal intellectuals "regarded themselves as the progressives of their era . . . [,] in their desire to model Argentina on the most modern aspects of Europe," or, in Sarmiento's case, the United States, as I will show, "they were often racist and elitist" (Lindstrom 89). Liberal writers of the period such as Sarmiento, Esteban Echeverría, and José Mármol seized upon Rosas's prestige among the popular classes, frequently mestizo or mulato in origin, to paint the Federales largely in terms of racial barbarism. In *Facundo, o, civilización y barbarie*, Sarmiento, for example, writes that the indigenous "American races" will never make good workers because they live "in idleness, and show themselves to be incapable, even when coerced, of dedicating themselves to hard and steady work." Similarly, he claims that the importation of African slaves into the Americas, which was intended to remedy the problems caused by the natives' supposed unfitness for labor, "has had fatal consequences." Sarmiento feels that the "fusion" of these two nonwhite groups with colonizers from Spain, "she that lags behind Europe," has created "a homogeneous whole that distinguishes itself through love of idleness and industrial incapability," suggesting the unfitness of the country's mixed-race population for productive capitalist economics (15).[11] Initiating a dubious Latin American intellectual tradition that would continue until the revalorization of cultural hybridity in the twentieth-century social-scientific work of Gilberto Freyre in Brazil, José Vasconcelos in Mexico, and Fernando Ortiz in Cuba, liberal writers such as Sarmiento would identify the Hispanic colonial legacy of race mixture among whites, Amerindians, and blacks as one of the causes of their countries' supposed barbarism.

This interest in negotiating the racial implications of New World republicanism ultimately would lead Sarmiento to look to the Jacksonian and Reconstruction-era United States for answers. Operating within the framework of Latin American *letrado* culture, which understands literature as an intervention into politics, Sarmiento would turn to North American writer James Fenimore Cooper for a model of how to Americanize European civilization.

Cooper's America and Sarmiento's América

Somewhat paradoxically, Sarmiento's Argentine foundational text, *Facundo: Civilización y barbarie,* takes inspiration from the North American Cooper.[12] The second chapter of *Facundo,* a section dedicated to a typology of "Argentine characters," famously begins with a meditation on *The Leatherstocking Tales,* Cooper's five-novel cycle on the rise of Anglo-Saxon economic and political hegemony over indigenous and Afro-descended populations in the late colonial and early republican United States.[13] The cycle's best-known installment, *The Last of the Mohicans,* tells the story of the Scottish Alice Munro and her half Afro-Jamaican half sister Cora, who journey through the North American wilderness during the French and Indian War (1754–63) in search of their father, a general in the British army. Accompanied by the southern creole Major Duncan Heyward and the Mohican Uncas, in addition to the archetypical white frontiersman Natty Bumpo, they are beset by a group of Hurons led by the chief Magua.[14] The novel ends with the deaths of Cora and Uncas at the hands of the Hurons and the suggestion that Alice and Duncan soon will marry.[15]

Reading *The Last of the Mohicans* from the opposite end of the hemisphere, the Argentine Sarmiento found himself uncannily at home with the folkways of British New York. Claiming that the novel is filled with "descriptions of customs that seem plagiarized from the pampas," he brags of being able to resolve various narrative situations in "*Los relatos de Leatherstocking*" at least as well as the North American author does (*Facundo* 22).[16] Later, Sarmiento suggests that there is "a font of poetry that is born of the natural accidents of a country and the exceptional customs it [sic] engenders" (22).[17] For that reason,

> If a spark of national literature can momentarily shine in the new American societies, it is that which results from the description of grandiose natural scenes, and above all of the description of the struggle between European civilization and indigenous barbarism, between intelligence and matter; the dominant struggle in América, which gives rise to peculiar, characteristic scenes far removed from the ideas in which the European spirit evolved, because dramatic devices become unknown outside of the country from which they are taken; and customs, surprising; and characters, original. (22)[18]

The bard of the struggle between civilization and barbarism, Cooper is "the only North American romancer to have achieved fame in Europe," precisely because he has transported "the scene of his descriptions beyond the circle occupied by the colonists who live at the limit between the barbarous world and the civilized one, to the theater of war in which the indigenous races and the Saxon race battle for possession of the land."[19] The "Saxons," Sarmiento was keenly aware, would win the war, an event that Cooper allegorizes through the tragic deaths of his nonwhite characters at the end of *The Last of the Mohicans*.

Not only was the North American Cooper to serve as a model for Argentine literature, but the burgeoning United States was to serve as a model for the Argentine nation-state, as Sarmiento makes clear in works such as *Viajes por Europa, África y América* (Travels through Europe, Africa, and America) (1847), *Las escuelas: base de la prosperidad en los Estados Unidos* (The schools: Basis for prosperity in the United States) (1867), and *Conflicto y armonías de razas* (Conflict and harmonies of races) (1883), among others. The westward expansion spurred by US president Thomas Jefferson's 1803 purchase of the Louisiana Territory from Napoleonic France, along with the acquisition of Florida from Spain in 1819 and the conquest of what is now the North American Southwest from Mexico in 1848 had dealt the final blow to the already moribund British-colonial system of aristocratic privileges in the United States. In his canonical *Frontier in American History*, Frederick Jackson Turner explains that the opening of vast western territories to settlement decreased class differences in the United States by expanding property ownership beyond the traditional landed gentry of the colonial and early-republican eras. Though he ignores the consequences of the Louisiana land grab for American Indians and Afro-descendants, Turner is clear on the relationship between this process and what has come to be known as Jacksonian Democracy.[20] "The frontier states that came into the Union in the first quarter of a century of its existence came with democratic suffrage provisions," as, now common, landownership could no longer be taken as a guarantor of civic virtue. This "had reactive effects of the highest importance upon the older States whose people were being attracted there" and "an extension of the franchise became essential" (30). Meanwhile, for white men of the previously subordinate classes, the possibility of land ownership that the Louisiana Purchase represented "meant that one's livelihood was not dependent on the goodwill of another, as was the case, presumably, with tenants, serfs, indentured servants, wage-workers, or chattel slaves, as well as women and children" (Howe 37). As a result, the republic was no longer considered "an integrated unity of social ranks but a society of individuals, often hostile and competitive, who believed they were both equal and unequal" (Langley 67).[21]

Sarmiento looked upon these developments in the northern country with awe, feeling that, carrying bourgeois democracy westward across the continent, the United States accomplished on the plains what Argentina had been unable to achieve in the pampa. To him, the United States presented itself as a rational, ordered society in which human willpower triumphs over the challenges posed by nature and disciplines the environment and the population in order to fill the overwhelmingly empty, barbaric New World wilderness with a civilization of its own industrious creation. As he writes in his laudatory *Viajes,* a travelogue of his journey to the United States: "These Yankees have the right to be impertinent. One hundred inhabitants per mile, four hundred pesos of capital per person, a school for every two hundred inhabitants, and five pesos a year for each child. Then there are the secondary schools; they prepare the spirit. For industry Boston has systems of railroads, canals, and rivers, as well as the coastlines. For thought she has the divinity school and forty-five newspapers, journals, and magazines. To make everything orderly, education."[22] The North American, then, "marks the territory with its civilized form and imposes order in the face of the natural environment and the primitive peoples who threaten to degrade the rational status of the modern subject" while the Argentine "is characterized by mixing and becoming confused with the natural environment" (Errázuriz 47).[23] Viewing the United States as the fulfillment of the New World's mythic promise of prosperity and social renovation, Sarmiento offers the northern country's particular form of racial capitalism, like Cooper's foundational novel of racial exclusion, "as a model for Argentina" (Katra, "Sarmiento en los Estados Unidos" 881).[24]

Gobernar Es Poblar

Sarmiento's meditations on Cooper's exclusionary novels, in which characters of color are expelled from the national family through death, point to the centrality of the racial disciplining of the national body for both liberal Argentina and the Jacksonian United States—an emphasis that Mansilla de García later would problematize. In Argentina, these racial republican ideas find their clearest expression in political thinker Juan Bautista Alberdi's famous maxim "gobernar es poblar" (to govern is to populate) in his 1852 *Bases y puntos de partida para la organización política de la República argentina* (Bases and points of departure for the political organization of the Argentine Republic).[25] An early articulation of what would become Latin American positivism and eugenics, Alberdi's text would influence his country's 1853 Constitutional Assembly, which even ordered the work reprinted (García Orza vi).[26] In the "Explanatory Pages" to the 1879 edition of *Bases,* Alberdi explains that "to govern is to populate in the sense that to populate is to educate, improve, civilize, enrich and grow spontaneously and rapidly" (22).[27] To populate, he continues, is "to instruct, educate, moralize, and improve the race."[28] For Alberdi, as for Sarmiento, this "population science" dictates that Argentine racial stock must be "improved" so that the country may gain "the knowledge and habit of self-government and the means of exercising it."[29] For that reason, prosperity can only be achieved if the country is populated "with people knowledgeable of industry and accustomed to work that produces and enriches" (24).[30] Much as Sarmiento views Argentina's difficult entry into bourgeois modernity as a result of the country's racially mixed history and, in his comments on Cooper, racializes the conflict between civilization and barbarism as a struggle between "the indigenous race and the Anglo-Saxon one," Alberdi adds that "to populate is to civilize" only when "the land is populated with civilized people"—that is, "with colonists from civilized Europe" (28).[31] Inspired by the burgeoning Anglo-Saxon empire in Cooper's United States, Sarmiento and Alberdi deem certain sectors of the Argentine population, such as the nomadic tribes of Amerindians and mixed-race *gauchos,* "uncivilized" and unfit to serve as a capitalist workforce for the bourgeois republic.

As a result, "the early liberal intelligentsia" in Argentina, like the pioneers of Cooper's Jacksonian United States, "demanded a purification of the race and sought a republican metaphor to protect the land from the expansion of indigenous peoples and undesirable 'others'" (Masiello 5). This process of racial "purification" emphasized immigration from Europe, which was encouraged specifically by the country's 1853 constitution and provided for in more detail by the 1875 National Immigration and Colonization Law. During Sarmiento's presidency alone, 280,000 Europeans would settle in Argentina in a state-sponsored effort to increase the country's "governable" white population.[32] Alberdi, for his part, would suggest the legalization of civil marriage in order to enable Catholic Argentine women to marry Protestant foreigners (Sommer, *Foundational Fictions* 103). The proposed rewriting of the marriage law points to the importance of reproduction and, with it, of motherhood and the raising of children for the proper exercise of citizenship to the nineteenth-century Argentine liberal project.

Republican motherhood was a central component of plans to govern through population in both Sarmiento and Alberdi's Argentina and Cooper's United States, as well as Mansilla de García's critique of these plans. Following canonical commentators on US republican culture such as Cooper, de Tocqueville, and Gustave de Beaumont, Sarmiento pays close attention to the lives of women, courtship practices, and child-rearing in the northern country.[33] The Argentine writer contrasts the circumscribed existence led by unmarried women in convent schools and paternal households in nineteenth-century Europe and Latin America with what he sees as the relative freedom of mobility and association enjoyed by single women in the United States, paying particular attention to the latter's supposed autonomy in choosing a husband:

> After two or three years of "flirting" [*flirtear*] (that's the verb the North Americans use), dances, walks, trips and coquetry, the girl in the story, one day at lunch, no big deal [*como quien no quiere la cosa*], asks her parents if they know a young, tall, blond machinist who was in the habit of visiting her once in a while (every day). They've been waiting for this introduction for a year. The point is that a new family bond has been agreed on, which the parents are only informed of right before it happens, even though all of the gossiping housewives in the neighborhood had already told them. The wedding celebrated, the couple hops the very next train, and goes out to show off their happiness in the forests, towns, cities, and hotels. (*Viajes* 349)[34]

Highlighting what he sees as the quintessentially North American nature of the archetypical story he relates through the use of the Anglicism "*flirtear*" (which, italicized, was still recognizably English at the time that *Viajes* was written), Sarmiento describes nineteenth-century US courtship rituals in ironically comical terms such as "the girl in the story," "como quien no quiere la cosa," and "once in a while (every day)."[35] On the one hand, this lighthearted narrative style reflects the author's belief in the innate simplicity and wholesomeness of the United States' Anglo-Saxon Protestant population, a view that he repeats often throughout his *Viajes* and upon which, he—like Cooper and de Tocqueville before him—believes that the success of the nation's democratic and capitalist institutions depends. At the same time, by resorting to comedy, a genre thought to have its origins in Greek fertility rituals, Sarmiento draws attention to the reproductive proclivity of the nineteenth-century North American population. The above-quoted passage is followed by a playfully risqué allusion to the archetypical couple's wedding night: "On the train one is forever seeing these charming couples of twenty-year-old youngsters embracing, resting their heads on one another's breasts, and giving one another such expressive caresses that they edify everyone around them, making them resolve to marry immediately, even the most confirmed of old bachelors. There can be no more insinuating propaganda for marriage than this fresh-air expression of matrimonial intoxication" (349).[36] It is the fruit of these "caresses," "insinuations," and "matrimonial intoxications" that interest Sarmiento: "Because of this a Yankee never reaches the age of twenty-five without having a large family, and I find no other way to explain the astounding propagation of the species on that fortunate soil. In 1790 the population consisted of 4,000,000 souls; in 1800, 5,000,000; in 1810, 7,000,000; in 1820, 9,000,000; in 1830, 12,000,000; in 1840, 17,000,000; in 1850 there will be 23,000,000" (349).[37]

This demographic delirium, too, is inspired by Cooper. In *The Travelling Bachelor; or, Notions of the Americans,* the US author proudly proclaims that "a great majority of the females marry before the age of twenty, and it is not an uncommon thing to see them mothers at sixteen, seventeen, or eighteen. Almost every American mother nurses her own infant. It is far more common to find mothers of eight, or ten children, at fifty, than mothers of two or three" (192). Prodigiously fertile, Anglo-Saxon women such as *The Last of the Mohicans*'s Alice, future mother of Cooper's Jacksonian republic, not only provide racially appropriate future settlers for the western territories—the stuff of Sarmiento and Alberdi's civilizational dreams—they raise morally upright citizens for the North American nation-state: "The first impressions of the child are drawn from the purest sources known to our nature; and the son, even long after he has been compelled to enter on the thorny track of the father, preserves the memorial of the pure and unalloyed lessons that he has received from the lips, and, what is far better, from the example of the mother" (Cooper, *Notions* 106). This interest in republican motherhood explains the racial exclusions at the end of Cooper's *Last of the Mohicans,* a novel typically read as a meditation on North American masculinity. In order to set a proper "example," the novel implies, mothers of the national family must be "pure" not only in "nature" but in race.

This emphasis on racial "purity" manifests itself in the energy that Cooper invests in keeping the half Scottish, half Afro-Jamaican Cora unreproductive in *The Last of the Mohicans.* Throughout the novel, the mulatta heroine feigns disinterest in the lascivious glances of the creole plantocrat Duncan—suitor to her white half sister, Alice—and emphatically refuses the Amerindian Magua's indecent proposal that she should "live in his wigwam forever" (586). Even this, however, is not enough for Cooper, and Cora must die before the novel's white protagonists can marry and give birth to the North American nation in the form of the couple's son, Duncan Uncas Heyward, referred to in a subsequent installment of *The Leatherstocking Tales* as "an officer of the States in the war of revolution" (*The Prairie* 122). Cooper's opting for a white foundational couple when presented with the possibility of emploting racially mixed origins for the nation helps to explain *The Last of the Mohicans*'s appeal to Argentine liberals obsessed with the capacity of republican mothers to raise a governable population.[38]

Republican Motherhood and the Possessive Investment in Whiteness

As Mexican critic Raúl Ianes Vera notes, unlike the nationalist writings of European romanticism, the foundational texts of the nineteenth-century Americas do not look for legitimacy in the region's traditional folkways. Rather, they seek to pare away the human materials that will be discarded from the construction of the nation. One wonders if Cooper doesn't get carried away with all this cutting. The almost random violence that precipitates Cora's death—stabbed by one of Magua's henchmen when the Huron chief is distracted—is senselessly melodramatic. What drives Cooper to such bloody narrative rage? Why does the possibility of racial hybridity perturb the Anglo-Saxon author so much? What is his possessive investment in whiteness?[39]

The racial politics manifested by the combination betrothal-funeral at the end of *The Last of the Mohicans* can hardly be dismissed as a narrative accident. Importantly, the novel was published just seven years after the First Seminole War, in which US forces, led by the same Andrew Jackson whose democratic model Sarmiento later would emulate, battled an interracial Afro-indigenous group in the newly incorporated

Florida. The exclusion through death of Cooper's indigenous Uncas and Afro-descended Cora at the novel's climax mirrors the US Army's subjugation and removal beyond the borders of the nation of the indigenous Seminoles and the Afro-descended maroons to whom they had offered refuge during the Floridian conflict. Much as the deaths of Uncas and Cora at the end of Cooper's novel allow the southern bridegroom Duncan to establish himself as the slavocratic patriarch of the new Anglo-Saxon nation, stripping the indigenous of their land rights in order to expand the plantation system, the expulsion of the Florida maroons as an outcome of the Seminole Wars served to uphold the neocolonial system of Amerindian removal, Euroamerican land tenure, and African chattel slavery upon which Jacksonian Democracy was predicated.[40] This dispossession was codified into law by the 1823 *Johnson v. M'Intosh* case, in which the Supreme Court ruled that Native Americans "can occupy but never own US territory," making it easier to clear the West of indigenous societies and open it to slave-based agricultural production (Goyal xvii).

Given the racial-capitalist nature of the US republican model, the alternative—that Cora, Uncas, and the Black Seminole Afro-indigenous alliance that they allegorize might engender an interracial national family to rival that of the white Alice and Duncan—must have struck Cooper and other Jacksonian North Americans as anathema. It is clear from the novel that the threat of an Afro-indigenous foundational marriage is at the forefront of Cooper's mind. In addition to her aborted romance with the Mohican Uncas, Cora repeatedly refuses the Huron Magua's "indecent" proposal to marry her and conceive mixed-race children similar to the Black Seminoles that were being born in Florida in the period in which Cooper was writing—a fate over which she willingly chooses death (589). This death is narrated in sexually suggestive language; Magua commands, "Woman . . . choose the wigwam or the knife." Moments later, he "recoiled a step, and one of his assistants, profiting by the chance, sheathed his own knife in the bosom of Cora" (862). The images of penetration that Cooper invokes while narrating the death of Cora point to the nature of the threat that she represents to the exclusionary logic of the novel, which resides in her potential to subvert North American racial hierarchies by giving birth to hybrid offspring.[41] These hypothetical children, like the Black Seminoles—and unlike the future mestizos of Mansilla's novel, as I will explain below—must be removed from the nation, as their presence would only undermine the social and political equality among white men through which the nation defines itself.

Yet, concerned as he is over Black Seminole threats to Anglo-American hegemony in Florida, Cooper also finds the energy to prohibit Cora's potential coupling with the white Duncan—a narrative development that draws attention to itself in the fact that the pair's unfulfilled desire to say more to one another "than cooler reason would approve" proves extraneous to the novel's central captivity plot yet does not play an important enough role in the narrative to warrant a subplot in its own right. In other words, Cooper creates sexual tension between Cora and Duncan for the sole purpose of prohibiting its release. Why?

Perhaps the answer is to be found in how the "intersection of ethnic diversity with property allocation" shapes the history of the colonial contact zone known as the US West (Limerick 27).[42] In a Jacksonian world in which the citizen is defined as a white male, to marry a white male to a nonwhite female is to admit the subaltern into the national body and to allow her hybrid offspring to become the legitimate inheritors of the wealth that he is recently free to make for himself using the territories and toil of nonwhites.[43] "Proscriptions on interracial marriage effectively meant that blacks [and other nonwhites] could not make any legally recognized claims as spouses to white wealth, since the laws regulating private wealth do not recognize nonmarital sexual coupling. Refusing to give legal sanction to marriage across the color line was an economic policy that aimed to stratify wealth racially" (Clymer 11). Antimiscegenation laws stripped female partners of color and their mixed-race children of the democratically equitable inheritance rights that Cooper in *The Travelling Bachelor; or, Notions of the Americans* identifies as the death knell for British aristocratic privileges (which were based on primogeniture and entailment) in the postindependence United States.

William Apes, a Methodist minister from an intergenerational mixed-race Pequod family, demonstrates the whiteness of property in his 1829 autobiography *A Son of the Forrest,* in which he complains that whites "had possession of the red man's inheritance, and deprived me of liberty" (38). Indentured to his white neighbors the Furmans, Apes is essentially adopted by the family; the grandmother even "allowed me to call her mother" (28). This does not save him from racist attacks, however, and the Furmans eventually sell their putative "son's" indenture and send him away (31). The autobiography uncomfortably demonstrates the racial limits of belonging to the national family in the early-republican United States, emblematizing the "possession of the red man's inheritance" and the "deprivation" of nonwhite "liberty" through the sale of Apes away from his supposed "mother."

Incidents such as this one demonstrate that, for Cooper to marry Cora to Duncan would be to undermine the foundations of Jacksonian racial capitalism, a system based on colonial regimes of land and labor. Moreover, "the fear of amalgamation aside," the injunction against miscegenation "also reveals a deeper anxiety that interracial intimacy would lead to social reform. Because of their race and gender, mixed-race women did not have a public voice, but . . . critics feared that they would influence men in power who could speak for them" (Manganelli 56). These men were not only the white husbands that they would marry but also the mixed-race sons that they would raise—the governable workforce that Alberdi was so interested in maintaining whitely industrious in order to foment Argentine economic development.[44] As Brenda O. Daly and Maureen T. Reddy point out, "Under patriarchal capitalism, motherhood is largely about private property: the children are property of the father who 'loans' them temporarily to the mother, whose duty is to raise those children according to the father's law" (8)—a law whose legitimacy is grounded in the illegitimacy of mixed marriages and the interracial children that they produce.

Thus, as critic George Dekker observes, the marriage of Alice and Duncan promised by the novel's conclusion and the racially pure citizenry to which Alice, as white republican mother, will give birth in the form of patriot Duncan Uncas Heyward highlight the unsuitability of the other possible foundational pairings—Cora and Duncan, Cora and Uncas, and Cora and Magua—that the text presents. Importantly, the common element in all these discarded interracial couplings is the mulatta Cora—herself an interracial subject—whose eroticized death at the narrative's climax allows her white half sister to assume the role of republican mother during the denouement. At the heart of the novel's libidinal logic, then, is the mixed-race Cora's supposed unsuitability for the task of reproducing the bourgeois-republican nation.

Cultural studies scholar Amy Kaplan identifies a link between the ideological construction of bourgeois-republican motherhood and the beginnings of the settler-colonialist model of North American imperialism in Louisiana and Mexico. "If, on the one hand, domesticity drew strict boundaries between the private home and the public world of men, on the other, it became the engine of national expansion, the site from which the nation reaches beyond itself through the emanation of woman's moral influence" as mother of the colonizing settlers in newly acquired territories (*Anarchy of Empire* 29). By turning the homestead into a home for their citizen children, white republican mothers such as Cooper's Alice "redefine the meaning of habitation . . . to make Euro-Americans feel at home in a place where *they* are initially the foreign ones. Domesticity inverts this relationship to create a home by rendering prior inhabitants alien and undomesticated and by implicitly nativizing newcomers. The empire of the mother thus embodies the anarchy at the heart of the American empire; the two empires follow a double compulsion to conquer and domesticate—to control and incorporate—the foreign within the borders of the home and nation" (34). This process relied on the "contraction of the domestic sphere to exclude persons conceived of as racially foreign within those expanding national boundaries" (42).[45] If North American domestic values were to be brought to colonized territories by civilizing republican mothers, mixed-race colonial subjects such as Cora—Kaplan's "racially foreign"—must not be allowed to raise the republican family and instill values other than those of Anglo-Saxon racial capitalism in the future voters. For similar reasons, Sarmiento's and Alberdi's racialized modernization projects hinged on the replacement of Argentine mothers of color with white Europeans. Eduarda Mansilla de García's *Lucía Miranda,* to which I now turn, would complicate these plans by locating race mixture at the beginning of the national genealogy by deploying a "Morisca" republican mother to vindicate particularly Hispanic forms of hybridity and coloniality that Sarmiento and others sought to replace with US-inspired modes of racial capitalism.

Lucía Miranda

His country's best-known liberal ideologue, Sarmiento would have a deep influence on nationalist discourse in Argentina in general and on the work of Eduarda Mansilla de García in particular (Batticuore 246). Having traveled to the United States when her husband, Manuel García, succeeded Sarmiento as Argentine minister to the northern country, Mansilla de García was in a position to observe and evaluate the racial-capitalist model narrativized by Cooper and that Sarmiento and Alberdi wished to import into Argentina.[46] She would explore her misgivings regarding this model and its implications for her country's colonial race structures in her 1860 historical novel *Lucía Miranda*.[47] A (paternalistic) rejection of the racially exclusive republicanism espoused by Cooper and Sarmiento, by casting the daughter of an Old Christian and a *morisca* as her protagonist, the novel breaks with the conventions of the Cooperian foundational genre that Sarmiento had proposed as a model for Latin American literature.[48] Instead, Mansilla's narrative vindicates as a civilizing force the hybridity of the Hispanic society that Sarmiento condemns in *Facundo*. The work thus represents an elite response to the northernization of Argentine society proposed by the country's liberals, endorsing creole neocolonialism while asserting the validity of South American tradition at a moment in which European and US paradigms were becoming increasingly hegemonic.[49]

The novel intervenes in the Argentine debate between provincialism and cosmopolitanism that I described earlier, steering close to the conservative cause without taking it up entirely. On the one hand, the story presents Spanish colonialism in a positive light that is sure to make twenty-first-century readers wince, stressing Spain's evangelizing mission in the Americas and portraying mestizaje as a hopeful resolution to the brutality of the conquest in a manner that the last several decades of decolonial scholarship have demonstrated to be problematic. In this way, the novel can be read as a vindication of the Hispanic traditionalism with which Sarmiento, for example, associated the Federales. On the other hand, the text displays a reverence for something that might be understood vaguely as "Western Civilization," for European high culture, and even—despite its embrace of mestizaje and the other—for whiteness.[50] In this way, the novel vindicates Spanish American society as the equal of the cultures of the Global North, questioning the civilization/barbarism binary that Sarmiento had drawn.

Ruy Díaz de Guzmán and the Lucía Miranda Myth

An Argentine tradition, the apparently apocryphal story of Lucía Miranda first appears in the *Anales del descubrimiento, población y conquista del Río de la Plata* (Annals on the discovery, settlement, and conquest of Río de la Plata), a colonial *crónica* written by Mansilla's distant ancestor Ruy Díaz de Guzmán as a counterdiscourse to Dominican Friar Bartolomé de las Casas's works denouncing the Spanish conquest (de Ángelis 1). Though penned in 1612, the foundational text was not published until 1836, as the first volume of the Neapolitan-born historian Pedro de Ángelis's *Colección de obras y documentos relativos a la historia antigua y moderna de las Provincias del Río de la Plata* (Collection of works and documents relating to the ancient and modern history of the provinces of Río de la Plata), an edited series of historical texts commissioned by the traditionalist Federal dictator Rosas in an effort to forge a cultural identity for the newly independent Argentine state (Marre 340–41). The collection celebrates "the colonial creole roots of the United Provinces of Río de la Plata" at a moment when traditional Hispanic values were under attack from the Europeanizing Unitarios (Lojo, "Lucía Miranda," 31).[51]

Set during the early conquest of the Timbú people of the Southern Cone, the story of Lucía Miranda features noble and ignoble Amerindians in the form of twin *caciques,* or indigenous chiefs, named Mangoré and Siripo. Like their counterparts Uncas and Magua in Cooper's canonical text, both brothers display sexual interest in Lucía. Siripo kidnaps the Spanish woman and makes her his slave but offers her liberty if she will agree to marry him, much as Magua offers to spare Cooper's Cora's life if she will accept a similar arrangement. Like Cooper's novel, too, the story of Lucía Miranda serves as a foundational historical romance for the future nation. In taking Lucía in marriage, the cacique Siripo would make her his queen and give her legitimate power over the indigenous Timbúes whom she and her husband, Sebastián Hurtado, have gone to South America to conquer and colonize (18). Her refusal of this offer reaffirms the values of Christian marriage and fidelity. Thus, even as the story narrates the failure of the first Spanish settlement in the Southern Cone, Lucía's sacrifice consecrates the New World soil for an eventual European victory in the name of the white national family. As an imperial captivity narrative in which the kidnapping of the woman of European origin allegorizes the nation under threat of penetration by racialized others, the *crónica* involves "a racist discourse of revenge in which the fear of rape and possession of white female bodies by indigenous men is used to justify the conquest and possession of native lands" (Hanway 86) and imagine a white national community through narrative.[52]

A traditional legend, the Lucía Miranda myth has resurfaced in Argentine literature time and again, normally at moments, such as the modernizing 1860s, when the human and geographic borders of the nation were in question.[53] The colonial Lucía represented "a safe, unproblematic hero" for the Argentina of the liberal age, as she "existed at a safe distance in the past, she was from the 'correct' race and class, and she was virtuously married" (Frederick, *Wily Modesty* 88). Much as in the case of Kaplan's North American West, "the desire by the growing [Argentine] nation to contain and put boundaries around lands that were still not under the control of urban Buenos Aires required a narrative that would re-create indigenous territory . . . as a space that belonged to the white nation" (Hanway 91–92). Works such as Echeverría's *Cautiva* and the traditional Lucía Miranda myth readily filled this void. In such a reading, "Lucia stands for the white Argentine nation that is considered to be vulnerable to indigenous attack" (Hanway 86) and her body, "kidnapped and later killed to maintain honor and fidelity, marks only the enormous distance between white culture and the representation of the indigenous as Other" (101).[54] In this way, the Lucía texts address "some of the major debates of mid-nineteenth century national discourse: the desire of white Argentines to expand into the pampas, the effort to prescribe the relationship between territory and citizenship, and the quest to reconcile a divided nation"—polemics with which Mansilla would dialogue and from the fault lines of which her own discourse would emerge (85).

The allegory's currency in the 1800s demonstrates that, as in Kaplan's settler-colonialist United States, the domestic sphere and the notion of republican motherhood were integral to the nineteenth-century liberal project in Argentina. While Mansilla supported her period's gender constructions of domesticity and maternity, in her novel, she articulates more nuanced views regarding the racial paradigms implicit in this liberal discourse, feeling that they closed the limited space that she believes the Hispanic tradition had left open for hybridity through the cultural pluralism of the Iberian Middle Ages and the tripodal mestizaje of Spaniards, Amerindians, and Africans during the New World colonial period.[55] In this way, the text questions the northern-inspired view of national motherhood promoted by Sarmiento and other nineteenth-century Argentine liberals.

Recent critics have pointed to the discourse of domesticity present in Mansilla's *Lucía Miranda* and the interracial marriage between a Spanish conquistador and an indigenous Timbú woman at the novel's conclusion as a—still racially hierarchical—contestation of Argentine liberals' patriarchal attitudes toward the country's Amerindian population. Building on those studies, I read *Lucía Miranda* in light of the nineteenth-century trans-American discourse on republican motherhood in order to consider the question of how the protagonist's "Morisco" origins intervene in the period's conflict between the defenders of Hispanic tradition and the proponents of European and North American modernity. I argue that the author uses the ethnically ambiguous figure of Lucía—an embodiment of the meeting of Christians, Muslims, Spaniards, Amerindians, and Africans in the Spanish empire—in order to vindicate colonial modes of cultural pluralism as a civilizing force in the Americas and reject North-looking liberal formulations of Argentina's Hispanic heritage as "barbaric." In this way, she makes room in the Argentine national family for the Hispanic traditions of ethnocultural hybridity derided by the Cooper-loving Sarmiento.

Lucía Miranda's Moderate Mestizaje

Daughter of Lucio Norberto Mansilla, a prominent general in Argentina's early-nineteenth-century wars with Spain and Brazil, and Agustina Ortiz de Rozas, Eduarda Mansilla was the niece of the Federal dictator Juan Manuel de Rosas, whose regime famously is attacked in Sarmiento's *Facundo*—a work with which she would dialogue critically in her novel *Pablo, ou la vie dans les pampas* (Pablo, or life in the pampas) (1869).[56] Despite her Federal heritage, however, in 1855, Mansilla married the liberal diplomat Manuel Rafael García Aguirre (himself the son of a prominent Unitario).[57] Written from a position of race and class privilege and gender marginalization, her reconfiguration of the republican motherhood trope subverts the racial-capitalist ideals for which Cooper and his Argentine admirers Sarmiento and Alberdi advocated by rejecting the gendered racial paradigms underlying their beliefs.[58] Casting off the neocolonial paradigms of Argentine liberals and the racial-capitalist model of US continental empire upon which they were based, Mansilla de García articulates a pluralist—yet patrician—vision of New World republican motherhood from the perspective of the hemisphere's southern peripheries.[59]

Originally published in serial form under the title *Lucía; episodio sacado de la historia argentina* (Lucía, an episode taken from Argentine history) in *La tribuna*, Mansilla's deployment of the colonial myth in the mid-nineteenth century intervenes in her era's debates regarding the value of traditional Argentine society versus assimilation to the political, economic, and cultural standards of the Global North. While not departing dramatically from the basic plot of its foundational source material, Mansilla's *Lucía Miranda* breaks with the uterine-nationalist logic of racial engineering typical of earlier adaptations of Ruy Díaz de Guzmán's myth, as well as the racial-capitalist thinking of Cooper, Sarmiento, and Alberdi by locating mestizaje at the center of her story of national origins.[60] A critique of the Argentine liberal emphasis on racial and cultural *blanqueamiento*, or whitening, Mansilla's *Lucía Miranda* often is read as reversing the racial order presented by much of canonical nineteenth-century New World literature: works such as Cooper's *Last of the Mohicans*, as well as the Argentine Esteban Echeverría's 1837 *Cautiva*, the Brazilian José de Alencar's 1857 *O guarany*, the Ecuadorian Juan León Mera's 1877 *Cumandá*, and the Cuban Cirilo Villaverde's 1882 *Cecilia Valdés* in which protagonists of color are either killed or confined before they have the opportunity to reproduce with whites. As scholars such as María Rosa

Lojo have noted, Mansilla breaks with this narrative tradition by identifying a possible foundational couple in the indigenous Anté and the Spanish Alejo, to whom "the whole pampa offers its immensity" as they flee Lucía's execution to carry on their relationship far from the interethnic violence for which the colonial encounter is known (359).[61] In this way, Mansilla optimistically imagines "the foundational moment for Argentine nation culture in the mixed-race couple's turn away from the martyr's pyre and toward a confrontation with the vast and newly empty landscape" (Moody 22). Through this interracial primal moment, the author interrupts liberal Europeanizing designs with her assertion of foundational mestizaje, providing a multiracial genealogy for a nation that soon would complete the genocidal Conquista del Desierto (Conquest of the desert) against the indigenous peoples of Patagonia.

Given that the contrast between Mansilla's mestizo-maternal *Lucía Miranda* and Cooper's *Last of the Mohicans*—in which nonwhite characters die before they can miscegenate and conceive a mixed-race nation—is so stark, it is worth considering how Mansilla's frontier captivity narrative might function as a counterdiscourse to Cooper's canonical example of the genre. Proposed, as I noted above, by the pro-Yankee Sarmiento as a model for New World literature at the opening of his foundational *Facundo,* Cooper's text was popular in nineteenth-century liberal circles and had been translated into both Spanish and French (the vehicular intellectual language of the nineteenth-century Latin American intelligentsia) at least twice by the time Mansilla wrote her novel, influencing the development of Romanticism, the historical novel, *indianista* literature, and the foundational historical genre in Latin American letters, as works by Echeverría, de Alencar, Mera, and Zorrilla de San Martín attest.[62] Given the North American text's importance to the nineteenth-century literature of Latin America—particularly through Sarmiento, who initiated the tradition in Argentina—it is difficult to believe that Mansilla would not at least have been thinking about Cooper's novel when she wrote *Lucía Miranda*. She clearly was aware of the book as, in *El médico de San Luis* (The doctor of San Luis), published in the same year as *Lucía Miranda,* she makes a point of noting that the protagonist's daughters own a copy of the North American author's works. More tellingly, in *Pablo, ou la vie dans les pampas,* written in French while her husband was working in the Argentine embassy in Paris, Mansilla describes her gaucho hero as dressed in "bas de cuir" (leatherstocking)—a clear allusion that proves that the writer was familiar with her North American predecessor's novelistic cycle when she penned her own frontier romances (26).[63]

Her decision to promote mestizaje where her North American counterpart prohibits miscegenation thus may be read as a tacit critique of the US-inspired paradigms of Sarmiento, Cooper's fan *número uno*. While Cooper locates the origins of the US nation in the joining of Anglo-Saxon Alice's and Duncan's hands in matrimony over the mulatta Cora's coffin, Mansilla de García's foundational novel opposes the northern-influenced *blanqueamiento* paradigm with her counterdiscursive narrative of foundational mestizaje, drawing attention to the country's hybrid history of intercivilizational encounter.

However, as scholars have pointed out, at the same time that it undermines liberal whitening paradigms, *Lucía Miranda* reproduces much of the colonialist rhetoric regarding indigenous Argentines found in hegemonic cultural discourses. Mansilla takes care to describe "some twenty or thirty Indians, their bodies almost naked, with their heads covered in feathers and so still [that] they looked like clay statues" (303), reproducing colonialist images of exotically nude natives that have been omnipresent in Spanish American letters since Columbus's *Diario de abordo*.[64] At another point, she references the "rebel nature" of an indigenous "child of the desert" (348), presenting the Timbúes as wild creatures of the pampa.[65]

Lucía, meanwhile, takes it upon herself to instruct the seemingly childlike Timbú women and correct their maternal "failings": "One of the things that the virtuous Spaniard most begged [of the indigenous women] was that they inspire respect in their children, teaching them [*educándoles*] from when they were young, respectful, and submissive because the Indian women had the most mistaken beliefs in this regard, judging motherly love to consist of permitting even the most unruly and shocking acts" (316).[66] Not only does Lucía offer instruction in the Christian faith, she schools the Timbú mothers on the importance of maintaining domestic order in their households. Combining the role of virtuous mother with that of teacher in a way typical of nineteenth-century New World literatures, much of Lucía's function in the novel seems to be that of national *educadora*, imparting the blessings of Western civilization to the future Argentines.

As is clear, if Mansilla admits nonwhites into the nation, it is as subordinates. This is demonstrated by Lucía's tutelage of the indigenous Anté, whom she teaches to be a good wife (109) and whose desire to dress in European fashion she does not discourage—domestic actions that indoctrinate the indigenous mother of the future mestizo nation in European canons of feminine comport (107). The marriage of Alejo and Anté that Lucía orchestrates thus represents, "a mestizaje in which the dominant masculine element (the father) is white and Christian, and therefore can give *shape* or *form* to the 'barbarous material.' To think the opposite (that Lucía had children with Siripo) would be to subvert the relations of domination and to humiliate the conquistador's culture by transforming it like a woman, into a penetrable object/body" (Lojo, Introduction 33).[67] Despite its focus on mestizaje, like the more traditional foundational romances, Mansilla's novel mobilizes domesticity in the service of settler colonialism.

Thus, while Mansilla's nation model certainly allows for alterity, as her incorporation of the marriage of Anté and Alejo makes clear, her persuasions are not egalitarian as much as patrician. "In essence, the author advocates for assimilation of indigenous communities to creole Argentina as complimentary to and more palatable than other methods including homicide and displacement" that certain US-inspired Argentine liberals were promoting at the time. Mansilla counters this with a "vision of an adaptable family-nation that would work together to ensure care for creole society's most vulnerable members, acknowledging and even celebrating its own mestizo origins" (Moody 23). Instead of the genocidal designs for which the Jacksonian Cooper and his admirer Sarmiento advocated, she offers a vindication of the Hispanic colonial order that her uncle Rosas claimed to defend against the liberals' modernizing reforms.

While critics traditionally have concentrated (rightly) on the relationship between Anté and Alejo to demonstrate Mansilla's endorsement of the traditional integration of society under creole hegemony, I want to draw attention to the hybrid figure of Lucía herself. How does Mansilla intervene in nineteenth-century Argentine conversations regarding race and national identity by scripting a protagonist of Morisco descent as allegorical mother of the nation?

Importantly, though the indigenous Anté is the only female character who lives to potentially reproduce at the end of the novel, it is the Spaniard Lucía who metaphorically mothers the nation to which Anté is poised to give birth. Upon arriving in the New World, Lucía effectively adopts Anté, arranging the latter's marriage to Alejo: "Lucía, who witnessed the budding love between the two young people, took special care in preparing the Indian's heart for the intimate and delicate enjoyment of that sweet affect, and with sermons tempered the fiery ardor of her savage soul. And, as time went by, the Spanish woman's heart transferred a portion of its delicate perfume to the young Indian" (318).[68] "Preparing the Indian's heart" for her Spanish husband by tempering "the fiery ardor of her savage soul," Lucía, like Kaplan's domesticating republican mother, participates in the colonialist civilizing mission in the Americas through the raising of children. Transmitting a "portion of her delicate perfume," the Spaniard is grafted onto the native, rendering Lucía an allegorical mother of the nation that Anté and Alejo will found.

This rhetorical function is made clear at the end of the novel, when she is burned alive as punishment for her refusal of the indigenous Siripo's violent advances: "The wind suddenly blows, its whining voice echoing in the distance; the flame, about to become extinguished, comes back with greater force. The bonfire lights again, it burns, it consumes everything in its reach. The neighboring trees burn. The trunk from which the disfigured cadaver hangs swings and falls. A moment more, and Lucía's and Sebastian's ashes mingle [*se confunden*] in a final embrace!" (359).[69] *Abrazados* and *abrasados* as they embrace in the embers, Lucía and Sebastián "mingle" to found the national line, at least symbolically. In the novel's allegorical economy, the immolated pair passes their foundational status to Anté and Alejo as the interethnic couple flees the wreckage around them to the pampa. This is evident from the text's final sentence: "The forest turned into ash; today no vestiges are left—the Timbúes moved camp the next day" (359).[70] In Moody's interpretation of the novel's conclusion, "Lucía's flaming body sparks a fire that spreads and clears away the wood, as if creating the Pampa from her funeral pyre and cleansing the symbolic space of its violent past and the impediments to creole occupation" (22). Lucía's and Sebastián's ashes thus destroy the wilderness and force the Timbúes to abandon the area, opening a space for Spanish colonizers to return to the Southern Cone and bring Argentina into what Mansilla views as the civilized fold of Western Christendom.

Miranda Morisca

However, Mansilla adds a level of nuance to this colonial model by locating her protagonist on unsteady ethnic terrain. While the colonial *crónicas* present Lucía Miranda ethnically as a Spaniard with no further qualification, Mansilla de García depicts her character as the illegitimate daughter of a Spanish nobleman by "a young woman of Morisco origin" (una joven de origen morisco) (159). A Christian descended from Muslims, Lucía's mother was impregnated out of wedlock by a "young gentleman" (jóven hidalgo), whose membership in the Spanish gentry indicates his Old Christian lineage. Importantly, while, as historian Diana Marre points out, there are more than twenty versions of the Lucía Miranda tale, making it difficult if not impossible to trace the source of any particular innovation, the heroine is not of Morisco heritage in any of the other iterations of the story of which I am aware. Moreover, as María Lojo shows, Mansilla appears to be the first writer to discuss the fictional Lucía's life before she arrived in the New World (Introduction). Why add this detail to the classic tale?[71]

Mansilla de García's decision to incorporate a Hispano-Arab character into her mestizo foundational historical romance clearly dialogues with the Orientalist discourse famously found in Sarmiento's *Facundo*, the foundational text on the conflict between European civilization and New World barbarism on the pampas. Deploying an eclectic set of Romantic tropes for describing alterity that will strike twenty-first-century readers as imprecise, Sarmiento seizes upon the nineteenth-century West's fascination with the "Orient," and the "readily available vocabulary of temporal and spatial otherness" that it had created (Beckman, "Bedouins" 43). He somewhat speciously describes the gauchos as "American Bedouins" engaged in "the same struggle between civilization and barbarism [that] exists in Africa" (14).[72] The sentence frames the alterity within the Argentine nation in terms of "Moorishness," a capacious category that, as I will explain below, at the time could be interpreted as either North African, Asian, or black. This ambiguous other, faced with the ungovernable vastness of the pampa, lives in a "savage," "cruel," and "tyrannical" world vaguely reminiscent of Black Legend tales about the Spanish conquest of the Americas. In a long passage Sarmiento explains:

> This extension of the plains paints civilized life with a certain Asiatic tincture. . . . The spirit finds an analogy between the pampas and the plains that lie between the Tigris and the Euphrates. . . .
> The overseer is a strongman [*caudillo*], like the chief of a caravan in Asia. . . . At the slightest sign of insubordination, the overseer unfurls his iron whip and rains blows over the insolent party that cause bruises and wounds; if the resistance goes on . . . , he jumps from his horse with his formidable knife in hand and quickly vindicates his authority through the superior skill with which he wields it.
> The man who dies executed by the overseer has no right to redress, as the authority of the one that killed him is considered legitimate.
> So it is that Argentine life begins to establish itself through the peculiar predominance of brutal force, the law of the strongest, limitless authority without responsibility on the part of those who rule, and justice administered without formalities and without debate. (*Facundo*, 14)[73]

Here Sarmiento racializes dictatorship as "Asian" (meaning Middle Eastern, or "Moorish," located between the Tigris and the Euphrates, beyond the borders of Europe). In the analogy that radiates from this comparison, the overseer of an Argentine ranch is likened to the chief of an "Asian" caravan, whom Sarmiento, following French Enlightened discourse, figures as violent and despotic.[74] Subordinates have no rights in this world, as sovereignty lies in the "authority" of the "caudillo." Argentina's "Moorish" barbarism is represented in these texts as a non-Western lawlessness and lack of restraint endemic to a country that Sarmiento and his liberal companions wanted desperately to make conform to North Atlantic canons of modernity.[75]

Sarmiento's Orientalist presentation of Argentina's colonial heritage as retrograde draws on northern European tropes for discussing Iberia that had been common since the Golden Age of the Spanish empire. "Although official discourse in Spain loudly renounced Moorishness, the westernmost reaches of Europe remained for many observers part of the Orient or Africa, and thus savage, cruel, or tyrannical" (Fuchs 117). Even as late as the nineteenth century, writers took inspiration in Spain's medieval history of Islamic rule under the Umayyad, Almoravid, and Almohad governments to exoticize the Hispanic world in terms of a "Moorishness" unassimilable to Western modernity, as Romantic texts such as Hugo's 1829 *Orientales* (the source of several epigraphs in Mansilla's *Lucía Miranda*) and North American Washington Irving's 1832 *Tales from the Alhambra* demonstrate.[76] Mansilla, for her part, was largely "independent" of these "guidelines followed by the Argentine Romantics who, like Sarmiento and Ecehverría, rejected all things Spanish" (Chikiar Bauer, *Entre ellos* 82).[77] While Sarmiento bemoans Argentina's Oriental "barbarism," Mansilla enshrines Hispano-Arab alterity in the national family through the Moorish descent of republican mother Lucía.

Significantly, upon arriving in the Río de la Plata region, Lucía is said to have set herself up like a "sultaness" (*sultana*) in her New World home, suggesting a relationship between the American colony's peninsular rulers and the medieval Moors (305). Similarly, while Mansilla de García's description of the conquistadors as a "small tribe" (*pequeña tribu*) echoes Sarmiento's reference to the gauchos as "American Bedouins," it lacks the critical tone found in *Facundo* (305). If the original Lucía Miranda legend is an allegory of national purity, Mansilla, through her hybrid maternal figure, celebrates the alterity at the origin of Argentina's national genealogy, the very colonial legacy that Sarmiento sees as an impediment to bourgeois-republican modernity.

Mansilla's engagement with Moorishness, then, simultaneously reinscribes and resemanticizes the well-known Orientalist representation of the Hispanic world found in Sarmiento's *Facundo*. While Sarmiento, echoing Black Legend discourse, uses the "beduino americano" as an empty signifier onto which he poetically projects his preoccupations regarding Argentina's "Oriental" "barbarism," Mansilla makes room for Hispanic approaches to alterity through the less-than-entirely-Western background of the national mother. Even if, with her Spanish furniture and books, Lucía has created "a stamp of culture still foreign to those remote lands," those very activities mean that she has set herself up like a "sultana" in her comfortable New World home (305).[78] Strikingly out of place in the sixteenth-century Southern Cone, the Romantic Orientalist trope dialogues with Sarmiento's poeticization of Argentine otherness while tracing a line of continuity between the splendor of Spain's intercultural Middle Ages and the civilizational mestizaje of the Golden Age *barroco de Indias* (305).[79] Lucía's identity as the daughter of an Old Christian father and a Morisca mother thus embodies a Hispanic history of hybridity that Sarmiento seemingly wished to replace with Cooper's US model of racial purity. The author may embrace what she sees as the supremacy of the Christian West through her use of colonialist tropes, but her novel asserts the validity of the specifically Hispanic variant of that tradition. In this way, she vindicates the cultural legacy of the colonial power that Argentine liberals of the period had condemned as "lagging behind Europe" (Sarmiento, *Facundo* 15).

Lucía's "Morisco" heritage proves to be the locus of multiple forms of hybridity. The peninsular character's Atlantic crossing reflects the fact that, of the few women granted royal licenses to travel to the Americas during the early sixteenth century, a large number were of partial Arab descent (Forbes 182). Also overrepresented among women traveling from the peninsula to the Americas during the early years of colonization were Iberian mulatas, daughters of African women enslaved in Spain, and their masters (Buscaglia-Salgado 85). This coincidence may explain how it came to pass that, in addition to the peninsular meaning of a Christianized Moor, in the colonial taxonomic system of racialized *castas*, the Iberian term "morisco" would come in some regions to refer to the child of a Spaniard and a *mulata*.[80]

The association of the Arab Morisco-descended Lucía with the black Moriscos of the castas system that I am proposing represents an against-the-grain reading of the novel, which does not make explicit allusions to blackness or African chattel slavery. Yet the topic of New World blackness and bondage appears in other texts that Mansilla worked on at about the same time that she composed *Lucía Miranda:* in *Recuerdos de viaje,* which discusses a trip to the United States during the 1860s; in her 1860 *Médico de San Luis,* in which freedmen appear as characters; and in her 1869 *Pablo, ou la vie dans les pampas,* which prominently features a black nursemaid. Meanwhile, her 1880 collection *Cuentos* contains a sentimentalist critique of slavery in the United States in a short story entitled "El tío Antonio" (Uncle Antonio). The integration of Afro-descendants into New World societies, then, was clearly a subject of interest to the author. Reading the polysemic term "morisco" in this context opens the door to a dialogue between *Lucía Miranda* and the racialization of Argentina's Hispanic traditionalism in terms of black "barbarism" that, as I will show, was common in the canonical liberal literature of the age. It also makes clear how Mansilla's text reconfigures the exclusionary racial-maternal politics of Cooper's *Last of the Mohicans* in order to critique the view of Argentina's Spanish American culture as inferior to northern modernity presented in works such as *Facundo.*

Argentine Blackness

Recent scholarship has explored how "whiteness prevailed in Argentina because of a system of racial classification and perception that broadened North Atlantic definitions of the category 'white' to include an array of racial origins, phenotypical variations, and shades of color" (Alberto and Elena 11). In his classic study *The Afro-Argentines of Buenos Aires,* historian George Reid Andrews postulates that, in the same way that, in Golden Age Spain, the children of Morisca mothers and Old Christian fathers inherited Old Christian legal status (Childers), in nineteenth-century Argentina, a similar process was applied to people of sub-Saharan African descent by census takers who systematically registered mixed-race people as white (Andrews, *Afro-Argentines* 64–92). As a result, "large numbers of Afro-Argentines" were "counted as white in official demographic records" (89). Among this group were people like Lucía, children of Afro-Argentine (that is, Morisca) women and the Italian immigrant men (among the oldest of the "Old Christians") who settled in the country as a result of the liberal whitening strategies that Mansilla questions in her novel. A skeptic of the liberal project, Mansilla would have been conscious of these official efforts to present her country's racial heritage as more European. Given the parallel Europeanization processes in the peninsula and along the Plata embodied in the dual meaning of the term "morisco" (a person of partial Arab or of partial African descent), the author's decision to cast a character of Morisco origin in the role of mother of the nation—through the very meaning(s) and associations of the word—intervenes in the racialized national discourse underlying the Europeanizing vision of maternity found in periodicals such as *La Aljaba*.[81] Having spilled considerable ink over the unfitness of Afro-descendants—overrepresented among the Federales—to raise future citizens, one might imagine that the liberal elites would take note of a Morisca mother in a work by Rosas's niece.

Though Argentina long has prided itself on being the most European country in the Americas, the nation's racial history is more complicated than this popular image suggests. Despite widespread present-day views of Argentina as a European nation misplaced at the southern extremity of South America, during eighteenth and nineteenth centuries, "the majority of the population [was] composed of blacks, mulattoes, and a variety of other *castas*" (Salvatore, "Integral Outsiders" 61). The 1778 census shows that, out of 24,083 inhabitants, there were 2,997 mulatos and 3,837 blacks in Buenos Aires. A generation later, at the time of independence, Afro-descendants had grown to over a third of the capital's population. The countryside, too, was largely black (Freixa 12; Grandin 27; Alberto and Elena 6). This demographic situation is a result of the (often underestimated) importance of human bondage in the country's economic history. Buenos Aires's opulent nineteenth-century mercantile class owed its primitive capital accumulation largely to the slave trade (Grandin 106–8); between 1777 and 1812, approximately seventy thousand enslaved persons entered Río de la Plata, constituting "the most important object of trade" in the region's interior (Borucki 2–3).[82]

Even as they were aligned with these urban import-export interests, anti-Rosas writers would express concern over the Afro-Argentine population's seeming alliance with the dictator. Importantly, "the peculiar relationship between Rosas and the Afro-Argentines was . . . one of the fundamental characteristics of his government" (Solomianski 103); the Afro-Argentine newspaper *El negrito* went so far as to open its 1833 inaugural issue with an anonymous poem in praise of Rosas (1–2).[83] The Argentine Generation of 1837 to which Sarmiento belonged resented the support that Afro-Argentines leant the government and came to associate the group with what they perceived as the Federales' barbarism. In *Facundo*, Sarmiento claims that "the blacks . . . endowed Rosas with a dedicated force of spies in the bosom of every family, servants and slaves, giving him, moreover, excellent and incorruptible soldiers" (218).[84] In another passage, he criticizes the Federal gauchos' participation in "a system of murders and cruelties only tolerable in Ashanti, in Dahomay, in the African interior," discursively blackening the "barbaric" Federalista popular classes.[85] Liberal writers Esteban Echeverría and José Mármol, too, "directed their anti-Rosas rhetoric against African Argentines," including racially demeaning descriptions of black Federales as a way to discredit the Rosas dictatorship in the short story "El matadero" (The Slaughterhouse) (1871) and the novel *Amalia* (1855), respectively. As Hanway summarizes, "To *unitarios*, African Argentines were barbarians, and spies for Rosas" (9).[86] In this way, even as it refers to the "Oriental" "backwardness" that Sarmiento saw as plaguing Argentina, Lucía's status as a Morisca associates her with the Afro-Argentine popular classes whom the country's liberal elites identified with the nation's supposed political immaturity.[87] It seems probable, then, that Mansilla's decision in her foundational romance to position a Morisca's daughter as mother of the nation represents a conscious rejection of the liberals' whitening paradigm via an assertion of a racial tradition that would prove problematic to the modernizing state. Thus, as it does with Anté, through the figure of the *media morisca* Lucía, Mansilla's novel questions prevailing ideologies by broadening the civic motherhood construct to create a space for the mestizaje constituting the colonial order that Sarmiento wished to modernize along northern lines.

Mansilla's racialized maternal figure reflects the reality of women of color acting as republican mothers despite liberal ideology. The Afro-Argentine María Remedios del Valle is a case in point. Having distinguished herself through her participation in the war for independence, del Valle frequently is referred to as "Madre de la Patria," a title that points to the importance of black women to the construction of the nation. Yet while today, the Día Nacional de los Afroargentinos y de la Cultura Afro is celebrated every November 8 in her honor, Argentine historiographers traditionally have paid del Valle little attention (F. Guzmán 9–10). This neglect began even during her life, as she struggled for years to obtain a pension from the Argentine government for her services during the war. These funds finally were granted only after numerous testimonies to her virtue—held, as the Cádiz Constitution made clear, to be exceptional among Afro-descendants (26). Importantly, not only was her virtue whitened, but her figure was, as well, as visual representations of the mulata del Valle frequently have depicted her as a white woman, an image more palatable to liberal tastes (49–50).

Thus, overwhelmingly allied with the Argentine conservatives—Rosas went so far as to lend del Valle his surname (F. Guzmán 8)—Afro-descended mothers could not reproduce the nation along the lines desired by liberals, as the 1833 folk poem "¡Viva la Patria!" by *payadora* poet Juana Peña, known to history only as a self-proclaimed "negrita muy federal," attests:

> La Patria se ve amagada
> De unos pocos aspirantes
> Que quieren sacrificarla
> Por salir ellos avantes
>
> Opongamos a su intento
> Nuestro pecho por muralla,
> Y reunidos los negritos
> Corramos luego a salvarla.
>
> Esto aconsejar debemos
> Las mujeres al marido
> Y las madres a los hijos
> En señal de agradecidos. (xxix–xl)
>
> (The Patria is threatened
> By a few ambitious men
> Who want to sacrifice her
> So that they can get ahead
>
> We oppose their intent
> With our breast as a wall
> And all of the blacks [negritos] united
> Run to save it.
>
> This is the advice
> That we wives should give to our husbands
> And mothers to our sons
> As a sign of their gratitude.)

Criticizing the liberals as opportunistic in their nationalist fervor, Peña asserts that it is her duty as a wife and mother to raise the Argentine national family according to more traditional values. In this way, by providing the nation with racially hybrid origins, the author marks her distance from the colonialist "Manifest Domesticity" that Kaplan identifies in North American novels of the period and to which Cooper owes the futuristic projection of his canonical foundational romance, as well as Alberdi's wish to govern Argentina by populating it with European progenitors. A symbol of colonial race mixture, Mansilla de García's Morisca Lucía Miranda, like the Afro-descended nursemaids of *La Aljaba* and the apparently pro-Rosas del Valle, threatens to subvert the bourgeois-republican vision of motherhood by raising the new Argentine nation-state's citizens with values that some would see more aligned with racialized forms of colonial "barbarism."

Moorishness and Race

Though the associations with blackness and Moorishness present in the polysemous term "morisco" are out of keeping with twenty-first-century racial taxonomies, the two categories have not always been considered distinct from one another. In his history of early modern racial categories, Jack D. Forbes overturns the common wisdom that dictates that the term *mulato* is a variation on *mula* ("mule" in Spanish and Portuguese) by suggesting that the word derives from the Arabic *muwallad,* which refers to a person of mixed Arab and non-Arab parentage. He supplies documentary evidence in which Moors are referred to as "mulatos" during the early modern period and suggests that the term gradually came to designate individuals of dark to medium complexion (131–90), especially darker-skinned Muslims (114). Other scholars have noted that, "derived from *moro,* . . . in the sixteenth century *moreno* became the general term used to refer to blacks and mulattoes alike" (Buscaglia-Salgado 51). This imbrication between the two categories would enjoy a long life in the Hispanic imaginary: as late as 1793, a Cuban officer serving in Haiti "scattered his descriptions with allusions to the Christian reconquest of Muslim Spain or to North Africa more generally, using terms such a 'Saracens' and 'seraglio' to refer to the black auxiliaries and their encampments. He compared [black Haitian military leaders] Biassou, who he said commanded 16,000 soldiers, and Jean-François, who commanded another 20,0000, to the emperors of Morocco and Algiers" (A. Ferrer, *Freedom's Mirror* 103). Similarly, in the world-literary sphere that Mansilla inhabited, blackness and Moorishness often appeared as discursively imbricated with one another, as indicated by the famous French aphorism "L'Afrique commence aux Pyrénnés" (Africa begins at the Pyrenees). Shakespeare's *Othello,* a popular play throughout the nineteenth century, too, is a canonical example of the collapsing of the two categories. Meanwhile, Portuguese chronicler Gomes Eanes de Zurara's fifteenth-century *Chronica do Descobrimento e Conquista da Guiné* (Chronicle of the discovery and conquest of Guinea), which presents a slippery distinction between North

African Arabs and sub-Saharan Africans, was rediscovered and published in Paris in 1841. Even the eponymous character of Mary Mann's *Juanita* (discussed in chapter 4 of this book) is an enslaved "Moorish" woman and, like Mansilla's Lucía, very fair in complexion.

By mentioning these facts, I do not mean to suggest that Spanish Moors "are" black. Indeed, "the phenotypical notion of race was emphatically not the main focus for Spaniards in the sixteenth century, particularly where Moors were concerned" (Fuchs 118). Nor do I wish to suggest that Mansilla is making a point about Argentina's racial composition that would have proven controversial to her contemporaries (who, as I have explained above, were well aware of Argentine blackness and dedicated considerable time to bemoaning the relationship between the Afro-Argentines and "barbarism"). Rather, I am noting that, in the nineteenth-century lettered sphere, the capacious concept of "morisco" spread across a wide and ambiguous semantic field that included both Moorishness and blackness without always drawing sharp distinctions between the two.

At the same time, because of popular associations of Spanishness with Moorishness, the "classificatory instability of 'Moor' as a broad marker of identity" called the whiteness of Spaniards and their descendants into question in the northern European imaginary (Windell 312). "In the anti-Spanish pamphlets that circulated furiously throughout Protestant Europe in the last decades of the sixteenth century . . . Spaniards were imagined as a miscegenated race, tainted by Moorish and Jewish blood" (Fuchs 117). Particularly in the literature of Renaissance England, Spanishness frequently was associated with blackness (123–27), "with Islam, with Africa, with dark peoples" (118). Fuchs contends that "it is important to recover the essentializing blackness of this cultural mythology." While "critics typically read it metaphorically, with black as a figure for Spain's cruelty and greed in the New World[,] it often refers in unambiguous terms to Spain's racial difference, its *intrinsic* Moorishness" (emphasis in original). Black Legend discourse thus represents "an attempt to render Spain biologically (if not visibly) black" (118). In Spanish American letters, these attitudes surface in the Cuban Cirilo Villaverde's 1882 novel *Cecilia Valdés,* in which a character comments to the creole protagonist that "your father, as a Spaniard, is not exempt from the suspicion of mixed blood. I suppose he is Andalusian, and the first black slaves came to América from Seville. Nor were the Arabs, who were more dominant in Andalusia than in other parts of Spain, of pure Caucasian race. Rather, they were African" (135).[88] Scholars such as María de Guzmán and John C. Havard, meanwhile, have shown that, by the 1800s, northern eyes had come to see Spanish American creoles in this dark light as well. More than a statement specifically of black or Arab identity, then, during the nineteenth century, the figure of the Moor signified Hispanic racialized difference from the Global North.

Inherently other to the northern metropolitan cultures of Europe and the United States, Mansilla's Morisco-descended Lucía ironically functions in the novel as the force that brings Western civilization to the Southern Cone. As I noted earlier, much of Lucía's work in South America consists of instilling European—particularly Spanish—culture and Christianity in her indigenous charges. For example, she enlightens the Timbúes by showing them that their shaman does not really receive messages from the spirit world, bringing Hispano-Catholic tradition to the indigenous Argentines (328–33). This evangelization takes a more domestic form at other points of the novel:

> Lucía took upon herself the pious task of instructing the simple women of the wilderness in the sublime truths of Christianity. Every day, with tireless perseverance, her determination took her to the huts of the Timbúes. There she could be seen surrounded by Indian women sitting on the grass, some with their children in their arms, others in an attentive pose with their hands crossed over their knees, their hair hanging loose over their backs. Their great eyes fixed on the young woman's visage, they would listen to her words of love and charity, which awoke dormant echoes in their souls, much as a child who repeats the first prayer taught by his mother and, without realizing, feels, at the bottom of his soul, a mystic revelation, which rises from his heart to his visage, casting a celestial glow. (316)[89]

Here, Lucía represents a traditionalist vision of motherhood that soon would be supplanted by modernizing reformers; more interested in the raising of good Christians than of future citizens, she shows more affinity to Fray Luis de León's *Perfecta casada* than to the articles published in *La Aljaba*. Yet, at the same time that Lucía's actions vindicate colonial gender and family structures, as discussed above, her place as metaphoric mother of the nation frames her within nineteenth-century discourses on the national family and republican motherhood (which cannot exist without a nation or republic and is therefore decidedly not a Spanish colonial construct). In this way, the ethnically hybrid character herself hybridizes Hispanic society's Marianist construction of motherhood with modernizing republican paradigms, ironically deploying mestizaje to further the cause of Europeanization.

The particular form that Lucía's hybridity takes is fundamental to Mansilla's worldview. The relationship between Lucía's parents does not trouble social hierarchies in early modern Spain, as the father is an Old Christian bearing both gender and ethnic privilege, while the mother is a Morisca and consequently marked as subordinate both as a woman and as a member of a marginalized ethnic group. As with Alejo and Anté, this gendered interethnic pairing reinforces the traditional paradigm of Hispanic domination of conquered others. The Catholicism practiced by both Lucía and her mother demonstrates this fact. Thus, even as it intervenes in nineteenth-century conversations on whitening, the vision of mestizaje that the novel endorses, ultimately, is bound up in the hegemonic structures of the day.

Curiously, the Morisco identity of Lucía's mother seems to reaffirm the character's whiteness as much as it problematizes her inclusion in that category. In the colonial castas system, after all, "de español y morisca sale albino," the offspring of a Spaniard and a Morisca is called an "albino," a term that paints Lucía's phenotype as whiter than her genealogy. Importantly, even as it positions her as a "sultana" in the Southern Cone, the text takes care to point out that Lucía is a "white Spaniard" (308, 345) and a "European woman" (341).[90] The narrator also describes Lucía's "pale cheeks" (284) and "moonish face" (*rostro de luna*) (338) and even drapes a white camisole over the character's bare back in the racially charged scene in which Siripo spies on the protagonist in her boudoir prior to her abduction (350). The novel's indigenous antagonist, for his part, calls Lucía "light of the pampa, star of the day" (353).[91] Indeed, Lucía's very name, which she shares with the maternal *educadora* of Peruvian Clorinda Matto de Turner's 1889 *Aves sin nido* (*Birds without a Nest*) (who also serves as an enlightened surrogate mother to indigenous orphans), means "light." The character's whiteness, moreover, is a condition of possibility for the plot, inscribing the novel within a long New World tradition of narratives concerning white women taken captive by indigenous men.[92]

This whiteness of the Morisca's daughter is at the center of Mansilla's opposition to the imposition of US-style bourgeois-republican modernity onto Argentina. The black blood of Cooper's Cora's always will threaten to "burst its bounds" (488), reducing the mulatta maiden to another feature of the American wilderness that must be cleared for Anglo-Saxon civilization to take root. Mansilla's hybrid Lucía, on the other hand, is the standard-bearer for Western civilization and Christianity in the Southern Cone; the author is careful to note in her description of the Espíritu

Santo settlement that Lucía and Sebastián's books "lent the rustic room a stamp of culture foreign to those remote lands" (305). Paradoxically transformed by her "impure" Morisco blood into an unpigmented *albina,* Lucía is in some ways even whiter than the novel's other whites. Thus, while liberal Argentine Romantics such as Sarmiento and Echeverría condemn the legacy of Hispanic colonialism as barbaric, Mansilla de García "vindicates and valorizes that tradition" (Chikiar Bauer, *Entre ellos* 82) as her "off-white" Morisca republican mother, an embodiment of the Spanish colonial legacy of mestizaje, becomes the force that civilizes the Southern Cone.[93]

Embodying Western civilization on its peripheries, Miranda, the character, is in many ways not unlike Mansilla, her creator. Distantly descended from an indigenous Guaraní princess who had married a Spanish conquistador, Mansilla de García belonged to a venerable old colonial family that had come to occupy a privileged position in the Argentine oligarchy, her remote racial alterity posing no obstacle for her standing as a member of the highest levels of the creole aristocracy. Like Lucía, too, she dedicated her life to European high culture, and, much as the Morisco-origin albina Lucía surpasses the Old Christian Sebastián in her knowledge of the Greek and Roman classics, Mansilla would win the praises of no less than Victor Hugo for her works produced in French (Lojo, *Lucía Miranda* 17) and eventually was offered a position at the Prussian court (15). If the liberals of her age sought to import white Europeans in order to make up for the "Oriental" customs and "African" "barbarism" of a Hispanic colonial population that included "Moriscos" in both meanings of the term, Mansilla through her Moorish-descended national mother suggests (however problematically) that Argentina's ethnoculturally hybrid colonial population can be as "white" as the "Europeans," who soon would immigrate to the country's shores, and just as able—perhaps even better able—to bring "civilization" to the "barbaric" Americas.[94] In this way, she vindicates a Latin American model of race hierarchization that considers culture as carefully as it does bloodlines. Regardless of what Sarmiento might think, Mansilla's person and *personaje* seem dedicated to demonstrating that the "blancos españoles" (355) to whom she refers as "europeos" (325, 326) are not beyond the limits of Western civilization; indeed, the epigraphs to the novel's chapters read almost as a catalog of the European canon, spanning Horace to Hugo, with both Virgil and Dante helping to guide the reader through Mansilla's history of South America. More than an affirmation of the traces of Arab or African blood flowing through the nineteenth-century Argentine national family, the polysemic term "morisco" provides Mansilla with a trope through which to critique efforts to turn Argentina away from its Hispanic colonial heritage and toward the racialized northern modernity that Cooper's *Last of the Mohicans* represented to Sarmiento.

El Sur

The author articulates her oppositional stance toward the modernizing northern bourgeois values espoused by Cooper, Sarmiento, and Alberdi in her *Recuerdos de viaje* (Travel memoirs) (1882), a nonfictional account of a stay in the United States not long after she wrote *Lucía Miranda*.[95] As critical of the United States as Sarmiento is laudatory, Mansilla dedicates her book to poking sardonic fun at what she sees as Yankee vulgarity and her own aristocratic aloofness toward republican democracy. The only place that the Argentine feels at home in *el Norte* is in the South, and she closes the work by confessing to having been a Confederate sympathizer:

> I was a Confederate [*sudista*].
> Despite the slaves? I will be asked. Despite them, I humbly reply, for that South, where slavery reined, was until then the monopolizer of elegance, of refinement, and of culture in the Union, a truth that the North recognized and proclaimed at every step in its social aspirations. (122)[96]

Mansilla de García's apology for the South—refined even as it was reprobate—in her seldom-studied *Viaje* contrasts with Sarmiento's condemnation of that region in his *Viajes*, a high-canonical text with which subsequent Argentine travelers to the United States such as Mansilla necessarily would have to reckon. Visiting a plantation outside of New Orleans, Sarmiento notes the difference between the slave quarters and the master's house and registers one of his rare critiques of the northern hegemon:

> This is the aristocracy of cotton balls and sugar bags, fruit of the sweat of slaves. Oh! Slavery, deep wound and incurable fistula that threatens to cover the robust body of the Union with gangrene! What a fatal error of Washington and the great philosophers who wrote the declaration of the rights of man [*sic*], when they left the planters of the South with their slaves. By what trick of fate are the United States, which in practice have made the most advanced progress in the feeling of equality and charity, condemned to wage the final battles against the ancient injustice of man to man, already won in the rest of the earth? (*Viajes*, 490)[97]

Explaining southern slavery as an exception to the Protestant ethic to which Sarmiento attributes North American economic success and political stability, the Argentine statesman points out that "the free states are superior in number and wealth to the slave states."[98] Mansilla de García, on the other hand, is happy to trade Sarmiento's northern "riqueza" for southern "refinamiento" and "humbly" declares herself to be a "sudista." Concluding her *Viaje* by embracing the South that Sarmiento rejects at the end of his *Viajes*, Mansilla once again turns her back on the northern-style capitalist modernity that Sarmiento wishes to inaugurate in Argentina.[99]

These North/South dynamics are key to Mansilla de García's geopolitical philosophy. The term normally used to refer to the North American Confederates in Spanish, "sudista," literally means "southist." The slippage between the two meanings points to the notion of an extended South, a transnational, traditional periphery of the Western Hemisphere encompassing both South America and the American South and existing in opposition to the modernizing centers of the "North," understood as both North America and the American North. Comparatist Tânia Franco Carvalhal explains that, in Argentine literature, the "South" "is reality and metaphor. A geopolitical reality that eventually reproduces, on the new continent, an originally European North/South opposition with the particular inflection that it gained in the second half of the nineteenth century, when the South, in addition to an opposition of wealth and poverty between regions, becomes tied to notions of Latinity, Catholicism, and decadence. In the constructed paradigm, this South is opposed to the Anglo-Saxon North, to Protestantism, to progress" (97).[100] The direct reference to the Confederate States of America aside, Mansilla de García's comments clearly register an opposition to a particular northern style of modernity. Instead, she embraces her "southern" identity (in the forms of ethnic hybridity, Catholicism, and colonial paternalism) in order to reject the Argentine liberals' efforts to assimilate the country to northern racial, cultural, and economic norms by promoting bourgeois-republican motherhood for white European immigrants such as Cooper's Alice while denying the maternity of Afro-descended women such as Cora.[101] Yet, despite the black overtones with which she paints the mother of the Argentine nation in her novel, here Mansilla de García looks the other way at North American slavery to embrace the southern cause in the name of what she perceives to be a threatened system of colonial values—a hybrid, peripheral modernity that, however unacceptable contemporary readers may find its racist presuppositions, acts as a counterdiscourse to the Yankeeization that the Argentine liberals such as Sarmiento and Alberdi advocated.

To state what is by now obvious, contradictions are constitutive of the work of Eduarda Mansilla de García, an author who protested social exclusion while praising slavocracy, who mobilized a character's metaphorical blackness in order to prove her whiteness, and who rewrote a US novel in order to reject US cultural influences. Yet, extraordinary as she was in many respects, Mansilla was hardly peculiar in her paradoxes. Rather, she embodies the aporias of the Latin American creole elites of her day, a group of people—conservatives and liberals—who rejected the colonialism of Spain and the United States while continuing to colonize their own subalterns. This ambivalent attitude toward racism and coloniality would prove central to public educación in the nineteenth-century Americas, as the following chapters will show.

3 Una Maestra Norteamericana in the "South"

LIKE THE previous chapter, the following pages probe Sarmiento's racially fraught plans to modernize Argentina through republican motherhood on a northern bourgeois-republican model, this time considering the educational sphere. Between 1869 and 1916, at least sixty-five North Americans—almost all of them female—arrived in Argentina with the intention of founding normal schools to instruct the country's youth in the ways of Anglo-Saxon civilization and bourgeois modernity.[1] As Sarmiento explains in his pedagogical treatises *De la educacion popular* (On mass education) (1849) and *Las escuelas: base de la prosperidad en los Estados Unidos* (The schools: Basis of prosperity in the United States) (1860), these values were considered necessary for the political and economic consolidation of Argentina as the country emerged from decades of civil war. The statesman saw North American teachers, by virtue of their nationality and gender, as ideal republican mothers able to implement this modernizing educational program in Argentina. Inspired by the Reconstruction-era migration of northern white women to the US South to establish schools for the freedmen following the abolition of slavery in the region, Sarmiento collaborated with the New England reformer Mary Mann, widow of the educationalist Horace Mann, to recruit a group of North American teachers for Argentina's new normal schools.[2]

With this racialized and gendered history of inter-American educational collaboration in mind, the chapter will turn to *In Distant Climes and Other Years* (1934), North American teacher Jennie Howard's memoir of her time in the Argentine schools. I argue that, writing during the opening years of the United States' Good Neighbor Policy of soft-imperialist hemispheric cooperation, Howard stakes a claim for herself as mother of the Argentine republic through her position as teacher. In a curious reversal of the foundational schemas presented by Cooper's *Last* of the Mohicans and Mansilla de García's *Lucía Miranda,* in *In Distant Climes,* the culturally hybrid maternal figure is presented as white, while the Hispanic children that she Anglicizes are, through their discursive equation with US freedmen, scripted as black.[3] Importantly, however, a close reading of the text shows that, even as Howard brings Anglo-Saxon modernity to Argentina, her Argentine pupils Hispanicize their North American teacher, suggesting that, as in *Lucía Miranda,* here, too, the liberal Argentine government's strategy of US-style whitening through republican maternal allegory met with resistance from the more traditionally Hispano-colonial sectors of the population.

Expanding on the notions of racialized republican motherhood elaborated in my discussion of Cooper and Mansilla, this chapter turns to child-rearing as it explores North American influence (and lack thereof) on educational reform in Argentina during the second half of the nineteenth century. Much like Mansilla's rejection of northern paradigms of bourgeois-republican modernity through her articulation of Confederate sympathies, Sarmiento's US teachers project was made possible by a hemispheric reading strategy practiced in both Argentina and the United States that drew parallels between the South American country and the North American South and between the Argentine rural masses and the US freedmen. While, at first glance, the rhetorical equation of the South American nation with the US South that this hemispheric mirroring implies represents the discursive codification of the country's peripheral status vis-à-vis the Global North, an examination of the US teachers project in the broader context of Sarmiento's transcultural thinking and a consideration of the less-than-reverent treatment that teachers such as Howard received upon their arrival in the Southern Cone suggests that nineteenth-century Argentine educational reformers' critical relationship with the United States was not mimetic—as is commonly thought—but, rather, instrumental, a tool at the service of Argentine nation building.

Background

Sarmiento's first visit to the United States, recounted in his 1847 travel narrative *Viajes,* represented the culmination of a world tour sponsored by the government of Chile, where the political firebrand had been forced into exile as a result of his vocal opposition to the traditionalist Rosas regime in his native Argentina.[4] Ostensibly, the Chileans intended for Sarmiento to gather information about educational practices in the Global North. More urgently, however, in the wake of the 1845 publication of the writer's inflammatory *Facundo* and Argentine demands for the agitator's extradition, the "Chilean government, fearing that Sarmiento's activism against Rosas and his prestige among Argentine exiles would strain foreign relations between Chile and Argentina" (Stavans xx), sought an excuse to unload the political exile onto countries where he could do less harm (Palcos, *Rasgos de Sarmiento* 110; Ard 39; González Echevarría 8).

Though the North American chapters are today the most widely read and commented upon, Sarmiento dedicates considerable space in his *Viajes* to recording his impressions of Europe, particularly France, which recently had restored the monarchy after the defeat of Napoleon.[5] If, as I explained in the last chapter, Sarmiento is rhapsodic about the seemingly equitable distribution of power and prosperity among the (white) population of the United States, in France he is repelled by the contrast between the nation's elites—the thinkers who inspired him in his opposition to Rosas and the Federales—and the masses that served them.[6] "¡Eh! ¡la Europa!," he sighs, "sad mixture of greatness and abjection, of knowledge and dullness at the same time, sublime and dirty repository of everything that elevates a man and that degrades him, kings and lackeys, monuments and leper colonies, opulence and savage life!" (*Viajes* 102).[7] Frustrated with the social inequality that he encountered in France during the Bourbon Restoration, Sarmiento left Paris for London (138–39).

It was in the British capital that, according to most scholars, the Argentine encountered the writings of North American pedagogue Horace Mann, to whose "sufficient ability, will, and influence to work such a good, enlightening public opinion and that of the government, concentrating and pushing the action of the enthusiastic friends of progress, pointing out the obstacles and guiding them down the righteous path that his long years of study, his travels and his daily devotions revealed to him," Sarmiento attributed the success of the Massachusetts Board of Education (*Las escuelas* 39–40).[8] Disillusioned with the frustration of the republican project in Europe following his experiences in Restoration-era France, Sarmiento decided to use the last of his savings to travel to the United States in search of Mann and the answers to his existential doubts regarding the promise of the bourgeois revolution in which he so ardently believed.[9] As the statesman would write to a Chilean friend a year after publishing his *Viajes,* "I have returned to another sun that does not eclipse, that no cloud hides: the United States. As theory, as fact, as power, as influence, as the future . . . I find the democracy there to be strong and internally consistent" (qtd. in Rojas 231).[10]

In the United States with Mann, then, Sarmiento "regained his enthusiasm" and definitively turned his back on Old World social models and, scholars long have held, sought cures for Argentina's civic ills in the burgeoning North American empire (Katra, "Sarmiento en los Estados Unidos" 863).[11] In addition to acting as a sort of patron for Sarmiento while he studied public education in the United States, providing the foreign visitor with letters of introduction to important pedagogues and facilitating his access to documents of interest (Sarmiento, *Viajes* 449), Horace Mann was to exert a profound ideological influence on Sarmiento's 1849 *De la educacion popular* and on the Argentine's thought in general.

Sarmiento returned to the United States as plenipotentiary minister in 1865, charged by President Bartolomé Mitre with "transmitting everything that can be of interest to improve and perfect our institutions and develop our moral and material progress, by sending books, memoirs and whatever he believes will be useful to that objective." Additional instructions specify that Sarmiento "should also try to make our country known and encourage commerce and immigration indicating the means he thinks necessary to consider, and be careful in his relations with the other diplomatic agents and immigration officials to make known the advantages our country offers" (qtd. in Patton 136).[12] The US public school system was of particular interest.[13] As the Argentine plenipotentiary confessed to US secretary of state William Seward in his letter of introduction, "Nominally I am minister to this country . . . but my real purpose is to study school systems here, which my travels twenty years ago convinced me are the best in the world" (qtd. in Luigi, *65 Valiants* 10). In keeping with this mission, Sarmiento soon began sending North American textbooks, teaching methodology, classroom furniture, and, eventually, teachers back to his native country. Years later, while serving as superintendent of schools, he would write that, "in terms of Educational Reports, Common Schools, Superintendents, etc., etc., our Jurisprudence and [our] antecedents [are] in the United States, from whence the law . . . and the system of common education have come to us" (Sarmiento, "Nota" 12).[14]

Public Education and School Reform in Nineteenth-Century Argentina

Though Sarmiento is by far the best known, he was, in fact, but one of many individuals—both Unitarios and Federales—working to reform the Argentine education system in the generations following independence

(Puiggrós, *Qué pasó* 39–52). On the one hand, Rivadavia "opted for the Napoleonic model that consisted of a pyramid whose apex was the university, which directed all educational establishments" and which would be centralized, naturally, in Buenos Aires.[15] This model "was not statist in the sense of modern, democratic public education. Rather, it had an absolutist character."[16] The more progressive of the rural caudillos, on the other hand, "preferred to promote provincial and local Juntas Protectoras de Educación [Committees for the Protection of Education], in which local citizens participated actively and defended the autonomy of provincial educational systems."[17] Similar to the notion of a "school board" in the United States, this system, if expanded, would have created a nationwide web (but not a centralized system) of public schools. Thus, while the caudillo project "linked the education of people in the provinces with national integration, Rivadavia aspired to form an enlightened and privileged minority" (Puiggrós, *Qué pasó* 58).[18]

Education would become a key political issue in the years following the Argentine civil wars, as evidenced by the fact that the "Instrucción Pública" sections of the yearly *Memorias del Ministerio de Culto, Justicia e Instrucción Pública* (Memories of the Ministry of Religion, Justice, and Public Instruction) typically run hundreds of pages longer than the reports from the ministry's other two departments. Earlier, during the dictatorship, traditionalist Juan Manuel de Rosas—excoriated in Sarmiento's 1845 polemic *Facundo*—had imposed ideological controls on education (Puiggrós, *Qué pasó* 60–61), which he saw as "more closely linked to order than to labor, to the ritualization of the regime than to the training of producers" (62).[19] Even as provincial caudillos promoted public education, Rosas "restored the *ancien régime*'s view that education was a privilege reserved for the gentry and associated elites" (Szuchman 124) by eliminating funding for public schools in Buenos Aires in 1839 (Batticuore 89). He eventually outlawed compulsory schooling completely (Batticuore 93), viewing public instruction as beyond the state's purview (Puiggrós, *Qué pasó* 61).[20] As a result, during the 1850s, only 50 percent of Argentine children attended school, most not for very long (Batticuore 90). The situation appeared dire by 1869, when, in the province of Buenos Aires, of 24,000 school-age children, only 6,663 were receiving formal instruction—and only eighty-four schools had been built for that purpose. Perhaps not surprisingly, of a national population of 1,737,036, over a million people were unable to read and write (Puiggrós, *Qué pasó* 75).[21] While these numbers may not have been particularly alarming in the international context of the time, Sarmiento viewed this state of affairs as dangerous.[22]

In *De la educacion popular* and *Las escuelas,* Sarmiento argues that Rosas's failure to meet his obligations regarding public education had condemned Argentina to languish atavistically in its semifeudal Spanish colonial "barbarism" while the Northern Hemisphere, particularly the United States, lunged avidly into bourgeois-republican "civilization." Under the liberal education plans of the decades following the civil wars that I discussed in the last chapter, this colonial heritage came under attack as the country's modernizing elites attempted to promote the values of bourgeois modernity through the public-school system, without which, they increasingly felt, "peace, labor, constitutional guarantees, family welfare, and wealth and virtue are impossible" (Barrondo 445).[23] A "vital question" for Argentine administrations during the last four decades of the nineteenth century, public educación was harnessed "as a political measure in the refining of institutions, as an economic measure in public wealth which grows under the empire of methodological thinking applied to the objects of nature that man transforms and puts to his advantage, and as a moral measure in the formation of the public criteria that makes possible and assures the welfare of human communities" (Wilde, *Memoria 1882* L).[24]

The Argentine liberals' educational reforms had mixed results. On the one hand, according to Director of Public Instruction Nicolás Avellaneda, between 1856 and 1872 the ranks of students enrolled in Argentine schools trebled (8). During Sarmiento's presidency alone, eight hundred schools were constructed and the number of students in the country increased by 233 percent (Rothera, "Civil Wars" 211). In the president's native San Juan, for example, the number of public schools jumped from eighteen in 1864 to forty-four in 1869 while the number of students grew from 1,405 to 6,113 in the same period (Avellaneda, *Memoria 1873* 8–39). On the other hand, the country's teaching force proved ill-equipped to handle this increased demand; as early as 1858, Sarmiento had predicted that, in Buenos Aires alone, at least six hundred people would be necessary to staff the public schools ("El Editor" 2). This situation persisted even as federal education expenditures quadrupled (Rock 130). In the provincial city of Entre Ríos in 1869, 101 teachers attended to 3,691 students while, in Mendoza, 205 teachers provided instruction for 7,485 students. In La Rioja, there were 104 teachers for 4,157 students at the same date and, in Santiago del Estero, 68 teachers supervised 3,812 students, while Tucumán employed only 130 teachers for 6,317 students (Avellaneda, *Memoria 1873* 8–39). The problem would become compounded as the government's educational reforms continued to yield results; twenty years later, between 1883 and 1884, full-time school enrollment across Argentina would rise by 13,910 students, and part-time enrollment would increase by 9,160 (Thwaites 81).

Finding the public education system suddenly overwhelmed with students, the national government would establish normal schools to prepare a teaching staff equipped to raise the country's youth as a bourgeois-republican citizen body. Argentine liberals turned to the United States for instructors for these new institutions. In a July 21, 1868, letter, Sarmiento would write to Minister of Justice and Public Instruction Eduardo Costa that it is necessary to "introduce new ideas, new practices," and that "this will only be achieved by transplanting the men who are to render effective the ideas, forms and institutions that have produced such astounding results there where they are the base of the political and social system" (157).[25] An extension of Alberdi's plan to govern by populating, the importation of human capital proposed in this letter would prove pivotal to Sarmiento's particularly New World brand of republican nation building.[26] The Argentine minister was especially influenced by a January 6, 1866, article in *Harper's Weekly* on the arrival of a group of New England schoolteachers to the Washington Territory (Luigi, *65 Valiants* 38). The article notes that the teachers were sent to replace an earlier group of female emigrants who, after arriving in the unincorporated lands, "were soon married, and there were none to take their places" ("Emigration to Washington Territory" 10). The sounds of their wedding bells echoing in his head, Sarmiento imagined the effects that a similar influx of Anglo-Saxon blood would have in his country, which he already had compared to the United States in his *Facundo*. He soon published an article in the Chilean newspaper *La Patria* posing "the question of seven hundred North American teachers in Argentina or Chile," arguing that they "would repair in ten years the ruin of three centuries" of backward Spanish misrule (Patton 148).[27] As a result of this plan, between 1860 and 1916 at least sixty-five North American schoolteachers (among them Jennie Howard, whom I will discuss below) arrived in Argentina, where they labored to establish a system of normal schools to train the country's teaching force (Luigi, *65 Valiants* 17).[28]

The "South"

Sarmiento would look to Mary Mann, widow of his hero, Horace Mann, for help finding North American republican teacher-mothers for his new normal schools. Upon returning to the United States as plenipotentiary minister, Sarmiento sought out his old friend in order to inquire about the possibility of translating her 1865 *Life of Horace Mann*, a biography of her late husband, into Spanish (*Vida de Horacio Mann* 299). Mary granted him permission, and returned the favor by preparing an English-language translation of *Facundo*.[29] Later, upon learning of Mann's efforts to send upper-class New England women to the US South in order to teach the freedmen, Sarmiento persuaded her to turn her efforts to recruiting a similar group for the Argentine normal schools.[30]

Mann was motivated to aid Sarmiento by what at the time was a common (though somewhat improbable) understanding of the conflict between the locally based traditionalism of the Federales and the centralizing modernization of the Unitarios in Argentina as a South American variation on the recent US Civil War. The reform of the US South long had been one of Mary's personal projects, having helped to hide one of John Brown's coconspirators after the ill-fated 1859 raid on Harpers Ferry (Valenti 202). Her *Juanita,* an antislavery novel set in the "southern" country of colonial Cuba, would be published posthumously in 1887.[31] As she notes repeatedly in her letters to Sarmiento, Mann saw the Federales, in their hostility to bourgeois republicanism, as the South American version of the slavocratic US South. In her English-language translation of *Facundo,* she even goes so far as to render the titles of two of the three chapters that Sarmiento originally had called "Guerra social" as "Civil War."[32] In a similar vein, in her preface, she refers to a possible Argentina redeemed from sectional strife as "the Union" (xxviii).

Curiously, while Sarmiento, unlike Mann, was familiar with both the US South and Argentina and therefore aware of the differences between the regions, the plenipotentiary participated actively in this questionable construction of Argentina as a deeper South. Particularly, Sarmiento's stay in the United States during Reconstruction had an impact on his views on race. "Sarmiento read US history selectively, in a way that significantly misunderstood its political conflicts, especially the Civil War, in the service of intervening in and shaping Latin American debates about democracy, education, and the design of political institutions" (Hooker 68; see also Rothera, "Our South American Cousin"). In *Las escuelas,* for example, he comments offhandedly that "the men of color of the United States are not more lacking in education than are the white inhabitants of our countryside" (11).[33] Similarly, in a July 21, 1868, letter from the United States to Eduardo Costa, Sarmiento writes that "the states where there were slaves are driven to continue in their backwardness by the same reasons—though to a lesser extent—as are we. The common people, or, the *poor whites,* as they are called here, do not worry too much about educating themselves" (*Escuelas* 155–56).[34] Othering his compatriots by equating them with North American freedmen and the US southern working poor, Sarmiento, like Mansilla de García (albeit with different political aims), constructs Argentina and the former Confederate States of America as parts of the same backward, racially marked "South" waiting to be civilized by northern bourgeois values.

This extended South paradigm in which Sarmiento's circle participates is more than a mere discursive construction. Among the North American teachers who went to Argentina, there were former employees of the southern freedmen's schools, members of prominent abolitionist families, and northern women seeking to earn livings after their husbands and fiancés had died in the Civil War. Teacher Fanny Wood, for example, had, in 1866, opened the first school for freedmen in Virginia, while Louise Coffin had taught in Little Rock, Arkansas, before immigrating to Argentina (J. Crespo 100). Teachers Annette Emily Haven and Bernice Avery of Winona, Minnesota, meanwhile, were inspired to travel to the Southern Cone after reading Mary Mann's translation of *Facundo* which, as I have noted, collapses the two Souths into one another (204). Similarly, Samuel Storrow Higginson, one of the few male US teachers in Argentina, "had served as chaplain to the Ninth Colored United States Infantry during the War Between the States" (Luigi, *65 Valiants* 35). Clearly drawn to northern reformist circles, in 1876 teacher Abby Ward married James Marsh, who had served as regimental quartermaster and first lieutenant of the Fifth US Colored Troops and whose family home in Oberlin, Ohio, had been a station of the Underground Railroad (94–95).[35] This migration of Reconstruction-era New England teachers farther south to Argentina indicates a slippage between the ethnoracial category of Afro–North American and the class category of Argentine campesino, racializing the latter, largely mixed-race group as black through the transnational discourse that I am laying out here. Indeed, as late as 1881, Paul Groussac, serving as principal of the Normal School in the provincial city of Tucumán, would inform the Argentine Congress that, when he began his job, the institution "resembled an American colored school" (442).[36]

The notion of "an American colored school" in the Argentine provinces will seem strange to readers familiar with Argentine guiding fictions that conceive of the country as an island of whiteness holding against a sea of South American mestizaje.[37] This traditional narrative casts the maestras de Sarmiento as northern missionaries ministering to the country's European immigrant population, newly imported under Alberdi's plan of government through population. Accounts of turn-of-the-century schools, however, tell a different story. An 1885 class picture included in the appendix to Sara Figueroa's *Escuela Normal de Paraná,* for example, displays mostly mestizo, indigenous, and Afro-descended faces.[38] It is thus Argentines of color, and not immigrants, toward whom the educational reforms of Sarmiento and his peers seem to have been targeted.[39] The paradox is apparent. On the one hand, as I discussed in the last chapter, Sarmiento in *Facundo* identifies the gaucho, racialized as African, as the locus of New World barbarism and later encouraged European immigration as a way to improve Argentina's racial stock. On the other, however, he also maintains the (still racially condescending) belief that the country's Afro-descended population—like newly emancipated US slaves in the freedmen's schools—can be capacitated for participation in the bourgeois nation-state through public education.[40] This can be seen in the negro Barcala episode included in "Vida del General Frai Felix Aldao," which replaced the third section of *Facundo* in the book's second edition. In contrast to the Afro-descended barbarians depicted in other sections of *Facundo,* or in Echeverría's "Matadero" (Slaughterhouse) or Mármol's *Amalia,* Sarmiento's Barcala fights for the cause of civilization:

> One obstacle, however, stood in the way of [Facundo Quiroga's ambition]. An inhabitant of Mendoza had raised a black creole slave who, from an early age, had shown a talent and clarity of thinking that is not uncommon to the descendants of the African race; he read and wrote and, raised next to his masters, in contact with them, and listening to their conversations, had received an education sufficient for the genius with which nature had endowed him to reveal itself at the first opportunity. He began as his master's assistant and, rising up the chain of command, eventually became the commander of a civil battalion, which put him into contact with the political notables of the day. Black Barcala is one of the most distinguished figures of the Argentine Revolution, and has one of the most impeccable reputations to have passed through this stormy period, in which so few have not wished to tear out the page from the book of their actions. Elevated for his merit, he never forgot his

color and origins; he was an eminently civilized man as far as his manners, tastes and ideas were concerned, and in Haiti he might have been counted among Pétion and his most notable men. What made Barcala a historical figure is his rare talent for organizing the corps and his ability to bring civilized ideas down to the masses. The mulatos and the common men were transformed in his hands; the officers and soldiers of his school were distinguished by the purest morals, the dress and habits of decent men, the love of liberty and enlightenment. In Mendoza the patricians took many years to erase the deep mark that Barcala left on the souls there, and in Cordoba the Revolution of 1840 against Rosas assembled a large infantry battalion, willing to fight to the death, thanks to a retreat lantern with the word *Barcala!* written on it.[41]

Educated, meritorious, and allied with the forces of civilization, the heroic Barcala appears in a better light than the "barbaric" gauchos that Sarmiento racializes as black. Through his participation in the war for independence and the conflicts between Federales and Unitarios that followed, as well as his positive influence on the other lower-class and mixed-race troops, he seems a model for the civilized nation that Sarmiento wishes to construct. The writer even goes so far as to compare Barcala favorably to Haitian president Alexandre Pétion, registering one of the few positive references to Haiti in nineteenth-century Spanish American nationalist discourse.[42] Relating the story of a slave turned potential president, the Barcala anecdote represents a Sarmientine example of the self-made man of North American bourgeois folklore who, lacking money or family background, by dint of assiduous study, manages to prosper and become a leader of his society, "a sort of Benjamin Franklin projected onto the discourse of race" (Garrels, "Sobre los indios" 107–8).[43]

Importantly, however, even as it cites an Afro-descendant as an example of republican virtue, the Barcala anecdote demonstrates the importance that Sarmiento places on education in the ways of northern civilization for the transformation of the racialized masses into productive citizens. If Barcala had shown talent from an early age, that talent, Sarmiento tells us, was only able to develop because the enslaved man was raised hearing the cultured conversations of his white masters. Afro-descended gauchos such as Barcala, it appears, can only be "redeemed" if whites oversee their educación.

Offensive though it understandably is to contemporary sensibilities, the Barcala anecdote does not seem to represent an isolated incident. Rather, the very difficulty that we face today in interrupting Argentina's guiding fiction of a nation of European immigrants with the historical fact of

Argentine blackness points to the "success of the local elites to achieve their national project of creating a 'modern' nation, which involved the cultural assimilation of the natives and the Afro-descendants into the supposedly superior and civilized European way of life" (Rodríguez and Geler 1). In the last chapter, I noted that large numbers of Afro-Argentines had aligned themselves with Rosas's traditionalist forces, as the Federal newspapers *El negrito* and *La negrita* attest. Yet, although it does not necessarily sit well with certain postcolonial paradigms, it is necessary to note that the liberals' plans for whitening *educación* also seem to have enjoyed a certain degree of prestige among some sectors of the Afro-Argentine population. The black poet Horacio Mendizábal, for example, would dedicate his 1869 *Horas de meditación*—a work deeply indebted to European cultural traditions—to then-president Sarmiento.[44] Similarly, written at the same time as the early *modernista* texts, Ida Edelvira's Rodríguez's 1887 narrative poem *La flor de la montaña* also would scale to the summits of European high culture, presenting the poetic voice as a sort of Prometheus conversant with Nietzschean philosophy. Critic Bonnie Frederick has noted that Rodríguez tellingly makes no allusions to her race in her work, passing unmarked into the lettered sphere (*Wily Modesty*). In this way, she embodies public *educación*'s goal of assimilating Argentina's nonwhite populations to the cultural standards of the Global North.

North American Women

With their experience preparing disenfranchised Afro-descendants for citizenship in the southern freedmen's schools, the newly imported North American teachers would have seemed the perfect republican mothers to rear Argentina's racialized popular classes with the civic consciousness displayed by Barcala and the northern bourgeois values that Mendizábal and Rodríguez reflect in their work. Like el negro Barcala, students from the racialized Argentine popular classes were to be civilized through education so that, in turn, they might preserve the nation from the "barbarism" that it had inherited from the semifeudal world of the colony. Article 1 of the July 8, 1884, Law 1420, which establishes Argentina's system of compulsory elementary education, states that the "primary school has the sole objective of favoring and directing simultaneously the moral, intellectual, and physical development of all children from six to fourteen years of age" (*Memoria del Consejo* 174).[45] Particular efforts were taken to "direct" children toward bourgeois industriousness. The motto of the normal school at Goya, for example, was "Labor omnia vincit" (Luigi, *65 Valiants* 157), a phrase that repurposes the maxim *amor omnia vincit* of the obscurantist colony's Latin Christian heritage for the values of the Protestant ethic that the liberal republic, through its focus on self-discipline and industry, wished to promote.[46] Similarly, in his March 11, 1881, "Nota al Gobierno de Santa Fé contestando la que dirijió sobre traslacion á la Capital de esa provincia, de la Escuela Normal que funciona en la Ciudad del Rosario" (Note to the government of Santa Fé answering the one sent about the transfer of the normal school operating in the city of Rosario to the capital of this province), M. D. Pizarro mentions plans to establish two or three "Escuelas de Arte y Oficios" (Vocational schools) in "the Republic's Costal Region and Interior, aimed at the industrial preparation and moral reform of poor street children and youths, whose laziness and vicious habits are a threat at present and constitute a true social danger for the future" (524).[47] Identifying "laziness"—held by Sarmiento and other reformers of the time as one of Spain's most pernicious legacies in the Americas—as a threat to the country's present and future well-being, the school sought to channel the energies of street children toward "industrial preparation," an activity that it linked to "moral reform." In the same vein, part 2 of the March 18, 1879, "Resolucion dictada en consulta hecha por el Director de la Escuela Normal de Tucuman, sobre esclusion de alumnos del Establecimiento" (Resolution dictated in consultation made by the principal of the Normal School of Tucuman on the exclusion of students from that establishment) states that the "the lack of application on the part of the student teacher will be considered a motive for expulsion from the School for reasons of bad conduct" (135), a dictate that codifies the work ethic of the northern bourgeoisie as a moral good and leisure (considered ennobling by traditional Hispanic society) as "bad conduct."[48] This emphasis on comport and morality resituates education/ción as a maternal practice, converting the teacher into a bourgeoise mother raising her children to be productive republican citizens.

Yet, precisely because these bourgeois values were to be imported from the Global North, traditional Argentine mothers such as Mansilla's Lucía Miranda would not do. While Sarmiento's respect for and devotion to his own mother, Paula Albarracín, are evident throughout his autobiographic *Recuerdos de provincia* (*Recollections of a Provincial Past*), the matriarch of the impoverished aristocratic family ultimately "is linked to a glorified colonial past that is also presented as an obstacle to nineteenth century progress" (Hanway 54). For Sarmiento, doña Paula represents the traditional precapitalist society for which he displays a love-hate relationship in *Facundo*. Rather than participate in the bourgeois cult of domesticity, which separated women from economic production while placing them in charge of national reproduction, Sarmiento's mother sustains the family through her engagement in cottage industry. She thus produces goods for the interior, interprovincial market, a colonial relic from the Viceroyalty of Peru that Sarmiento and his modernizing allies among the Unitarios sought to supplant with European trade.[49] Like the Romantic lives of the gauchos, Sarmiento admires the system that produced his mother but feels that it must yield to the world-historical forces of bourgeois republicanism and market integration. Much of his *Recuerdos* chronicles Hispano-criolla doña Paula's encounter with this northern modernity in the form of her children, metaphors for the future.

Though Sarmiento clearly loves his mother, as I have noted earlier, he sees the Hispanic traditionalism that she embodies as an impediment to Argentine development. For Sarmiento and the Argentine liberals, Spain, the colonial motherland, had shown herself unfit for the task of raising republican citizens.[50] An August 17, 1839, editorial in *El zonda,* a periodical that he published in his native San Juan, draws on the same Orientalist tropes that, as I explained in chapter 2, the author mobilizes in *Facundo* to present Spain as a bad mother to her New World children. Responding to a letter from "a mother" (una madre de familia) published in a previous issue, the editors note that "our dear mother, Spain, was conquered by the Moors, who held her in their power for more than 700 years and, if they did not leave her anything of their religion and language, at the very least they left her their Oriental customs" ("Correspondencia" 56).[51] These customs are detailed in Sarmiento's autobiography, which describes the architecture, furnishings, and culture of the author's childhood home—remnants of a world fated to pass, as the book's very title, *Recuerdos,* indicates.

Most pernicious among these "Oriental" ways was the "complete degradation" of women, in whose "angelic forms" Sarmiento alleges, the traditionally "Arab" Hispanic culture "sees nothing but an instigation of the animal passions," a prejudice that has led to the barring of females from educational institutions ("Correspondencia" 56).[52] Meanwhile, among "the other peoples of Europe who have not been dominated by Arabs and Moors," Sarmiento claims, women are considered men's equals.[53] There, women's intelligence is recognized, and they are encouraged to study so that they might prove better mothers, more able to instill bourgeois discipline in their progeny. In the North Atlantic, Sarmiento states, the mother "gives [her child] his first ideas. Instruct her, so that she may make him happy with a wise educación. Teach her the bases of morality, so that she may guide his moral conduct and teach her daughters to adopt habits in keeping with their state of civilization."[54] Repudiating the Morisca mother whom Mansilla de García later would defend in *Lucía Miranda,* here Sarmiento proposes a new mother for the Argentine republic, one who will raise her children not in the "barbarous" ways of Hispanic colonial obscurantism but in the bourgeois-republican modernity of northern "civilization."

In discursive terms, Sarmiento would replace his degraded Argentine madre with the dignified North American maestras, exchanging Mansilla's Lucía Miranda for Cooper's Alice Munro. For some of the maestras, this charge proved as literal as it did rhetorical. Not content simply to teach Argentine children, Clara Armstrong, for example, adopted a few (Morgade, "¿Quiénes fueron?" 54). Other teachers, such as Mary Gorman, the first US educator to arrive in Argentina, eventually married, settled, and raised families in their adopted country. Like Cooper's Scottish Alice, they became both metaphorical and literal mothers of the nation.[55] Sincere though she undoubtedly was in her decisions, the discourse surrounding the maestras had preconditioned Gorman to assume this role as bourgeois-republican matriarch. Sarmiento understood the emigrant normal teachers as white republican mothers raising the nation's children with the capitalist and democratic values of the North, pedagogical variations on Kaplan's "Manifest Domesticity."[56] By scripting the Anglo-Saxon female schoolteacher as civilizing republican mother to Argentina's "atavistic" youth, Sarmiento mobilizes public educación— "an army of twelve thousand teachers" in the words of one school administrator—as a technology for overcoming the country's supposed impediments to bourgeois-republican consolidation (Torres, "Informe de la Escuela Normal" 1882, 283).[57] Yet, if the maestra was conceived as the mother of the bourgeois Argentine republic, how can that mother be a North American foreigner?

Jennie Howard

With difficulty. In *In Distant Climes and Other Years,* her 1931 memoir of her time in Argentina, US teacher Jennie Howard performs the liberal government's scripting of the northern educators as bourgeoise white mothers of a racialized, backward-looking southern nation, even as she (consciously or not) registers Argentine folk resistance to that narrative.

A graduate of the Framingham, Massachusetts, normal school in 1882, Howard was selected to teach in Argentina by "the Boston head of the banking house of Samuel B. Hale, fiscal agent in Buenos Aires for the Argentine government" (Luigi, *65 Valiants* 135) and Clara Armstrong, a maestra de Sarmiento on a recruiting expedition to the United States (Howard 24).[58] She would spend the next five decades in Argentina, training teachers and making friends. One of the last three North American normal teachers to retire, upon returning to the United States in 1928, she would pen her memoirs, telling the story of how—she believed—she maternally guided Argentina's progression from underdeveloped backwater to one of the wealthiest countries in the world (Chavarria 360).

Though the events that she narrates occur primarily in the late nineteenth century, Howard's memoir was published in 1933 as the Good Neighbor Policy was replacing the "Big Stick" military interventionism that had marked the United States' relationship with Latin America during the previous generation with a strategy of hemispheric partnership and cultural exchange.[59] *In Distant Climes* appears with a prologue written by Mrs. Robert Woods Bliss, wife of the US ambassador to Argentina, suggesting endorsement of the text by the political class that implemented this new phase of North American imperial entanglement in the Americas.[60] Part of "the explosion of written and visual representations of South America coincidental with the emergence and diffusion of Pan-Americanism" (Salvatore, "Enterprise" 76), the book presents "South America as a land caught in a perpetual state of childhood, unable to reach the political maturity required to sustain stable and democratic governments" without US intervention as a result of "the region's atypical racial mixture, economic 'backwardness' and lack of 'civilization'" (83).

In keeping with the good-neighborly paternalism of the times, Howard emphasizes the North American teachers' role in Sarmiento's successful plan of consolidating bourgeois republicanism through educational reform. Accordingly, she dedicates her book to "my co-workers and companions living and dead whose courage and enthusiasm rose to answer the call for help in implanting under the Southern Cross in the Argentine Republic the educational ideals of Horace Mann through the patriotism of Sarmiento." In this way, she contrasts the North Americans' active "courage and enthusiasm" with the Argentines' passive "call for help," subordinating the Argentine Sarmiento to the northern Horace Mann as the prophet of modernity "under the Southern Cross" (Howard 2). Howard's belief in northern protagonism in Argentina's civilizational process is made clear by the chapter entitled "A Rip Van Winkle Awakening"

(115–21). Using a canonical 1819 US text by Washington Irving—often cited as the initiator of a distinctly North American literary tradition and the propagator of the myth of a racialized, romantically traditionalist Hispanic world—to frame the story of Argentina's modernization, the chapter suggests that "progress" in the South American country is a northern cultural enterprise. Howard feels that, like Rip Van Winkle, who famously falls asleep in the colony and awakes in the republic, Argentines, through their exposure to North American education, have exchanged the "barbarous" semifeudal world of Hispanic traditionalism for "civilized" northern bourgeois modernity.

From the text's first pages, it is evident that Howard in her narrative functions as a metaphorical mother guiding the young Argentine republic through the process of civilizing reform. In her prologue to the work, Bliss warmly notes that Howard referred to the students as her "boys" (12), as though she were talking about her own sons. This maternalist discourse creates a germinal role for Howard in the narrative of Argentina's development, as can be seen in her description of a celebration for the twenty-fifth anniversary of the founding of the normal school at San Nicolás:

> When [the North American teachers] found themselves at the head of the long rows of tables at the banquet, looking down at the representatives of every class since the inauguration twenty-five years before, men and women, many married with families, occupying posts of dignity and usefulness, coming at that time to place the flowers of affectionate remembrance and gratitude at the feet of those who had tried to lead them to higher ideals of manhood and womanhood, for those American teachers all the years of exile from their homeland, the dark days of discouraging labor and the occasional ingratitude were quite blotted out and forgotten. (86)

Leading their students to "higher ideals of manhood and womanhood," the North American teachers are cast by the narrative as guiding mothers to a "discouraging" and ungrateful Argentine people, condescendingly presented as growing into adulthood under their tutelage. As many of those students are now "married and with families," the teachers are transformed by Howard's discourse into nurturing matriarchs who have helped their descendants to found their own properly bourgeois-republican families and propagate the national line. This rising generation comes of age with the Argentine nation. As Howard writes toward the end of her text, "If thirty years mark a generation, then a marvelous transformation such as has taken place in Argentina within a like period has seldom, if ever, been seen" (115). Under their North American republican mother, she feels, the new Argentine generation has grown up along with a modern society of "schools and colleges of all kinds" (119).

The North American teachers' maternal aid in this process seems to have consisted of bringing the bourgeois discipline desired by Sarmiento and Alberdi to Argentina. In the "Biographical Appreciation of Miss Howard by an Ex-Pupil," which serves as an introduction to the book, an anonymous former student notes that, among Howard's accomplishments before arriving in Argentina, the teacher had taken charge of "a boys' school where the lack of discipline was so lamentable that no teacher with sufficient courage could be found to undertake the task." Under her guidance, however, the school "became known as a model establishment, noted for the culture and good conduct of its pupils" (qtd. in Howard 19). Positioned at the beginning of the text, this anecdote posits all of Argentina as a similarly unruly school waiting for Howard to reform it.

This disciplining process makes up the bulk of the travel narrative. The book reads almost as a catalog of the tropes of underdevelopment—dirt, disorder, and dysentery—typically found in the writings of explorers surveying the Southern Hemisphere's potential for economic exploitation by the North. In these writings, "Spanish American society ... is relentlessly indicted for backwardness, indolence, and, above all, 'failure' to exploit the resources surrounding it" (Pratt 150). In an unappetizing description of the country's culinary customs, for example, Howard writes:

> Vegetables, with the exception of mandioca and onions, were scarce, and the weeks sometimes passed without seeing a potato. . . . This lack of vegetables was not because the earth would not produce them, but because the people who could do it were too lazy to drop the seed into the earth. Milk was rare and when obtainable, an expensive article. When it was brought from a distance into the town, it was conveyed in large cans on horse-back, and as the usual constant gait of the horse was a brisk trot, by the time the milk reached its destination it had been well churned, and the bits of butter on the top of the milk were sometimes fished out by the hand of the vendor and offered to the client as a great delicacy. (50–51)

Here, in addition to the unhygienic "delicacy" about which Howard ironizes, Argentine unproductivity is contrasted not only with the fecundity of the soil, but with the "brisk trot" of the horses that bring the milk. Not only is the supposed indolence of the Argentines counterpointed against the bounty of their natural environment (soil and horses), it is juxtaposed with the industriousness of Howard herself, who, in the teacherly gesture of pointing out the Argentines' error, is the one who finally "drop[s] the seed into the earth" in order to cultivate a more productive citizen body.[61]

This lack of interest in disciplining nature becomes even more apparent when the teachers arrive in the provincial city of Paraná and stay "at a hotel kept by a Frenchman": "He gave them the best accommodation possible, which was an ill-smelling, dark room where a naturalist would have found a rich field for study, as there was scarcely any class of insect which had not made a habitation in it. Their New England instincts awakened, the Americans exerted themselves to the utmost to dislodge the other inhabitants, although Don Juan insisted that he had the room entirely evacuated before the ladies arrived" (39–40). Here, Howard's ironic reference to "naturalists" suggests that squalor and vermin are in Argentina's "nature." The text juxtaposes this filthy, undisciplined South American "nature" with the teachers' "New England instincts," which impel them to sanitize the space, "dislodg[ing] the other inhabitants" from the room in the same way that they labor to stamp out stereotypical Hispanic backwardness in the country.

Importantly, while the text originally states that the hotel is "kept by a Frenchman," Howard Hispanizes the owner semantically after he fails to meet her middle-class New England standards of comfort and seemliness by referring to him derisively as "Don Juan" (which is probably not his real name if he is French). Perhaps not coincidentally, this would-be mother of the Argentine nation renames the French innkeeper after the literary archetype of libidinal indiscipline, someone not fit to reproduce the bourgeois-republican family that the northern teachers have come to South America to found. Immortalized in English-language letters by Lord Byron's canonical poem (1819–24), the Romantic don Juan embodies "Latin" distance from northern bourgeois modernity. By renaming the French innkeeper after the mythic Spanish libertine, Howard racializes his incompatibility with her notions of discipline as typically Hispanic.

The innkeeper's sudden slide down the Pyrenees from French to Spanish reflects the racialization of North-South dynamics that occupied a central role in the nineteenth-century US public sphere.[62] Imbibing these intellectual currents, Howard, like the Argentine school administrators who compared the country's campesinos to North American freedmen, views her South American charges in racial terms, as evidenced by her use of the ambiguously capacious phrase "Latin race" twice in the book (81 and 110). In her ethnographic description of Argentina, for example, she defines the gaucho as "a mixture of Indian and Spanish blood, that of the Indian predominating" (90). Like Sarmiento and Groussac, she cannot resist drawing parallels between Argentine and North American racialized groups and states that the gaucho "spoke in a low voice, and like our North American Indians never expressed any emotion" (91). Even as she insists on the gauchos' indigenous heritage, a member of the post-Reconstruction generation, Howard concludes her description with a comparison with US blacks; the gauchos' "diversions," the author claims, "were card-playing, horse-racing, dancing and singing to the accompaniment of his guitar, from which he was rarely separated, and which was to him what the banjo is to the negro" (93). This choice of details is significant. While the gaucho cattle hand (presented in Sarmiento's *Facundo* as African), like the Afro–North American agricultural laborer of the period, might be more naturally presented as occupied with physical labor and "rarely separated" from his or her tools, Howard has chosen to focus on the group's leisure, once again highlighting the stereotypically "Latin" laziness that she criticizes in other passages. Thus, much like Sarmiento in his evaluation of the gaucho's "barbarism," here Howard racializes the Argentines' supposed moral failings—the indolence that she so fiercely criticizes—as black.

Howard's ethnographic description of the provincial city of Corrientes, site of her first teaching assignment in Argentina, presents this mixed Afro-Latin racial heritage as being at odds with bourgeois modernity. She observes that, while "there were some families in Corrientes of pure Spanish descent," "others traced their lineage back to the Moorish Kings of Spain, and very proud they were of their aristocratic ancestry." "These families," she notes, "were usually people of fortune and, with retinues of a dozen or more servants, lived in a truly patriarchal style, the servants marrying and with their children and grandchildren continuing for generations under the same roof, each member generally having his or her particular attendant" (52). Echoing Sarmiento's Orientalist depictions of life in the "barbaric" world of provincial Argentina, here Howard associates "Moorish" cultural retentions (cast by Sarmiento as "African") in Corrientes with city's premodern economic habits—shared, as she was surely aware, with the semifeudal antebellum South.[63] These customs include the cohabitation of multiple generations of multiple families of servants and served under the same roof, which runs counter to the modern northern *ethos* of bourgeois individualization and personal consumption that she seeks to promote in Argentina.

Moral value, too, is attached to the Argentines' racial backgrounds, particularly with regard to mestizaje. Howard writes that "the Argentine women, as a rule, have black eyes, veiled with thick, long lashes and a creamy skin and are much addicted to the use of face powder" (59). The description paints the "creamy" Argentines as "off-white," a fact that they try to hide with copious applications of cosmetics. This artifice lends them a disquieting air, as their true complexion, like their "black eyes," is mysteriously "veiled" from Howard's Anglo-Protestant moralizing gaze. Not content with this verbal description of her pupils, Howard includes photographs of them in her book (74). The decision is a curious one, given the additional effort for her and expense for the publisher that finding and printing the photographs entails, especially because Howard's students do not play a protagonic role in her narrative.[64] Importantly, the students' mixed racial backgrounds stand out in these images, as the poor contrast and resolution of the nineteenth-century black-and-white photographs serve to darken the Argentines visually. Following the custom of the time, most of the female students wear white dresses, which contrast starkly with their dark hair and eyes and make their olive-colored faces appear as an intermediate tone between white and black. The only exceptions are two students (perhaps in mourning), who appear in the foreground of one of the pictures wearing heavy black dresses. These women also wear black gloves and hold dark leather books, thereby creating a wall of blackness that partially blocks the view of the students dressed in white, a visual metaphor for what Howard views as the morally degenerative effects of race mixing.

Perhaps from delicacy, the author chooses not to discuss the aspects of this "degeneracy" that prove most problematic for her bourgeois-Protestant domestic worldview. Argentine historian Félix Luna, on the other hand, informs his readers that "girls from Corrientes, mixtures of Spaniards and Guaranis, were not prudish when it came to enjoying their love and sex lives. They went about gracefully, dressed in white, with bare feet . . . ; they joked with men, managed to please them with no concessions to modesty and found clever excuses for discrete solitary meetings with their lovers. No one worried about a bride's virginity; young women could marry after having had children by different fathers without anyone becoming upset" (Luna 5:67–68).[65] Sexually undisciplined, the *correntinas* would have appeared to Howard as the female counterparts of her innkeeper don Juan. If, as Alberdi argues, to govern is to populate, then the potential families that the *correntinas* and don Juan might found seem unlikely to produce industrious citizens for the newly consolidated bourgeois republic.

Not surprisingly, then, Howard turns her disciplining imperial eye to the future mothers of the Argentine nation, reserving particular criticism for the bodies that will bear the republic's next generation of citizens. She quips that "the Argentines [of the 1880s] considered stoutness in women to be a mark of beauty and judged by this standard, their ladies were all charming, for after the age of twenty-five they formerly grew enormously heavy because of their appetite for sweets and their distaste for any exercise" (59). Showing the same lack of restraint in their consumption of sugar as, according to Luna, in their choice of sexual partners, the female Argentines' "appetite for sweets" becomes a metaphor for the want of bourgeois discipline that incapacitates them for virtuous republican motherhood.

The North American teachers, however, had domesticated the future mothers of Argentina by finding better outlets for their students' libidinal energies, such as "calisthenics . . . together with walking, rowing, fencing and other games," which had an "effect upon the women of the present day, who are more graceful in figure and less burdened with superfluous flesh" (59). This physical discipline, in turn, had a positive impact on Argentine women's reproductive capabilities. Two sentences after detailing the exercise regime implemented by the US teachers in the girls' schools, Howard comments that Argentine women "usually marry between the ages of eighteen and twenty-five, and are pleased to have large families of children whom they love intensely [*sic*]. The greater the number of children she has, the prouder the mother. One family of eighteen children sat down at meals with their father and mother, four others having died" (59). Juxtaposing this vision of fertility with the US teachers' interventions into Argentine women's health, Howard suggests that, much like Mansilla de García's Lucía and Anté, the Northern Hemispheric women have disciplined the libidinously unrestrained *correntinas*' "superfluous flesh" and molded them into proper republican mothers.

The text makes this supposed relationship between the North Americans' labors and the Argentines' maternity apparent when Howard writes of "two intelligent girls" who "learned English [and] went to the United States for two or three years to study methods of educational work," embarking physically upon the same journey that the other students in the US teachers' schools were making intellectually. Upon their return, they "created a model common school in Buenos Aires." One of them later married "a distinguished educationalist of that city" and became "prominent in many up-lift circles and is the head of the 'Child Welfare Work.'" Howard concludes her comments by noting that this former student has "adopted a Belgian orphan, thus practically carrying out her ideals" (112)—the ideals that the North American teachers had taught her. Here, the text establishes a genealogical relationship between immersion in northern culture, teaching, and republican motherhood, emblematized by the adoption and raising (which, in Spanish, would be the polysemic verb *educar*) of the Belgian orphan—an act that legally incorporates a representative of northern culture into the Argentine state. Exercising leadership in the educational field and raising northern children in a southern clime, Howard's Argentine protégée becomes a metaphorical mother of the modernizing republic.

By elevating the former normal student to the status of republican mother, Howard situates the US teachers who have made this ascension possible at the beginning of Argentina's republican genealogy, echoing Sarmiento's claim that Mary Mann was the "grandmother of [the] Argentine common school education" that would lead the country to bourgeois modernity (qtd. in Luigi, *65 Valiants* 14). Howard's view of this foundational function of the North American teachers can be seen at the memoir's end, when the elderly author describes a celebration that her former students, now adults, have organized for her saint's day: "They were nearly all married, with families of their own, and some who lived far away had not met their former teacher for two or three decades" (106). Here, Howard presents herself as a republican matriarch whose children have formed proper marriages, doing their part to continue her work in reproducing the bourgeois nation. In the metaphoric economy of this passage, these offspring have gathered to pay homage to their aging mother and recognize her role in national foundation. The generation of students that lived Argentina's "Rip Van Winkle awakening" has grown up, founded new families, and now looks back fondly on the teacher that raised them to their current level of civilization.

This incident can be thought of as the culmination of Howard's efforts and of those of her fellow North American teachers, as is made clear by the fact that it appears at the end of a chapter entitled "Resumé of the Work of the American Teachers." Written, as I noted above, during the era of the Good Neighbor policy, this image of a North American mother of the Argentine republic—a benevolent figure to whom respect and allegiance are owed—is replete with imperial connotations. Howard suggests that her Argentine children have obligations toward their Anglo matriarch, as is made clear when the teacher explains how they help to support her economically during her retirement (107).

Howard (mis)represents the saint's day, a traditional celebration in many Catholic countries held on the date on the liturgical calendar honoring the saint for whom one is named, as an imperial pageant of filial obsequiousness throughout the text. The author glowingly informs her readers that, every year

> on the Saint's Day, which generally was the birthday and always the name-day of the Argentines, many servants were seen wending their ways to the house of the saint's name-sake with trays of flowers, in the centre of which reposed a gift, sometimes of much value, the whole covered with a square of hand-made lace, work of the Argentine women. At the close of such a day, the rooms of the American teachers resembled the house of a bride during her wedding, filled with gifts and flowers and with visitors who came to wish them great happiness in the coming year. (63)

Honored with flowers delivered by fawning southern servants—an imperial allegory if ever there was one—here the North American teacher is figured as a bride, as a prospective mother of the Argentine republic. This gifting of flowers functions as an emblem of imperial relations in Howard's depiction of her 1928 name-day celebration, as well: "Suddenly and quietly there entered the hall the wife of the American Ambassador, Mrs. Robert Woods Bliss, followed by the bearer of a large basket of most beautiful flowers, brought not alone in honor of the American teacher but also to show gratitude to all those Argentine ex-pupils for the great kindness and affection shown to one of her country-women" (106–7). Officiated by a representative of the US embassy, who applauds the Argentines' efforts to honor their maternal North American teacher, the scene serves as an allegory of neighborly relations between the United States and Argentina.

Yet, despite the unequal imperial relations allegorized here, to consider the North American teachers project a case of unidirectional cultural imperialism is to miss the Argentine students' nuanced agency in the proceedings—an agency of which Howard seems unaware. In the episode that I have just discussed, the author presents the economic support that her former students filially extend to her as a token of the love that her now-enlightened peripheral subjects have for their metropolitan matriarch, evidence of their new-found respect for the northern bourgeois-republican culture in which she has raised her Argentine charges. What she apparently does not recognize is that economic support of aging parents, rather than a sign of their appreciation for the Anglo-Saxon bourgeois modernity that she has brought them, is an old Hispano-feudal custom that her students reproduce as they adopt the North American teacher as their mother. In other words, it represents the sort of "Latin" intergenerational interdependency that the teacher condemns as "Orientally" anticapitalist in her description of upper-class Correntinos. Importantly, Howard must rely on this aid from her former students because she does not have biological children of her own; unmarried, she apparently has remained a virgin in Argentina. In this way, looking beyond the confines of Howard's Protestant New England heritage, the Argentine students' supposed adoration of their matriarchal teacher can be read as a variation on the Roman Catholic cult of the Virgin, a maternal figure traditionally honored, like Howard on her saint's day, with offerings of flowers.

Importantly, Howard's students do not celebrate her "birthday," as per the Anglo-Protestant tradition, but her "saint's day," in accordance with Hispano-Catholic cultural norms. In substituting the saint's day for the birthday, the Anglo teacher's life story (what happens from birthday to birthday) is resituated within the cultural framework of the Roman Church, a shift that undermines the narrative of northern assimilation that Howard seeks to inscribe in her text. While the Anglo Howard attempts to raise her Argentine children in the ways of the Protestant ethic, through this repackaging of her life in terms of Latin Christianity, her students reassert the authority of Hispano-Catholic tradition.

Equally important is the date of the celebration, June 24, as it means that Jennie Howard's saint's day was already a folk holiday, both the Catholic Feast of St. John and the Guaraní celebration of the solstice. Did the students' party for Howard supersede the traditional gathering, or was the event incorporated into the customary festivities, which would have been held on that day with or without Howard? The text offers no clues, suggesting that the author was unaware of the greater cultural significance of her saint's day. In the Northern Hemisphere from whence Howard hails, the date marks the beginning of summer and, in this way, commemorates the triumph of light over darkness, an astrological allegory of the maternal teacher's civilizational activities in the barbaric Argentina. Howard's Southern Hemispheric students, however, would have understood the date to signal the beginning of winter, a period of darkness, perhaps symbolizing the death of traditional Hispanic colonial culture in the modernizing Argentine nation-state that Sarmiento and others had envisioned or emblematizing the economic turmoil that, by the late 1920s in which the scene takes place, the liberal government's reliance on foreign investment would bring to the country.[66] In this against-the-grain reading, Howard does not colonize the Southern Hemisphere for northern Anglo civilization but, instead, finds her own northern narrative colonized by the counterdiscourse put forth by her racialized southern children.

Thus, despite Sarmiento's efforts and Alberdi's catchphrase, in this case, to populate is not necessarily to govern, and the only thing that teachers have in common with mothers is that they are often disobeyed. Howard's rebellious students were not an isolated case in turn-of-the-century Argentina. In his 1886 report on public education in Mendoza, C. N. Vergara notes that compulsory education laws frequently were ignored in that province due to the vast distances separating children's homes from the institutions that they were required to attend (545). In the same year, Alberto M. Larroque cited similar reasons for low school attendance in Santiago del Estero province, adding that "in certain areas of the Province, the indigenous class either does not know or speaks the national language very poorly, making it necessary for the teacher to have Quichua" (683).[67] Significantly, I have found no evidence that the government attempted to recruit teachers fluent in Quichua or that the Department of Public Instruction sought to take Argentina's indigenous and Afro–New World histories and cultures into account as it drafted the national curriculum. In this context, like Eduarda Mansilla de García's colonial-traditionalist novel, Howard's students' efforts to insert their teacher into the metanarrative of Hispanic Catholicism represents a conservative critique of this liberal disregard for Argentine national realities. Sarmiento and Alberdi may have wished to import Cooper's Alice as mother of the nation, but, like Eduarda Mansilla through her "Morisca" Lucía Miranda, other Argentines preferred someone more like themselves and fashioned their own culturally hybrid Cora out of Howard.

Conclusion: Cannibal Colonials

This passive-aggressive struggle for discursive authority between Howard and her mixed-race students would transpire at the same time that Argentine elites negotiated between the peripheral position to which the capitalist world system had consigned their country and their desire to avoid imperial domination. Taking an ambivalent stance toward their identity as a comprador bourgeoisie, Argentine liberals certainly imported some of the sociocultural patterns of bourgeois republicanism—often racial in nature—from northern countries such as the United States, yet they did so selectively. In the inversion of typical relations between the periphery and core of the capitalist world system that Howard's story and others like it perform, the raw materials of the Protestant ethic are exported from the northern metropole in order to be processed into an uneven, hybrid modernity in the southern territory and then reexported back North as evidence of Good Neighborly intercultural cooperation.[68] Though hardly utopian, the South-centric reading that I am proposing here, by identifying the origins of Southern Cone resistance to US imperialism a generation or two before scholars commonly locate them, reveals Argentine agency in a way that the common view of early-republican creole *letrados* as Eurocentric "cultural vassals" of the Global North does not.[69]

This critical stance toward northern modernity appears clearly in the introduction to the 1869 *Memoria* (most likely penned by Avellaneda, the director of public instruction at the time), which criticizes the US Constitution on the grounds that "it makes no provisions for the education of the people, and ... the federal powers have long shown themselves to be insensitive or indifferent to the supreme need of the Nation." However, "It is noteworthy that the Argentine Constitution has shown itself to be more farsighted in this regard than the American Constitution, which it almost always adopts as a visible model."[70] The author proudly notes: "The Argentine Constitution, reflecting a movement of ideas whose stamp honors our name, happily departs from its credited model on this grave point and takes the promotion of public educación as one of the duties and functions of the Government that it organizes in order to bring about the ends proudly stated in its preamble with a program for our futures. Thus, the Constitution has established the Department of Public Instruction as one of the executive branches of government" (iv).[71] The Argentine constitution takes its US counterpart as a "visible" and "credited model," but the country's lawmakers also make visible their own credit in improving on that model. In 1884, for example, Wilde would boast of "the number of Normal Schools with respect to the total population," which is "superior to ... that of the United States" (Wilde, *Memoria 1884* 1:241).[72] The late nineteenth century thus saw a situation in which Argentines "articulated a vision of the two Americas as each other's natural interlocutors," as "political equals who should establish a horizontal intellectual dialogue and mutually beneficial exchange of ideas and models." This view moved "beyond claiming that the United States was a model that Latin America should follow, to a vision of mutual learning between political and intellectual equals" (Hooker 89). Like Jennie Howard's students, the Argentine liberals were not afraid to assert their own values when they felt them to be superior and to reframe northern narratives of bourgeois-republican modernity within a southern sociocultural context, even as they put those narratives to the service of Sarmiento's dream of northern-style political and economic consolidation through public educación.

I began this project with the somewhat unsophisticated intention of presenting the maestras de Sarmiento program as a precursor to the US invasions and occupations of Cuba, Puerto Rico, the Philippines, and Guam during the late nineteenth and early twentieth centuries. As I will show in chapter 5 of this book, like the Sarmientine US teachers project and the freedmen's schools of the Reconstruction-era South, these post-1898 efforts involved mobilizing armies of northern teachers to educate the children of southern, peripheral territories in bourgeois-republican ideology. It is perhaps no surprise, then, that, in 1901, three former maestras de Sarmiento would travel to New York in order to establish a normal school for teachers from occupied Cuba, tying Latin America's two extremities together in the imperial inter-American state system as parts of a racialized, extended South under the maternal guidance of the northern United States. In this way, late-nineteenth- and early-twentieth-century Argentina was incorporated into the imperial designs that inter-American scholars already have identified elsewhere in the hemisphere.

Yet, this simplistic reading raises as many questions as it answers. Most obviously, there is the inconvenient fact that the United States was not a major imperial power in the Southern Cone during the late nineteenth century: the foreign investments were chiefly British, the foreign cultural influences were chiefly French, and the foreign people disembarking in the port of Buenos Aires were chiefly Italian and Spanish.[73] Most importantly, as historian Karen Leroux points out, the maestras program was led by the Argentine government, complicating any reading of the project strictly in terms of US imperialism ("Self-Strengthening").

Indeed, North Americans represented marginal—and marginalized—players in nineteenth-century Argentine education. Despite the sums wired by successive directors of public instruction to diplomats in the United States to pay for the transportation of North American teachers to Argentina and the gallons of ink spilled in correspondence between Sarmiento and Mary Mann, among others, in their efforts to recruit teachers for the Argentine normal schools, the North American educators enjoyed little institutional support upon arriving in South America.[74] Rather, they were often paid in arrears, placed in subordinate positions, subjected to verbal abuse by the choleric Sarmiento, and held in contempt by much of the general population due to their Protestant beliefs (Luigi, *65 Valiants*). Thus, instead of serving as the harbingers of bourgeois-republican modernity that Sarmiento envisioned, the normal schools "ran into longstanding contrary traditions, such as the separation of males and females in the public sphere, the denial of school education and professions to women, fathers' preeminence over children's activities, and prohibitions on private, male tutors' close association with female students" (McMeley 105). Meanwhile, a cursory glance at the employment information included in the *Memorias* from the period reveals that, despite the rhetoric regarding North American women as ideal educators, Argentines made up a clear majority of people teaching in and administering the normal schools during the period under analysis here.[75] Even at the Escuela Normal de Maestras de la Capital, as late as 1880, there were no US teachers on the staff (Caprile, "Informe de la Directora" 500). Tellingly, the schools known to have employed maestras de Sarmiento almost never mention them in their annual reports. When, in 1889, the contracts of the US maestras de Sarmiento working in Paraná expired, instead of their contracts being renewed, the North American teachers were replaced by their Argentine students (Figueroa 106). The importance of the maestras, then, appears to have been more mythical than material.

The point of such a myth is puzzling, as it denies the Argentines of much of the credit for their own success. After all, many of the innovations that the Argentine liberals attributed to Horace Mann already had been attempted in the Southern Cone long before Sarmiento met the North American pedagogue; by Sarmiento's own admission, the Colegio de Educandas in Salta, Argentina, had been training female teachers since the 1820s (Sarmiento, "Informe" 10).[76] Even more significantly, despite Sarmiento's constant praise for Horace Mann, the notion of local public schools, as I mentioned earlier, was not introduced into Argentina by the liberal statesman following a US model but had already operated in the South American nation in the form of the caudillos' Juntas Protectoras de la Educación (Puiggrós, *Qué pasó* 67–71). Historian Silvia Roitenburd, meanwhile, notes that Argentine educational reformer Juana Manso already had been disseminating progressive educational ideas in the Southern Cone independently of Mann and Sarmiento when the US teachers project began.[77]

Intriguingly, Sarmiento seems to be the author of many innovations that he later attributes to Mann. In 1839, a full decade before his trip to the United States, the Argentine reformer opened a school for girls in his native San Juan, the statutes of which sought to foster the same sort of bourgeois discipline for which, three decades later, he would turn to the North American maestras (Bunkley 108–10). Sarmiento's address at the school's opening ceremony foreshadows much of the rhetoric that later would come to be associated with the North American teachers project. Like the normal schools that the US teachers eventually would found, the Colegio de Pensionistas de Santa Rosa represented the sort of modernizing de-Hispanicization effort aimed at the future mothers of the republic that Mansilla de García opposed, an "admirable proposition of emancipating from the baneful customs of the old metropole that part of the people in whose bosom social transformation, progress, and well-being take root" (Sarmiento, "Apertura" 5).[78] Similarly, while living in exile in Chile, in 1842, Sarmiento had been involved in the creation of the first normal school in Latin America, almost thirty years before the earliest US teachers in Argentina would open the Escuela Normal de Paraná (Bunkley 181–92).[79] Moreover, in an 1881 article in the *Monitor de educación común,* he claims (erroneously) that this institution predates its counterparts in the US ("Chile" 80).[80] Even if, as Roitenburd suggests, Sarmiento initially was exposed to Horace Mann's educational philosophy while exiled in Santiago de Chile in the early 1830s and not while traveling in London in the mid-1840s as scholars commonly contend, the influence of North American thinking on his southern educational reform is less direct than a simple reading of the writings from his time as plenipotentiary, the *Memorias,* or Howard's memoir would suggest.[81]

Why would Sarmiento credit the Manns with reforms that he was already carrying out on his own? Why would the Argentine liberals draw so much attention to the importation of North American republican maestras into the Argentine schoolrooms if those teachers were never to take full command of the country's educational system? Why go through the trouble of positing Argentine campesinos as the structural equivalents of North American freedmen and importing everything from textbooks to tables to teachers from the United States? Why insist on the similarities between Argentina and the US South when the two regions are so obviously different from one another?

Another, better-known example of Sarmiento establishing a specious northern genealogy for his plans to modernize South America may help to answer these questions. In his "Advertencia del autor" (Author's notice) in the first edition of *Facundo,* the writer, fleeing to Chile in order to escape Rosas's henchmen, scribbles the French quote "on ne tue point les idées" (one does not kill ideas) on the wall of a cave, much to the consternation of his monolingual pursuers. The incident is often cited as an example of Sarmiento's instrumental and expropriatory relationship with northern cultures, given that he incorrectly attributes the quote to French journalist Hippolyte Fortoul, though it seems to be his own invention. Some commentators have pointed to this "quotation," which provides an unstable point of origin for Sarmiento's slippery foundational text, as an example of the author's "ostentatious, secondhand culture" (Piglia 17).[82] A mere token, the apocryphal French quote serves to locate Sarmiento intellectually in Paris—which French literary theorist Pascale Casanova has identified as the "meridian" of the nineteenth-century intellectual world—and not in the peripheral early-republican Southern Cone. However, Sarmiento does not simply exchange Spanish-colonial cultural hegemony for its French counterpart; rather, by writing his own quotation in French, he presents his peripheral self as the equal of the European metropole. The misattribution of the quote to Fortoul, then, may be read, not as an example of gauche colonial subservience, but as what cultural studies theorist Néstor García Canclini would call a "strategy for entering modernity."

I want to argue that, much as he borrows intellectual prestige by quoting in French (the language of nineteenth-century cultural and political aristocracies) throughout *Facundo,* in other discourses Sarmiento borrows political prestige by referencing North American bourgeois-republican social thought, a model whose viability had been tested and proven by the recent US Civil War. The United States, then, is not the "modelo acreditado" as much as a *modelo acreedor*—not credited, but a creditor—from which Sarmiento and his companions borrow as they seek legitimacy for reforms that, in reality, respond principally to local concerns. The maestras de Sarmiento, then, can be thought of as a form of cultural finance capital, borrowed from the North in an attempt to develop the southern nation.[83] Perhaps more than another incident of US exploitation of the Global South, the maestras project represents, in Leroux's words, an act of Argentine "self-strengthening."

I suspect that most contemporary scholars will share my ethical unease with the model of cultural borrowing that I have just described. After all, even as it bolstered Argentine bourgeois-republican modernity—the strong public education and large middle class that caused the country to stand out among its Latin American neighbors for much of the twentieth century—as I discussed in the last chapter, that development, articulated through the racial allegory of the northern republican mother, was predicated on Amerindian genocide and Afro-Argentine discursive disappearance. Yet, while the criminal effects of Sarmiento's northernizing plan on southern populations of color should not be ignored or excused, they do have to be understood in context if they are to be understood at all. Sarmiento's scheme to northernize Argentina takes place at a moment in which the Global North was ravaging the South. Across the Atlantic, in the Africa to which Sarmiento frequently compares Argentina, for example, Europe was taking advantage of the continent's lack of a northernized republican bourgeoisie to divide the territory among the great colonial powers for purposes of a particularly savage form of capitalist exploitation.

One cannot help but wonder, then, if Sarmiento's efforts to create a northern-style republican bourgeoisie were not part of an—admittedly flawed—attempt to spare his country the fate of outright domination that at the time was befalling other areas of what would become the Global South.[84] After all, while visiting the United States in the 1840s, he had witnessed firsthand the effects of Mexico's failure to manage (initially peaceful) Anglo incursions, culminating in the loss of one-third of the country's territory to the northern giant. Later, he would write to Mary Mann criticizing the United States' decision not to invoke the Monroe Doctrine during France's 1862–67 occupation of Mexico, noting that "when North Americans see us wrapped in clouds of so much disorder, not only do they ignore us but they do not value us" (qtd. in Ard 116). Meanwhile, in *Las escuelas,* he admonishes that "the United States need to say that they are a country that spans between two oceans and two treaties" (300), thereby eliminating the possibility of further territorial expansion.[85] Alberdi, for his part, would identify the United States as a greater threat to the sovereignty of Spanish American nations than Europe, stating that "*annexation, absorption* by the neighbors is the deaf conquest by which they are threatened" (qtd. in Satas 118).[86] Thus, while Argentine liberals welcomed North American aid—and trade, which began to pick up during the 1850s and '60s (H. Peterson 191)—they feared that Anglo disdain for Latin America represented a threat to the sovereignty of the hemisphere's other republics.

In some ways, the "self-strengthening" borrowings of northern cultural and economic capital by Sarmiento and other like-minded liberals were victims of their own success. In the closing decades of the nineteenth century, after the nation-state had consolidated around free trade with Europe and whitening through genocide against peoples of color, a group of wealthy and conservative agro-exporters rose to social, political, and economic prominence after expanding their ranching interests into newly conquered indigenous territories. As a result, Argentine capitalist development became reliant on latifundial agriculture and assumed a much more peripheral model than the US-style industrialization and middle-class expansion that Sarmiento had sought to implement (Leroux, "Self-Strengthening" 64). Positivists, the leaders of the *Generación del*

1880 rejected Sarmiento's and Alberdi's plans for a practical, utilitarian public school system that would prepare the masses for participation in a democratic society and production in a modern economy. Thinkers of this generation similarly would dismiss the normal teachers as "one of the noxious plagues that Sarmiento left us" (Alier vii).[87] Many shared school inspector T. P. Ramos Mejía's view "that the Normal Schools in general do not meet their aim, that the results that they produce do not justify the sacrifices that their upkeep demands, not only because the number of graduates every year is miniscule, especially in the men's schools, but also because their graduates tend to come away with a deficient professional preparation" (38).[88]

This critique of normalism would find a pointed articulation in conservative writer Manuel Gálvez's *La maestra normal*. The 1914 novel presents readers with a female schoolteacher of scandalously illegitimate birth who is seduced, impregnated, and brought to ruin by a mulato coworker. Significantly, the text suggests that the teacher's "downfall" is the result of the strictly secular training that she has received at a normal school (314). In this way, Gálvez questions how normal teachers could raise the sort of bourgeois-republican national family that Argentine liberals sought. Perhaps not surprisingly, as late as fifteen years after the normal program began, many graduates had trouble finding work as schools continued to hire teachers without education degrees, leading Wilde to call for a reduction in the number of state-sponsored normal programs (*Memoria 1882* xlix). Instead, Argentine policy makers favored the Europhile and traditionalist education of the elite *colegios nacionales*, designed to meet the needs of "an oligarchy that had decided upon a model of reproduction based on income from land, which required a small workforce and excellent relations with European buyers" (Puiggrós, *Sujetos* 98).[89] Thus, "more than a continuity, what really existed was a rupture between the educational thinking elaborated by emigrants from the Rosas period (Alberdi and Sarmiento) and the educational actions taken after 1880" (Tedesco 10).[90] Undemocratic though this "asphyxiation" of Sarmiento's economic and socio-cultural gains may have been (Puiggrós, *Sujetos* 80), it ushered in a period in which Argentina would become one of the world's strongest economies and seek to establish itself as a regional leader.[91]

During this belle epoque, Argentine elites would rely on Sarmiento's and Alberdi's legacy of racial and cultural whitening through immigration and educación in their efforts to overcome their status as colonized compradors and broker a more central place for themselves in world affairs. In a 1913 article entitled "Agasajos a Roosevelt" (Feting Roosevelt), the dean of the medical school at the Universidad de Buenos Aires would note that "the Monroe 'attitude' was created 91 years ago, when South America was inorganic, when her countries, including our own, were but gaucho-political rotten states, constantly in danger of seeing their flags and interests humiliated by the frequent appearance of foreign warships" ("Documento 5" 228).[92] Condemning the early Spanish American republics as "gaucho-political rotten states," he alludes to the racial and cultural legacies of colonialism that the liberal education project attempted to stamp out. Now, thanks to public educación, "This is a European pueblo, because the mass has absorbed the Indian and the black and the mestizos, through the successive development of the generations, today are as White and pure as they were Indian and black in their origins! Today in any corner of the country . . . you will find the same palpitating European feeling that you so admire in Buenos Aires. Our progress in that sense is uniform: it may be less rich in some areas, but all have the same European characteristics!" (229–30).[93] With these words, he ties public educación to whitening as part of an Argentine self-strengthening that renders the presence of "foreign war ships" unnecessary. It is important to note that the writer is not lacking in gratitude to that which renders the presence of "foreign war ships" unnecessary: the United States, which "with the Monroe 'attitude' protected us in our infancy and then transformed our education systems" (231).[94] Ironically, he credits the United States with lending Argentina the cultural finance capital necessary to exploit its human resources and produce a sovereign bourgeois republic that no longer needs imperial protection.

In this context, Sarmiento's collaboration with Mann on the racialized teachers project can be seen as an early effort to put the northern cultural capital that she represents to the use of Argentine development. The terms of the transaction are uneven at best, as Mann's emotional investment in Latin America leads her to produce the 1887 novel *Juanita*, in which she treats the region as a racialized and childlike extension of the US South ripe for "reeducation" through invasion, occupation, and colonial modernization. This ideological current would serve to justify the 1898 war between the United States and Spain for control of Cuba. Indeed, turn-of-the-century Cuba's colonial relationship with the United States—also articulated in terms of racialized family allegory—would prove the very antithesis of what Sarmiento desired for Argentina, confirming the statesman's fears regarding what northern powers might do to developing racialized southern nations, as I now will explain.

4 Foundational Frustrations in Cirilo Villaverde, Mary Mann, and Martín Morúa Delgado

LIKE ARGENTINA, nineteenth-century Cuba would look north to the United States during its efforts to break free from Spanish cultural, political, and economic obscurantism.[1] As in the South American nation, this modernizing project required the negotiation of tensions between autochthonous and imported racial paradigms through the allegory of the national family. However, Cuba's relationship with the northern hegemon would prove much more fraught than that of Argentina, and the twentieth century would dawn not over a consolidated nation-state but a US protectorate. On the Caribbean island, then, the Cooperian racialized national-family allegory that Argentine liberals had cannibalized would not serve as the discursive bedrock of the bourgeois nation-state; rather, the northern vision of Latin American creoles as racially degenerate children to be raised and educated by white North American republican mothers would lock Cuba within a US imperial grip from which it would struggle to escape.

This chapter examines how the novels *Cecilia Valdés, o la Loma del Ángel* (1882), by Cuban creole Cirilo Villaverde; *Juanita, A Romance of Real Life in Cuba Fifty Years Ago* (1889), by North American Mary Mann; and *Sofía* (1891), by Afro-Cuban Martín Morúa Delgado—three stories of interracial relationships set against the interimperial backdrop of the 1898 Spanish-Cuban-American War—complicate the racialized allegory of republican motherhood by deploying incest, procreation, and child-rearing as tropes to debate the racial question that Cuba's looming independence from Spain was fast rendering urgent and inevitable: Would creoles and Afro-descendants be members of the same republican national family? I will conclude by looking at how, as an Afro-Cuban, Morúa Delgado expropriates the reproductive maternal trope from white authors Villaverde and Mann in order to resist both

Cuban creole and North American designs for Cuba's future after independence from Spain.

The chapter builds on the interest that the field of inter-American studies has shown in the 1898 conflict, in which the United States intervened in Cuba's anticolonial struggle against Spain in order to transform the Caribbean island into its protectorate, a status that continued until 1934. Dubbed the "Spanish-Cuban-American War" by historian Phillip Foner, the war represents a key moment for hemispheric relations, marking the definitive collapse of Spain's overseas empire and the contemporaneous consolidation of the inter-American state system under Washington's rising star.[2] These events would derail Cuba's decades-long quest for sovereignty and eventually contribute to the 1959 revolution against US imperial influence.

In his widely anthologized essay "Nuestra América" ("Our America") (1891), Cuban poet and patriot José Martí looks to mestizo nationalism to ease the racial tensions endemic to postabolition, pre-independence Cuba, caught between Spanish and North American colonial gazes. In his passionate prose, Martí condemns the racist hypocrisy of "those born in América, who are ashamed of their mother because she wears an Indian smock, of the mother that raised them and deny—the scoundrels!—their sick mother and leave her alone on her sickbed" (87). In this way, he rejects the exclusionary logic of earlier foundational texts such as *The Last of the Mohicans, In Distant Climes and Other Years,* and, to a lesser extent, *Lucía Miranda* by scripting a woman of color into the role of national mother.[3] Born of an Indian mother, the body politic of Martí's "Nuestra América" cannot be exclusively white. Rather, the writer turns away from narrative justifications for creole hegemony such as those found in varying degrees in the foundational texts of Cooper, Mansilla de García, and Howard, in which women of color are either killed or culturally disappeared before they have an opportunity to give birth to the nation. Instead, Martí in his essay suggests that "the genius would have been in making brothers, with charity of heart and the founders' daring, of the headdress and the professor's gown" (90)—a fraternal form of integration that, historian Ada Ferrer argues, the Cuban *independentista* army was achieving on the battlefield at the time (*Insurgent Cuba*).[4]

This rosy reading of Martí's foundational text as a racial-democratic manifesto—popular among both multiculturally aware new Americanists and solidarity-building Cuban Marxists—has been contested as a rhetorical device to cover up the social marginalization of black and Amerindian populations in Latin America, declaring the region to be racelessly mestizo at a moment in which peoples of color still lacked basic rights and resources. (Filing antidiscrimination suits against the colonial government, Afro-Cuban leader Juan Gualberto Gómez, for example, may have been confused by Martí's contention that "there is no race hatred because there are no races").[5] Thus, despite the national family raised by an Indian mother that Martí imagines, in recent years, critics have attacked the Cuban thinker's notion of "nuestra América mestiza" (our mestizo América) as yet another racially exclusive discourse, noting that the "nosotros" (we) dressed in "epaulets and professors' gowns" (charreteras y togas) that the author interpellates is creole. Afro-descendants and the indigenous remain at the margins: "The silent Indian circled around us," and the black, off to the side, "sang among the waves and the beasts" (90).[6]

Perhaps because of the interpretive ambiguity to which it gives rise, the Martían vision of a nonwhite national mother raising an interracial citizen body—however insincere it may or may not be—has inspired scores of writers from across the hemisphere. In the context of Cuba's late-nineteenth-century gravitation away from Spain's imperial orbit and toward that of the United States, several authors would attempt to reconsider earlier New World foundational romances such as *The Last of the Mohicans* and *Lucía Miranda*, contemplating what might happen if whites and nonwhites—the headband and the professor's gown—really were to embrace one another as the siblings that Martí had envisioned. In *Cecilia Valdés* (1882), *Juanita* (1887), and *Sofía* (1891), creole Cirilo Villaverde, North American Mary Mann, and Afro-Cuban Martín Morúa Delgado, respectively, express pessimism toward Martí's mestizo fraternity through the theme of interracial incest. The texts rescript the foundational historical romance genre in order to question whether the star-crossed relationships between their white and mulata protagonists represent an impetus or an impediment to national consolidation. Through the foundational plot, the works discussed in this chapter, like *The Last of the Mohicans* and *Lucía Miranda*, ultimately take up the question of whether a culturally and racially hybrid woman can serve as mother of the republic, this time by imagining—or, more to the point, by electing not to imagine—the destinies of the children that she might bear. Considered together, the works offer a nebulous vision of Cuba's national future: in creole Villaverde's *Cecilia Valdés*, the child of the mixed-race Cecilia and her white half-brother Leonardo Gamboa mysteriously drops out of the narrative as soon as she is born; in North American Mary Mann's *Juanita*, a group of Cuban creoles are educated by a Massachusetts governess rather than fall into the hands of their slaves; and, in *Sofía*, Afro-Cuban Martín Morúa Delgado unsettlingly critiques the other two authors' deployments of the republican-mother trope by introducing miscarriage as a metaphor for nonviability of creole and North American plans for postcolonial Cuba. The sharp divergences among fates of the children in the creole, US, and Afro-Cuban novels indicate the differences among the various postcolonial identities that were being imagined for Cuba through the allegory of national motherhood at the turn of the nineteenth century—incommensurabilities that would mark public life in the postcolonial state from the 1898 war's conclusion to the present day. Thus, like the Cuban nation itself, Villaverde's, Mann's, and Morúa's projects encounter the same racial stumbling block that Martí's vision of "nuestra América" tried vainly to remove.

History: Autonomy, Annexation, and Independence

Cuba's protracted struggle for independence from Spain spans the entire nineteenth century and includes movements such as the 1810 Constitutional Conspiracy and the 1823 masonic Soles y Rayos de Bolívar Conspiracy, which sought to make the colony part of Gran Colombia (present-day Colombia, Panama, Venezuela, and Ecuador), as well as multiple filibustering expeditions and movements to annex the island to the United States throughout the 1800s. Prominent among these was Venezuelan Narciso López's 1850 conspiracy to incorporate Cuba into the northern country as a slave state, in which Villaverde participated, resulting in his eventual exile.[7] Cuba did not, however, play a major role in the 1820s independence movements that liberated most of the Spanish Main from the imperial Crown. While some have sought to condemn the Cuban elite for its seemingly belated adoption of nationalist principles, other scholars have cautioned against projecting the values of the nation-state onto the colony, an ideological anachronism that risks casting Cuba's "late" independence as a failure (Sartorius 9). Historians traditionally have contended that, the Haitian Revolution still a clear memory as the Hispanic island filled the void in the world sugar market left by the newly liberated French colony, white Cubans feared that the withdrawal of metropolitan troops from Havana would create the ideal conditions for a slave revolt, as happened during the 1812 Aponte Conspiracy and the 1844 Conspiración de la Escalera.[8] Newer studies have painted creole elites in a more protagonic light. Ada Ferrer suggests that the "decision to remain Spanish was one dictated less by fear . . . than by self-interest"

(*Freedom's Mirror* 15–16). The historian postulates that, as New Spain was rebelling against the metropole, creole elites, rather than risk the possibility of abolition (in 1810, *independentista* Miguel Hidalgo had declared slavery illegal in Mexico), pledged their loyalty to the peninsula in exchange for certain guarantees, including the expansion of the slave trade and the right to engage in international commerce (269). Among the last Spanish Americans to win independence, nineteenth-century Cubans would see themselves crippled both politically and economically by the metropole's slow and half-hearted adoption of liberal reforms (the very reforms that Sarmiento and his ideological comrades in Argentina sought to implement through a cultural distancing from the peninsula).[9]

Of course, not everyone accepted Cuba's place in the Spanish empire, which, they felt, clung to a feudal and obscurantist tradition as other nations embraced the Age of Revolution's promise of republican rights. In his 1882 *Cecilia Valdés,* Villaverde complains that "the press had remained silent since 1824, there was no citizen militia, the town halls had ceased to be popular bodies, and not even the shadow of liberty was left, since in 1825 it was declared by decree that the country was under a state of siege, and a permanent Military Commission was instituted" (289).[10] Perhaps the greatest resentment was caused by the final abrogation of the Constitución de Cádiz in 1837, which led to the expulsion of Cuba's delegates from Spain's lawmaking body, the Cortes. "The result of this political project was that the metropole was incapable of granting Cuba any of the Fundamental Rights: in economic terms, free trade; in social terms, the equality of white creoles and Peninsular Spaniards; in political terms, the representation of the country in the power structures of the Spanish State" (Andioc 4:xiv).[11] To add to this geopolitical mix, as the 1800s progressed, Cubans would experience the twin pressures of British abolitionist intervention and US economic absorption and imperial gazing.[12]

These three tendencies—dissatisfaction with Spain, antislavery, and annexation—would intertwine over the course of the nineteenth century to produce the knotty conflict over the island's independence. Carlos Manuel de Céspedes's 1868 Manifiesto de la junta revolucionaria de la Isla de Cuba (Manifesto of the revolutionary junta of the island of Cuba), written at the beginning of the Ten Years' War for Independence from the Iberian metropole, for example, called for "universal suffrage to insure the sovereignty of the people" and "gradual slave emancipation with compensation to the owners."[13] The end of the Ten Years' War and subsequent Guerra Chiquita, or "Little War" (1879–80), inaugurated a period of nuanced political debate. While the wealthiest members of the creole upper class, hesitant to abandon the protections for slavery for which they had bargained, went back and forth over the question of the colony's relationship with the metropole, more modest landowners and the popular classes were divided between *autónomos,* who wanted more independence for Cuba within the Spanish empire; *anexionistas,* who hoped for annexation to the United States, where many of their number lived in exile; and *separatistas* (sometimes also called *independentistas*), who sought sovereignty for the island. To complicate matters further, many supporters of independence in fact wished for Cuba to proclaim independence as a first step toward eventual annexation to the United States—a path that came to be nicknamed the "Texas model."[14]

All these plans were marked by strong racial overtones and *independentista* José Martí's famous disavowal of race politics (seconded, as I will show below, by Martín Morúa Delgado) are largely a reaction to this situation. While "the nationalist strivings were fundamentally at odds with the demands of a sugar economy that continued to depend heavily upon slave labor, the possibility of slave emancipation posed other problems. What role the island's sizable African population, once freed, might play in a fledgling republic was indeed a hotly debated issue" (Kutzinski, *Sugar's Secrets* 18). Chiefly upper-class in membership, El Partido Unión Constitucional (the Constitutional Union Party), for example, contended that Cuba, because of its mixed racial composition, must remain fully under Spanish domination. They were particularly concerned about the island falling under the rule of *mulatos,* whom they presumed to be resentful of both whites and blacks. Additionally, the Partido feared that the United States might take advantage of the confusion to dominate and repopulate Cuba (Helg, *Rightful* 48). The mulato question proved equally vexatious for the *autónomos,* who were uncertain as to whether or not to grant political rights to mixed-race individuals (59). Meanwhile, creole annexationists "were willing to develop an alliance with US expansionists in part because the Creoles saw themselves as whites in the Americas fighting a European power." This understanding was not universally held, however, as "a segment of the U.S. population, including some antislavery and antiexpansionist writers, saw Creoles as hybrid people incapable of governing themselves" (Lazo, *Writing* 156–57). Anglo-American beliefs regarding the creoles' racial inferiority would play no small role as, in 1898, the United States, bowing to pressure from the yellow press, intervened in the colony's final independence war, which Cubans had initiated in 1895. The United States would occupy the island for the four years following the peninsular power's surrender and reinvade it on multiple occasions thereafter. The racialized disagreements among creoles, Afro-descendants, and US Americans—whether Afro-Cubans were members of the national family and whether creoles were white in the same way in which Anglo-Americans were—are at the heart of the three novels that I now will discuss and of the political debates over public educación and Cuba's status as a sovereign republic analyzed in the following chapter.

Cuban Antislavery Writing

The antislavery movement in Cuban letters is considered to have been initiated by Domingo del Monte, a creole intellectual and son-in-law of sugar baron Miguel de Aldama. In 1834, recognizing the constitutive relationship between bondage and coloniality in Cuba, del Monte founded an antislavery literary salon dedicated to the nationalist cause. The *tertulia*—which was constituted largely by men who, like del Monte, had a stake in the colonial slave system that they ostensibly wished to reform—began by organizing the translation of French antislavery texts (L. Williams 16). The group rapidly developed into a forum in which creole liberals could read and discuss antislavery works out of earshot from the colonial censors (Ocasio 63). Many scholars hold that, though anticolonial and antislavery in orientation, the reforms proposed by the del Monte group were driven largely by the creoles' political and economic self-interest. In addition to calling for the suppression of the slave trade, "a measure that halted the growth of the black population and presupposed a gradual abolition of slavery," the *tertulianos* promoted the immigration of European workers as a means of whitening the population. The *delmontinos*' interests extended beyond race and slavery, however. Members of the group also sought to "obtain from the Crown a cessation of the colonial status in favor of an autonomous regime, reorganize sugar agriculture, renovate transportation and communications, end vagrancy and vice, promote scientific study and reform the educational system" (Benítez Rojo 104).[15]

This uneasy relationship between self-interest and altruism would be characteristic of the works produced by the tertulia. While calls for full abolition were a rarity in del Montean texts, the denunciation of slavery as a sign of Cuba's moral debasement under Spanish colonialism was a central theme, as works such as Félix Tanco y Bosmeniel's 1838 "Petrona y Rosalía," Juan Francisco Manzano's 1840 *Autobiografía de un esclavo*, and Anselmo Suárez y Romero's 1877 *Francisco. El ingenio, o las delicias del campo* make clear. "Since Cubans were supposed to be identical to Spaniards" during this colonial moment, "a narrative founded on a notion of Cubanness that acknowledged the cultural contributions of the non-Hispanic element violated the rules of decorum to which writers in Cuba were expected to give allegiance" (L. Williams 4). On the one hand, then, antislavery in these texts ironically serves the cause of creole hegemony, as the feudally oppressed slave functions as a figuration of the Cuban nation "enslaved" by Spain's obscurantist colonialism (Sartorius 7). On the other, "In the act of creating and representing subjects," creole antislavery writing "encouraged identification and identity formation and thus undermined metropolitan authority" (Fraunhar 46). This ideological ambiguity would shape *Cecilia Valdés,* as I now will explain.

Cecilia Valdés

Written over the course of more than four decades, Cirilo Villaverde's *Cecilia Valdés* represents a textual embodiment of the racial concerns clustering around Cuba's drawn-out struggle for independence. After penning two early versions in 1839—a short story and a novella—Villaverde published the work in its definitive form in 1882 in New York. The novel also was sold in centers of Cuban reformist activity such as Key West, Madrid, Paris, and, of course, Havana (Lazo, *Writing* 171). Set in the Havana of Villaverde's youth, *Cecilia Valdés* tells the story of the illicit relations between the creole aristocrat Leonardo Gamboa and the mulata Cecilia Valdés, who, unbeknownst to them both, is his half-sister.[16] The relationship ends in tragedy when Leonardo, after marrying the creole heiress Isabel Illincheta, is murdered by José Dionisio, an Afro-Cuban rival for Cecilia's affections. Through the machinations of Leonardo's mother, doña Rosa, Cecilia is interred in a mental institution as punishment for the crime.

The novel in its definitive form initially appears to be a foundational romance in which the eponymous heroine allegorizes a mixed-race Cuban pueblo struggling against the Spanish colonial patriarchy. The mulata Cecilia's embodiment of *cubanía* is made clear by Villaverde's constant references to her as a "little bronze Virgin," a turn of phrase that compares her to Cuba's patron saint, La Virgen de la Caridad del Cobre, the Virgin of Charity of Cobre (101). (Literally "copper," Cobre is a town in eastern Cuba.)[17] According to legend, the Caridad del Cobre saved an interracial group of fishermen—named Juan Blanco, Juan Negro, and Juan Indio—from a storm off the island's coast. Offering protection from the extremes of the New World environment to representatives of all races, the Caridad del Cobre functions as a mother to the Cuban people. Through her association with the "copper" Virgin of Charity, the figure of Cecilia presents a vision of an Afro-Cuban woman as a possible mother to the interracial nation, an idea to which the birth of her child near the end of the novel gestures.

At the same time, however, by qualifying Cecilia as a "little bronze Virgin," Villaverde also associates the character with the Yoruba deity Ochún, who traditionally is clad in yellow. Though syncretized with the Virgin of Charity in the Afro-Cuban religion Santería, Ochún represents feminine sexuality in the Yoruba pantheon. This can be seen in the stereotypical tropes of debauched mulata libidinousness through which the novel often presents Cecilia. Significantly, she first is introduced as she walks the streets unchaperoned, a behavior that readers at the time would have viewed as sexually illicit. The narrator in this scene describes Cecilia's body with a voyeuristic level of detail (particularly unsettling, given that the character is only twelve years old at the time) (73–75). Though the syncretization of the Virgin of Charity and Ochún is internally consistent within the cultural logic of Santería, from the point of view of the Hispanic tradition within which Villaverde wrote his *costumbrista* novel, Cecilia's association with the Virgin Mother is cancelled out by the non-virginal terms in which she is described. Ironically, through her affiliation with the Virgin of Charity, the text situates Cecilia as a mother to an interracial Cuba at the same time that the interracial associations of the Caridad del Cobre with Ochún render Cecilia a morally unfit mother to that nation. This aporia is reflected in the plot by Cecilia's pregnancy by her half-brother Leonardo, which positions her as a potential mother of the Cuban nation, even as it is shrouded in incest and illegitimacy. In both cases, the conditions of possibility are also the conditions of impossibility. This semantic and structural instability shapes the slippery race politics of Villaverde's canonical novel, as I now will explain.

In this section, I will contrast this constitutive instability with the foundational imperative of earlier creole romances such as *The Last of the Mohicans* and *Lucía Miranda* that I discussed in chapter 2. I explain how Villaverde's text breaks the rules of the trans-American foundational romance genre by deploying interracial incest (a trope for the paradoxical copresence of difference and sameness) as a narrative containment device, revealing the nation's would-be foundational parents—a creole and a mulata—as unable to reproduce under circumstances propitious to the founding of the interracial nation, a political dream deferred whose fruitful realization seemed increasingly complicated as the nineteenth century progressed. I argue that interracial incest and the problematic vision of republican motherhood that it suggests serve in the 1882 novel as a late-nineteenth-century reaction to the Americas' earlier foundational texts and the (frequently ill-fated) creole national projects that they justified—both of which, Villaverde fears, fail to take seriously the complexity of the New World republics' entrenched racialized political economies. After considering the difficulty of giving birth to Cuba Libre in Villaverde's novel, the section concludes with a discussion of an alternate republican mother that the author proposes for the Cuban nation: the white exiled revolutionary Emilia Casanova, his wife.

Foundational Cecilias

In both of the two 1839 *Cecilia* texts and the final 1882 novel, the narratives' inconclusive natures result in the protagonists' inability to reproduce under circumstances conducive to the founding of the interracial nation. While the definitive *Cecilia Valdés* frequently is lauded as a masterwork of the abolitionist genre, neither of the 1839 versions expresses direct antislavery sentiment, possibly in order to avoid problems with censors on the island colony in which Villaverde still lived (Álvarez García 319; Shulman xvi; Luis, *Literary Bondage* 100). Instead of the realistic depictions of slavery that scholars such as César Leante find in the 1882 edition, the first 1839 publication (known as "La primitiva *Cecilia Valdés*") is marked by the Gothic romanticism characteristic of Villaverde's earlier works, such as the short stories "La peña blanca" (The white crag) (1837) and "El ave muerta" (The dead bird) (1837) and the novel *El penitente* (The Penitent) (1844).[18] The text does not pay specific attention to race but tells the tale of a lower-class girl who disappears mysteriously after being seduced by a young man from the creole upper classes. Critics have read the story as criticizing creole elites' disregard for the popular classes, written by a member of the Delmontean group that would advocate for social reforms such as public education (Harney).

The second "Cecilia" was published in book form by the Editorial Cuba Intelectual. Prepared for the del Monte tertulia, the *costumbrista* text at first glance appears to promote a racially integrated national project. Upon closer inspection, however, the unfinished novella shares the reticence "La primitiva *Cecilia Valdés*" to express direct abolitionist sentiment (Kutzinski, *Sugar's Secrets* 18; Shulman xxiii).[19] The work ends somewhat abruptly when Leonardo, ostensibly in love with Cecilia, attempts to convince his friend Diego Meneses to court Isabel so that he may be free to pursue his new romantic interest. By having Leonardo go to the length of jilting his white betrothed for a mistress of color, Villaverde—however improbably—suggests the possibility of an integrated future for Cuba, gesturing at an interracial foundational romance between Leonardo and Cecilia. Yet the notion of racial reconciliation through romance in the 1839 novella will appear problematic to anyone familiar with the history of nineteenth-century Cuba, the second-to-last country on earth to abolish African chattel slavery. Meneses, too, finds Leonardo's declaration that he will leave wealth and standing behind for his "mulata santa" unlikely, and goes to bed. Undeterred, Leonardo then turns to his friend Pancho Solfa:

> And he was talking a good part of the night, heatedly, but fruitlessly . . . because, as a man of pithy education . . . it was not easy to convince him. Gamboa gave it his vanity and painted castles in the sky which collapsed under the crude positive dialectics of a law student. Sleep surprised both young men in the course of the battle, like the kick of a police officer, and threw the glove at the distracted drinkers, laying them half-naked in bed and interrupting the last words in their throats, leaving them open mouthed [*con la boca abierta*]. (245)[20]

The first (and only drafted) volume of the 1839 edition ends here, "con la boca abierta." There is no second volume in the true sense—the canonical 1882 *Cecilia Valdés* is radically different and by all rights its own, separate work from the earlier versions. The foundational romance of racial reconciliation that Leonardo proposes is—quite literally—unable to reach completion: the participants have fallen asleep midsentence, their very utterances left unfinished, to say nothing of their half-baked schemes; despite Villaverde's evident plans to write more (the term "Tomo I" appears on the book's cover page, promising another installment that the author never delivered), the uncompleted text, like Leonardo, is left with its mouth hanging open. That Villaverde was unable to finish what he started and marry Leonardo to Cecilia points to the difficulty of imagining interracial alliances in the Cuba of the 1830s and '40s; just five years after volume 1 was published, following the discovery and foiling of the Escalera slave conspiracy, the incipient community imagined by Villaverde's novel would be decimated by the recrudescence of caste boundaries and the repression of Cuba's free community of color.

Thus, if the short story ends mysteriously with the disappearance of its female protagonist, removed from the public sphere before she has had the chance to enter it fully, the novella dead-ends with the male protagonist in a drunken stupor, as unable to close his mouth as the author is to close the narrative. Both versions, then, resist Sommer's foundational paradigm: the short story presents Cecilia as a "fallen woman" but stops short of suggesting that she has had a child that might embody the future nation; the novella does not place Leonardo into an appropriately reproductive marriage with either the creole Isabel or the mulata Cecilia but instead leaves him half naked in bed with two other men. If, as Imeldo Álvarez García argues, Villaverde's earlier texts show the inner workings of the colonial state, it seems that that state—dominated, as the del Monteans were well aware, by plantation economics and the fear of slave revolt—is unable to unite its creole and Afro-descended populations in order to produce a nation.

Incest as Revolution

The same problematic consolidation of the national family through narrative manifests itself in the 1882 version of *Cecilia Valdés*. Significantly, Latin American *independentista* rhetoric typically condemned Spain for paternalistically treating the *americanos* as children, casting the king of Spain as "more an overprotective father than a remote tyrant" (Felstiner 159)—a trope that, in *Cecilia Valdés,* is reflected in the tensions between peninsular father Cándido Gamboa and his creole son Leonardo. Doña Rosa, the boy's mother, comments to her husband that her son reacts to Gamboa's purchasing of a title by stating that "nobility bought with the blood of the blacks that you and the other Spaniards stole in Africa in order to condemn them to eternal slavery was not nobility, but infamy, and he looked upon the title of nobility as the greatest blot on his honor."[21] The Spanish-born father responds by angrily exclaiming, "Isn't that the creole blood boiling in his veins! The piece of trash would start the beheadings with his own father if we ever had on the Island the same kind of uprising that we had on the Mainland" (422).[22] In this way, the intergenerational family conflict is elevated into an allegory of the political struggle over Cuba's colonial status, transforming, as literary scholar Vera Kutzinski notes, Leonardo's decision to disobey his father through his affair with his mulata half-sister Cecilia into a revolt against the colonial patriarchy (*Sugar's Secrets,* 32). The novel makes this clear when Cecilia states that she is "very independent and I will never consent to someone ruling me, much less a stranger" (243).[23] Not coincidentally, the Spanish word for "stranger" (*extraño*) is related etymologically to the word for "foreigner" (*extranjero*). In the context of the foundational novel, the play on words transforms the creole's desire for the mulata into an allegory of the interracial Cuban nation asserting its freedom from Spain.

Villaverde's deployment of the incest trope only makes these national-allegorical family dynamics more complicated. Drawing from Sigmund Freud's 1913 *Totem and Taboo,* which postulates the origins of civilization in the blood guilt of a mythical band of troglodytic brothers who killed their father, the clan's alpha male, in order to break his sexual monopoly on the tribe's women (their mother and sisters), critic Gabriel Croguennec-Massol notes that "in many foundational tales, the story begins with a transgression" (6).[24] In this case, it is the creole son's transgression against his peninsular father, Cándido Gamboa, whose opposition to the relationship between Leonardo and Cecilia is misattributed as an expression of his own "twisted desires" toward the young woman (Villaverde 617; see also 414).[25] As the foundational act of transgression with which the history of Cuban nation-state begins, "incest in *Cecilia Valdés* lends the work a foundational aspect, representative of a society still under construction" (Croguennec-Massol 6).[26] Punning on the Spanish term for star-crossed love, *amor imposible,* Doris Sommer postulates that the novel is "about impossible love, not because blacks and whites should not love each other—after all, they are mutually attractive and produce beautiful children—but because slavery" (and, with slavery, the Spanish colonial patriarchy that upholds the institution) "makes it impossible" (*Foundational Fictions,* 128). In this way, "sibling incest" and the union of black and white colonials can be "interpreted as the victory of revolutionary *fraternité* over the tyrannical father" of the metropole (Sollors 319).

In this Freudian reading, in which the incest prohibition represents an exercise of paternal authority by limiting the son's sexual access to the women of the clan, Leonardo and José Dionisio, his Afro-Cuban rival for Cecilia's affections, are, despite (or perhaps because of) the racial difference between them, locked in a fratricidal struggle to assume the colonial father's authority over Cecilia, who, as a mixed-race woman, comes to allegorize a Cuban nation that, in theory, may be possessed by either the Spanish patriarch's black or white sons.[27] Once the anarchic blood crimes—Leonardo's symbolic overthrow of peninsular authority through his defiance of Cándido and José Dionisio's murder of the creole aristocrat Leonardo—are consummated, civilization, in the form of the rule of law (embodied by the interlocking prohibitions against incest and patricide), may manifest itself in the founding of the Cuban nation-state.

Following this argument to its logical conclusion, by killing the creole Leonardo, the Afro-descendant José Dionisio should gain control of the Cuban nation that the mixed-race Cecilia represents and is able to reproduce. As another mulato character says consolingly to the unrequited José Dionisio earlier in the novel, the monopoly that white men enjoy over women of color due to their class and social status cannot last forever, and "some day it will be our turn" (205).[28] The only antislavery text "to include a mulato killing a white man" (Luis, *Literary Bondage* 118), the dramatic resolution of *Cecilia Valdés* should signal "an end to historical exploitation of black and mulatto women"—and, by extension, the nation that they allegorize—"by white men" (117). At first glance, then, it seems that Villaverde presents nonwhites as the catalysts and rightful heirs of Cuban independence and the republic that it will engender. This arrival of "our turn" should find its natural metaphorical expression in José Dionisio achieving "alpha" status and gaining access to Cecilia's national-allegorical body.

That is not how the novel ends, however. The psychoanalytic anticolonial reading of the text is predicated on Leonardo's erroneous belief that he is competing sexually with his father don Cándido for his sister Cecilia. However, the fact that Leonardo is mistaken as to his father's true intentions means that the novel's climax cannot represent a Freudian wish-fulfillment fantasy of a new racial or political order emerging from the ashes of the Spanish colony. Rather, both José Dionisio and Cecilia are imprisoned—that is, removed from society—for Leonardo's murder and, dead, Leonardo is hardly in a position to inherit his peninsular father's place in colonial society, leaving the question of future national consolidation in this foundational historical romance narratologically open. With his foundational protagonists either deceased or confined, Villaverde, in a departure from the typical function of the Latin American historical novelist, runs the national family's "line of generation" into the wall of incest, signaling not the "formal path" toward a nationally consolidated future but, rather, a dead end (Jitrik, "De la historia" 16), a variation on Leonardo's open mouth at the end of the 1839 novella.[29]

Foundational Fictions Unfounded

Thus, "unlike the other nineteenth-century novels that Doris Sommer has studied so well, in Villaverde's novel there is no love story that allegorically represents national unification. Instead, there is a love story that ends in national dissolution" (Gelpí 56).[30] While, in urging star-crossed lovers toward interfactional *alianzas* (both "alliances" and "wedding rings"),

Villaverde's narrative of national dissolution re-creates the deep structure of the foundational historical romance, this imitation of the genre only serves to turn its structural conventions against themselves, narrating not the consolidation of a class or the foundation of a nation but the frustration of those occurrences. This frustration, I will argue, reflects the fraught racial reality of late-nineteenth-century Cuba as well as Villaverde's own uncertain stance vis-à-vis the increased participation of Afro-Cubans in colonial society under the leadership of the likes of Juan Gualberto Gómez's Directorio Central de Sociedades de Color and the insurgent commanders of the revolutionary army, known as the *mambises*.

Importantly, while, in Villaverde's seemingly foundational novel, the incestuous relationship between the creole oligarch and the Afro-Cuban subaltern is consummated, it is outside of marriage. While "the child is a recurring theme in many of the antislavery narratives and a symbol of the country's future" (Luis, *Literary Bondage* 51), the scandalous origins of Leonardo and Cecilia's daughter lend an air of illegitimacy (in all senses of the term) to the project of national consolidation. That the child's illegitimacy is intended to speak to the condition of the entire Afro-Cuban population is underscored by the fact that, as critic Juan Gelpí points out, Villaverde renders his exacting reproductions of Afro-Cuban dialect in italicized *bastardilla* (literally "little female bastard"), which "denotes... the character who, by not conforming to the linguistic standards or laws of nineteenth-century Cuban Spanish, gives away his or her identity as a bastard, which in this case would be someone who is not a 'legitimate child' of the Cuban patria" (Gelpí, 51).[31] Indeed, it is precisely the daughter's racial status that produces her illegitimacy, as race is the factor that renders marriage between Leonardo and Cecilia difficult. Historian K. Lynn Stoner has argued that the notion of illegitimacy itself carried racial and class connotations in Cuba. The legal distinction between children born within and those born outside of marriage would continue until the 1959 revolution, and efforts to reform this law would result in some of fiercest legislative battles that the new republic would see. Threatening racial and economic hierarchies, Leonardo and Cecilia's mixed-race child cannot serve as the ideal citizen for an imagined future community and drops out of the story the sentence after she is born, leaving the narrator's mouth open and the issue of national consolidation that the daughter embodies unresolved.

Villaverde's inability to find a place for the child of a free black mother and a rebellious creole father in his novel of national origins thus reflects the author's uncertainty as to the role of free blacks in the national

Foundational Frustrations 137

family.[32] It is important to note that the "pattern of exploitation" that had produced the mixed-race Cecilia's almost white phenotype has a transgenerational quality. "It began with Magdalena Morales, Cecilia's great-grandmother" and supposedly "will end with Cecilia's daughter," as "both 1839 versions state that the exploitation will end in the fifth generation.... Villaverde omitted this information from the 1882 edition because neither the emancipation of slaves in 1886 nor the liberation of Cuba from Spain in 1898 had occurred during the proposed fifth generation" (Luis, *Literary Bondage* 117). This suggests that the same history of racial marginalization will continue into the future. At the same time, however, it is important to recognize the political gains that Afro-Cubans were making during the period. In 1878, for example, racial restrictions on suffrage were abolished, while in 1881 (a year before Villaverde's novel was published), interracial marriage was reinstated—a legal change that could have rendered Cecilia and Leonardo's child a legitimate member of the national body (Helg, *Our Rightful Share* 27).[33] Perhaps most importantly, in 1880, as Villaverde was readying his manuscript for press, the Spanish Cortes passed the Ley de Patronato, a plan for the gradual phasing out of slavery, thereby mitigating the fear of slave revolt that long had thwarted Cuban independence movements.

Thus, at the same moment when Afro-Cubans rapidly were gaining social and political agency in the extratextual world, Villaverde raises the possibility of protagonism in the national narrative, but presents the option as unsavory. In much the same paradoxical fashion that Cecilia's association with the Caridad del Cobre/Ochún situates her as the mother of the nation at the same time that it disqualifies her from virtuous motherhood, Villaverde suggests that, in a wealthy sugar colony in which slavery is the economic engine of the would-be bourgeois republic, whites and blacks are (as it were) already in bed together and, thus, cannot unite to found a legitimate nation. "The pillar of the nation" is thus "a blurry origin, an incest" that is "inevitable, both by the very motor of the slavery system and by the deep psychological structure of which it is an effect" (Méndez Rodenas 85). By 1882, two facts would have been clear to Villaverde: (1) that Afro-descendants soon would be full members of the Cuban national family, at least in legal terms, and (2) that, given that the plantation economy was the basis of the nationalist bourgeoisie's wealth, full racial equality could only undermine the economic bases of the nation. On the one hand, creole elites and the Afro-Cuban masses are, in a sense, "married," as the success of the plantation economy depends upon an indissoluble union to which both are equally integral.

On the other, the colonial-economic nature of the relationship means that the equality that the indissoluble union between masters and slaves implies would, paradoxically, dissolve that union. Given Villaverde's involvement in revolutionary and (later in life) antislavery activities, it is noteworthy that his novel does not gesture toward these coming changes by commenting on the fate of Cecilia's child.

Instead of optimism about the future, the novel takes the more difficult path of meditating on the "epistemological and psychological split" caused by the fact that the "fundamental contributions of Africans to Cuba and Cuban identity, both economically and culturally, could neither be ignored nor incorporated" (Fraunhar 80). In many ways, the character of Leonardo embodies this "split." When Leonardo attacks his father's participation in the slave trade as "the greatest blot on his honor," doña Rosa, the boy's mother, defends her husband, countering: "Oh, son! Would you throw away so much luxury, and stop enjoying such comforts if your father stopped working?" (Villaverde 255).[34] As it turns out, vehemently though he may speak against the slave trade and the Spaniards who run it, Leonardo is addicted to the "luxuries" that the system makes possible, as his machinations to obtain from his mother eighteen ounces of gold with which to buy a new Swiss watch make clear (187-94). It is no surprise, then, that, despite his rebellious comments to his father earlier in the text, Leonardo is invested in maintaining the hierarchies of slaveholding society, as can be seen in Villaverde's description of the creole's brutal whipping of a slave for failing to follow orders: "That soul had lost its feeling; only that arm seemed to move. Iron, it did not tire of striking him" (260).[35] Leonardo, like many creole reformers, such as del Monte and even Villaverde himself, critiques colonial slavery at the same time that he depends on that system for his existence. Significantly, the character ultimately abandons Cecilia after the birth of their child—the future that the narrative cannot quite imagine—when he confronts the fact that his mulata mistress was not, as he ruminates, "his equal" (634). Instead, Leonardo choses the wealth and status that plantation heiress Isabel would bring him.

Though more sincere than literary libertine Leonardo, the Villaverde family, too, would embody the contradictions of the anticolonial elite. The author was married to Emilia Casanova, the daughter of the pro-independence slavocrat Inocencio Casanova y Fagundo, whose net worth in 1869 was valued at 3,402,300 pesos (Hernández González 50). The couple seems to have lived with Emilia's family in Oak Point, New York (Horrego Estuch, *Emilia Casanova* 26) for a period, and Villaverde notes in his *Apuntes biográficos de Emilia Casanova de Villaverde* (Biographic notes on Emilia Casanova de Villaverde) that they also spent significant time at the Casanovas' country estate in West Farms, New York. The author records Emilia's efforts to have her father transfer his money to US banks when the war in Cuba threatened his finances, indicating how entrenched the couple was in the very system that they sought to overthrow.

Despite her family's possessive investment in colonial slavery, however, Casanova proved a tireless advocate for the intertwined causes of independence and abolition, positions to which she eventually persuaded Villaverde. The Casanovas' New York homes became the sites of revolutionary meetings, the family stored arms in their basement, and Inocencio Casanova even had a tunnel built from one of his houses to the coast in order to send supplies to Cuba during the Ten Years' War (Horrego Estuch, *Emilia Casanova* 26). These beliefs cost Casanova personally. "Money came from the family budget for multiple resources for both expeditions . . . , to help recently arrived emigrants, or to help defenseless families in Cuba. They also bought arms to give to noted military chiefs such as Máximo Gómez" (Cairo 236).[36] While claims that, by the conclusion of the Ten Years' War, Emilia Casanova "lived in virtual poverty" (Cairo 236) are probably exaggerated (after divesting himself of his slaves, Ignacio used the money to acquire at least two properties in New York and a mining interest in Pennsylvania), it is undeniable that the Casanova and Villaverde families' participation in the separatist movement was not in their best economic interest (Hernández González).

A consideration of these rarely mentioned facts requires us to (perhaps unfashionably) give what credit is due to creole revolutionaries such as Casanova and Villaverde, who advocated for abolition and independence even as they profited from the status quo. Villaverde's ideological development is a particularly striking case. His youthful collaboration with filibusterer Narciso López indicates his initial "annexationist position and tacit approval of slavery in a post-Spain Cuba" (Lazo, *Writing* 107), perhaps emblematized by the decision to name his son "Narciso" (Cairo 232). Yet, the writer "ultimately renounced annexation, denounced the United States, and wrote critically about slavery" (Lazo, *Writing* 177). The author's "Revolución de Cuba vista desde Nueva York" (Cuban revolution as seen from New York), for example, criticizes the Junta Central Republicana de Cuba y Puerto Rico as representing exclusively the monied interests of the Western half of the island, many of whom supported annexation to the United States (32–33). Scholars have suggested that Villaverde may have participated in an "unofficial anti-slavery circle" in

New York in the 1850s (Albín, Corbin, and Marrero-Fente 91) and that, later, "by supporting Céspedes and other rebels, . . . [he] explicitly embraced the antislavery cause" (Luis, *Literary Bondage* 107). Importantly, this altruistic conversion did not occur until after the author had married Casanova and united his economic fortunes to those of her family.[37]

Yet even the most visionary among us have blind spots. In a July 25, 1871, letter in English to the editor of the *Daily Telegraph* (later published in Villaverde's *Apuntes*), the revolutionary Emilia Casanova would write that "we Cubans . . . are fighting for dear liberty for ourselves and for thousands of poor African slaves, as well as for entire independence" (qtd. in Villaverde, *Apuntes* 158). As in Martí's "Nuestra América," here, too, it is not clear whether or not blacks are included in the phrase "we Cubans." While Casanova desires "liberty" for the "poor African slaves," one wonders how they will be incorporated into a national project that, grammatically, articulates "dear liberty for ourselves," for "poor African slaves," and "entire independence" as three separate desiderata. Participating in the antislavery, nationalist activities that they financed with money originating in the Casanovas' sugar estates, the Villaverdes must have realized that the underlying unity between creoles and Afro-descendants functioned simultaneously as the basis for and the bane of national consolidation. This real-life ambiguity manifests itself through the instabilities that characterize *Cecilia Valdés,* and Leonardo reflects the contradiction that Casanovas and Villaverde (albeit more sincerely) embodied. These paradoxes also shape the novel's narrative structure, as I now will explain.

The Miscegenation Was the Incest That Couldn't Bear

The interracial incest in Villaverde's novel thus manifests the internal contradictions of liberal elites that feel discontented with the present system but (like most of us) cannot imagine a world in which it does not exist. Leonardo and Cecilia's mixed-race, inbred child functions as "the emblem of a disturbance at the origin," the socioeconomic structures thwarting national consolidation (Méndez Rodenas 99). A "natural" development from the biological notion that the ability to reproduce fertile offspring mutually defines two organisms as members of the same species, marriageability in nineteenth-century literature functions as a trope for sameness or, in social terms, equality (what Leonardo ultimately decides that he does not share with Cecilia). Blurring the dividing line between difference and closeness, "the narrative anxiety of miscegenation reflects fears that the races may not be inherently different" as "interracial attraction presumes the humanity and sameness of the Other" (Rosenthal

133).³⁸ The Cuban author's paradoxical mobilization of miscegenation and incest, the only two blood crimes prohibited by the state (Sollors 320), undermines the racial binary upon which New World societies were founded (318), canceling out the prohibition against marriage when there exists too much difference between partners with the mutually exclusive prohibition against marriage when there exists too much sameness (Fischer, introduction xxiii). Incest and miscegenation are not discrete phenomena in Villaverde's novel; rather, the former is a figuration of the latter, a tropological expression of the too-close relations between the supposedly distinct races in the political economy of the plantation Americas.

In Villaverde's novel, this paradoxical condition can be seen when, upon the birth of their child, Leonardo, as I mentioned above, notes that Cecilia "was not his wife, much less his equal" (634)—a thought that denies the very sameness between Cecilia and Leonardo that the birth of their child would suggest.³⁹ Cecilia and Leonardo may appear to be *personas de la misma especie* (people of the same kind/species) but, according to the text, like the horse and the donkey, though they can reproduce, they are not "iguales" and, an aberration, their child is unable to continue the line of national generation and falls out of the narrative. In keeping with the term's alleged derivation from the word for "mule," in the text, race mixing *mulataje,* like incest, fails to produce (socially and politically) fertile offspring.⁴⁰ As the disappearance of her child suggests, Cecilia's "womb is a tomb" (Kutzinski, *Sugar's Secrets* 31) where the Cuban national-republican project—economically dependent on the racial subordination of the child to whom she has given almost impossible birth—is laid to rest. Born to repeat the same cycle of racialized exploitation as her mother, grandmother, great-grandmother, and great-great grandmother (Méndez Rodenas 100), Cecilia's problematically absent child cannot function as an allegory of interracial national consolidation. If anything, her presumed phenotypical whiteness—the child is fifteen-sixteenths white—symbolizes the marginality of Afro-Cubans to the national project.

The Road Not Taken

However, despite its ultimate flight into whiteness, *Cecilia Valdés* would seem to present a black national mother in the figure of María de Regla, the enslaved Afro-Cuban wet nurse whose suffering at the hands of the Gamboa family serves as a catalyst for much of the novel's action. The character is obligated to stop nursing her own daughter, the black Dolores, so that she may provide milk for Adela, Cándido's legitimate daughter by his creole wife, and—in secret—the mixed-race Cecilia.

Villaverde takes care to point out that, "as they grew up together, as, in reality, they drank the same milk, despite their different places in society and races," the three baby girls "loved one another as sisters" (303).[41] Nursing the triethnic group of *hermanas de leche* when creole and mulata mothers prove unable to do so, the black María de Regla appears as "the 'real' mother of all the children in the novel" (Luis, *Literary Bondage* 116). Villaverde makes this clear when a character refers to the enslaved woman as Adela's "madre" (505). Another claims that María de Regla is Cecilia's "true mother" (384).[42]

The racial and gender construction that black wet nurse María de Regla embodies "calls into question the concept of family and motherhood" found in other texts from the period, which present republican motherhood in terms of whiteness (Luis, *Literary Bondage* 116). While, as I explained in chapter 1, reformers such as Sisto Sáenz de la Cámara advocated that upper-class white women avoid racial "contamination" by nursing their own children, Villaverde reveals the enslaved black woman as the force that nourishes the interracial national family (a fact that, taken as an economic metaphor, explains Leonardo's internal contradictions, as discussed previously). "Symbolically," then, María de Regla functions as "the mother of the Cuban people." Villaverde is clear about the racial relevance of the character's maternity. In the same way that Cecilia is associated with La Caridad del Cobre/Ochún, María de Regla's name "suggests both the Virgen María [Virgin Mary] and the Cuban black Virgen de Regla, known ... as Yemayá" in Santería, in which she functions as a maternal figure (Luis, *Literary Bondage* 116). Culturally as hybrid as the national children that she nourishes, María de Regla symbolically invokes both European and African visions of divine motherhood. This nomenclatural symbolism specifically links María de Regla's national maternity to her African origins in Villaverde's metaphorical economy, positing her, in principle, as the black mother of the interracial Cuban nation.

Yet here, too, the text is ambiguous. Like the black servants in the racist prescriptions for child-rearing proffered by Sáenz de la Cámara and others, María de Regla lacks the requisite virtue for republican motherhood. Villaverde is careful to note that the character's numerous romantic intrigues have been the cause of much discord at the sugar mill (514, 521–22). This "chronicle of María de Regla's sexual slips suggests that their scandalous aspect resides in their unsettling effect on the socioeconomic order of the sugar plantation. The acknowledged rivalry among white men for María de Regla's sexual favors not only carries with it the threat of undermining the existing racial hierarchy through the birth of a mulatto child, but the male workers' quest for sexual access to the female slave also drains their energies away from the economic enterprise of sugar production" (L. Williams 173).[43] Much like Cecilia, who suggests the potential for social leveling through *mulataje,* María de Regla's racialized sexuality represents a threat to the political-economic order of the island. Perhaps for that reason, the novel's omniscient third-person narrator takes an ironic attitude toward her attempt to elicit sympathy from the Gamboa family and finally—after twelve years of exile at the sugar mill—return to her husband in Havana, dismissing the character's efforts by calling her a "conspirator" (624). While María de Regla finally does reveal the truth of Cecilia's origins to doña Rosa, it is not to save the protagonists from incest but in order to "obtain full pardon for her sins" (635)—not out of concern for her national-allegorical children, but out of self-interest.[44] A destabilizing social force in her sexualized lack of virtue, despite the nourishment that she provides to the novel's black, white, and mulata characters, María de Regla is not equipped for the sort of moral motherhood that creole reformers desired for the nation.

Importantly, even as the name María de Regla references an intercultural form of maternity, it also, in its mention of "la regla" (the menstrual period), alludes to moments normally associated with infertility—a connection made all the stronger by the way that lactation defines the character's place in the novel. Thus, though she seems at times to serve as a spiritual mother in the text, María de Regla, through this very function, is unable to act as an actual mother in the novel. (Indeed, she is not allowed to nurse her biological daughter and is banished from the Gamboa household when it is discovered that she has been doing so in secret [527]). In much the same way that Leonardo in his fight with his father rails against the very slave system to which he owes his existence, the conditions creating María de Regla's spiritual motherhood render more literal modes of maternity impossible. Like the incarcerated Cecilia, then, María de Regla is an unlikely candidate for mother of the nation. Her role in setting the novel's plot in motion renders her central to the narrative, but her very involvement in the sordid tale of incest is a sign that she lacks the citizen virtue necessary for republican motherhood. The character is both inside and outside the national narrative, which focuses primarily on its white characters and the "vengeful mulata" (636), failing to mention her in the denouement in which the other characters' ultimate fates are revealed (Padula 24).[45] More than anything, María de Regla is an allegory of the enslaved women to whom colonial society has denied national motherhood.

This should not be read as a simple racially exclusive wish-fulfillment fantasy, however. Importantly, despite Cecilia's interment and María de Regla's moral disqualification, the white Isabel—unlike Alice following Cora's expulsion from the imagined community in Cooper's *Last of the Mohicans*—does not become the mother of the Cuban nation, either. Rather, secluded in a convent, she is, physically, as removed from society as Cecilia in her asylum and, more tellingly, rendered permanently unable to produce legitimate children for the national family. By triangulating his foundational romance plot through incest, Villaverde manages to frustrate the national motherhood of his black, white, and mulata characters. How, then is the nation to be born?

American Gothic: Interracial Incest and the Foundational Fictions

In order to understand the stakes of the interracial incest plot that disqualifies Cecilia, María de Regla, and Isabel from becoming mothers of the nation, it is necessary to read the 1882 foundational text as "part of a history of transnational writing that contradicts the novel's insistence on the Cuban nation as a local formation tied to the island" (Lazo, *Writing* 170). More than a Cuban national novel, *Cecilia Valdés* is a hemispheric text, a work well aware of the foundational romance genre circulating throughout the Americas at the time of its writing. Even though he had lived four decades outside of Latin America when he published the definitive version of *Cecilia Valdés*, it is likely that Villaverde would have been familiar with foundational texts such as Argentine José Mármol's 1852 *Amalia* and Chilean Alberto Blest Gana's 1862 *Martín Rivas*. Much as, as Anne Fountain argues, it was in the cosmopolitan New York of the late nineteenth century that José Martí learned about the other countries of *nuestra América*, it seems inevitable that Villaverde would have read Latin American literature while living in the northern metropolis. After all, the nineteenth-century northeastern United States was a major center of Spanish-language publishing; the first edition of the anonymous *Jicoténcal*, the first Spanish American example of the historical genre to which the 1882 *Cecilia Valdés* belongs, for example, had been published in Philadelphia in 1826.[46] Despite the author's claim in the prologue to the definitive 1882 edition that, for years, the only novelists that he read were Walter Scott and Alessandro Manzoni, the 1882 version of *Cecilia Valdés*—unlike its 1839 precursors—is littered with Spanish words not commonly used in Cuba, pointing to the Cuban émigré's wide reading in the developing Spanish American literary canon during his exile (Rodríguez Herrera 164–65). Even if he had not encountered Latin American foundational texts, Villaverde would have been familiar with their North American counterparts; James Fenimore Cooper's works already were known in Cuba before Villaverde went into exile (de la Torriente 128) while, working as a writer, translator, and publisher in the nineteenth-century New York literary scene, he likely would have read *The House of the Seven Gables* (1851), in which Nathaniel Hawthorne, a celebrated member of the American Renaissance, first theorizes the "romance" genre.[47]

Yet *Cecilia Valdés* departs from the national romances of both Anglo and Latin America through the trope of interracial incest, which was becoming increasingly common in Latin American "foundational" literature as the nineteenth century—bloodily marked, as the Argentine case makes clear, by racialized battles between reformers and traditionalists—wore bleakly on.[48] Interracial incest serves in this context as a sign of late-nineteenth-century society's "neurotic" incapacity to advance beyond colonial race divisions (Luis, *Literary Bondage* 117–18), indicative of "a nation in a state of arrested development, unable as yet to reconcile the mixed-up, mixed-race world as it is with the binary order—white/black, us/them, civilized/barbaric—that the West had touted since the Enlightenment" (Sheffer 14). While incest is a common motif in Western Romanticism, the trope takes on special resonance in the racially heterogeneous environment of the Americas, where it becomes "a fictional vehicle to explore perceptions regarding the transition from hierarchical to more egalitarian societies" (Kristal 403), as texts such as the Puerto Rican Alejandro Tapia y Rivera's 1867 drama *La cuarentona* (The quadroon), the Argentine Juana Manuela Gorriti's 1861 short story "Si haces mal, no esperes bien" (If you do ill, don't expect good), the Ecuadorian Juan León Mera's 1877 novel *Cumandá*, and the Peruvian Clorinda Matto de Turner's 1889 novel *Aves sin nido* (*Birds without a Nest*)—all of which discuss romantic relations between white and mixed-race half-siblings—attest.[49] These interracial incest texts mirror the foundational historical romances' interest in cross-factional alliances yet ultimately reveal those alliances to be unviable (again, the mulata as a *mula* unable to reproduce legitimately and found the nation).[50]

The preponderance of the interracial incest trope during the late nineteenth century suggests an evolution (or perhaps a devolution) in the foundational fictions model as the genre struggled to incorporate the New World's racial realities. In chapter 2, I explained that James Fenimore Cooper's *Last of the Mohicans* and Eduarda Mansilla de García's *Lucía Miranda* deploy mixed-race female characters in order to affirm the contributions of people of color to national life while simultaneously upholding racialized (neo)colonial hierarchies inherent in settler-colonial societies. Yet, later texts, such as the Cuban *Cecilia Valdés*, the Ecuadorian *Cumandá*, and the Peruvian *Aves sin nido*, display less sanguine attitudes toward national consolidation along racial lines. Written in nations like Cuba, Ecuador, and Peru, where racialized black and indigenous non-wage labor proved an obstacle to economic and political modernization, these works deploy the trope of interracial incest precisely in order to problematize the creole nationalisms expressed by writers like Cooper and Mansilla de García.[51]

A newspaperman, Villaverde would have been only too aware of the failure of Reconstruction in Cooper's United States and the struggle between the colonial racial order and the genocidal depredations of national consolidation in Mansilla de García's Argentina. Importantly, interracial incest texts by Villaverde, León Mera, Matto de Turner, and others were written as the nation-state project was stumbling in much of Latin America—witness the defeat of *independentista* forces in the Ten Years' War in Cuba, the debilitating contest between liberals and conservatives in Ecuador, or the War of the Pacific in Peru. They thus might be thought of as counterdiscourses to the foundational romances proffered by the previous generation of nationalist writers such as Cooper, whose racially exclusive nationalism would have proven unacceptable in a late-nineteenth-century Cuba, where, as I have explained, Afro-descendants were making considerable political strides. In transforming the foundational fictions' romance plot into an unsavory tale of *amor imposible* and refusing the genre's traditional resolution of national foundation through cross-factional *alianzas*, Villaverde and other late-nineteenth-century writers use the trope of interracial consanguinity to ask whether these earlier nation-building models might be—like incest and *mulataje*—unviable. Much as interracial half-siblings Leonardo and Cecilia are the same and yet different, national consolidation appears desirable, but the preexisting economic relations from the colonial period complicate further proximity. While Leonardo tragically fails to grasp this fully, Villaverde, sworn enemy of the plantocracy on whose largesse he lived, is all too aware of the structural political-economic contradictions that have thwarted national consolidation in Cuba and in other nations of the Americas. By "failing" to write a foundational romance, Villaverde draws attention to the fact that, given the circumstances, he cannot write a foundational romance.

The unsavory incest trope that Villaverde uses as a metaphor for the impossible nation fits into a broader tendency toward the antimodern grotesque in late Cuban antislavery writing, which "can be read as local resurrections of the Gothic tradition: a literature of horror taking place in the plantation, with the modern boiler house in lieu of medieval architecture, slave quarters instead of dungeons, and the overseer playing the role of the Inquisitor" (Goldgel Carballo 4). The Gothic in these texts serves to draw attention to the incompatibility of local socioeconomic realities with the nation-state paradigm that writers such as Villaverde hoped—against both hope and their own best interests—to inaugurate in Cuba, one of the last slave colonies in a region in which the republican nation-state model had yielded mixed results.[52] If Villaverde's three *Cecilia*s refuse to come to their logical narrative conclusions (national consolidation through legitimate foundational marriage), it is important to remember that, so, too, did the process of nation-building in Cuba and other racialized colonial and neocolonial New World societies for much of the nineteenth century.

Ultimately, then, Villaverde's unfinishable opus is a meditation on the structures that render its own completion—and the national consolidation that that would allegorize—impossible: the narrative structures that drive the romance plot are interrupted by the kinship structures that push Leonardo and Cecilia toward each other at the same time that they pull them apart. These, in turn, function as allegories of the social structures thwarting *alianzas* between creoles and Afro-Cubans, whose identities, structurally, can intertwine only if they remain separate. *Cecilia Valdés*, then, is a novel not of foundation as much as frustration.

Emilia Casanova de Villaverde and National Motherhood: A Tale of Two Cecilias

While Cecilia, Isabel, and María de Regla are all barred from assuming the role of republican mother in the novel, elsewhere in his oeuvre, Villaverde does put forth a candidate for mother of the Cuban nation: his wife, Emilia Casanova de Villaverde. Members of the upper echelons of the plantation elite, the creole Casanovas moved to the United States after their proindependence activities caused problems for them in colonial Cuba (Horrego Estuch, *Emilia Casanova* 18–19; Cairo 232; Hernández González 53). Emilia Casanova participated actively in the movements for abolition and independence from exile, taking part in an intense letter-writing campaign to build support for Cuba Libre across Spanish America and Europe and advocating for the revolutionary cause before President Grant in the United States, all the while tending to her family. Initially more left-leaning than her husband, Casanova "allied herself with the more radical wing of the revolution, calling early on for full abolition, democratic representation for the island's lower classes, and total independence" (Lazo, *Writing* 134). At her side, the canonical writer began "to move away from the US-Cuban Creole coalition that had been at the center of efforts by the Cuban Council and Narciso López until 1851. Villaverde had concluded that the people of Cuba must fight to appreciate a hard-won victory for self-rule" (175). Converting the canonical writer to the views that he espouses in *Cecilia Valdés,* a work that she urged her husband to finish and may have helped him to write, Emilia Casanova de Villaverde might be thought of as the nationalist mother of the novel on the mother of the nation (Horrego Estuch, *Emilia Casanova* 23–24).

Villaverde, for his part, is open about Casanova's foundational role in his life and in the cause of Cuba Libre in his anonymous *Apuntes biográficos de Emilia Casanova de Villaverde* (1874), a brief hagiography of his wife followed by a selection of her letters that he claims (rather dubiously) to have taken for publication without her knowledge. Tellingly, Villaverde is careful to cast Casanova, who was well known in political circles, in maternal terms. He points out that her "possession of certain comforts and position in a class that, generally speaking, does not stand out for its motherly feeling did not keep her from nursing her three children during their childhoods, or from serving them as a devoted nanny and wise governess until they reached maturity" (28–29).[53] Unlike the fictional doña Rosa, then, Emilia Casanova engages in the sort of enlightened maternal practice that nineteenth-century creole reformers advocated.

By the same token, in keeping with the gender mores of the day, Casanova's revolutionary activities are presented in the *Apuntes* as an extension of her maternal identity. In a July 14, 1869, letter to an "unknown gentleman," Emilia writes that she "assisted the cause of the patria the best [she] could from here, given [her] position as a woman with a family" (45).[54] For example, in one incident, she requested, "in the name of the mothers of Cuba, intervention from the US government in favor of the young medical students who had been condemned to prison in Havana" (16).[55] Similarly, in an October 4, 1870, letter to Céspedes on the Liga de las Hijas de Cuba (League of the daughters of Cuba), she writes that "our sacrifice will be useful if we manage to spur men to heroism and if the fame of our deeds fills our adored patria with glory" (96).[56] Despite her extensive activities outside the home, these passages suggest that Casanova's greatest contribution to the Cuban cause has been that of raising future citizens, a task for which *Cecilia Valdés*'s Isabel has proven unwilling and María de Regla unfit. Villaverde may not be sure of the fate of Cecilia's child, but Emilia's child is the revolution.

Importantly, the author takes the time to discuss Casanova's intriguingly named friend Cecilia Pita de Valdés, whose efforts to hide patriots from the Spanish government caused her to be condemned to La Paula—the same prison where the fictional Cecilia Valdés finds herself at the end of Villaverde's classic novel. Of course, Villaverde first wrote about his character Cecilia Valdés in 1839, well before he would have met the real-life Cecilia Pita de Valdés—but that makes his decision to discuss her in the *Apuntes* all the more relevant, particularly because Cecilia's confinement in La Paula is not included in either of the 1839 versions of the story. Villaverde explains that Cecilia Pita de Valdés's daughter later was arrested for burning papers, possibly letters from Emilia, thereby establishing a parallel between the two women, who literally become partners in anticolonial crime (90–91). A double for Emilia Casanova, the real-life Cecilia (de) Valdés, mother to yet another revolutionary, steps in to fill the republican-maternal role that the fictional Cecilia Valdés is unable to play.

It thus seems that, even as he remained ardently antiannexationist, if Villaverde sees any hope for Cuba Libre, it is in the émigré community, in the labors of people like Emilia Casanova and Cecilia Pita de Valdés. Importantly, the author explains that, while his *Apuntes* conclude in 1876, Casanova continued to write her letters until Cuba's defeat in the Ten Years' War in 1877 (231)—an event that "drove Villaverde back to *Cecilia Valdés*" (Lazo, *Writing* 177) and pushed him finally to finish the novel. Given these circumstances, the 1882 text can be read as "an attempt to seize the nation at a moment when it appears to Villaverde that the military battle . . . has been lost to Spain" (170). Cuba Libre may have been defeated, but the struggle continues from abroad. These transnational geopolitical circumstances produce a situation in which the black María de Regla, the apolitical white Isabel, and the mulata Cecilia see their national motherhood frustrated and creole exiles such as Emilia and the *other* Cecilia must fill the role of republican mother. If national foundation is interrupted by the incestuous relations among the races at home, abroad, another romance is being written. Mary Mann and Martín Morúa Delgado would contemplate the limits and possibilities of this transnational *historia,* as I now will show.

Juanita

Begun in the 1830s, but not edited until a year after the author's death in 1887, North American Mary Mann's 1888 *Juanita* was published to commemorate the recent abolition of slavery in Cuba (Havard, *Hispanism* 120). Inspired by a trip to the western Cuban province of Matanzas to work as a governess on a coffee plantation while her sickly sister Sophia convalesced under the Caribbean sun, along with her Reconstruction-era collaborations with Sarmiento, the novel represents the culmination of Mann's lifelong interest in Latin America.[57] Set, like *Cecilia Valdés*, during the period of Miguel Tacón y Rosique's rule as captain general of Cuba, the novel—in which a mixed-race slave, raised by her masters as though she were their child, falls in love with Ludovico Rodriguez (*sic*), the son of the plantation family—if less lurid, is strikingly similar to Villaverde's canonical novel. Though Juanita and Ludovico are not blood siblings, they have been raised as brother and sister, and Mann draws attention to the fact by noting that Ludovico turns to Juanita "as to a sister to supply his little wants" (76). Perhaps more significantly in the context of the interracial incest texts discussed above, Juanita's quadroon status raises the question as to who her father and grandfather were—a question that the novel never indulges (I. García 154). Unlike Villaverde's Cecilia and Leonardo, however, Juanita and Ludovico do not consummate their relationship and reproduce. Ludovico does propose marriage, but Juanita rejects his offer on the grounds that "it will ruin his earthly life" (211), echoing the logic of Villaverde's Leonardo when he contends that Cecilia "was not his wife, much less his equal" (634). In the end, Ludovico marries Carolina Fernandez (*sic*), a white heiress, and Juanita raises the creole couple's child when its mother dies, presumably as a consequence of her moral dissipation.

The Extended South: Fictions Founding Another Nation

Regardless of whether she read Villaverde's canonical text, Mary Mann clearly was familiar with the foundational interracial romance genre that was spreading rhizomatically throughout the Americas at the time, as well as the transnational trope of the tragic mulatta. The image of the mixed-race slave resisting her master's advances reflected in Juanita's relationship with Ludovico was a common topos in del Montean texts such as Anselmo Suárez y Romero's *Francisco* (1880) and Félix Tanco y Bosmeniel's "Petrona y Rosalía." Similarly, the figure of Juanita bears strong similarities to the heroines of other antislavery texts written throughout the Americas. Light-skinned enough to be mistaken for white, like the Zoe of Irish American Dion Bouciault's *Octoroon; or, Life in Louisiana* (1859), the Julia of the Puerto Rican Alejandro y Tapia Rivera's drama *La cuarterona* (1867) and the Isaura of Brazilian Bernardo Guirmarães's abolitionist novel *A esrava Isuara* (Isuaura the slave girl) (1875), Juanita has taken advantage of her privileged upbringing in the masters' house to rise above the cultural level of the white characters in the text. And, like her Puerto Rican and Brazilian counterparts, she must reject the hand of a white man due to her racial origins.[58]

Yet *Juanita* differs from these other New World texts in the ends to which it deploys the tragic mulatta plot. Mann thus does not write an allegory of her own nation but of that of a foreign colony that the United States was coveting at the time of her book's publication. The New Englander's ability to write a foundational romance of the Cuban nation is predicated on the discursive, cultural, economic, and political assimilation of Cuba to the United States over the course of the nineteenth century. In the novel, Cubans are incorporated into the US national family through the maternal figure of Helen Wentworth.[59] A visitor to Cuba from Massachusetts who is meant to embody the novel's moral voice, she draws constant comparisons between the two regions throughout the novel.[60] Curiously, not only do the Cuban characters in *Juanita* speak fluent English (which was common among nineteenth-century Cuban elites), but the New Englander Helen, for reasons that the novel never explains, arrives in Cuba already conversant in Spanish. The lack of linguistic difficulties experienced by the diverse characters in the novel suggests an interchangeability between the United States and Cuba, as if one were a mere extension of the other.

This discursive assimilation of Cuba to the United States was not unusual in the nineteenth-century North American lettered sphere. "The latest Western Hemisphere rebellion against European colonialism, some ninety miles off American shores, could not help but receive anything less than the enthusiastic popular support of the first independent nation of the Americas. For the better part of the Cuban conflict, Americans had indulged themselves with fanciful if faulty historical analogies, detecting in the Cuban struggle a drama not unlike the American war for independence." For the North American reading public, "both the personalities and the issues of the Cuban conflict were understood through the use of historical surrogates and appeals to the national hagiography. Máximo Gómez evoked George Washington, Tomás Estrada Palma in the United States corresponded to Benjamin Franklin in France. The Assembly of Jimaguayú in 1895 found its counterpart in the Continental Congress in 1776" (Pérez, *Cuba between Empires* 187–88).

These rhetorical gestures were underpinned by the intense US presence in Cuba. During the nineteenth century, North American interests "owned and operated sugar estates, coffee plantations" (such as the Morell plantation on which Mann had stayed as a young woman), "tobacco farms, and cattle ranches" on the island. As a result of this heavy investment, "between 1846 and 1862, the US-born population of Cuba almost doubled: from 1,260 to nearly 2,500" (Pérez, *On Becoming Cuban* 20). Meanwhile, during the California Gold Rush, Cuba acted as a rest stop en route to the isthmus of Panama and a slew of American-owned "bars, brothels and bistros" to accommodate visitors from the United States appeared on the island (23). Other North American transients and émigrés on the island during the 1800s included criminals, corrupt politicians, and ex-Confederates (23–24).

At the same time, "during the middle decades of the nineteenth century, about two thousand [Cuban] young men enrolled annually in US schools"—a situation registered in *Juanita*, as I will discuss later. "Families reluctant to send younger children alone to the United States brought North American instructors to Cuba, principally tutors and governesses" (Pérez, *On Becoming Cuban* 34), such as the young Mary Peabody or Helen Wentworth, her novelistic counterpart. Important though these educational exchanges were, perhaps the largest group of Cubans in the United States were political exiles such as José Martí, Cirilo Villaverde, and Martín Morúa Delgado, who, as Rodrigo Lazo explains in *Writing to Cuba,* worked in the northern country to produce anticolonial newspapers, in that way uniting the United States and Cuba in the *independentista* imaginaries of both countries. These factors, combined with the relatively high incidence of intermarriage between Cuban and southern US plantation families, made it easy for Mann to locate Cuba beside Howard's Argentina in the "extended South" (Guterl). Accordingly, much as Jennie Howard has full confidence in her South American students' gratefulness toward their northern teacher and her modernization efforts, Mann is quick to assert that Cubans "showed strong inclination to be annexed to the United States" (*Juanita,* 208).

These annexationist views inform *Juanita*'s foundational function and move the novel, somewhat like *Cecilia Valdés,* to postulate competing versions of republican motherhood for the contested colony in the forms of the Afro-Cuban Juanita, her creole mistress Isabella, and the North American governess Helen Wentworth. On the one hand, like Villaverde's Cecilia Valdés, Cooper's Cora Munro, Mansilla de García's Lucía Miranda, and the racialized Argentine *campesinas* whom Jennie Howard replaces, Mann's Juanita is a mixed-race candidate for the role of national mother. This becomes evident at the end of the novel when Ludovico, realizing that his debauched creole wife Carolina will die in childbirth, asks Juanita to look after their newborn child:

> "Will you take care of it for me, Juanita? I fear its mother is dying."
> She held out her arms for it.
> "God bless you, Juanita, and I will take care of you both."
> He stopped and kissed her forehead, and rushed from the room, to find that Carolina had breathed her last.
> Ludovico was thrown back into his old home by the death of Carolina, and devoted himself to his father and to watching over the motherless little ones that surrounded him. He said little to Juanita, but looked upon the miracle of her love for this child with reverence and awe. He truly felt that he had had no wife,—that he was the victim of an empty delusion. There was something in the atmosphere of Juanita's presence that forbade his approaching her on terms of former ease, but it purified and ennobled him to witness her devotion to her charge. She allowed no one to share the care. No vigils wearied her. But her figure rounded into the proportions of perfect health and symmetrical beauty, and as the time approached when they were to go to Helen, even melodious song, such as had been the natural language of her childish days, was heard to issue from her lips when she was conscious of no presence but that of the child. As Mrs. Warwick expressed it, she had "turned into a mother!" (207)

In this long quote, Juanita is "'turned into a mother'" as Mann transfers Carolina's maternity to the enslaved woman—an event rendered all the more evident by the fact that Ludovico's kiss and Carolina's death are related in the same sentence. It is as if, suddenly widowed, he takes a new wife who promises to raise her stepchild as her own. As Ludovico is the heir to the coffee plantation that functions as a microcosm of Cuban society in the novel, this scene may be read as the primal moment in the forging of a new national family out of the union of creoles and Afro-descendants—precisely the groups that had rebelled against the Spanish Crown in the 1860s and '70s and that would rebel again less than a decade after the text's publication.

That said, Mann's opinion on the common Cuban practice of interracial unions as expressed in the *Cuba Journal,* the collected set of letters that Sophia and Mary sent home from Matanzas, was at times less tolerant than the one she seems to defend in *Juanita*.[61] In a May 12, 1834, letter to her mother, she writes that "in general Americans who reside here are much worse than the Spaniards, in as much as mulatto women are generally the mothers of their children, & even preside at their table—this is of course double infamy to the unfortunate children" (209). Hardly welcoming Afro-descended mothers into the national family, Mann follows the lead of Cooper, Mansilla de García, and Villaverde in marshalling death to police the racial borders of the nation. Even then, the New England author neutralizes the threat of miscegenation long before Juanita is mistakenly captured and accidentally burned alive as part of a colonial attempt to suppress a slave revolt (that is, the inclusion of people of Juanita's condition in the national family). No more than a paragraph after Juanita inherits Carolina's position in the national family, Mann proclaims that Ludovico "felt that he had no wife," stripping Juanita of her title of metaphorical mother. While he feels "reverence and awe" toward Juanita, he cannot draw nearer to her because of her "forbidding atmosphere"—that is, the prohibition against the sort of closeness that Juanita's forming a new national family with Ludovico would entail, the same prohibition that blocks Cecilia and Leonardo's union in Villaverde's novel. Importantly, as I already have mentioned, when Ludovico finally does find it in himself to ask for Juanita's hand in marriage, she refuses. Pages later the character dies, immolated on the pyre of colonialism.

Thus, as in *Cecilia Valdés*, in *Juanita*, too, all Cuban female characters prove unable to assume the role of republican mother (I. García 150). The deaths of the potential Cuban mothers represent a racialized moral statement on Mann's part. "Carolina's self-destructive appetite for pleasure represents a Creole decadence unfit to govern effectively, and Juanita's inter-racial desire for her master runs against the conflict between Creole elites and the rebels" (R. Rodriguez 161). Instead, Juanita is replaced in her maternal role by the white North American Helen Wentworth. A former classmate of Ludovico's mother, Isabella (who also perishes near the end of the novel), Helen raises the Rodriguez children after the other three mother figures die. Given the US government's open desire to annex Cuba and avoid the creation of a black-majority republic ninety miles from its borders at the time that the novel was written, it cannot be coincidental that the North American Helen manages to usurp the maternity of the creoles Carolina and Isabella and the Afro-Cuban Juanita. As with Alice's replacement of Cora in the role of republican mother in Cooper's *Last of the Mohicans* and Jennie Howard's training of the future mothers of Argentina, here, too, an Anglo-Saxon woman moves into the United States' imperial peripheries in order to rear the national family in the ways of North American civilization.

Much as, in her letter to her mother, Mann expresses concerns regarding the propriety of Cuban mulatas bearing and raising their white partners' children, in *Juanita* she voices similar doubts regarding the moral aptness of creole wives for such a task:

> Marriage in these classes is but a nominal thing, and if these ties are violated within the circle of one's visiting cards little opprobrium is attached to the violation. The social position is in no wise altered by it.... The fact that left-handed families bear the sobriquet of *Holy Families* shows the average morality of society in the colonies, with perhaps some distant conception that there is something sacred in true affection.
>
> It is impossible not to be aware that the institution of slavery deepens and extends these social evils in all communities. But where married women are obliged to reconcile themselves to the facts of concubinage, prevalent in all slave communities, and this, of course, even without the excuse of sanction of affection, perverted though it may be, the fountains of all virtue are poisoned, and it is only because the average civilization of Christendom is higher than that of savage life, and that some measure of intellectual cultivation withholds mankind from the last degradation, that society does not lapse back into barbarism. It is indeed only barbarism a little refined and gilded. (55; emphasis in original)

Here Mann considers the effects of slavery on the moral health of the national family. A common theme in reformist literature in both the United States and Cuba during the nineteenth century, the critique of slavery as a cause of moral degeneration in whites, despite Mann's anachronistic use of the present tense, would have been a moot point by 1887, as the peculiar institution already had been outlawed in the United States for over two decades and in Cuba for a year by the time *Juanita* was completed. Not surprisingly, then, slavery is not the only culprit in Mann's analysis. The New Englander writes that "the institution of slavery deepens and extends these social evils," choosing verbs ("deepens and extends") that indicate that Cuban society would have been corrupt regardless—slavery has merely made the situation worse. For that reason, in addition to her critique of slavery, Mann's meditation on the term "holy family" betrays a typical Anglo-Protestant disdain for the supposed hypocrisy of Catholic religiosity, while her appeal to the discourse of civilization and barbarism at the end of the excerpt echoes the Sarmientine characterization of Latin America already found in Mann's translation of *Facundo* some twenty years before *Juanita*'s publication.

Thus, Mann's reservations concerning the moral health of Cuba stem not only from the island colony's slave economy but also from its Hispanic cultural inheritance. As Lazo argues in his study of the novel, "Cuban

Orientalism ... divided Anglo-American readers from the island's racially mixed population" ("Against" 182). This can be seen in Mann's discussion of what she views as the promiscuous nature of creole ladies, which reiterates a long-held US stereotype regarding Latin American—but not slaveholding Anglo US southern—women. The New Englander expresses similarly unflattering views on Cuban women throughout her novel. Plantation mistress Isabella, for example, is portrayed as cowed by convention and unable to take charge of the degenerate moral situation on her estate. In a much-commented-upon passage, she expresses her ambivalence regarding the corporal punishment of slaves to Helen: "They must feel that there is an inexorable power over them, or they would kill us all. The most faithful are not to be trusted in extremity. How can we expect them to be faithful if they see a chance of liberty for themselves? They might not take into account the retribution that would come upon them. Oh, my dear Helen, I felt just as you do when I first came home [after years at a US boarding school], but I have resigned myself to necessity. What else can woman do?" (35). Yet, despite the Cuban Isabella's dreary views as to what women can do, the North American Helen does not hesitate to act. While Isabella and her husband "did not interfere" with the overseer's whipping of a slave, Helen, "as if impelled by energies that had never before been roused, darted from the piazza, and seized the arm of the wretch who was inflicting the punishment" (33).[62] Mann is sure to suggest that the differences between Helen and Isabella's reactions are more ethnocultural than personal; Isabella confesses to her friend that she "felt just as you do" after her years in the United States, but that her reintroduction into Cuban society had worked to temper her moral outrage at the abuses of the slave system. "As Mann understands it, . . . Cuban conventions deny women their ability to speak against vice and thus exercise moral suasion, particularly in their primary role as moral educators of their children. Cuban mores thereby corrupt the domestic sphere by preventing women from benefitting family and community" (Havard, "Mary Mann's" 148). The text seems to ask how Cuban mothers can possibly educate children for republican citizenship when they are unable to benefit their own slaves and servants.[63]

Perhaps Isabella herself recognizes this, for Mann informs the reader that the creole plantation mistress "had lived too long in America to be willing to give her child into the care of a negro slave" (25)—"so fruitful a source of corruption in a slave community" (51)—and had instead, in a gesture strikingly similar to the Argentine maestras de Sarmiento program with which Mann collaborated, hired a North American governess.

While it was not uncommon in the nineteenth century for Cuban children to have North American governesses (Mann herself had traveled to Cuba to work as one, after all) or to be sent to US boarding schools, it is difficult to ignore that Isabella's creole children have been entrusted to Anglo-American tutelage precisely so that they will not be raised by blacks.

The strategy eerily echoes the annexationist rhetoric of the period, which advocated for North American control of Cuba in order to prevent blacks from gaining power on the island.[64] An Anglo character in Martin Delany's *Blake* (1859), one of the earliest African American novels, voices these sentiments more openly when he states that "the colony as it now stands" represents "a moral pestilence, a blighting curse, and it is useless to endeavor to disguise the fact; Cuba must cease to be a Spanish colony, and become American territory. Those mongrel Creoles are incapable of self-government, and should be compelled to submit to the United States" (62). Here, Cuban racial realities are presented in terms of contagion, "moral pestilence" and "blighting curse" that infects even the creole elite, which finds itself "mongrelized" by the racial plague supposedly endemic on the island. Beneath the seeming similarities between Cuba and the US South that Mann's imperial rhetoric has used to domesticate the island, Delany claims, lurks a radical racial alterity that has the potential to strike down hierarchies within the United States.

Mann's imperialistic rescripting of the allegory of the national family, in which both Afro-descended and Hispano-creole mothers are replaced by Anglo nursemaids, then, might be thought of as an effort to contain and assimilate Cuban otherness as a justification for North American intervention on the island. The text presents Cuba not as a romantic partner to the United States, existing in a relationship that (even if unbalanced in gendered terms) implies a certain equality between the nations but as an immature and racialized child in need of a North American govern-ess. In this way, the novel "presciently portrays the pattern of race relations that the United States seeks to impose upon Cuba" (Windell 303). The text was written during the preamble to the 1898 imperial moment in which William H. Taft, head of the US colonial administration in the Philippines, infamously would refer to the Filipinos as "our little brown brothers" needing a fifty- or one-hundred-year education to prepare themselves for democracy. During the same years, British poet Rudyard Kipling would urge North Americans to look after "Your new-caught, sullen peoples,/Half devil and half child" (vii–viii) and Jennie Howard would feel compelled to instill the Protestant ethic in "Latin" schoolchildren. Mann's metaphor of child-rearing evidently was in keeping with the racially infantilizing imperial spirit of the times.

As it turns out, comparisons of Cubans to children abounded during the period. Walter Barker, the North American consul in Sagua la Grande, for example, writes that the Cubans' "chief virtue is that they are not of a turbulent nature, and can (when understood) be made as tractable as a child, controlled as a child with kindness but firmness," concluding that "the present generation will not prove equal to self-government" (qtd. in Pérez, *Cuba between Empires* 272) and will need guidance from the United States following independence from Spain. More damningly, Orville Platt, who later would author the Platt Amendment assigning protectorate status to Cuba, wrote that "in many respects they are like children[.] They are passionately devoted to the sentiment of liberty, freedom, and independence, but as yet have little real idea of the responsibilities, duties and practical results of republican government" (qtd. in Pérez, *Cuba between Empires* 272). Meanwhile, George M. Barbour, the American sanitary commissioner in Santiago, predicted that "under our supervision, and with firm and honest care for the future, the people of Cuba may become a useful race and a credit to the world" but cautions that "to attempt to set them afloat as a nation, during this generation, would be a great mistake. We must wait until the children of today are old enough to think for themselves, and absorb American ideas" (qtd. in Pérez, *Cuba between Empires* 272).

Thus, the northern-style educación offered to the Rodriguez children by Helen Wentworth in *Juanita,* like the labors of Jennie Howard in Argentina, cannot be divorced from their imperial context. This is made clear when the young Rodriguezes accompany Helen to Massachusetts at the end of the novel in the same way that the real-life Morell children accompanied Mary Mann and her sister Sophia back to Salem and how, as I discuss in the next chapter, young Cuban women would travel north to study in US normal schools after the 1898 war (S. Hawthorne 633). Mann is sure to demonstrate how the Rodriguez children profited from their years in the North and dedicates considerable space to (somewhat condescending) explanations of their efforts to implement the Protestant ethic on their plantation upon returning South to Cuba: "It soon came to be understood that skilled labor was remunerative, for whoever proved himself capable was paid something." The housekeeper "was now told that she would be paid a small stipend for her services and for her nice pastry work and the candying of fruits, in which she excelled; and Ludovico encouraged her to be thrifty of the money which might buy her freedom at a future time, for he now constituted himself his people's banker, and showed them the books in which he recorded their work," and the slave "Solidad [sic] excelled in sewing, and the prospect was held out to her that she should have the charge of the annual sewing" (220). The message is clear: under US tutelage, the underdeveloped child Cuba—emblematized in racial terms by the slaves who are persuaded to save for their freedom, the Afro-descendants whose fate bedeviled Villaverde's liberal heart—can attain a level of political liberty and capitalist maturity that it cannot under Spanish colonialism or unmediated creole domination. Like Jennie Howard, the North American educator in Argentina, Mann sees the New England schoolteacher as the rightful mother of the "southern" nation, sent to guide her "benighted" children into the light of "Yankee" civilization.

Sofía

Background: The Morúa Law

As the cases of *Cecilia Valdés* and *Juanita* make clear, the tension between independence and annexation stemmed largely from a concern among whites on both sides of the Straits of Florida that, a numerical majority, Afro-descendants would gain political power in an independent Cuba. The son of a Basque migrant and an African-born freedwoman, Martín Morúa Delgado was a fervent defender first of Cuba's rights within the Spanish empire and, later, of the island's sovereignty. He would hardly remain silent as he read Villaverde's creole and Mann's imperial allegories of the future Cuban national family.[65] Rather, throughout his oeuvre, the mulato author would counter the basic presuppositions of these discourses, accepting their terms while resignifying their meanings in order to reveal the racial shortsightedness of both creole nationalist and US imperial thought.

An antianexationist traveling, like Villaverde and Martí, in US exile circles, Morúa Delgado would oppose North American imperialist attitudes such as those reflected in Mann's "tutelage" metaphor in his 1882 "Ensayo político, o Cuba y la raza de color" (Political essay, or, Cuba and the colored race). Originally written as a Spanish-language pamphlet directed at the Cuban exile population in New York, the essay criticizes the questionable republicanism of "Texas-model" "liberals" who, like Mann, claim that "the people have not been educated/bred for independence" and that "our salvation lies in annexation to the United States."[66]

Speculating as to what ideas might drive them to "leave one dependency behind to fall into another," Morúa accuses the annexationists of wanting to profit personally from a transfer of colonial power on the island, privileging "personal convenience over the public good."[67] Countering the notion found in Mann's *Juanita* that the Spanish colony is unprepared for self-government and in need of foreign guidance, Morúa affirms that "Cuba is very capable of establishing the same liberties as the United States."[68]

Why, then, he asks, "should we envy today what we can inaugurate by ourselves tomorrow?" Taking up the same child metaphor that structures *Juanita* and much of the US-imperial discourse of the day, Morúa mocks the notion that, in order to be *educada*, Cuba, like a young girl from the creole upper classes, must be sent to a North American convent school, querying sarcastically, "and when she is educated/all grown up [*educada*], what do we do? Take her back?" The possibility of recuperating Cuba from its imperial schoolteachers strikes Morúa as unlikely: "How long will her educación last, with us paying—as surely we will pay—her tuition?" he wonders ominously (Morúa, "Ensayo" 101–2).[69]

Morúa attacks the racial logic of colonialism throughout his essay, which dismantles the US imperial and Cuban creole supposition that the island's large Afro-descended population rendered it unfit for self-government. The author argues that "the colored race is not opposed to liberty," furnishing as evidence "the infinite times that it has resisted suffering the impositions that only through the rule of the strongest have been administered to it. Holland, England, France, and Spain herself are among the witnesses who will only confirm what we are saying" (69).[70] Using what, as will become apparent, was a common rhetorical strategy for the author, here Morúa adopts the tropes of creole discourse in order to deconstruct hegemonic logic from within: the possibility of subaltern rebellion is not a reason to delay national liberation; blacks love liberty, as the high incidence of Afro–New World uprisings demonstrates.

That said, Morúa is careful to exorcise the specter of Haiti, a country to which he dedicates considerable attention in the introduction to this essay and throughout his oeuvre.[71] Writing in the aftermath of the 1879–80 Guerra Chiquita, a war against Spain misinterpreted at the time as an Afro-Cuban racial uprising (Luis, *Literary Bondage* 140–41), Morúa refuses to frame Caribbean slave revolt in terms of race war: "Everyone, although some try to hide it, knows perfectly well that, once placed in the same condition as other men, blacks will not make attempts against the lives of whites," he writes in an obvious reference to "the horrors of St. Domingo," the 1804 extermination of the white French population of postrevolutionary Haiti. Instead, according to Morúa, "Everyone knows, much as they feign the opposite, that the blacks of Cuba do not feel any hatred towards whites." Rather, they look with opprobrium on "the wretched chain that holds them in servitude; they detest that degrading domination that all peoples have suffered and detest; and, like all peoples, they will shake it off once and again until they destroy the haughtiness of their oppressors, be they whiter than ermine or blacker than the calumny to which they are the object" (75).[72] For Morúa, Afro-Cuban rebels such as Villaverde's José Dionisio, who kills plantation scion Leonardo in a struggle for possession of the mixed-race nation, do not seek to overthrow whites but slavocracy.

Similarly, to the traditional colonialist view that "Cuba will be Spanish or she will be African," the author answers that those who believe that "Cuba will not be happy if she is not the slave of Spain" are "sadly mistaken" (97).[73] While Morúa's comments mirror the common upper-class reformist metaphor of Cuban creoles as "enslaved" to the semifeudal Spanish imperial state, the Afro-Cuban author does not use the language of slavery to postulate the presence of the island's Afro-descended population as a hindrance to independence.[74] Rather, throughout the article, he points to the continuation of slavery in colonial Cuba when the peculiar institution has been abolished in other, more "civilized" (to use Sarmiento's term) nations as a sign, not of Cuba's unfitness for self-government, but of the Spanish metropole's inability to bring modernity to its colonies. If it took "Enlightened England" eighty-four years of "the crudest debates" in order to "define the black as a man," the backward Spaniards "have been trying to resolve the same issue since 1814" with little progress (64).[75]

Rather than an impediment to independence, Morúa sees colonial racial divisions as an imperial strategy to prevent Cubans from rebelling against Spanish rule: "It seems that only Spain heard the Florentine politician when he said *Divide and conquer!*" (80).[76] If Cuba is to achieve sovereignty, however, instead of allowing racial tension to act as a deterrent to independence, it is necessary that whites believe in "blacks' love" and blacks in "whites' sincerity"—themes central to *Sofía,* as I will show. The union that results from "this frank and practical expression of both sentiments will bring independence to our island before long, with no consequence other than the rebirth of public wealth and the spurring of general progress"[77] (63). Thus, in a true break with the legacy of Spain's racist colonial system, an independent Cuba "will not recognize differences among her citizens, who will enjoy the same rights; free all, all equal and brothers like children of the same mother, the patria, Cuba" (52).[78] This "equation of Cuba, common mother, and homeland is a strong foundation for his project of equality and the basis of his homeland of integration" (Kornweibel 100). Metamorphosing black and white Cubans as sons of the same mother, "la patria, Cuba," Morúa echoes the familial allegories structuring texts such as *Cecilia Valdés* and *Juanita* in Cuba, or *The Last of the Mohicans* in the United States and *Lucía Miranda* and *In Distant Climes* in Argentina. Yet, Villaverde, Mann, Cooper, and Howard deploy the racialized national family allegory either to promote creole or racial-imperial visions of the nation or to question the possibility of interracial national consolidation. In Morúa's maternal patria, on the other hand, "the reality and metaphor of familial relations between blacks and whites is an important cornerstone to the creation of a unified Cuban nationality that was understood beyond the terms of black and white" (Kornweibel 100). Like Martí through his mythological mother dressed in "an Indian smock," Morúa turns the elite writers' trope against itself and imagines a republican community that will be open to black and white members of the national family alike (63).

Morúa sought to safeguard this racial openness during his time in the Cuban Senate, where he led an effort to block imperial US attempts to restrict suffrage to the island's white population. Yet, despite Morúa's virulent opposition to colonial and neocolonial discrimination against Afro-descendants, he was equally opposed to the Afro-Cuban movement led by Juan Gualberto Gómez and the Directorio Central de Sociedades de Color, which, in his article "Factores sociales," he dismisses as "completely useless" and "ridiculously pretentious" (229). The Directorio, he feels, is based on "the absurd principle of popular division." On the one hand, there are "blacks with their supplicant diplomatic corps and their autonomous organization within the current colonial administration," and on the other, "whites, *denying* more or less openly, the *requested* rights, or *granting* them, ostensibly with a degree of protective generosity, not as one who *recognizes* a right, but as one who *bestows* a more or less deserved honor upon a particular collectivity. And that is precisely what we must resist" (230).[79] By accepting the terms of the color-coded caste hierarchy, Morúa feels that racial politics continue to uphold white protagonism in the island's affairs, giving the creoles the power to grant or deny blacks rights that should have been conferred automatically at birth. For those reasons, the author concludes that "anything that means grouping individuals of one class together in Cuba so that they can improve their condition, constitutes a partiality that inevitably will be highly prejudicial to the country in general; because grouping fractions together will do no more than accentuate the dividing barrier that degrades all of us and perpetuates the racial line that kills the progress of Cuban society" (227–28).[80]

This universalist, Martí-esque approach to raceless citizenship would lead Morúa to oppose the sort of political organization around race practiced by his political rival Juan Gualberto Gómez. While serving in the Cuban Senate after the war, he would propose the now-infamous "Ley Morúa" (Morúa Law), an amendment to Article 17 of the Electoral Law, which declared that "under no circumstances will a group consisting exclusively of individuals of a particular race or color, nor of individuals of a particular class based on birth, wealth, or profession be considered a political party or independent group" (*Obras completas,* vol. 3, *Integración cubana* 239–40).[81] Though his views might prove contentious among social organizers today, for Morúa, the prohibition against race-based parties represented a necessary safeguarding of republican political institutions. By banning the "privileges" characteristic of the Iberian ancien régime, the senator hoped to interpellate Afro-Cubans into the public sphere as rights-bearing citizens and not—as he explains in "Factores sociales"—a feudal-colonial collective that could be granted or denied entitlements at the whim of its creole overlords. While the idea to add other, nonracial categories to the amendment may have come from Afro-Cuban congressman Lino D'ou, the effect is consonant with the ideas that Morúa expresses in his essays (Guillén 262). The amendment reads as an attempt to replace the traditional Hispanic hierarchical corporatist society (the castas of the colonial period) with a state composed of citizens who were equal before the law. Rather than drawing distinctions of *calidad,* or rank, among members of the national body, here "the Africans who were slaves" are invested with the "the status of Cubans" (*Obras completas,* vol. 3, *Integración cubana* 239–40).[82] In this way, Morúa proposes an early version of the racial democracy that many Latin American republics—however problematically—would celebrate as the twentieth century progressed. Yet, regardless of what the author's intentions in sponsoring the amendment may have been, in 1912, after his death, the law was applied brutally against the Partido Independiente de Color when government forces massacred thousands of members of the Afro-Cuban political party in the eastern province of Oriente.[83]

Morúa's authorship of the law used to justify the massacre, together with his begrudging support of the Platt Amendment, have caused his name to live in infamy in Cuban history.[84] A close reading of his novel *Sofía* (1891), however, offers a more nuanced picture. Widely considered to be an Afro-Cuban adaptation of *Cecilia Valdés*, *Sofía* was published after the author became disenchanted with exile politics, returned to Cuba, and converted politically from separatism to autonomism (Guillén 248–49; Zettl 15).[85] Though many of the ideas espoused in this text still prove uncomfortable to contemporary sensibilities, the novel, like the essay "Ensayo político" mentioned above, adopts the trope of national motherhood organizing creole and North American discourses on the future of Cuba—such as *Cecilia Valdés* and *Juanita*—in order to reveal the exclusionary nature of both projects. While the scholarly view of *Sofía* as an Afro-Cuban counterdiscourse to *Cecilia Valdés* is well established, by situating Morúa's work in a hemispheric context, I hope to reveal how the author responds to the creole racial republican philosophy taking root throughout the Americas during the late nineteenth century and, particularly, to draw attention to the Afro-Cuban writer's opposition to US annexationism.

Sofía *as a Rewriting of* Cecilia Valdés

Given the Martían emphasis on national unity that Morúa Delgado expresses in "Ensayo político" and "Factores sociales"—beliefs that led him to author the now notorious Ley Morúa—it will come as no surprise that the writer should object to the ambivalent racial politics that underlie Villaverde's *Cecilia Valdés* and similar nineteenth-century foundational texts. "The complaint Morúa has against *Cecilia Valdés* is due principally to Villaverde's use of his personal ideology, the dominant ideology, rather than realism as the basis for his narrative" (Zettl 102). In his 1891 essay "Las novelas del Sr. Villaverde" (The novels of señor Villaverde), Morúa critiques the creole writer's canonical text on the grounds that "throughout the work one sees the censurable and deliberate effort to justify the dividing lines that are drawn and preserved by colonial exclusivism." For example, "the author accepts the established order, and follows the unfortunate argument of those who attempt to move up while still holding down the people that the colonial regime that they are fighting to the death has placed under their feet" (33).[86] Other "flaws" in the 1882 novel include "its implausible depiction of the slave's situation, its representation of stock characters whose behavior lacked credible motivation, and the improbable plot driven by the need to withhold knowledge of their kinship from the protagonists embedded in a social network of gossip and frequent interaction" (L. Williams 160–61).

The improbability of Cecilia and Leonardo not discovering that they are siblings is a particularly contentious point for Morúa and subsequent critics of Villaverde's novel. Leonardo appears unable to take the possibility seriously, even suggesting it as a simple joke at one point, once again rejecting the possibility that Cecilia could be "his equal" (Villaverde 413). However, as Doris Sommer points out in her essay "Who Can Tell? Villaverde's Blacks," "There are characters in the novel who can and do tell the story straight to those who will hear it. They are the black slave informants: Dionisio, the lonely cook in the Havana house, and his wife María de Regla, the wet-nurse . . . ; she is banished to the plantation because she knew too much." For Sommer, the effectiveness of Villaverde's incest narrative is premised on white privilege:

> Each time a pale protagonist (or reader) turns a deaf ear to the slaves' stories Villaverde exposes the inability to listen as a dissembled gesture of control which keeps the text of Cecilia's life conveniently blank, that is, white. The gesture is one of those defensive denials that end by destroying the deniers. To defend the privilege that comes with whitening out her history, Cecilia and other presumptively white characters must ignore the details that make her so compromisingly colorful, so available for the final tragedy of misfired affairs. And to protect our expert reading, readers are also tempted to ignore competitors. Rather than defer too soon to the authority of black narrators, readers tend to flatter themselves as collaborators of the prudent white one who frames the novel. (192)

The novel's Afro-descended characters know of Leonardo and Cecilia's secret consanguinity, but the mysterious tone that pervades the text is predicated on the reader only trusting the white characters, who are not privy to the scandalous incest that drives the plot. As Leonardo states in a conversation about an injured slave: "One should never believe entirely in what blacks say" (452).[87] Ostensibly seeking to criticize colonial racism, the text ironically incorporates that very same racism into its narrative technique. This has implications for the racial balance of power in late colonial Cuba: "If the secret is to be exposed or mentioned, then it should happen through the white narrative voice and not the black voice, for if the black voice were to have such dynamic power, it would occupy the site of national narration, and, at the same time, fatally expose the already tenuous myth of white Creole racial purity" (Nelsen 65). In this way, critics note, the colonial caste system that Morúa excoriates is upheld in Villaverde's novel through the division of society into groups that are licensed to speak and groups that are not.[88]

In light of Morúa's essay lambasting Villaverde's canonical text, literary scholars long have considered *Sofía*—published, like Martí's canonical "Nuestra América," just one year after "Las novelas del Sr. Villaverde"—as a critical adaptation of *Cecilia Valdés*.[89] In his effort to "correct" the creole text, Morúa Delgado in his *Sofía* "invert[s] the logic of *Cecilia Valdés* while keeping the same plot structure" (Sommer, "Who?" 69). "Fill[ing] in the holes in Villaverde's narrative," Morúa denies "that narrative of its power to consolidate a national image on the basis of . . . racially exclusionary representations" (Nelsen 72). While the protagonist of Villaverde's tale of mistaken identity is a mixed-race woman who can pass for white, Morúa writes about a white woman who unwittingly passes for mixed race. The unrecognized illegitimate daughter of a Spanish slave trader living in Cuba, Sofía is mistaken for mulata after her father's death and, through a somewhat unlikely series of confusions, kept as a slave in her family's house, where she is raped and impregnated by her (also white) half-brother, Federico. While, in Villaverde's text, Cecilia and Leonardo's child simply disappears from the narrative as soon as she is born, Sofía suffers a miscarriage and then dies from shock when she discovers the secret of her origins. In this way, Morúa interrupts hegemonic racialized national familial discourse—so important to *Cecilia Valdés* and *Juanita*—not only by discrediting it morally through Sofía's rape, but by showing, through Sofía's miscarriage, that the foundational pair fails to found anything.

Sofía as Mulata

Curiously, though *Sofía*'s mistaken identity plot may strike the reader as just as improbable as that of *Cecilia Valdés*, in "Las novelas del Sr. Villaverde," Morúa dedicates many pages to taking the creole writer to task for his supposed lack of mastery over the realist mode of literary production, subordinating "notions of realism" to "his beliefs about the status of the ethnically different in Cuban society" (L. Williams 184). The novel announces its realist intent in its very title, which means "knowledge" in Greek, suggesting a view of Cuban slavery from within that Morúa, the son of a formerly enslaved African, felt himself more capable of presenting than creoles such as Villaverde. To achieve that, he turns to a strategy that he had already employed in essays such as "Ensayo político" and "Factores sociales" and mimics the tropes of creole antislavery writing from across the hemisphere in order to show the limits of that discourse.

A fluent reader of Spanish, French, Italian, English, and Portuguese, as well as the artificial language Volapük, Morúa in his novel critically adapts the hemispheric tradition of creole writings on slavery in order to reveal what he sees as the discourse's racist presuppositions (Guillén 247). For example, his story of a white woman mistaken for mulata and wrongly enslaved without the necessary legal documents resembles the tale of the real-life Salomé Müller as it is recounted in George Washington Cable's 1889 *Strange True Stories of Louisiana.* Similarly, as I mentioned earlier, the trope of the mixed-race woman involved in real or imagined incestuous relations with her creole half-brother can be found in works from throughout the Americas by reformist authors such as Félix Tanco y Bosmeniel (1838), Juana Manuela Gorriti (1861), Alejandro Tapia y Rivera (1867), Juan León Mera (1877), Cirilo Villaverde (1882), Clorinda Matto de Turner (1889), and, later, the Afro–North American Pauline Hopkins (1902).[90] In *Sofía,* Morúa demonstrates an ironic awareness of these other texts; one of the characters comments offhandedly on men who, "having a wife and children, and lording it about like they were high and mighty," pay for "houses and treats for stray mulatas" and baptize "with their name children of adultery" who "practically wind up forming matches" with their legitimate children (184)—a phenomenon much more common in novels than in real life.[91] Similarly, Federico, the ne'er-do-well son who rapes Sofía, has his literary antecedents in Villaverde's Leonardo and the Ricardo of Anselmo Suárez y Romero's *Francisco,* as well as the Fernando of Tanco y Bosmeniel's "Petrona y Rosalía." Sofía, meanwhile, a light-skinned slave in possession of breeding superior to that of her masters, participates in the same tragic mulatta tradition as Mann's Juanita.[92]

Thus, as in *Cecilia Valdés* and *Juanita* (and, in other geographic spaces, *The Last of the Mohicans* and *Lucía Miranda*), in *Sofía,* too, the body of the ethnically hybrid woman becomes a surface on which to draft the possible contours of Cuba's future citizen body. Yet, while Morúa's recycling of the most common topoi of hemispheric antislavery works—interracial incest, the debauched plantation scion, and the tragic mulatta—allows his text to repeat "what has already been said without exactly coinciding with it," the author adopts these elements oppositionally, turning the metaphor of slavery and the trope of interracial incest inside out through Sofía's secret white identity (L. Williams 163). In this way, he "tricks the implied reader to make false assumptions" in order to reveal the biases and double standards that underlie those assumptions (Zettl 23).

As many critics have noted, the effectiveness of the reformist tragic mulatta trope lies in the readiness with which a white reading public identifies with these cultured and light-skinned heroines. "Playing upon the race pride and sentiments of the Caucasian group, [antislavery] novelists placed in the forefront the near-white victim of slavery and asked their readers: Can an institution which literally enslaves the sons and daughters of the dominant race be tolerated?" (Bullock 281). Morúa, however, forces his "Caucasian" readers to confront their "race pride" by presenting them with a "tragic mulatta" whose "tragedy" is that she is not a mulata at all. If "the bastard Negro who could pass for white threatened the difference between those within the cultural covenant and those without" (Arbery 397), Morúa's inversion of the topos (an illegitimate white woman who can pass for black) renders that covenant arbitrary, as the existence of passing on either side of the color line exposes the racial binary itself as a construct.[93]

This "absence of difference without sameness" (Arbery 400) upon which Morúa's tale of mistaken identity and race-bending *mulataje* is based is featured prominently in the novel. Though secretly white, Sofía is described as "trigueña" (olive-skinned) with such mixed racial features as a "head sporting shiny, wavy, magnificent black hair" with a round face "of very fine features" and "lit by two almond eyes with black pupils" (12).[94] If this phenotypical ambiguity might be dismissed by the fact that, as explained near the end of the novel, Sofía's mother was from the Canary Islands, which are geographically part of North Africa, such an explanation only serves to undermine the supposed whiteness of Cuba's white elite. At another point, Morúa notes that Sofía closely resembles her legitimate sister, Magdalena, whose whiteness no one doubts. Time and again, the novel mobilizes the idea of *mulataje* to question the immutability of racial categories, such as when the eyewitnesses to a murder disagree over whether the perpetrator was white or mulato (282) or when another enslaved woman comments to Sofía, "You know full well that, some more and some less, all of us trace our nobility through the master's kitchen" (17).[95] On the one hand, it seems as though Morúa were attempting to prove the Martían assertion that "there is no race hatred because there are no races." On the other, the trivialization of racial lines that the differences in Sofía and her sister Magdalena's respective social standings demonstrate serves to critique the exclusivity of the creole national and North American imperial projects found in *Cecilia Valdés* and *Juanita*. After all, in an arbitrary racial classificatory system in which whites are also Afro-descended and slaves can be of European origin, why can't Cecilia and Juanita be mothers of the Cuban republic?

Critique of the Creoles

By drawing attention to the arbitrary nature of the conventions that distinguish Magdalena from Sofía (the same conventions that bar Villaverde's Cecilia and Mann's Juanita from marrying into the national family), Morúa suggests that many creole reformers of the time indulged in hypocrisy. His harshest comments are reserved for the *independentistas* and *anexionistas,* whom he at one point dismisses as "cruddy democrats" (73).[96] This criticism of elite reformers was hardly unfounded. Many of the exile papers that Morúa would have read during his time in the United States unproblematically defended creole claims to sovereignty, ignoring the question of slavery on the island and largely refusing to discuss race altogether (Lazo, *Writing* 142–43). "Although most white separatists agreed with Martí that without massive Afro-Cuban participation in the struggle against Spain, independence would never be achieved, many of these whites fully adhered to the ideology of white supremacy" (Helg, *Our Rightful Share* 45). Morúa attempts to unmask this ideology in "Las novelas del Sr. Villaverde" when he criticizes the way in which *Cecilia Valdés* relates the execution of Panchita Tapia, a white woman garroted for the murder of her husband. While Villaverde views this display of sovereign violence as particularly brutal because it was carried out against a white woman, Morúa considers the creole author's view to be racially short-sighted. Much as, in *Sofía,* he deploys an enslaved white woman in order to explore the racism underlying the tragic mulatta trope, here Morúa queries, "What morality does señor Villaverde attempt to establish with such a demoralizing sentence? Where is the justice in this judgement? Who is he writing for? What is the author trying to establish or consolidate?" (32).[97] Invoking issues of establishment and consolidation, Morúa asks for whom the creole author Villaverde writes his foundational national narrative; that is, he wonders for whom the creoles wish to found the nation.

Understandably unsympathetic to the aporias that ultimately undo Villaverde's Leonardo, Morúa questions the sincerity of white Cuban liberals throughout *Sofía*. He takes care to note that the reformers, ostensibly antislavery and prodemocratic, inappropriately employ familiar second-person singular Spanish verb forms when addressing the slave Sofía and complains that "those modern freethinkers do not realize their own inconsistency, as Esladislao did not when he spoke with such familiarity to Sofía," asking, "Would he have done so if he were unaware of her poor social state?" (164).[98] Similarly, describing a meeting of creole reformers, the author comments that, "inspired by the presence of Sofía, who had waited on the table, they spoke of slavery and the reforms underway. Some of them regretted that 'such a fine little mulata (*mulatica tan buena*) was a slave'" (121).[99] Here the speakers are opposed not to slavery but to the enslavement of an attractive, light-skinned mulata (*una mulatica tan buena*). Even more damning is the white Magdalena's response upon discovering that Sofía is her sister: "Then Sofía wasn't a mulata, she wasn't a slave? And she had been taken for one, and sent to the sugar mill for them to punish her. She had been whipped, and her sisters had consented to it" (140).[100] Like Villaverde's outrage at Panchita Tapia's execution, Magdalena's concern here is not the abuse of power itself but the fact that that abuse has been perpetrated against a white woman. Here again Morúa exposes the racism behind the common creole reformist strategy of using phenotypically white slaves to elicit sympathy, criticizing the white liberal readers' inability to apprehend and accept difference, requiring the other to be similar to themselves in order to feel compassion.[101]

Morúa uses this constant theme of creole misrecognition of the enslaved in order to expose the racial exclusions underlying the hemispheric interracial incest trope that Villaverde deploys in *Cecilia Valdés*. While Leonardo's incestuous desire for Cecilia is disguised as a fetishization of the Afro-Cuban female body, Federico's lust for his white sister Sofía is revealed as emblematic of creole self-absorption, as "the pursuit of racial purity that leads to the cultivation of desires for endogamy and, at the limit, incest" (Fischer, Introduction xxiv). Much as Federico pursues a white woman in his efforts to dominate a black one, the creole reformers have advocated for black emancipation from bondage in order to secure white emancipation from colonial "slavery." Sofía's miscarriage at the end of the novel, then, can be understood as a suggestion on Morúa's part that nothing viable will come of the racial self-interest found in creole reformist projects. In this way, the novel sheds light on the dark side of creole modernity.

Failed Futures and Future Failures

In *La familia Unzúazu* (The Unzúazu family), a 1901 sequel to *Sofía*, Morúa continues his practice of resignifying elite nationalist discourse when, in an inversion of the racial and family dynamics of the first novel, the creole rapist Federico's white full sister Ana María is raped and impregnated by the slave Liberato. This child, too, is miscarried. Perhaps Morúa, in his universalist fervor, rejects the sort of violent racial fanaticism embodied by the rapes of Sofía and Ana María, instead striving for a Cuba in which neither Spanish, creole, nor African elements will dominate. Yet, if this is the case, why would the author not express his wish for a Martían *América mestiza* by resolving the narrative tensions laid out in his novels through the birth of a mixed-race child? Why does he stop short of rewriting Villaverde's ending, in which the disappearance of Leonardo and Cecilia's daughter in many ways embodies creole unease around interracial consolidation under a mixed-race national mother, feelings for which Morúa is open in his disdain?

Instead of functioning as a corrective to Villaverde's pessimistic view of race relations, the national project that Sofía and Federico's or Ana María and Liberato's children would emblematize is shown to be unviable, "miscarried" by what Morúa views as the racially exclusionary plans of hypocritical creole reformers and US imperialists expressed in texts such as *Cecilia Valdés* and *Juanita*. The temporal progression among the novels under discussion in this chapter is important. If Villaverde's and Mann's texts take place in the 1830s, Morúa's novel is set in the last decades of slavery, when the separatist movement was reaching its height. The children who were born under ignominious circumstances to mixed-race mothers and hidden away in *Cecilia Valdés* and those raised with so much care by Anglo-American governesses in *Juanita*, by *Sofía* and *La familia Unzúazu*, have grown up and are ready to take part in the struggle against Spain. Read in this context, the miscarriages in Morúa's novels suggest that the plans laid by creoles and North Americans over the course of the independence struggle—fundamentally flawed in the problematic ways in which they do and do not include the racialized Cuban masses—will, in the end, bear no fruit.

As it turns out, the only child born between Morúa's two novels is that of Magdalena, Sofía's look-alike sister who grew up at a boarding school in Philadelphia, and Eladislao Gonzaga, a Cuban separatist who has returned to the island after a long exile in New York (and is thus a member of the group of whites such as future president Tomás Estrada Palma who, historically, would step in to create the country's US-backed leadership class following the war). Rather than an enslaved woman such as Sofía or even an island aristocrat such as Ana María, the only possible mother for the Cuban nation, it would seem, is an Americanized creole, a sort Emilia Casanova de Villaverde without the radical ideology.[102] Does Morúa side with Mann, then, and see Cuba's future as born out of an alliance between creole elites and the forces of North American colonization? Given

172 *Foundational Frustrations*

that the author paid for the publication of his second novel with the honorarium from his service in the Cuban Asamblea Constituyente, or Constitutional Congress, in which he thwarted US efforts to deny the vote to Afro-Cubans and only agreed to support the Platt Amendment when compromise failed (Horrego Estuch, *Martín Morúa Delgado* 169), it seems unlikely that he should hold such an optimistic attitude toward North American imperialism.[103]

A conversation between Gonzaga and Magdalena in *Sofía* gestures at Morúa's complex views on Cuba's relationship to the United States:

> "I repeat," Eladislao said, "that that necklace is lovely, and your beauty truly brings its artistic value out. Was it made abroad?"
>
> "No," Magdalena responded, clutching the hanging star between her tiny fingers, "it was made wholly in Cuba, and I myself sketched the design. It has been executed to my liking."
>
> "It really is a work of art, Miss. . . . Is that the American seal?"
>
> "Maybe," the young lady answered spritely. "I didn't want to hang an eagle on the empty point so as not to complete the American design." (136–37)[104]

Ostensibly nationalistic, Magdalena—who, like the creole children in Mann's *Juanita*, was educated in the United States—is proud not to have bought her necklace abroad, but to have had it designed "a su gusto" (to her liking). Yet, as Gonzaga's comment demonstrates, her liking is indistinguishable from North American fashion. In such a situation, her refusal to place an eagle on the necklace, rather than a defiant gesture, becomes a meaningless token, not unlike the nominal sovereignty experienced by the *república mediatizada*, the postindependence US-protectorate state accepted by some members of the creole upper class during the early twentieth century.[105]

Importantly, Magdalena and Gonzaga do not marry—in fact, Gonzaga is already married to another returned exile, América. Her Martían name echoes the possibility of a new, racially democratic social order, the existence of which, scholars have argued, was thwarted by the North American intervention that Gonzaga's union with Magdalena seems to hail (Ferrer, *Insurgent Cuba*). Once again reappropriating the structures of hegemonic discourse to reveal the limits of creole nationalist thought, Morúa shows the creole child of Gonzaga and Magdalena—a sign of the betrayal of América—to be just as illegitimate as the mixed-race daughter of Villaverde's Leonardo and Cecilia, even if Uncle Sam has agreed to act as its godfather. In much the same way that he initially opposed but eventually voted for the Platt Amendment, Morúa in his novel objects, but ultimately understands that the next generation of Cubans will consist of Villaverde's creole elites entrusted to the tutelage of Mann's maternal-imperial schoolmasters. As the new century broke over US-occupied Cuba, such a conception of republican motherhood would cease to be metaphorical, as I now will explain.

5 "La Dignidad de la Mujer Cubana"
Racialized Gender Allegory and the *Intervención Americana*

As I EXPLAINED in the previous chapter, with the Spanish-Cuban-American War of 1898, the allegory of the Cuban national family would assume a transnational character, as Villaverde considered the country's racially fraught identity from the perspective of the post–Civil War United States and writers such as Mann and Morúa Delgado contemplated how the United States might intervene—for better or for worse—in the island's complex interracial dynamics. This transnationalization of the Cuban national-family allegory would cause Spanish American and US racial categories to collide with and complicate one another, as the creole characters deemed unworthy of self-government in Mann's *Juanita* might attest. More than that, however, Hispanic and Anglo-American gender constructs would also influence and, in turn, be influenced by the transnational family romance formed from the debris of the *Maine*. What emerges in the closing years of the nineteenth century and the beginning of the twentieth is an imperial allegory in which the United States is scripted as masculine, active, and paternalistic, while Cuba appears as a passive female on her way to motherhood—an allegory that Cubans alternately would reinscribe and resist, as I will show.

What happens to the national-allegorical daughter of Villaverde's Cecilia and Leonardo in this new "national" family? Esteban Borrero Echeverría, a writer and physician who would assume the role of Cuba's secretary of public instruction in 1901, offers a grim answer in a March 25, 1900, letter to novelist Nicolás Heredia. Employing the allegorical mode that he later would use in his 1905 short story "El ciervo encantado" (The enchanted stag), Borrero Echeverría draws a comparison between the recent death of his infant child and the frustration of Cuban independence:

My poor daughter sacrificed in the flower of youth, at my own hand as I plowed the way for the patria. Long though I may live, I will die before I am consoled of your death. Great and desolating though it may be, no pain of mine can ever be equal to that which overwhelms me when I think that the feeling of moral solidarity also may die in the Cuban consciousness. This feeling should be the support of the *fulcrum* of political consciousness, if that consciousness is finally able to constitute itself among us. Mutilated, if there is some accident mutilating us (and I think everyone knows what I mean), we should fight to put our soul back together. (Letter to don Nicolás Heredia)[1]

Lamenting the time that he took away from family life in order to "plow the way for the patria," Borrero Echeverría feels frustrated that, like his daughter, Cuban independence, too, has died prematurely. Ironically, this death is the result of "some accident," a mordant critique of US intervention in the war against Spain that the cryptic comment "I think everyone knows what I mean" only half conceals.

Importantly, at the same time that Borrero Echeverría bristles under US military rule, he also considers Cuban responsibility for the situation. "If for any reason, in times of peace, there does not persist among a pueblo the feeling of social solidarity that determined and made possible union in war, everything will have been lost for all, much as the fruit of conception is lost in miscarriage (*aborto*)."[2] In this reference to "aborto," Borrero Echeverría echoes the end of Morúa Delgado's *Sofia,* in which miscarriage serves as a metaphor for the unviability of creole nationalist projects that do not take the island's Afro-descended population sincerely into account.

In many ways, Borrero Echeverría embodies the ambiguous position of Cuban creoles—situated between Afro-Cuban popular classes on the one hand and North American imperial forces on the other—during the 1898–1902 US occupation of the island, known in Spanish as the *intervención americana*. Despite the fact that the Teller Amendment to the declaration of war against Madrid expressly prohibited US acquisition of the Spanish Caribbean territory, "no purpose was as central to American policy calculations during four years of military occupation as preparations for the eventual annexation of Cuba." US military rule aimed to provide "an opportunity to Americanize the island, organize national institutions compatible with the American political system, and recruit local allies" in order to "create the conditions setting into motion the forces leading ultimately to annexation" (Pérez, "Imperial Design" 4–5). Historian Marial Iglesias Utset notes that, "against the backdrop of the symbolic vacuum produced by the end of more than 400 years of Spanish colonial domination, strong nationalist and patriotic currents and a contradictory process of Americanization of institutions and customs emerge simultaneously" (Iglesias Utset 14).[3] These complex years would see Cubans ponder the relative merits of the racial-patriarchal structure of Spanish colonial society, the raceless citizenship articulated by some wings of the independence movement, and the white-manhood democracy represented by the US republican model. Like their Argentine counterparts during the transition from colonial tradition to republican modernity, in order to forge the interfactional "moral solidarity" that they felt was missing in Cuba, Borrero Echeverría and other thinkers of his generation would turn to public educación.

The formation of future citizens was central to the turn-of-the-nineteenth-century Cuban national project; exiled in New York, creole letrado Cirilo Villaverde and first president Tomás Estrada Palma both would work as teachers while José Martí, in addition to his labors at the chalkboard, in 1889 served as editor of a didactic children's magazine called *La Edad de Oro* (The golden age). The educational terrain would become the site of battles between annexationists in the colonial US military government and Cuban proponents of cultural and political autonomy during the occupation period. Perhaps more so than in Argentina, educational reformers in Cuba would insist on the moral, rather than intellectual, aspects of public educación, especially for students of color, as lettered elites sought to produce a citizen body capable of the self-government that the imperial United States at the time was denying the island.[4]

Paradoxically, Cuban educational reformers would seek North American aid in establishing a school system capable of resisting US imperialism. Between 1900 and 1902, thousands of Cuban teachers were sent to the United States in order to study democratic education with the aim of training students for citizenship upon their return to the island (Pérez, "Imperial Design" 15). In its emphasis on civic education, this program, like the system implemented in Argentina a generation earlier, posited the female schoolteacher as republican mother while making explicit the foreign formation of the national teacher-mother. This link between Cuba and Argentina is more than a mere parallel. As I will explain, several of the teachers at the Anexo Cubano of the normal school in New Paltz, New York, were invited to the institution after having served as maestras de Sarmiento in Argentina. Triangulating the relationships among Cuba, the United States, and Argentina discussed in the rest of the book, the story told in this chapter reveals the previously unexplored link between

"La Dignidad de la Mujer Cubana" 177

Sarmiento's racialized modernization-through-education initiative and North American imperialism in Cuba. This trinational cooperation between US imperialism and Latin American creole neocolonialism, in which Anglo mothers of the Argentine nation prepare racialized Cuban women in New York for republican motherhood, demonstrates how the North American, Argentine, and Cuban national-familial discourses become entangled as Latin American states brokered with the rising US empire in the late nineteenth and early twentieth centuries.

The chapter concludes with a discussion of how the Cuban normal students at New Paltz engaged the racialized and gendered imperial metaphors that underlay their stay in the United States and, metonymically, Cuba's new place in the US imperial orbit. Through a discursive analysis of the little-studied "Sección cubana" that the Cuban teachers published from 1901 to 1902 in the institution's periodical, *The Normal Review*, I show that, emphasizing their personal dignity, the Cubans consistently sought to represent themselves as independent bourgeoise white women. Admittedly problematic, this depiction acts as a counter-discourse to US imperialist rhetoric of the war period, which tended to racialize Cubans' supposed indolence and nonconformity to middle-class Anglo-American canons of masculinity and femininity. Obviating any racial difference from Anglo North Americans by scripting themselves as white and insisting on their dignity as female professionals, the Cuban teachers inscribe themselves within the "New Woman" paradigm current in the turn-of-the-nineteenth-century northeastern United States. In this way, the Cuban teachers at New Paltz revisit and revise the racialized maternal discourse found in the other texts that have been discussed in this book—ideas to which the Cuban nationalist group that sent them, the North American imperialists who hosted them, and the former maestras de Sarmiento who taught them all had subscribed.

Race, Gender, and Empire in 1898

The Rough Riders, Theodore Roosevelt's 1898 memoir of his experiences commanding the First US Volunteer Cavalry during the war, is a paradigmatic articulation of the imperial racial and gender paradigms that would influence North American policy toward Cuba in the coming years. The book exemplifies "a racially encoded gaze that served to metamorphose the rival imperial power 'Spain' into the colonizer and the Anglo-Saxon colonizer . . . into the superior, virile civilizer" (Saldívar, *Trans-Americanity* 64), as is made clear when the author notes that he was reading Demolin's treatise on "Anglo-Saxon Superiority" during the campaign.[5] In the memoir, this superiority is embodied in the figure of Allyn Capron, "who was, on the whole, the best soldier in the regiment . . . the ideal of what an American regular army officer should be." According to Roosevelt, this ideal is "tall and lithe, a remarkable boxer and walker, a first-class rider and shot, with yellow hair and piercing blue eyes," an almost Wagnerian archetype of the Germanic warrior (47).

As cultural historian Gail Bederman explains, late-nineteenth-century North Americans understood manliness in terms of self-control and capacity for leadership. These qualities, in turn, justified white males' patriarchal right to rule over women, children, and nonwhites (12). This "linking [of] whiteness to male power was nothing new," as, until the Fourteenth Amendment in 1868, "American citizenship rights had been construed as 'manhood' rights which inhered to white males, only." Nonwhite men "were forbidden to exercise 'manhood' rights—forbidden to vote, hold electoral office, serve on juries, or join the military. . . . The conclusion was implicit but widely understood: Negro males"—and, by extension, all nonwhite males—"were less than men" (20). Classified, like women and children, as dependents in many states, nonwhite males occupied a subordinate status vis-à-vis white men. Roosevelt's blue-eyed Capron, for example, had "under him one of the two companies from the Indian Territory and he so soon impressed himself upon the wild spirit of his followers, that he got them ahead in discipline faster than any other troop in the regiment," painting his "superior" Anglo-Saxon virility as stronger than the indigenous soldiers' unmanly wildness. Similarly, Roosevelt notes that, while "no troops could have behaved better than the colored soldiers . . . they are, of course, peculiarly dependent upon their white officers" (47).[6]

In contrast to the virile virtues of the Nordic Capron, for Roosevelt, the Cuban insurgents represented "a crew of as utter tatterdemalions as human eyes ever looked on, armed with every kind of rifle in all stages of dilapidation." He dismisses the group as "nearly useless" (75). This attitude regarding the insurgents' "uselessness" is most likely predicated on the *independentistas'* defeats in the earlier independence struggles known as the Guerra de los Diez Años (Ten Years' War) and the Guerra Chiquita (Little War) and their inability in US eyes to stop the abuse of the island's civilian population, which had been forced into unsafe and unsanitary reconcentration camps by Spanish General Valeriano Weyler y Nicolau (Pérez, *Cuba in the American Imagination* 85). North American "power brokers and opinion makers . . . detected in allegations of Spanish mistreatment of women a violation of the very responsibility by which men were held accountable and indeed the very obligations upon which the moral claim to patriarchy rested. If manly men in the United States failed to respond and vindicate the honor of American manhood, that, too, would signal a break of the responsibility of patriarchy" (81). For Roosevelt, then, "The United States was engaged in a millennial drama of manly racial advancement, in which American men enacted their superior manhood by asserting imperialistic control over races of inferior manhood" (Bederman 171), stepping in to protect the Cuban civilians that the insurgents had proven unable to defend.[7]

Perhaps not surprisingly, Roosevelt's reading of the *independentista* army's behavior contradicts the way that Cuban historiography remembers the period. In Cuban national mythology, *mambí* freedom fighters constitute an important nationalist symbol of resistance against colonial rule, one that, as Iglesias Utset explains, the US military government after the war would go to considerable lengths to contain. In contrast to Roosevelt's emphasis on the superiority of white, Anglo-Saxon manliness, many *mambises* featured in the pantheon of national heroes, such as Antonio Maceo and Guillermo Moncada, were Afro-descendants. The virile image of the fearless black *mambí* has persisted in Cuban culture through the post-1959 period and survives in texts such as Esteban Montejo's 1966 testimonial *Biografía de un cimarrón* (*Biography of a Runaway Slave*) and Humberto Solás's 1968 film *Lucía*.[8]

That said, the *mambí* forces were by no means exclusively male and "legends about the better-known mambisas [female *mambises*] have become part of the Cuban national identity, and they symbolized the efforts of nameless heroines" of the wars against Spain (Stoner 26). These women "presented their daughters with examples of heroism, durability, integrity, ingenuity, self-sacrifice, and combativeness during the campaigns against Spanish rule.... Mambisas, while remaining wives and mothers, left the protection of their homes, went into the *manigua,* and took up arms in support of national sovereignty" (13).[9] Like that of the Afro-Cuban *mambises,* this historical agency of Cuban women is minimized by Roosevelt. When, after the war, the Rough Riders encounter a group of civilian refugees from the Spanish reconcentration camps, the soldiers, "for all their roughness and their ferocity in fight, were rather tender-hearted than otherwise, and they helped the poor creatures, especially the women and children, in every way, giving them food and even carrying the children and the burdens borne by the women" (193). Apparently feeling that the women were unable to manage by themselves, Roosevelt's Rough Riders provided them with much the same paternalistic care that the United States would imagine itself as affording Cuba after Spain's withdrawal. The only female characters (and nameless, at that) in Roosevelt's hypermasculine, homosocial narrative, the Cuban civilians here do not appear qua women but as figurations of the Latin nation under "manly" Anglo-Saxon tutelage. The complex racial and gender dynamics between the United States and the Afro-Cuban popular classes on the one hand and Cuban creole elites on the other that texts such as Borrero Echeverría's letter and Roosevelt's *Rough Riders* suggest would influence how the trope of republican motherhood developed, helping to structure both interracial and international relations during the Occupation period, as I now will explain.

Public Educación
Educational Reform under the Military Government

After Cuba's supposed rescue from effete Spanish colonialism by virile Anglo-Saxon soldiers, public educación would be mobilized to form republican citizens out of the colonial masses. While US imperial influence necessarily left the deepest marks on urban elites, the "reform of public education, especially of elementary education, would affect thousands of schoolchildren of every class, sex, and race, all over the country" (Iglesias Utset 117).[10] Under US military governor Leonard Wood, "schools were opened all over the island—within six months the number increased from 635 to 3,313. . . . Enrollment increased tremendously. In 1900, slightly more than $4,000,000 was spent for education." This sum represented "one-fourth of the national budget" (Foner 2:459) and included funds set aside for the creation of the new Facultad de Pedagogía at the University of Havana. "By the end of Wood's administration, there were 3,800 public schools with a total enrollment of 255,000 and an average daily attendance of 160,000" (2:460). If, in 1894, 800 teachers taught 34,579 students on the island, by 1901, those figures had risen to 3,613 teachers for 172,273 students—a testament to the importance of public instruction to the assimilationist goals of the military government (Varona, *Instrucción* 23).

The North American colonial administration considered public education to be "an unparalleled opportunity through which to promote in Cuba the attitudes and values compatible with larger American objectives" by urging the country's young people to "abandon traditional values and acquire new habits" (Pérez, "Imperial Design" 7). Wood believed that "by controlling the management of what was taught on the island," he "could encourage the students to influence their parents to call for the annexation of Cuba by the U.S.," a process known as "annexation through acclamation" (Minichino 225).[11] After the staunchly antiannexationist Alexis Everett Frye resigned from the position of superintendent of public schools on the island, the more imperialist Lieutenant Matthew H. Hanna was appointed to the role. A former schoolteacher from Ohio, Hanna openly sought to model the Cuban educational system on that of the United States (Foner 2:462–63). Under Hanna, public education became a device to "inculcate American principles," absorbed through the study of translated North American textbooks (Foner 2:463). Additionally, "the introduction of courses of study normally found in the United States, including civics education and the study of English, the restructuring of the school calendar, the introduction of teacher examinations, and school regulations crafted from Ohio law" made their way to the list of North American cultural impositions on Cuban education. "Further changes included the introduction of United States–style teacher requirements specifying courses of study to be used in Normal Schools . . . , licensing requirements and processes, school textbook selection, classroom furniture design, procurement, and distribution, selection of student assessment methods, English language instruction, the introduction of summer schools for teacher training, and the insertion of a new schedule of school holidays" (Minichino 124–25).

These changes represented an effort to penetrate "Cuban society at its most fundamental level for the purpose of arresting the development of an autonomous and potentially rival national culture" (Pérez, "Imperial Design" 7). During the US occupation, public schools remained in session on the anniversaries of important events in Cuba's revolutionary past (Iglesias Utset 81), while "history texts recorded the American version of the Cuban revolutionary war," in which, as Roosevelt makes clear, "Cubans had contributed little to their own independence" (Pérez, "Imperial Design" 11–12). Meanwhile, the obligatory study of English was implemented in the island's schools in an assimilationist effort to pave the way for eventual annexation (Iglesias Utset 117–25). Thus, much as public education during the period was being mobilized within the US metropole to bring immigrants, freedmen, and Native Americans into the fold of Anglo-American bourgeois-republican values and culture, so, too, was it deployed on other racialized subjects in the nation's imperial peripheries.

Wood's administration marked the high point of education in Cuba for years to come. Yet the US foray into cultural imperialism achieved mixed results. The plan to implement widespread instruction in English, for example, was frustrated by a lack of available teachers and perhaps of interest on the part of the Cubans (Iglesias Utset 128–29). Indeed, Cubans often repurposed US imperial education to their own ends. For example, schools may have been open on what otherwise would have been national holidays, but teachers used those days to teach the history of the Cuba Libre movement (81). Similarly, the importation of the North American daily school schedule provided opportunities to salute the Cuban flag and sing the national anthem (193). This dynamic of imperial imposition and colonial reappropriation would characterize the intervention period, as I will show.

Blackness and Bourgeois Republicanism

For their part, reformers in late-nineteenth- and early-twentieth-century Cuba, "believed that just rule evolved out of democratic order and an educated populace. Nearly all agreed that rational thought had to replace mystical faith and that public schools should teach new positivistic values to young patriots" (Stoner 35). Not unlike Sarmiento and his peers in Argentina, Cuban elites were quick to note the inadequacy of their country's educational system for the task of republican nation building, which US colonialism suddenly had transformed into a question of national preservation. By all accounts, public education on the island had been languishing for generations. In the colonial period, "schools were poorly funded and ill-equipped; teachers were often inadequately trained and always poorly paid. It was not uncommon for teachers to supplement meager salaries with remuneration directly from the more well-to-do parents of their students. Nor was it uncommon for teachers to pay the rent of school buildings out of their own earnings" (Pérez, "Imperial Design" 6). As early as 1831, Domingo del Monte had noted that "public instruction is almost nonexistent in our countryside, and the founding of a school there could be considered a service of utmost importance to the State" ("Exposición" 258).[12]

Most damningly for elite nineteenth-century reformers, teachers often were recruited from "the humblest classes," including "old freedmen" (Figueras 321), especially Afro-descended women (García Pons 555–57).[13] While, until 1863, teachers at state-run schools were required to demonstrate their racial purity by presenting a *certificado de limpieza de sangre* (Huerta Martínez, *Enseñanza* 220), much of the education on the island occurred in informal institutions called *escuelas de amigas*. Known disparagingly as *"migas"* (which literally means "crumbs"), these schools were staffed by unlicensed teachers, frequently free women of color (Huerta Martínez, *Enseñanza* 133–36). The *escuelas de amigas* proved particularly offensive to the sensibilities of creole liberals. As early as 1830, del Monte would complain of "these *amigas'* imperfect learning; ordinarily directed by women of color, or so crassly ignorant, uncivil and totally inept for the role that they intended to play, that in the end it was impossible to benefit from them" ("Exámen de niñas" 403).[14] In 1836, the governor of Bayamo similarly would voice concerns that the high number of women of color teaching in his city imperiled children's moral development (del Monte, "Informe" pt. 2, 318). Even Villaverde in *Cecilia Valdés* would find it important to point out that there were "more schools . . . served by teachers of color than by whites" during the period, adding the fact to his inventory of Spain's colonial failings (535).[15]

Official support for public education in Cuba improved only marginally as the nineteenth century progressed and power in the metropole went back and forth between liberals and conservatives.[16] Responding to this situation, in his proindependence manifesto, Céspedes would complain of the "restrictive system of education" that imperial Spain had adopted in the hopes of rendering Cubans "so ignorant that we are unaware of our sacred rights" (Céspedes).[17] Meanwhile, in his "Memoria sobre el estado de la Instrucción primaria en 1881" (Memory on the state of primary instruction in 1881), Cornelio Coopiner reports that, though, as a colony, Cuba was subject to the same compulsory education laws as Spain in 1881, even as the *separatistas* plotted from exile and Cirilo Villaverde's *Cecilia Valdés* was being typeset on the New York presses, only 1 out of every 42,997 Cubans attended school. Perhaps not surprisingly, as late as 1888, as much as 63.9 percent of the population of Cuba was illiterate (Foner 1:23n). Hoping to improve the situation, during the war with Spain, the rebel government had required school attendance for children over the age of eight living in areas under insurgent control (1:137–38). Unfortunately, these efforts proved unsuccessful. "A census of Cuba taken on the basis of an order issued on August 19, 1899 showed that the number of children under ten who had attended school was only 40,559, and the number who had not attended was 316,428" (Foner 2:430n).

Eager to ameliorate the problem, in an 1899 letter signed by teachers Diego Torres and Domingo Frades, the Asociación de Maestros y Amantes de la Niñez de La Habana (Havana association of teachers and lovers of children) petitioned Wood's predecessor John R. Brooke, the first US military governor in occupied Cuba, for the creation of a Secretaría de Instrucción Pública ("Documento importante").[18] Improvement came at a frustratingly slow pace. Alexis Everett Frye, who served for a time as superintendent of public schools under the military government, would claim that in 1901, of 330,000 school-age children, only 143,000 were enrolled in educational institutions.[19] A year later, serving as first superintendent of public instruction under the Republican government, Borrero Echeverría would claim that, during the 1902–3 academic year, of 500,000 school-aged children, only 152, 934 were enrolled in school (Borrero Echeverría "Instrucción").[20]

The implications of these seemingly incredible statistics were not lost on Cuban educational reformers. A year after the Treaty of Paris, soon to be secretary of public instruction Enrique José Varona would identify two "vital problems" facing the Cuban people: "the material reconstruction of the country and the reform of mass education. Without stable public wealth, we will have no independence; without real mass education, we will have no democracy" ("Segunda" 1).[21] These two problems are related, as "it is materially impossible for a people to operate democratically if seventy-five percent of the population is ignorant of the fundamental letters and if the standard of life barely raises beyond that which is strictly necessary. A country like this hands the masses over to the impulses of demagogues instead of bringing citizens to choose among political programs or decide wisely who should apply them" (1).[22] Perhaps not surprisingly, Varona opposed universal suffrage (de la Fuente 59).

As in Sarmiento's and Alberdi's Argentina, public education in turn-of-the-nineteenth-century Cuba would aim to instruct the island's popular classes in the "civilized" bourgeois-republican values necessary for participation in a capitalist economy and democratic government. Puerto Rican *independentista* Lola Rodríguez de Tío inadvertently registers the racial overtones of the movement for public educación in her poem "A los niños cubanos," published in the March 15, 1900, edition of *La escuela moderna:*

> La luz disipa la tiniebla densa
> y de rasgar de la noche el negro velo,
> el alba es esperanza y recompensa
> al despertar en el azul de Cielo!
>
> Así también la humana inteligencia
> que va sirviendo al porvenir de guía,
> con el noble ejercicio de la Ciencia
> vence el error en inmortal porfía.

(The light dissipates the dark shadows
and, upon tearing from the night her black veil,
the dawn is hope and recompense
upon awakening in the blue of the Heavens!

So too does human understanding,
which serves the future as a guide,
with the noble exercise of Science
defeat error ever insisting.)

The references to the "light" and the "shadows" in this poem obviously draw on traditional Platonic, Catholic, and Hispanic metaphors for binaries of knowledge and ignorance, good and evil, and peace and disquiet. At the same time, the historical context of the Spanish Caribbean in the early twentieth century lends the "black veil" an inevitable racial connotation. This becomes clear in the next stanza, in which the poet plays with the slippery term "slavery" (which here can refer both to ignorance and bondage or lack of rights), proclaiming that "la nueva juventud no será esclava/si entona el gran hossana [sic] del progreso" (the youths of today will not be slaves/if they sing the Hosanna of progress).[23] She exhorts the Cuban schoolchildren, newly emancipated from their "slavery," to develop the Protestant work ethic in which Roosevelt had found them lacking:

Obreros del saber! Ceñid la gloria,
vosotros que sembráis tan ricos dones,
no hay empresa más digna y meritoria
que ganar para el bien los corazones.

Fecunda es la labor! La alegre infancia
tributo os rendirá. Tras la faena
recoge el labrador en abundancia
la rubia mies de la campiña amena.

(Laborers in knowledge! Hold fast to glory
ye who sow such rich fruits,
there is no enterprise more dignified or deserving
than to win hearts for good.

Fecund is the labor! Happy infancy
will render tribute onto you. After the task
the laborer will collect in abundance
the blond grain of the pleasant fields.)

Through education, Cubans are transformed from feudal-colonial "slaves" to capitalist-republican "workers." The nation's "black veil" is "torn" and the "blond grain" of civilization is harvested, financing the country's development into a bourgeois republic.

These polysemic metaphors of light and darkness would become common as creole reformers ambivalently expressed concerns that Cuba's racialized past would prove a hindrance to democracy—a pressing concern as Roosevelt, Wood, and others regarded the island with imperial eyes. In a 1905 letter to Varona, Borrero Echeverría writes of "the shadows that darken the moral and artistic consciousness of the country," a discrete racial reference that becomes more direct as he continues, speaking of "the dark moral existence of the lowest layers of colonial society." These "dark shadows" are dangerous, he argues, because "among that larger group, undignified by elevated political aspiration and contaminated by all sorts of concupiscence, our historical baggage is not particularly healthy. In good things and in bad, our soul is the labor of our race" ("Carta").[24] In a 1900 article, pedagogue Luis A. Baralt would employ the same metaphor of racial "darkness," arguing that education helps a student to see "the sad state of darkness and slavery in which he finds himself and to spy that which he is destined to be" (89).[25] Equating lack of education with "darkness" and "slavery" in a country that had only abolished African bondage fourteen years previously, Baralt racializes the popular classes upon whose supposed ignorance he fears the republic may founder.

Afro-Cuban education long had proven a fraught issue in Cuba. While the Spanish government had ordered the establishment of integrated schools early in the nineteenth century, in practice, many Cuban authorities refused to educate black children (Huerta Martínez, *Enseñanza* 115). Rather, some creole plans for public education appear to have been designed deliberately to bolster the racial values of the plantocracy. In wake of the Haitian Revolution, Francisco Arango y Parreño and Nicolás Calvo, for example, "proposed the establishment of free public schools in the countryside. . . . The schools would soften the habits of rural whites, from whose ranks would be hired plantation overseers who, as a result of that education, would be more cognizant of long-term interests and less likely to abuse slaves, thereby helping to minimize the threat of insurrection and resistance" (Ferrer, *Freedom's* 42). Here, instruction is conceived not to welcome blacks into public life but better to safeguard slavocratic hegemony. Segregated schools finally were established for free children of color in 1842 (Huerta Martínez, *Enseñanza* 32). Still, the number of children educated in them was small, and the percentage grew even smaller as the number of freedmen increased over the course of the nineteenth century.

The effect that the newly emancipated slaves would have on the island's political life caused particular concern. Like the Argentine liberals of Sarmiento's day, turn-of-the-nineteenth-century creole reformers in Cuba sought to correct the "defects" of the country's Afro-descended masses in order to build a "civilized" bourgeois republic. The Ley Moret, which granted freedom to all children of African chattel slaves born after July 4, 1870, required masters to provide moral instruction and occupational training to free-born children (Cowling 160–61). Meanwhile, Article 21 of the 1871 Reglamento Orgánico de Instrucción Primaria en la Isla de Cuba (Ordinances on primary instruction on the island of Cuba) decreed that basic instruction be made available to "boys and girls of color with the object of them receiving basic primary education," with particular attention to "moral and religious aspects" (11).[26] Equal parts egalitarian and condescending, the law's emphasis on blacks' morality and religion echoes sentiments common among creole educational reformers of the time.[27]

The question of education for the *raza de color* would become especially pressing after the granting of voting rights to Afro-Cubans in the country's 1901 constitution. While levels of school completion in general were low across Cuban society, the figures for Afro-Cubans, even after the 1871 Reglamento Orgánico de Instrucción Pública, were particularly discouraging. In 1881, Coopiner would state that, while 1 out of every 29,772 white Cuban children received an education, only 1 out of every 47,272 black children attended school. Twenty-two years later, Borrero Echeverría reported with equal alarm that, per 101,331 white children, Cuba educated the even more paltry sum of 51,603 Afro-descendants—slightly more than half. The consequences of this poor distribution of the island's limited educational resources are hinted at in pedagogue Manuel Rodríguez Valdés's racially inflected fear that "if, after the fall of slavery, rich source of our disgraces, our popular classes are to continue as victims of the moral slavery of ignorance, it must be agreed that the country will have to drag an existence rather similar to that of primitive people behind it, in the fashion of a traveling trade post [*factoría*]" (*Educación popular* 35–36).[28] Equating ignorance with slavery, Rodríguez Valdés expresses creole elite fears that a Cuba in which the vote was extended to "primitive" blacks lacking the "civilization" necessary for republican government would serve as a new African *factoría* (a trade post, particularly one used by slavers), a colonial economic zone in which northern foreigners exploited a racialized southern population.

The question of racialized subjugation by northern imperial powers after Cuban independence from Spain was understandably at the front of creole thinkers' minds in the period leading up to and following 1898. Hearing the jingoistic cries of hawks such as Roosevelt and Wood and "mindful of the U.S. hegemon and its equation of political stability in the island with a particular racial status quo" (Branche, *Colonialism* 213), Borrero Echeverría in 1897 would meditate on the political vulnerability to which Spanish colonial "enslavement" had subjected Cuba. Perhaps inspired by the intellectual decolonization proposed six years earlier by Martí, the reformer warns that "whoever thinks that all that is necessary is to become independent in order for a people (no matter how superior its intellectual aptitudes may be) to be free . . . is in great error."[29] Rather,

> It is always and all occasions necessary and just to *educarse*: to prepare the spirit for a purified moral culture and intelligence for the selection of ideas that it will gather for the better life that awaits it. It is necessary to be able to receive the guest in a dignified and profitable fashion; not everything lies in subduing the foreign enemy. It is necessary at the same time to battle against and to cast from ourselves the worst enemy, the one in our home, the one that we carry with us: vicious habits, ignorance in any of its disgusting forms. Viciousness and ignorance are, doubtlessly, the heaviest chains with which ages of corruption and ineffective, inattentive, and impious government has sought to bind our spirit. ("San Carlos")[30]

Here, Borrero Echeverría draws a distinction between political independence and independence of spirit, emphasizing the importance of education to the latter. This spiritual education enables a people to distinguish between the enemy within and the enemy without. Writing as Cuba sought to extricate itself from the grasp of Spain while avoiding that of the United States, Borrero Echeverría in these comments suggests the need to expel the "enemy at home"—the vice and ignorance associated with the Spanish colonial regime—while finding a "dignified and profitable" way to greet the North American "guest" (who, he hopes, will leave soon). Repeating a topos common in Cuban literature since the del Montean writings of the 1830s, Borrero Echeverría in his reference to "chains" likens foreign control of Cuba to slavery.[31] Yet, given the lack of success that the country had had in educating the freedmen, this notion of colonial "enslavement" is more than metaphorical. Instead, the writer sees a clear link between

"*La Dignidad de la Mujer Cubana*" 189

Cuba's former status as a slave society and the island's potential to become an exploitable *factoría* for the North.

Borrero Echeverría would speak more directly about the link between slavery and colonial vulnerability in other writings. In an undated manuscript, he laments that "Cuban Society, built on the unsteady base of slave labor, today is weak and teeters before the strike caused in her by a political idea—infecund in its infortune, even as it is generous—and seems to dissolve in the face of the social conflict that dispossessed her of her slaves and, like one who has lost the way and blindly takes the first path that presents itself to his stunned eyes, here, too, we move in blindness" ("Apuntes").[32] Here, the island's inability to come to terms with the slave heritage at its "base" is linked to political "blindness" or a lack of republican sensibility. Like Morúa Delgado, who figures the island's political future in terms of miscarriage, Borrero Echeverría employs the metaphor of "infecundity" to gesture at the truncation of Cuban independence by the US Army. The writer is even more explicit about the relationship between race and coloniality in "Los cursos pedagógicos de verano" (Summer pedagogical courses), in which he worries that the "social and political hybridity of the Intervention submits us to tremendous trials, the gravity and danger of which are magnified in this conflict by the state of penury, of misery (I would even say *of hunger*) in which a people, our people, has entered, unprotected. Among the shadows of her emaciated mind she caresses the beautiful and moving illusion of political sovereignty."[33] Through his reference to dark "shadows" and use of the unusual term "hibridismo," the writer subtly suggests a link between Cuba's racial "hybridity" and the "illusory" sovereignty of the "intervened" nation, trapped between formal colonialism and full independence. Deemed by Roosevelt and others to be racially unfit for self-government, Cubans found themselves politically subordinated to the United States.[34]

Fears of North Americans' racially condescending attitudes toward Cuba on the part of Borrero Echeverría and others were not unfounded. In a November 16, 1899, speech in New York, Brigadier General William Ludlow, military governor of Havana, stated that "to grant universal suffrage to such a population would hopelessly prejudice the entire future of the island" and render it a "Hayti No. 2," citing the nineteenth century's perennial example of a black state supposedly fallen into barbarism (qtd. in Mirabal 142). Wood was more explicit in an April 12, 1900, letter, in which he wrote McKinley that "we are dealing with a race . . . that has steadily been going down for a hundred years and into which we have got to infuse new life, new principles and new methods of doing things" (qtd. in de la Fuente 40).[35] Similarly, much as Sarmiento and his North American collaborators viewed their Argentine campesino students as the structural equivalents of US freedmen, Samuel Small, a North American school administrator in the sugar-producing province of Matanzas, compared Cuban academic institutions to "the old field schools for the south from 50 years past, a comparison to schools used for children of slaves" (Minichino 178).

Borrero Echeverría's comments thus reflect the tensions between "the culture of an elite that advocated for a 'civilized' Cuba (in the image of the nations of the West) and the popular understanding of expressions of cultural identity" during a period in which "Cubans find themselves obligated to attempt to 'pass' a sort of civility 'exam' before the self-erected tribunal of the US interveners" (Iglesias Utset 94).[36] Like their Argentine counterparts during the same period, turn-of-the-century Cuban elites attempted to project an image of a white nation in an effort to ward off northern imperialism. This wish to keep up appearances of whiteness dates from at least the earliest moments of the occupation. Under the mistaken belief that the end of Spanish colonialism would lead to greater liberty to engage in Afro-Cuban religious practices, a group of *ñáñigos* organized an independence celebration for January 1, 1899. "The participants paid dearly for the error of confusing the end of Spanish sovereignty with the coming of an era of full liberty," and the *ñáñigos*' drums were silenced by a whitening discourse that accused them of "illicit association" (Iglesias Utset 237).[37]

Incidents such as this clearly reflected racist attitudes toward the Afro-Cuban popular classes on the part of creole elites. At the same time, the potential of the imperial United States to impose its post-Reconstruction racial order in Cuba was real. Afro-descendants generally enjoyed more rights in occupation-era and republican Cuba than they did in the United States, yet US businesses operating in the country resisted the local government's orders to desegregate (Iglesias Utset 115–16). Creole and Anglo-American racism would combine forces in 1912 when, in response to a violation of the Morúa Law prohibiting race-based political associations, the Cuban government would accept US military support in putting down a rebellion of the Partido Independiente de Color. Between three thousand and six thousand people died in the massacre that ensued.[38]

Thus, fearing racialized barbarism and the northern imperialism that it often serves to justify—and keenly aware of the colonial bonds that the United States was tying around their country as they wrote—Cuban *letrados* during the intervention looked to public educación as a means of keeping the island out of greedy Anglo-Saxon hands. In her poem "A la niñez de Cuba" (To the children of Cuba), published in the November 10, 1900, issue of the *Revista de Instrucción Pública,* Aurora Silvestre de Feliu urges:

> Poned ¡Oh! niños! la primera piedra,
> Haced de Cuba la NACIÓN MODELO
> Y sed gigantes en la nueva Atenas
> Ya que la Europa nos llamó Pigmeos.
>
> (Lay, Oh children! the first stone,
> Make of Cuba a MODEL NATION
> And be giants in the new Athens
> Since Europe has called us Pygmies.)

According to Silvestre de Feliu, by educating themselves, the children of Cuba can show the nations of the north that their countrymen are not small and exploitable African "Pygmies" but a "NACIÓN MODELO," equals of the colossal US city on a hill. Employing a strategy that Sarmiento had pioneered in Argentina a few years earlier, Cuban *letrados* would mobilize public school teachers against the occupying US Army, hoping to "civilize" the island's racialized colonial population in order to avoid the same fate of imperial subjugation that was befalling the "Pygmies" of Africa at the time.

Educación and Republican Motherhood

Like their Argentine counterparts, Cuban reformers felt that, while it was incumbent upon the mothers of Cuba to guide the country away from the legacy of Spanish colonialism, that very history made it impossible for them to do so. In his 1898 *La mujer cubana,* Diego Vicente Tejera, founder of the Cuban socialist party, would assert that, even though "the Cuban woman is in an excellent position to serve as an educator," she is unable to fulfill this function because "she, like us, suffers from the defects and vices of the colonial tutelage to which we have been vilely subjected" (7), such as the supposed indolence and disorder that Cuban reformers of the period sought to eradicate.[39] Tejera takes his ideas on colonialism and maternity one step further in his "Educación en las sociedades democráticas," which metaphorizes Spain as a bad mother:

> Educación for public life should have as its base that educación that parents begin as soon as their child awakes to reason; the outlines of the citizen must already be present when the child leaves the home. And here, before the

spectacle that I spy on the horizon of our future agitation in a free patria, here is where our educación suddenly appears before my eyes in all of its deformity and deficiency. The brutal regime of Spain to which we have been subjected has not prepared us, nor could it have prepared us, for the exercise of our rights and liberties, nor has it allowed us even to acquire great domestic virtues. (7)[40]

Juxtaposing the comments on the proper raising of children with a reference to "the brutal regime of Spain," Tejera suggests that, unlike Cooper's Alice Munro, the memoirist Jeanie Howard, or Mann's Helen Wentworth, the Spanish motherland has not raised her children with "domestic virtues," nor has she prepared them for the republican "exercise of rights and liberties." How, then, can Cuban women instill in their children the bourgeois values necessary for capitalist economics and republican rule?

The question became even more pressing in the case of those most brutally affected by the immorality of Spanish colonialism, the newly liberated Afro-Cuban masses. Even the late-colonial Afro-Cuban press had expressed concern for the ability of black women to perform responsible republican motherhood. Like those of the creole intelligentsia, "the majority of elite [black] women's writings emphasised the connections between education, motherhood, and patriotic duty" (Brunson 489). Often they reflected the same biases, too, as "elite women of African descent employed modernising gender norms in order to counter negative attributes associated with blackness and to affirm their identification with the values of upper-class whites," in some ways resembling the Afro-Argentine poets Horacio Mendizábal and Ida Edelvira Rodríguez mentioned in chapter 3 (481). In a November 30, 1888, article in *Minerva: Revista quincenal dedicada a la mujer de color* (Minerva: Biweekly magazine dedicated to women of color), freedwoman María Angela Storni, for example, questions the ability of Afro-Cuban women to fulfill the demands of republican motherhood. Echoing Varona, she complains of "the state of moral decadence in which we live for lack of enlightenment." She worries that, without access to education, Afro-Cuban women, like Villaverde's fictional Cecilia Valdés, will not be useful "for more than the pleasures of dance," nor will they fulfill the "sacrosanct duties of the home." Devoted to the philosophy of republican motherhood, she feels that this enlightened domesticity is the "greatest need . . . of the race to which I belong," which recently had been granted citizen status (3).[41] To ameliorate the problem, Storni proposes the creation of an "*Association for the teaching of the women* of our race, where, girls as well as fully formed women, all of us can learn all that is necessary and indispensable for the fulfillment of our duties, an Association that responds to our moral needs" (4).[42]

In the same issue, another Afro-Cuban female contributor, América Font, asks if an ignorant woman "can be the teacher of her offspring." "Intellectualism and culture," she writes, are "very strong elements that women must have at their disposal in order to guide their children down the path of righteousness." Font therefore encourages her female readers to "escape from the slavery of ignorance," as "to be free [one] must be instructed, for where there is no instruction, there is no freedom" (3).[43] Appearing in an Afro-Cuban magazine, the equation of ignorance with slavery here has a clear racial undertone. True freedom—from captivity or from colonialism—the author believes, cannot exist without proper educación at the hands of a virtuous republican mother.[44]

Of course, Afro-Cuban women raised virtuous republican citizens all the time, even when they did not belong to the educated petite bourgeoisie like the contributors to *Minerva*. Antonio Maceo's mother, Mariana Grajales, for example, "became the legendary model of motherhood and patriotism" in postwar Cuba for encouraging her ten sons to take up arms against Spain (Stoner 20). Guillermo Moncada's mother, Dominga, meanwhile, "was the object of Spanish aggression for her own contributions to rebel insurrection. . . . Moncada sustained herself and her children . . . as a midwife and, like Mariana Grajales, taught her sons to fight for independence" and was herself imprisoned on more than one occasion for her participation in the war (26). Nonetheless, as the *Minerva* articles indicate, Afro-Cuban women were widely held as unsuitable for republican motherhood, an attitude also manifested in Villaverde's *Cecilia Valdés*.

Instead, Cuban elites felt that "other women would be needed in order to instill the kinds of 'morals' in children that their ex-slave mothers were unable to provide" (Cowling 167). For that reason, Article 22 of the 1871 Reglamento Orgánico de Instrucción Primaria en la Isla de Cuba decreed that "teachers in the schools for colored children should be from the white class," an obvious affront to the Afro-Cuban "migas" in whose hands much popular education informally had been placed (11). The timing of the 1871 school law, issued one year after the Ley Moret granted freedom to children born of enslaved mothers, suggests that white teachers were intended to pick up where the Afro-descended mothers left off, raising Cecilia Valdés's national-allegorical children with values that she was considered unfit to instill.

New Paltz

The question of where to find these teachers proved difficult in the post-Spanish period. Del Monte had advocated for the creation of normal schools on the island ("Informe" pt. 2 24), and famed educator José de la Luz y Caballero had tried unsuccessfully to establish one in 1838 (Huerta Martínez, *Enseñanza* 247–50). While an 1863 law required formal pedagogical training for all educators (Curnow 20), by the end of the colonial period, only three teacher-training institutes existed in Cuba, the last two of which were not founded until 1891 (Huerta Martínez, "Escuelas normales" 195)—and these institutions were closed for most of the US occupation, apparently due to cost (Minichino 195). To make this personnel shortage worse, a sizable percentage of the teaching force had emigrated from the island during the violent war years, leaving schools largely unstaffed (Pérez, "Imperial Design" 6).

Unlike the Argentine Sarmiento, however, Cubans rejected the importation of North American teachers, eliminating that strategy as a possible solution to the problem (Iglesias Utset 129). "Instead, the United States decided to Americanize the teachers" (Pérez, "Imperial Design" 12) and, starting in 1898, the nongovernmental Cuban Educational Association began sending Cubans to the United States for secondary and postsecondary education (Iglesias Utset 117–20). The program soon was replicated by other organizations, as well as the military government, which famously sent a group of Cuban school teachers to Harvard University in the summers of 1900 and 1901.[45] The plan worked and, two years into the occupation, the number of teachers in Cuba had swelled to three thousand (Pérez, "Imperial Design" 15).

Yet, while "virtually all" of Cuba's public-school teachers "participated in some educational program in the United States" (Pérez, "Imperial Design" 15), those teachers were overwhelmingly white. Perhaps influenced by Spanish-Cuban-American War propaganda texts, such as Mann's *Juanita*, that emphasized the African heritage of the racially mixed Cuban population, US schools receiving Cuban students found "only certain Cubans . . . fit to be 'Americanized.'" This meant that "darker skinned Cubans could not gain admission to a number of American universities and colleges." The University of Missouri, for example, explicitly stated that "the offer [of admission] is not extended to the Cubans that may be Negroes'" (qtd. in Foner 2:464). Similarly, of the 1,237 Cuban teachers to travel to Harvard (Iglesias Utset 132), only ten were of African descent (González Lucena).[46] The effects of this civic-intellectual whitening would continue into the early-republican period; as late as 1915, 90 percent of students at the normal school for women in Havana were white (de la Fuente 147–48).

Havana to New York via Buenos Aires

These white teachers were charged with instilling bourgeois-democratic values in the children of Cuba by Hanna's August 1, 1900, school law, Civil Order No. 368, mandating "civic instruction" for secondary school students (Minichino 173).[47] Cuban pedagogical reformers sought support in this endeavor from the State Normal School at New Paltz, New York (today the State University of New York at New Paltz), which recently had implemented a "school city" system "of student self-government" (Gill, *School City* 4) designed to instill the duties of democratic citizenship in its pupils. While other "school cities" existed in New York, Columbus, Chicago, Philadelphia, Great Britain, Mexico, and the US-occupied Philippines, "New Paltz had the most completely developed school city anywhere." The school distinguished itself from similar institutions through the creation of "a higher level—the school state" complete with a bicameral campus senate (Lang and Lang 54).

Developed by pedagogical reformer Wilson Gill (Gill, *School City* 5) and first implemented by teacher Bernard Cronson at PS 69 in New York in 1893 (Minichino 305), the school city model aimed "to give students an opportunity to develop a system of controlled freedom in terms of the greatest value for the improved functioning of the entire school" (Klotzberger 60). Like the Cuban reformers discussed above, Gill through his school city model sought "to cultivate in the individuals to be educated a good conscience, and to secure for them a wise and resolute self-government and the desire and ability to co-operate for the common good; or, in other words, a good character" (Gill, "School City" 19). This meant that students must be trained "as citizens, not as subjects" in order to prepare themselves for participation in republican government (21).

Gill was quick to understand the potential of his innovation, which was "widely used in immigrant neighborhoods of New York City to promote the acculturation process" (Pérez, "Imperial Design" 9), to spread US republican values to the territories newly acquired from Spain: "If it is desirable that adult Porto Ricans, Filipinos, and our own countrymen, shall understand full citizenship, it will be a great aid to such understanding if there is placed before them, wherever there is a school, a working model of that kind of government and citizenship which is desired" (Gill, *Social* 7–8). Wood agreed, feeling that the school city model "tends to develop the child's idea of his civic responsibility and . . . will send him out of school much better fitted to assume the duties of a citizen of a republic" (qtd. in Gill, *School City* 24). Impressed with the innovations at New Paltz, Wood invited Wilson Gill to visit Cuba and "work with school authorities there to develop citizenship education in the Cuban schools" (Klotzberger 64; see also Lang and Lang 55). He eventually would found some thirty-six hundred school cities in Cuba (Minichino 313), a "system of moral and civic education" that would "indoctrinate [the] children [of Cuba] into a system completely different than anything their parents had experienced" under Spanish colonialism (314–15).[48] In order to staff these institutions, "an arrangement was made with the New Paltz Normal School of New Paltz, NY. Sixty Cuban women were sent to the school for a two year program of studies paid for by the Island's treasury" (267).[49]

The sudden presence of so many Cuban students on the New Paltz campus necessitated the recruitment of bilingual teachers. For these, the school administration turned to the maestras de Sarmiento, North American teachers who by that time had thirty years of firsthand experience with Hispanic language and culture in Argentina. The Southern Cone nation rapidly was gaining fame as a regional success story in late-nineteenth- and early-twentieth-century Latin America. In an 1887 article, Cuban educator Bruno V. Miranda would credit the South American country's meteoric economic and social progress to the investment that it had made in public instruction. After almost a generation of quality schooling for the masses,

> her industry flourishes astoundingly. She has great factories of cloth, glassware, smelting, and machinery, in addition to industries in paper, earthenware, typography, distilling of brandy and liquor, salting and curing meat, and printing—she is one of the countries with the most newspapers per inhabitant. Buenos Aires is eminently mercantile, letters flourish there, her University and Medical School are well-attended, her normal schools are the best in Spanish America. Her Education Law is one of the most complete. She has numerous charities, various theaters, railway lines and street cars, public libraries, a museum, a stock market, banks, magnificent squares and a splendid racetrack. (18–19)[50]

The writer claims that the other Latin American republics have been unable to replicate Argentina's rapid rise to regional prominence because "they lack a Sarmiento to make them see the urgent and primordial need to distribute in all directions the benefits of mass education" (19).[51] Given this widespread international opinion, it was no wonder that the architects of Cuban educational reform would turn to the maestras de Sarmiento, the same people who, according to legend, had effected such positive change in the admirable Argentina.

The group of returning maestras was headed by Clara Armstrong, who had recruited Jennie Howard for the Argentine schools years before (Howard 24) and who had been recommended to Ida McKinley as an ideal headmistress by fellow maestra de Sarmiento Mary Gorman Sewell, the first lady's former schoolmate (Luigi, 65 *Valiants* 109). A native of New York, Armstrong, who arrived in Argentina in 1879 (Chavarria 386), had been "the first woman to found a normal school in South America" (Luigi, 65 *Valiants* 106) and formerly had headed the normal schools at San Juan and Catamarca, Argentina (107).[52] "Her Argentine experience made her the inevitable person for this job. . . . Two of the teachers she had taken in 1883 from Indianapolis to Argentina joined her at the Cuban Annex—Rosa Dark . . . and Amy Wales" (109). Employed at the model school at the Escuela Normal del Paraná, Argentina (Avellaneda and Leguizamón; Figueroa 128), following her 1883 arrival in Argentina (Chavarria 383), Wales, "who had come into an independent income, gave without pay six hours of teaching every day" (Luigi, 65 *Valiants* 109). Dark, in addition to serving as assistant principal (109), taught Spanish and methodology at the Anexo (145).

The return migration of these maestras de Sarmiento back north brings full circle the hemispheric efforts to install bourgeois-republican government through public educación in the hands of maternal teachers inculcated with Anglo-Saxon culture. It links the project's origins in the United States after abolition and the Civil War to the restructuring of Cuba after abolition and the Spanish-Cuban-American War through the consolidation of the liberal Argentine state following that country's racialized factional conflicts. Yet, if the maestras de Sarmiento project in Argentina had constituted a form of "soft," largely cultural, imperialism that some might not consider imperialism at all, the initiative's Cuban sequel, proposed by the interventionist US military government, openly worked toward the consolidation of North American hegemony in the hemisphere. In this context, the Anglo-Saxon Clara Armstrong is deployed by US imperial forces and their creole collaborators to fill the vacuum left by the racially incapacitated Cecilia Valdés as mother to the mulato Cuban nation.[53]

Autumn of the Creole Patriarch

As Cuba ultimately was granted protectorate status instead of annexation and statehood, North American women such as Armstrong, in the end, would not be able to serve as national republican mothers, but, instead, as trainers of the mothers of the new republican nation. Not surprisingly, drawing on the same gendered metaphors found in *The Rough Riders,* discourse surrounding the New Paltz project would insist on the teachers' femininity. The Cuban teachers are consistently referred to using feminine noun and adjectival forms (i.e., "las maestras cubanas") in the Spanish-language "Sección Cubana" of the *Normal Review* even though one of the Cuban students was male, which would have made the masculine plural (i.e., "los maestros cubanos") the grammatically correct form with which to refer to the group. Curiously, this practice—which, under other circumstances, might be dismissed as a simple linguistic slip—continues in a November 1901 article written by the lone male student, Bernardo de la Rionda, who feminizes himself through his relation to the female teachers. In his account of the Cuban teachers' excursion to the countryside, he writes:

> The beautiful Miss Peligero, Editor-in-Chief of the Sección Cubana, has sentenced me to the harsh punishment of writing this note, a punishment that I deem unreasonable for my crime of being the only Cuban man to have blissfully left behind the happy sensations of his modest home to come and contemplate how the precocious [*pre coz*] and fecund intelligence of the Cuban woman grows in this land of wonders [*esta tierra de grandezas llena*], where education is worshiped. But, obsequious to the dictates of Beauty, I am pleased to obey, even though it is impossible for me to paint the picture that I am asked in all the splendid tones of its true colors. (27)[54]

On the one hand, the passage can be read as a suggestive wink at the reader regarding the male Cuban writer's seemingly privileged experience alone in the New York countryside with his beautiful female compatriots. However, de la Rionda does not refer to the Cuban *maestras* simply as beautiful but as "intelligent" and "fecund." This odd turn of phrase suggests that, under Armstrong's guidance, the teachers have ceased to be the children as which Cubans are figured in *Juanita* and other imperial texts and are poised to become teacher-mothers to the nation.

Cuban masculinity, however, does not fare as well in de la Rionda's article. In a reversal of traditional gender dynamics, de la Rionda self-effacingly presents himself as subordinate to Srta. Peligero, who has imposed the "harsh punishment" of writing the article on him. Yet, while the "intelligent" and "fecund" female teachers are prepared for their future mission as mothers of the nation, de la Rionda is quick to mention his inadequacy to the journalistic task presented to him. The text thus links the intellectual precociousness of the Cuban women—figured as "fecundas," or sexually and intellectually mature, capable of reproducing and raising the nation—to the masculine anxiety of the inept Cuban male author, who, apparently one of the "tatterdemalions" whom Roosevelt criticizes, seems to lack the talents that he praises in his female counterparts. So unsettling is the female teachers' precociousness that, in the original document, the word "precoz" appears with a mistakenly placed space between the syllables "pre" and "coz," in part indicating that the term made the typesetter nervous and distracted, and in part—through the emphasis accidentally placed on the syllable "coz" (which, by itself, refers to a backward kick, as from a horse), suggesting the slap in the face to de la Rionda's traditional male privilege that the female teachers' precociousness represents.[55] Rather than being delighted with Cuban femininity, de la Rionda feels threatened in his own masculinity. Unable to "paint the picture that I am asked" (with all the phallic symbolism that painting implies), he is rendered impotent by the wonders that he sees.

Importantly, when, in the article, the teachers meet with (the somewhat ironically named) Mr. Smiley, an Uncle Sam–like school official, a female student is able to express her sentiments in "correcto Inglés" while de la Rionda must avail himself of his principal Srta. Armstrong's "faithful" and "capable" interpretation skills in order to make himself understood. Thus, not only does de la Rionda fret about losing the male privilege associated with traditional Hispano-colonial patriarchy, he registers anxiety about his ability to communicate with and incorporate himself into the new North American imperial patriarchy that Smiley embodies. This becomes apparent when the writer notes that he has left his "modest home" for "esta tierra de grandezas llena" (this land of wonders) (29). On the one hand, the contrast between the "modesty" of Cuba and the "wonders" of the United States suggests an attitude of colonial subservience. On the other, the archaic-sounding hyperbaton in the Spanish syntax ("esta tierra de grandezas llena") recalls the Golden Age of Spanish peninsular literature, or the New World *barroco de Indias,* a period associated with the Spanish imperial glory in the Americas that, in North American eyes, had decayed, justifying the transfer of Cuba to the burgeoning US empire.[56] This linguistic trace of Spanish colonial grandeur in the narration of the Cubans' meeting with Smiley frames de la Rionda's feelings of emasculation in an interimperial context. As in Roosevelt's *Rough Riders,* here, too, the supposed inferiority of "Latin" masculinity would appear to justify Cuban subordination to the United States.

This masculine rivalry between Cuba and the United States explains why, despite his inadequate English, it is de la Rionda—and not one of his more fluent female compatriots—who is chosen to address Mr. Smiley. In his speech, the male teacher gratefully recognizes the North American "as father of these . . . future teachers of their patria. This recognition, poor though it is, is a faithful reflection of what Cuba feels for the American Nation, which has granted her such valuable help in reaching her independence which, under her beneficent shadow, she hopes to see consolidated forever" (29).[57] Even as he assumes the traditional patriarchal role of spokesman for the Cuban national family—the "future teachers of their patria"—it is only so that he can cede that place to Smiley, now the "father" who will take the Cuban nation "beneficently" under his imperial "shadow." In this scene, then, the colonial creole patriarch, heir apparent to Villaverde's Leonardo Gamboa, hands control of the feminized Cuban nation over to the paternalistic US empire. In this rhetorical economy, de la Rionda's inability to perform the task in English is a sign of what Roosevelt and others had seen as the "uselessness" of the Cuban male and the traditional Hispanic order that he represents. Like the Cuban scouts of *The Rough Riders,* who run away as soon as the manly North American troops arrive, de la Rionda appears to bow out of history and signs the article not with his imposing aristocratic name, Bernardo de la Rionda, but simply "B. de la R.," erasing his colonial patriarchal identity behind a cloud of initials. In this article, as in Roosevelt's text, the Cuban nation, embodied by the women who will reproduce and raise it, once again finds itself under North American protection.

Yet, despite the imperial allegory that I have just narrated, it is obvious that de la Rionda, in all likelihood a member of the powerful, trinational Cuban-Spanish–North American family of sugar barons with multiple mills and close ties to US capital by the same name, is a willing actor in the allegorical transfer of power that he describes.[58] So, too, is Borrero Echeverría, who enthusiastically supported plans to send Cuban teachers to the United States. As in the case of Sarmiento, who cited the United States as a model for innovations of his own invention, Cuban creoles of the intervention period worked simultaneously with and against the United States in order to forge their own version of bourgeois-republican modernity—or, at least, to define their own place within the racial-imperial dynamics governing the island's geopolitical relations. This new system would give rise to a hybrid—and, perhaps, morally unsatisfactory—form of republican modernity.

The Hombre Nuevo *as a New Woman in Cuba*

At the same time that de la Rionda seemed to cede his patriarchal rights over the future mothers of the Cuban nation to the hypermasculine forces of US imperialism, certain Cuban female teachers were asserting their rights as Cuban women through the bourgeois individualism that they were absorbing during their sojourn in the northern metropole. An anonymous article entitled "Nuestros deberes como futuras maestras de Cuba" (Our duties as future teachers of Cuba) from the inaugural October 1901 edition of the Spanish-language "Sección Cubana" of the *Normal Review* embodies "the confrontation between colonial values and customs and the political and cultural representations sponsored by the interventionist authorities" affecting "the entire symbology of daily existence" (Iglesias Utset 15).[59] The piece argues that Cuban teachers at New Paltz should

> try to make the most of the short time we have for our instruction here, attempt to investigate, observe, and profit from the advances and advantages that that instruction enjoys, so that we later may put them into perfect practice in our country; and, at the same time, instruct ourselves and prepare ourselves for the difficult task that teaching holds for us. We should watch our behavior so that no one may justly find fault in us, as here we represent, first, our own dignity; secondly, that of our family names [*apellidos*] and of our parents; and thirdly, dear friends, that of our countrywomen, that of the women of Cuba, that of the teachers of Cuba—in a word, that of the Cuban people.
>
> We must show this country that we know how to manage the representation of all these dignities. This is my wish and I think that it should be that of any woman who holds herself to be a true Cuban. (16–17)[60]

The notion of the teachers' "dignity" expressed here clearly echoes traditional Hispanic notions of the *mujer honrada* (honorable woman). This echo is rendered all the louder by the reference to "our family names," a blood pride that Spanish essayist Julio Caro Baroja associates with traditional Hispanic culture and that French theorist Michel Foucault would see as distinctly feudal-aristocratic. Tellingly, however, the writer frames her discourse in terms of "dignidad" and not "honradez." The cultural logic of "honor" historically is associated with the "social hierarchies of the ancien régime, . . . consequently implicated with inequality and exclusion, as the necessary condition for [the hierarchy's existence] is that not all have access to it." Dignity, on the other hand, is "universal and egalitarian, belonging to democratic societies [and] includes everyone," part of a cultural modernity that the Spanish colonial state often resisted (Figueiredo 190).[61]

Thus, in the case of the Cuban maestras, the transition from honor to dignity represents a movement away from Spanish cultural norms and toward US modes of self-identification. While the Hispano-feudal tradition of "honradez" is, according to Caro Baroja, associated with the collective blood pride enjoyed, for example, by Villaverde's Gamboa family, "another factor will lend a new dimension to the notion of recognition that emerges with democracy. The particular conception of identity that emerges at the end of the eighteenth century sees identity as individual and particular" (Figueiredo 190).[62] The way in which teachers are to demonstrate their "dignidad" by dedicating themselves to their work—"striving" to "prepare themselves" for "the difficult task" of raising and educating the future republican citizens—suggests that the writer is articulating her identity as an individual in terms of the conception of self-realization through personal effort and hard work born, according to Max Weber, of Protestantism and capitalism. Leaving home unchaperoned to travel to the United States in the hope of integrating herself into the workforce as a teacher of North American republican values, the anonymous writer participates in the public sphere with an economic and political agency prohibited to privileged-class Cuban women at the time. She engages the world not as an honorable member of her family but as an autonomous bourgeois subject, focused on "first, our own dignity"—that of the maestras as individuals.

Paradoxically, much as she asserts her bourgeois individuality, the author does not sign her name to the article, instead interpellating herself through the group identity of "nosotras," the feminine form of the Spanish word for "we." The individual "dignidad" mentioned in the piece is collective, belonging not only to the teachers themselves but also to their "parents," their "apellidos" (family names) and, ultimately, to the "mujer cubana" and the "pueblo cubano" that she represents in the inter-American metaphoric economy in which the author, like Roosevelt and de la Rionda, participates. Thus, the dignified actions that these "mujeres cubanas" undertake as bourgeois individuals also must be read as signs of Cuba's individuality—that is, its sovereignty, which was being disputed between Havana and Washington at the same time that the article was published. This imperial context becomes apparent in the article when the writer calls upon her compatriots to "show [the United States] that we know how to manage the representation of all these dignities" of which imperial discourse had cast them as incapable.

Not coincidentally, the notion of dignity—or being a "mujer honrada"—to which the anonymous author appeals was coded as white in both the US and Latin American cultural spheres of the time, as historians such as Elizabeth Dore (11) and Peter Wade (154) have pointed out and as the concern expressed by creole reformers over Afro-Cubans' moral capacity for responsible, productive citizenship discussed earlier in this chapter demonstrates. This construction of blacks as lacking in "dignidad" is apparent in a December 15, 1888, article in *Minerva,* in which the author complains that, for four centuries, Afro-Cuban women such as Villaverde's Cecilia Valdés have been "object of the whims, the diversion, the plaything of . . . treacherous and cruel men" (Cecilia). The hour has come, she writes, for Afro-Cuban women to lift "our heads indignantly [*indignadas*] and make titanic efforts to reconquer the dignity that I beg Heaven to concede to *all* our sisters."[63] She exhorts Afro-Cuban women—*indignadas* as a result of their status as enslaved and lower-class and popular perceptions of their sexual availability—to "reconquer" their "dignity" through participation in bourgeois publications such as *Minerva.* Importantly, the author signs her article with the pseudonym "Cecilia," even though her real name, Úrsula Coimbra de Valverde, and portrait appear on the edition's title page. Both obvious and deliberate, the pen name links the voice in the article to the heroine of Villaverde's famous novel, published just seven years earlier. In this way, the author reclaims for Afro-Cuban women the "dignidad" racialized as white that Villaverde's protagonist, racialized as *de color,* is denied by articulating "a vision of womanhood in which women of African descent merited respect" (Brunson 484).

This denial of "dignidad" to Afro-Cuban women had become a central trope of Cuban nationalist writing, which—from Félix Tanco y Bosmeniel's "Petrona y Rosalía" (1838) to Anselmo Suárez y Romero's *Francisco* (1880) to Martín Morúa Delgado's *Sofía* (1891), in addition to Villaverde's *Cecilia Valdés*—routinely had allegorized the country as a mixed-race, lower-caste woman sexually abused by a scion of the Spanish colonial patriarchy.[64] These Gothically unpalatable national narratives mobilize traditional gender constructs to ask under what the circumstances Afro-Cuban mothers such as Petrona, Dorotea, Cecilia, or Sofía—outraged by the racial brutality of Spanish colonialism—could rear a stable republican citizenry. In all likelihood a creole, the anonymous author of the *Register* article, by presenting the view of the "dignidad de la mujer cubana" as residing in the adoption of a bourgeois discipline readily available only to whites, revises the ethnic and gender terms of nineteenth-century Cuban nationalist thought. Influenced by the new role demanded of women by liberal reformers such as the Manns, Sarmiento, and their followers at New Paltz, the writer rejects the racialized debasement of Cuban women implicit in the older nationalist model. Instead, she accepts—however begrudgingly—the imperial romance laid out by Mary Mann, who had been so instrumental in the early careers of the teachers at the Annex, by looking to the United States for the education of Cuba's future citizens, suddenly rescripted as white and bourgeois, following the "dignified" condition of their maternal teachers.[65] In this revised national narrative, the Gamboas, Villaverde's debauched creole patriarchs, have been replaced after de la Rionda's surrender by Mr. Smiley, who arranges an Anglo-Saxon imperial educación for Cecilia's offspring, who have been repainted as white by the anonymous maestra's discourse.

This discursive lightening of Cecilia's daughters, the Cuban teachers, in the anonymous article comes at a moment when US imperialists such as Mary Mann, Theodore Roosevelt, and the occupying military government were pointing to the Latin island's mixed-race heritage as a sign of unfitness for self-rule.[66] Thus, even as they inscribe themselves racially as docile creole pupils within Mary Mann's model of imperial educación, the New Paltz students' representation of Cuban women in terms of dignified whiteness serves as a tacit rejection of their subordinate place in North American racial-imperialist discourse. However problematically, by disavowing their discursive blackness and insisting on a "dignity" associated with whiteness, the maestras cubanas refuse to be "Pygmies" (in Silvestre de Feliu's terminology) and instead represent themselves as white women, the racial equals of their Anglo-American protectors.

It is no surprise, then, that these "white" Cuban women should behave as their supposedly more emancipated North American counterparts do. Unlike the Cuban women "rescued" by the Rough Riders, the article's anonymous writer actively participates in the building of the new, post-Spanish Cuba, much like the real-life mambisas whom Roosevelt has written out of existence. In this way, she uses her status as colonial apprentice in the metropole to penetrate a public sphere from which both Cuban nationalist and US colonialist discourses had marginalized her. Her adoption of Anglo-American gender roles thus signifies more than simple submission to US imperial paradigms. As historian Kristin Hoganson explains, "manly" Anglo-Saxons such as Roosevelt were inspired to invade Cuba "because they feared that chivalric standards were endangered within the United States," largely as a result of the gradual entrance of North American women into public life. "Many of those who fretted about a decline in chivalry regarded the assertive New Woman" populating turn-of-the-century North American cities "as evidence of that decline, for at the heart of chivalry was the juxtaposition of feminine vulnerability and masculine power" (45).

> Those who spoke of national struggle and national survival generally believed that these depended on powerful men who did not shirk arduous challenges and domestic women who dedicated themselves to raising the next generation of vigorous heroes. To Darwinian theorists, new gender arrangements prompted fears about Americans' evolutionary fitness. . . . When bicycle-riding, bloomer-wearing, college-educated, job-holding New Women refused to serve as foils to traditional masculinity, conservative men began to fret about the future of the 'American race' and, beyond that, about their place in it. (12)

To North American men feeling threatened by changing gender paradigms in their own country, Cuban women such as Roosevelt's displaced war victims seemed "to be perfect feminine foils for assertive American women" (46). An article in the *New York Times,* for example, marveled that "the 'New Woman' is altogether unknown in Havana. There is not even a woman's club there. In fact, in this regard the city is actually medieval" (qtd. in Hoganson 46).

Breaking with this romantic image, the Cuban teachers would travel to the United States in order to learn how to be modern, bourgeois-republican mothers of their nation's future citizens. Indeed, in the years following the US occupation, Cubans would apply the term "new woman" (in English) to "emancipated ladies and young women" who "work 'in the street' as typewriters in offices or nurses in hospitals," menacing the male egos of both Cuban and North American patriarchs as they went about their newfound business (Iglesias Utset 14).[67] Much like the male anti-Spanish *filibustero* writers studied by Rodrigo Lazo, by exercising masculine agency (ironically, as a new woman), the Cuban teacher in the *Register* article protagonically seizes republican citizen agency—scripted by Roosevelt and others as white and male against a foil of racialized "tatterdemalions"—and subverts discursive paradigms of colonial submission (*Writing*).[68] Thus, not only does she reject the notion of the country's to-be-conquered-ness by breaking with the traditional representation of Cuba as an exploitable *mulata* and painting Cuban women as white, she attempts to conquer the male power that Roosevelt had associated with Anglo-Saxon virility for Cuban women, thereby undoing the racial and gender allegories used to justify US colonialism in Cuba.[69]

In its morally ambiguous project of using US gender paradigms to mobilize the teachers' white-creole privilege against the discursive encroachments of US imperialism, the anonymous normalist's article prefigures much of the racial tension that would characterize the early twentieth-century Cuban protectorate: a country that—as scholars such as Aline Helg, Alejandra Bronfman, and Gillian McGillivray, among others, have demonstrated—adopted republican electoral politics while outlawing race-based political parties and encouraged European immigration while suppressing Afro-Cuban cultural practices, a country that would build a nationalistic bourgeoisie through a dependent, semifeudal economic system as it sought sovereignty and acceptance on the world stage. Meanwhile, the participation of the returning maestras de Sarmiento in the New Paltz project demonstrates the importance of the local crisis over Cuban sovereignty to the hemispheric movement toward racialized republican maternity that I have been describing throughout this book. The particularly neocolonial form of bourgeois republicanism that these teachers would seek to inaugurate implied a reconsideration of gender roles in Latin America, as the maestras de Sarmiento and their Cuban apprentices at New Paltz pushed women farther into the public sphere by scripting the formerly private activities of childbearing and childrearing as nationalist questions of racial survival. Yet, at the same time that, as bourgeois-republican teacher-mothers, some Latin American women—ironically, through their female biological sex and feminine social gender characteristics—entered the masculine territory of public life, Latin American territory became discursively feminized as a result of penetration by a US military represented in hypermasculine terms by figures such as Roosevelt. In literature, this rescripting of gender roles would have a profound impact on the traditional foundational romance genre which, not coincidentally, would decline at about the same time that the Stars and Stripes rose over Cuba. Indeed, the United States would become an obligatory reference for Cuban nationalist texts in the following century, often presented as an imperial antagonist that the racialized and neocolonial Cuban nation must combat in order to regain masculine agency. This can be seen in postrevolutionary works such as Che Guevara's *El socialismo y el hombre en Cuba* (1965), Roberto Fernández Retamar's *Calibán* (1971), and Alejo Carpentier's *Consagración de la primavera* (*The Rite of Spring*) (1978). Through the imperial educación of republican teacher-mothers in Cuba, the racialized allegory of the national family eventually gave way to the racialized allegory of the transnational family.

Conclusion

THIS BOOK has considered how creole neocolonialism and US imperialism became entangled through the figure of the racialized republican teacher-mother in the nineteenth-century Americas. North American James Fennimore Cooper's *Last of the Mohicans* inaugurated a hemispheric tradition of foundational romances condemning mulat(t)a maternity, of which Cuban Cirilo Villaverde's *Cecilia Valdés* is among the most famous. Meanwhile, convinced that Afro-descended mixed-race women such as Cooper's Cora and Villaverde's Cecilia could not raise proper bourgeois-republican citizens, a group of New England women teaching freedmen in the US South became part of an inter-American circulation of teaching personnel that would help to draw the racial contours of the Argentine and Cuban nation-states in a Western Hemisphere increasingly under US domination.

While this book has concentrated on foundational discourses in literature and education during the nineteenth century, it is important to recognize that the racialized trope of republican motherhood would have a long and varied life in New World nationalist rhetoric. Long viewed as a rupture with the creole-centric nation building found in the earlier works that I have discussed here, later Latin American mestizo-nationalist texts would attempt to complicate the discursive whitening projects of Cooper, Sarmiento, Mansilla de García, Howard, and Villaverde by locating mothers of color at the beginning of national narratives. This racially resemanticized republican mother trope surfaced in José Martí's 1891 defense of the national mother dressed in "an Indian smock," Mexican thinker José Vasconcelos's disquieting interest in racialized reproduction in his 1925 "Raza cósmica," and essayist Octavio Paz's casting of modern-day Mexicans as "children of Malinche" in his 1950 *Laberinto de la soledad* (*Labyrinth of Solitude*). In Chile, some critics have argued, Nobel laureate Gabriela Mistral came to represent a queer mestiza mother for the nation—one who had pursued a career in teaching, no less (Fiol-Matta).

As I discuss in chapter 4, this reracialization of the republican mother trope, too, has been criticized as exclusionary. Disappearing nonwhite mothers into homogenizing nationalist metanarratives by discursively transforming them into the ancestors of the modern-day mestizo middle classes, mestizaje has been decried as a technology for invisiblizing and controlling present-day populations of color. Argentina is a particularly potent example of this process of whitening through mestizaje—precisely because the country is not strongly associated with populations of color in the popular imaginary. By disavowing nineteenth-century black intermarriage with immigrants in an act of selective historical amnesia, Argentine organic intellectuals fashioned a "white legend" of a European national genealogy that would forever exclude women of color from the national narrative, replacing the "negrita muy Federal" with a Lucía Miranda of conveniently downplayed "morisco" origin.[1]

At first glance, Brazil represents a counterdiscourse to the whitening paradigms found in other locations throughout the Americas. In 1926, Rio de Janeiro newspaper editor Candido Campos began a campaign to build statues throughout the country honoring the Mãe Preta (Black Mother), an archetype of the Afro-descended wet nurses and nannies who historically raised many white children in Brazil (Seigel 207). Reversing the condemnation of black wet nurses that characterized much of the hemisphere's nineteenth-century liberal discourse, the Mãe Preta movement represents black women as selfless nourishers of the white national family (211). Yet, as historian Micol Seigel points out, at the same time that it located the black maternal figure as the historical base of Brazilian national identity, the Mãe Preta campaign framed the black national mother as existing only in the past (211). Marked by a certain *saudade,* this discourse celebrated vanishing black childcare workers at a time that the profession increasingly was being occupied by European immigrants. In this way, like the maternal construction of mestizaje in Spanish America, the mythic Mãe Preta in Brazil bolstered early-twentieth-century triumphalist discourse on the country's supposedly inevitable cultural and racial whitening (212).[2]

The status of Afro-descended mothers would prove even more complex in Cuba. As a North American protectorate, the island would experience tensions between the racial entropy unleashed by the independence movement and the logic of apartheid carried into the country by the US Army. In her *Reyita, sencillamente: testimonio de una negra cubana nonagenaria* (translated into English by Anne McLean as *Reyita: The Life of a Black Cuban Woman in the Twentieth Century*), María de los Reyes Castillo Bueno explains how, following in the tradition of the nineteenth-century *escuelas de amigas*, she taught briefly at an informal neighborhood school, only to lose her position to the standardizing demands of the centralized system of public education established following the US intervention. Stripped of her post, Reyita would be forced to work as a hotel maid, conscripted into domestic labor by Cuba's early-twentieth-century postslavery economy. Later, she would marry a white Spaniard and give birth to mixed-race children who would comprise the first generation of revolutionary subjects. One, a sailor, would die in the 1960 explosion of *La Coubre*, which the text paints as a sacrifice of heroic Cuban youths to the forces of US imperialism. Meanwhile, her daughter, Daisy Rubiera Castillo, would become an organic intellectual, serving the revolutionary state as an anthropologist and transcribing her mother's oral narrative for publication.

The book presents a complex vision of Afro-Cuban maternity. By raising exemplary revolutionary subjects, Reyita, like the Brazilian Mãe Preta, is figured very clearly as mother of the nation in a way in which few Afro-descended women in the Americas have been. Yet, married to a Spaniard, she conceives her children through the same process of mestizaje that nationalist discourses throughout Latin American have mobilized as a means of whitening the nation. Perhaps the greatest complication, however, is the role of the Cuban revolution in the text. On the one hand, the revolution has opened up new opportunities for the Afro-Cuban working classes, as evidenced by daughter Daisy Rubiera's academic prominence, which creates the conditions of possibility for Reyita to tell her story and claim subjectivity for herself as a black woman within nationalist discourse ("una negra cubana," as she asserts in her book's title). On the other, as a government employee, Rubiera's participation in the production of the testimonial text necessarily directs Reyita's words through (still largely white) official channels. While it is neither realistic nor desirable to expect the text to espouse the embryonic bourgeois individualism found in the writings of the New Paltz *maestras*, a reader cannot ignore that Reyita's story—sincere though it may be—reproduces hegemonic narratives about the revolution ending racial exploitation in Cuba. As with José Martí's mother in an "Indian smock," Reyita's alterity (at least as far as literary production and reception are concerned) is not a self-justifying experience in and of itself but is subsumed into a larger discourse on interracial nation building.

Women of color would have an even more difficult time incorporating themselves into North American national narratives. In the US discursive sphere, mixed-race mothers proved unable to recover from Jefferson's expulsion of Sally Hemings from his republican family, emblematized by Cooper in the virginal death of the mulatta Cora at the end of *The Last of the Mohicans*. In the late twentieth century, Cora's revenant, the equally fictitious "welfare queen," would rise to haunt social policy debates as "an omnipresent icon of motherhood gone wrong, a nationally recognized media villain" (Douglas and Michaels 181). Importantly, the way in which the mythic welfare mother's motherhood "goes wrong" is racialized. "Particularly with regard to Black solo mothers, the misrepresented public image grows out of and contributes to the tendency to focus on that family style as deviant, amoral, or pathological," rhetoric that echoes the nineteenth-century liberal campaign against Afro-descended wet nurses discussed in chapter 1 (Geiger 249).

Political scientist Franklin D. Gilliam Jr. explains how the welfare mother came to be racialized as black in the popular imaginary:

> This narrative script skillfully locating the "intersection" of race and gender was given its most public voice by then-candidate Reagan on the 1976 campaign trail. During that election Reagan often cited the story of a woman from Chicago's South Side who was arrested for welfare fraud. . . . The implicit racial coding is readily apparent. The woman Reagan was talking about was African-American. Veiled references to African-American women, and African-Americans in general, were equally transparent. In other words, while poor women of all races get blamed for their impoverished condition, African-American women commit the most egregious violations of American values. This story line taps into stereotypes about both women (uncontrolled sexuality) and African-Americans (laziness).

For the United States of the 1970s and '80s, the racialized "welfare mother" became an embodiment of the degenerate values that historically marginalized subjects were thought to pass on to their children. This tropological specter supposedly menaced a traditional bourgeois-republican "American way of life" that already was teetering in the aftermath of the civil rights movement, the forced confrontation with the reality of imperialism represented by military debacle in Vietnam, and the oil crisis. Legal dependents of "the system," socially abject Afro-descended welfare mothers and their children were members of the national family in a way that proved threatening to the bourgeois republic's self-image.

The popular connection between "welfare mothers" and African American women to which Gillman points is particularly troubling in light of the fact that Linda Taylor, the historical basis for the myth of the welfare queen, was, by all accounts, "a racial Rorschach test" (Levin, "Welfare Queen"). A United Press International article describes Taylor's ambiguous phenotype by stating that "her skin is sallow—like a medium yellow—and she has no features that make her peculiar to any racial background. She can pass as Filipino. She puts on a black wig and becomes a Negro, and with other makeup and wigs, she passes for white" (qtd. in Levin, *Queen* 40). Meanwhile, a December 1974 story in the Gannett News Service describes her as "either black, white, or Latin, a native of the U.S., Haiti, England, or South Africa" (qtd. in Levin, *Queen* 55). While, as journalist Josh Levin explains in his recent book on Taylor, she probably was biracial, born of an extramarital relationship between a white woman and a black man in 1920s Tennessee, this fact—a well-held secret—was not evident from her appearance, as the newspaper articles that I have just referenced demonstrate.

Importantly, while Reagan never refers explicitly to Taylor as black, he locates her geographically in the racially coded "South Side of Chicago," implying a racial identity that he had no way of confirming but that spectators watching images of her trial on the nightly news had no trouble accepting. This points to the way in which visions of acceptable and unacceptable forms of motherhood had become color-coded in the North American petit bourgeois imaginary. "Reagan implied that Taylor was a stand-in for a whole class of people who were getting something they didn't deserve" (Levin, *Queen* x), as though her "mere existence gave credence to a slew of pernicious stereotypes about poor people and black women. If one welfare queen walked the earth, then surely others did, too" (152).

Media studies scholars Susan Douglas and Meredith Michaels note that the rise of the racialized welfare mother myth is contemporaneous with the "new traditionalist movement" in the United States (188). Promoted by magazines such as *Good Housekeeping* and the phenotypically Anglo-Saxon pop cultural icon Martha Stewart, new traditionalism sought a return to domesticity for middle-class white women in the years following the race- and gender-based social movements of the 1970s.[3] Thus, at the same moment that the media (however regressively) focused on white women's traditional gender role of raising good republican citizens, they also, through the opposite myth of the welfare queen, suggested the supposed inadequacy of women of color for that task. Racializing proper and improper ways to raise children much as nineteenth-century liberal elites throughout the Americas had, late-twentieth-century North American media suggested that "only white, middle-class women could wear the halo of the Madonna and transform the world through their moral influence and social housekeeping" (O'Reilly 5). Like Cora Munro and Cecilia Valdés, lower-class mothers of color were asked by this discourse to remove themselves and their children from the national narrative.

And not just the narrative. The welfare mother/new traditionalist binary took shape near the seeming end of the United States' long but often silent eugenics movement. Women of color, particularly those receiving public assistance, were especially "targeted . . . for compulsory sterilization" (Levin, *Queen* 47); as late as the 1990s, Louisiana state legislator and former Ku Klux Klan leader David Duke "suggested that women on welfare be paid to get birth control implants" (327). Angela Davis reports that, by 1970, "20 percent of all married Black women ha[d] been permanently sterilized. Approximately the same percentage of Chicana women had been rendered surgically infertile. Moreover, 43 percent of the women sterilized through federally subsidized programs were Black" (219). In 1972 alone, the federal government had funded between 100,000 and 200,000 sterilizations (218) and, "by 1976 some 24 percent of all [American] Indian women of childbearing age had been sterilized" (218). Puerto Rican women, however, hold the record for the highest rate of forced sterilization in the world: some 33 percent of the island's female population by the 1970s.[4]

It thus seems that, at some point, US elites ceased to be content with Cooper's allegorical expulsion of the mulatta Cora from his foundational romance and turned to more material methods of preventing women of color from reproducing the imperially expanding national family. Susan Sheehan's feature article "A Welfare Mother," published in the September 29, 1975, edition of the *New Yorker,* overtly links race and certain stigmatized forms of female gender performance to maternal unfitness and US empire through the figure of the New York Puerto Rican "Carmen Santana (fictitious name), a welfare mother" (42). Here, the "fictitious name" draws attention to Sheehan's racialized gender biases. Noticeably Hispanic, the surname "Santana" resembles both the English word "Satan" and its Spanish cognate "Satanás," marking the character as an underworldly social undesirable. Meanwhile, the first name "Carmen" recalls the eponymous protagonist of Prosper Mérimée's 1845 novella and Georges Bizet's 1875 opera, a canonical figuration of the supposedly undisciplined sexuality of the "Latin" female. This imperative to understand Santana in racial terms becomes clear when, on the second of forty-two pages, Sheehan pauses to point out that her subject has inherited her grandmother's "dark eyes, wide nose, mulatto complexion, curly black hair, thick lips, broad face, and prominent cheekbones" (44). "Welfare mother" Carmen Santana appears as a sort of Nuyorican Cecilia Valdés, daughter and granddaughter of degenerate mulatas and unable to reproduce an acceptable bourgeois republic, as evidenced by her own granddaughter's "bilingual vocabulary of four-letter words and her ferocious knack for biting other children" (74).

Like her nineteenth-century forbears in Argentina and Cuba, the Afro-Latina Carmen is subordinated as a mother to an imperial United States. Throughout the article, seemingly well-meaning Anglo social workers, like the teachers in Sarmiento's Argentina and occupation-era New Paltz, attempt to correct Santana's maternal failings. (Significant attention is paid, for example, to the proper way to use baking soda to clean a refrigerator.) However, despite these efforts, the situation appears irredeemable, largely because of Carmen Santana's telling "failure to get her children to school regularly" (Sheehan 55) or provide them with a proper educación. "When he was fifteen and in the seventh grade," son Felipe "dropped out of school, and soon became addicted to heroin" while his brother Vicente "is now in the seventh grade—he has failed a year—and may well drop out of school before the year is over." Most damning, however, is her ironically (and also "fictitiously") named daughter "Inocencia," who, like Cecilia Valdés, has followed her mother's path and "dropped out of the seventh grade in October of 1971, when she was thirteen and was three months pregnant with her first child" (55). Sheehan leaves no doubt as to the negative effects that this cycle of poor educación will have on the nation; another son, Rafael, is in trouble after having gone absent without leave from the army (64). Showing the racialized "welfare mother" to be a transgenerational financial burden and threat to the security of US empire, Sheehan suggests that bourgeois-republican motherhood should not be left to women of color.

The Santana anecdote, like the comments on race and "welfare queens" that frame it, is in many ways a story already known to academics and activists. However, situating it at the end of a discussion of racialized republican motherhood elucidates the relevance of nineteenth-century discourses to contemporary conversations.[5] An inter-American flashpoint, the Carmen Santana anecdote draws attention to two common-sense narratives about New World bourgeois republicanism that *Imperial Educación*'s focus on the entanglements of nationalist and transnational discourses interrogates: (1) that the bourgeois republic, in its ideal form, represents the most inclusive system of social organization possible and (2) that nationalism and imperialism are antithetical to one another.

By echoing nineteenth-century discourses on mothers of color in the early post-Fordist era, Sheehan's article problematizes the wide belief that the race-based exclusions that characterize North American history are discrete events occurring in a distant past, mere detours on the triumphal march of bourgeois republicanism toward an egalitarian millennium. This reading of US history—the one that most contemporary readers will have absorbed in high school—holds that the original sins of Amerindian genocide and African chattel slavery are isolated errors that, once corrected through civil rights legislation, will in no way detract from the greatness of "the greatest country in the world." Now that DNA testing has proven that Sally Heming's descendants are, indeed, members of the national family, we can nod our self-satisfied heads and assert comfortably that all lives really do matter without worrying about how the Hemmings might inherit from Jefferson. If the discourse surrounding "welfare mothers" seems rhizomatically reminiscent of attempts to racialize the national line of descent by Cooper, Sarmiento, Mansilla, Howard, Mann, Villaverde, Borrero Echeverría, or Wood, that (all right-thinking people concur) is more coincidental than constitutive. Taking the nation as its "natural" limits, this logic insists that New World bourgeois republicanism is not predicated on racial exclusion (i.e., that it could somehow be tweaked to be made inclusive), even if the similarities among the experiences of countries as different as the United States, Argentina, and Cuba strongly suggest the inherence of racial marginalization to the model that they all adopt.

The early ideologues of New World bourgeois republicanism were less sanguine about the Americas' potential for meaningful racial democracy than many of us are today. At the funeral for Cora and the indigenous Uncas in Cooper's foundational *Last of the Mohicans*, Munro, moved by the mourning cries of the Amerindian women in attendance, instructs the multilingual white frontiersman Hawkeye to tell them that "the Being we all worship, under different names, will be mindful of their charity," and "the time shall not be distant, when we may assemble around his throne, without distinction of sex, or rank, or colour!" Hawkeye counters that "to tell them this . . . would be to tell them that the snows come not in the winter, or that the sun shines fiercest when the trees are stripped of their leaves!" (340). Founded on the colonial expropriation of indigenous land and African labor—as the very funeral scene in which the conversation takes place allegorizes—New World society, Hawkeye asserts, cannot produce inclusive republics.

To take Hawkeye's comment seriously is to invite an uncomfortable series of questions: What does it mean that our current political and economic institutions do not exist in spite of historic racial crimes but, rather, because of them? By this I mean, without their wealth in Amerindian land and African labor, how could the republican bourgeoisies of the United States, Argentina, and Cuba have developed? What would have become of Jacksonian democracy, in which an abundance of cheap land led to the removal of property requirements for suffrage, had the purchases of Louisiana and Florida and, later, the Mexican Cession not opened indigenous territories to white settlement and black bondage? And how did the gobbling of those "inferior" Latin regions by Anglo-Saxon bourgeois republicanism affect racial hierarchies in other parts of the Americas? Does the bourgeois-republican model allow for racial democracy in the colonies turned nation-states that populate the map of the Western Hemisphere? That is, can Lucía Miranda and Cecilia Valdés ever be mothers of mixed-race republics, or do their stories just reinforce the metanarrative of coloniality?

I suspect that many readers will wish to salvage as much as possible of the bourgeois-republican project and end this book on an optimistic note. I want to offer some resistance (if not necessarily outright rejection) to the narrative opiate of the happy ending, however. At first glance, nineteenth-century Haiti seems the most obvious example of a New World nation-state model that does not rely on creole hegemony. The country, after all, had no considerable population of native-born whites, offered automatic citizenship to any Afro-descendant arriving on its shores, and declared all citizens to be legally black in its 1805 constitution.[6] Indeed, derived from the French word for "white," the Haitian Kreyòl term *blan* means "foreigner," a semantic shift that would seem to dislodge whiteness from the hegemonic space that it occupies in the rest of the hemisphere. Yet, at the same time, as discussed in chapter 1, a Francophile *mulâtre* elite exerted a heavy influence on Haitian national life for much of the nineteenth century. Their Euro-leaning worldview would be embodied in the figure of the white republican mother in Émeric Bergeaud's 1859 novel *Stella*.

Does anything, then, really undermine the structural whiteness of bourgeois-republican national families in the nineteenth-century New

World nation-states? Was the paradigm's hegemony really a teleological given, as we tend to narrate it in the early twenty-first century? In addition to the monarchical models that flourished briefly in Haiti, Mexico, and Brazil, the extreme federative system that dominated the Southern Cone until the consolidation of the Argentine nation-state stands out as a possibility ultimately discarded by history. José Gervasio Artigas, a *Federal* normally credited as the founder of modern-day Uruguay, abolished slavery in the country and instituted land redistribution (Rock 91), in this way building interclass and interracial support among the enslaved, free blacks, and poor whites (Andrews, *Afro-Latin America* 15). Fears that Artigas's democratic reforms would inspire slave revolt led the Portuguese empire to invade from Brazil in 1816 (Rock 92) and, in retaliation against Artigas's radicalism, local *hacendados* sided with the invading army (Andrews, *Afro-Latin America* 15). Clearly, the bourgeois-republican nation-state was anything but the operative frame of reference to which these actors looked.

In the Argentine Confederation, meanwhile, Federales under President José Justo Urquiza (1854–60) organized racially integrated public schools resistant to European influences (Puiggrós, *Qué pasó*, 25–38; Solari 123). As early as 1829, the Federal government of Córdoba had made special provisions for the education of mixed-race *pardos* (Solari 96), ordering that they be instructed in grammar, drawing, and mathematics by the same teachers who taught white students. The government also set aside two scholarships for secondary education for students of color (J. Paz 105–6). Meanwhile, in the provincial city of Juyjuy, a group of Catholic priests, traditional defenders of Federalism, founded a teacher-training college for girls in 1858 (Solari 127).[7] Does this mean that the Federales were the true proponents of a radically democratic gender and racial order of the New World nineteenth century? Given their defense of the patriarchal world of the cattle *estancia* and the endurance of slavery throughout the Rosas dictatorship, it hardly seems so, yet it appears that their political-economic models opened the door to other forms of association that liberalism closed off.

In the extended Caribbean, Martin Delany's 1859 *Blake, or the Huts of America*, too, presents a radical alternative to the creole models of political association based in the nation-state championed by the hemisphere's bourgeois-republican elites during the 1800s. An African American counterdiscourse to Harriet Beecher Stowe's 1852 *Uncle Tom's Cabin*, Delany's novel rejects the images of black passivity for which the classic abolitionist text is known. The plot instead involves an Afro-descended

West Indian man who is wrongfully enslaved in the US South and eventually travels to Cuba, where he becomes involved in "a bold design to wrest from Spain the Island of Cuba, and instead of a Castilian, establish a Negro government" (270). The main character's travels through the circum-Caribbean provide him with a broader field for exercising agency than does the setting of Stowe's novel, in which Uncle Tom's boundedness to the plantations of the South becomes a sign of his inability to act of his own volition. Other characters in Stowe's text do, of course, travel to Canada and Liberia, but they have limited interactions with the people there. Delany's novel, on the other hand, imagines a transnational alliance among the enslaved in the US South and Spanish Caribbean (two of the final three sites of legalized African chattel slavery in the Americas). The characters thus bypass the New World political structures in existence at the time, which had limited their agency by scripting them as noncitizens, as people unable to defend their natural rights for themselves, as Stowe's novel infamously makes clear. For cultural studies scholar José Buscaglia-Salgado, "a project for a Caribbean federation . . . was the mulatto alternative" to the hegemonic creole-nationalist paradigms of the nineteenth century, which were marked by the "persistence of colonial institutions of racial differentiation," as Afro-Cuban Martín Morúa Delgado's 1891 *Sofía* points out (xxii–xxiv). Yet, like the thousands of slave revolts and maroon colonies that ride the undercurrent of New World history, the "mulatto alternative," to quote Raúl Coronado, ultimately represented "a world not to come," a possible past that never came to pass. Perhaps inevitably, then, *Blake* fell prey to a more extreme version of *Cecilia Valdés*'s fate, and the novel was never finished, its serial publication suddenly discontinued.

Throughout this book, I have considered how the entanglement of creole neocolonialism with US imperialism impacted the racial-political projects that emerged in the Americas throughout the 1800s. That idea subverts another narrative: that of the seeming success of US bourgeois-republicanism as an isolated exception in a Western Hemisphere otherwise characterized by creole corruption. Much as Susan Sheehan, in the forty-two pages of her exposé, fails to mention that Santana's visaless migration to New York and seemingly unrestricted ability to access federal welfare benefits are the results of North American colonialism in Puerto Rico, common sense casts the seemingly divergent fates (and, believing in the self-congratulatory narrative of the triumphal march to equality, one would not question how divergent they really are) of bourgeois republicanism in the United States and Latin America as proof of Anglo virtue (Roosevelt's "manliness") and Latin vice (oh, those "tatterdemalions"!). It is this superiority of the US natural aristocracy that draws racial degenerates such as Santana to the northern country's shores as they attempt to escape colonial haciendas established by marauding Spanish priests and their creole-aristocratic acolytes in the throes of a gold fever far more delirious than the one that led Anglo settlers into newly "acquired" California in 1849, we are told. The histories of the United States and Latin America are thought of as thoroughly disentangled from one another. Reflective of geographically, political-economically, and—most importantly—racially isolated realities, they are best studied as separate academic specializations having nothing to say to one another.

This attitude reinforces the view that Latin American neocolonialism represents the revisiting of the Iberian parents' colonial sins on their New World children, nothing more. It is inconceivable that the debauched Latin feudocrats might alternately react to, against, or in conjunction with US imperialism, as I have argued that the nineteenth-century Argentine and Cuban elites did (perhaps not without a certain degree of self-interest). Bourgeois republicanism is not racially imperialist, and the proof is that Anglo-American empire is racially superior, this story goes. Yet, Sarmiento's comments on the Mexican Cession, like the concerns of Borrero Echeverría and other Cuban educationalists regarding how the United States viewed the island's racialized masses, points to the imperial entanglements of racial republican projects throughout the hemisphere. In the scenario that I am describing, creole elites in Argentina and Cuba, concerned about preserving their own place in the social hierarchy in the face of US imperialism, mobilized public educación as a means of preventing their countries from suffering, like Carmen Santana and the Puerto Rican colony that she embodies, constant intervention by Anglo-Saxons unconvinced of their ability to raise a proper bourgeois-republican citizenry.

Would the creoles have erected racial hierarchies without the threat of US imperialism? The 1812 Constitución de Cádiz, which refused automatic citizenship to Afro-descendants, as well as the somewhat half-hearted antislavery of the Cuban del Monte group and the negative representations of Afro-descendants found in the works of the Argentine *Generación del 37* point to an autochthonous racism in nineteenth-century Latin America existing without northern intervention. Yet, by putting the national and transnational experiences into dialogue with one another, we can see that the particular policies adopted in Argentina and Cuba during the late 1800s and early 1900s, especially in the educational sphere, suggest that the specific shapes that those racial structures took responded to inter-American geopolitical concerns.

Here, too, one might ask what other possibilities there may have been besides the creole national projects that became hegemonic across the hemisphere. Much as, according to Buscaglia-Salgado, federation existed for a time as an alternative to the bourgeois-republican nation-state in its contemporary form, I want to consider how the diasporan frame might contest imperial logic with an-other model (*un modelo otro*) of transnational mobilization. The concept has enjoyed a broad currency in postcolonial studies of the Atlantic World in recent decades, theorized by Édouard Glissant and Paul Gilroy, among others. In literature, the theme is taken up in texts such as US-Afro-Panamanian Cubena's 1981 *Chombo* (a derogatory term for a person of Afro-Caribbean descent in Panama) and its 1991 sequel *Los nietos de Felicidad Dolores* (The grandchildren of Felicidad Dolores). These two novels explore Afro–New World identity beyond the nation-state construct by following the migration of a group of West Indian laborers to Panama during the construction of the canal and the subsequent denial of Panamanian citizenship to their descendants, who later would migrate to the United States and then back to Central America. In this way, they reveal the national and imperial forces structuring the lives of Central Americans of West Indian descent while at the same time presenting images of Afro-Panamanians exerting agency while maneuvering within those confines.

In many ways, the transnational frame represents an obvious paradigm for discussing the lived experience of Afro-descendants in the Americas, as "diasporas and the African diaspora principally are the quintessential transnational units, unevenly distributed and defined, shaped in opposition to nation-states and in contested collaborations across national lines" (Seigel xiii). Literary scholar Ifeoma Kiddoe Nwankwo, for her part, has written about the radical possibilities of black cosmopolitanism, noting that Afro-descendants in the nineteenth century were denied cosmopolitan subjectivity by an inter-American slavocratic intelligentsia concerned about the potential for transnational slave revolt embodied by the Haitian Revolution (10). Black cosmopolitanism thus is "born of the interstices and intersections between two mutually constitutive cosmopolitanisms— a hegemonic cosmopolitanism, exemplified by the material and psychological violence of imperialism and slavery . . . , and a cosmopolitanism that is rooted in a common knowledge and memory of that violence" (24). This theme of a radical cosmopolitan diasporan identity based in shared experience appears in Afro-Colombian Manuel Zapata Olivella's monumental *Changó, el gran putas* (1983). Translated into English by Johnathan Tittler as *Changó, the Biggest Badass*, the novel traces the history of black resistance to colonialism from sixteenth-century Yorubaland to the funeral of Malcolm X, articulating a notion of identity that refuses passive circumscription by any one continent, language, or class, much less any particular bourgeois-republican nation-state.

The intersection of diaspora and gender, too, has been the subject of multiple novels during the last two generations. In the United States, Gayle Jones's 1975 *Corregidora* follows the transnational journey of several generations of Afro-descended women in one family from Brazil to the United States in order to lay bare the ways in which national projects throughout the Americas have depended upon the abjection and exploitation of black women's bodies. Martinican writer Maryse Condé's 1986 *Moi, Tituba . . . sorcière noire de Salem* (*I, Tituba, Black Witch of Salem*) takes on a similar project as it traces the eponymous character's journey from Barbados to Massachusetts and back again with allusions to Africa and the Lusophone Americas. The difference between these works and the mestizaje texts mentioned above is noteworthy. Octavio Paz's Malinche is forever captive to the mestizo-nationalist cultural politics of the Mexican Partido de la Revolución Institucionalizada, while José Martí's mother in an "Indian smock" cannot escape being a pawn to Havana and Miami's dueling imaginings of the patria. Whatever else she is now free to do, Reyita cannot directly criticize the intersectional racism and sexism existing under the revolutionary state. Jones's and Condé's characters, however, challenge the traditional exclusion of women of color from New World national narratives—ironically, through a story that exceeds the limits of any one nation. Perhaps that is the point.[8]

An eye to the entanglements among the racial discourses emanating from and circulating through the United States, Argentina, and Cuba in the long nineteenth century reveals a transareal network of political, cultural, and human exchanges. Gaining colonial connotations as a result of the expansion of slavocracy into formerly Amerindian and "Latin" Louisiana and Florida, the foundational literary discourse of bourgeois-republican motherhood, racialized as Anglo-Saxon, inspired changes in educational policy in the settler-colonialist Argentine nation-state. Later, Cubans, hoping to avoid the political absorption suffered by other Latin territories peripheral to the United States, would seek to emulate Argentina's success in transmitting northern paradigms of bourgeois-republican motherhood to racialized masses. By including Argentina and educación among the entangled threads of inter-American cultural relations, this story expands the usual cast of characters of hemispheric studies, showing how often-overlooked actors such as mothers and other *educadores,* in addition to novelists and statesmen, helped to shape racial paradigms and imperial relations in the nineteenth-century Americas.

To state what I hope is obvious, this is not a happy story. Sarmiento's bourgeois Argentine republic, predicated on physical and cultural genocide on the one hand and foreign debt on the other, distributed its economic and political bounty most unevenly. The Cuban protectorate state would have trouble finding a place for Cecilia's children. As I revise this manuscript in the wake of the summer 2020 protests against police brutality (two generations after the Civil Rights movement), the fact that black (and Latinx and Native and Asian and queer and the list goes on) lives matter is proving a revelation to many in the United States (probably not for the last time). What I do want to show is that these historical exclusions are part of the deep structure of New World society and not solely the result of misguided actions on the part of evil elites. They stem from the inherent paradox of the postindependence Americas: that, due to the expropriation of Native lands and African labor upon which it depends and the entanglements of Anglo-American economic, political, cultural, and social capital throughout the hemisphere, New World bourgeois republicanism always already exists within a racial-imperial context. What that fact means for us today and how we might best respond are topics that merit further exploration.

Notes

Preface

1. Throughout this book, I will use the term "republicanism" to refer to political systems in which public office is not hereditary but elective. Such a system is composed of citizens recognized as possessing inherent rights, as opposed to aristocrats enjoying inherited privileges. In the Americas, the construction of race as a system of social and political inclusion and exclusion complicates the republican rejection of heredity as the basis for conferral of sociopolitical agency.

2. Jefferson spoke or read English, Latin, Greek, French, Italian, Spanish, Anglo-Saxon, and some German (Monticello.org).

3. For a discussion of Jefferson's conflicting views on race, see Kendi, 79–158. For a fictional account of the lives of Hemings's and Jefferson's descendants, see William Wells Brown's *Clotel; or, the President's Daughter* (1853), widely considered to be the first Afro–North American novel.

4. For a more extensive discussion, see chapter 1 of this book. I use "New World" as a synonym for "the Americas" throughout this book, fully aware of the term's fraught history. While, obviously, no "world" is newer or older than any other and no one people ever "discovers" any other, the particular forms of racial coloniality that arose after October 12, 1492, were, indeed, new and distinctive, marking a turning point in the entangled histories of the Americas, Europe, and Africa. For more on the term "New World," see Greene, "Wanted," 339. On coloniality, see Quijano.

5. Throughout this monograph, I have preserved the original nineteenth-century orthography in English and Spanish when the editions that I consulted do so. Nineteenth-century Spanish spelling, in particular, differs markedly from contemporary Spanish in conventions governing the use of diacritical marks.

Introduction

1. "Colonizar el país con sus propios habitantes y, para tener colonos decentes, instruirlos en la niñez." I have standardized Rodríguez's atypical typography and punctuation. Unless otherwise indicated, the translations appearing in this monograph are my own.

2. "La ignorancia de los principios sociales es la causa de todos los males que el hombre se hace y hace a otros."

3. "El magisterio es una profesión, el que reemplaza a los padres de familia [y] ejerce las funciones de padre común." The Spanish word "padre," of course, can be translated as both "parent" and "father." Interested in the relationship between public education and republican motherhood, I have chosen to translate the term as the more inclusive English word "parent." I will discuss the maternalization of the teaching profession later in chapters 1, 3, and 5 of this book.

4. "El grado de ilustración y moralidad."

5. The *Diccionario* defines the verb *educar* as: "1. tr. Dirigir, encaminar, doctrinar; 2. tr. Desarrollar o perfeccionar las facultades intelectuales y morales del niño o del joven por medio de preceptos, ejercicios, ejemplos, etc. Educar la inteligencia, la voluntad; 3. tr. Desarrollar las fuerzas físicas por medio del ejercicio, haciéndolas más aptas para su fin; 4. tr. Perfeccionar o afinar los sentidos. Educar el gusto, el oído; 5. tr. Enseñar los buenos usos de urbanidad y cortesía" (1. v.t. Direct, orient, indoctrinate; 2. v.t. Develop or perfect the intellectual and moral faculties of a child or young person through precepts, exercises, examples, etc. Educate the intelligence, the will; 3. v.t. Develop physical forces through exercise, rendering them more apt for their purpose; 4. v.t. Perfect or sharpen the senses. Educate tastes, the ear; 5. v.t. Teach the rules of etiquette and courtesy).

6. "La instrucción, esto es, la adquisición de conocimientos, no es más que una mitad de la Educación. La otra mitad es la cultura, ó sea el cultivo que da por resultado el desenvolvimiento de nuestras facultades. No significa otra cosa el vocablo *educación*, que, derivado del latín, dice bien claro que no se trata de imbuir ideas ni de inculcar conocimientos, sino de sacar lo que está dentro del alumno, desarrollando por medio del ejercicio los gérmenes que dormitan en su mente, convirtiendo en actualidad lo que antes existía como posibilidad y potencialidad." Emphasis in original.

7. "La educación prepara el perfeccionamiento del individuo, desarrolla y fortalece sus facultades, suaviza sus instintos, dirije sus pasiones, modera sus impulsos desordenados, al de sacrificarse á sí propio en obsequio de sus semejantes."

8. "Enseña al hombre ciertas cosas, le dá capacidad, talentos, abre á sus ojos las páginas del gran libro de la naturaleza y penetra los secretos de esta y difundiéndose luego en ciencias, artes, en profesiones y oficios, convierte en objetos útiles las primeras materias que suministra la tierra."

9. "La educación prepara al hombre para el cumplimiento de sus deberes y la instrucción le enseña cuales sean estos. La educación le inspira el deseo de ser útil á sus semejantes y la instrucción le facilita los medios de poder realizar este deseo. La educación hace nacer en su alma el pensamiento del amor de Dios, y la instrucción abre el camino por donde ha de llegar este Supremo Sér, y le facilita recursos para honrarle y reverenciarle cual se merece, poniendo en práctica ese amor cuya semilla hizo nacer en su alma el primer destello de educacion."

10. "La instrucción superior a la medios de existencia o la clase social podría ser peligrosa si no la acompañase la educación."

11. "La instrucción se refiere á la cultura intelectual; la educación al moldeamiento del carácter."

12. "En el alma del alumno los principios de una vida correcta"; "la cultura intellectual."

13. "La relación madre-niño, una madre-ama de casa con poder moral sobre su esposo e hijo, un hijo que adquiriría importancia capital para la sociedad, el Estado y la 'raza' y a cuyo cuidado de crianza quedaba dedicada la vida de la madre." Emerging in the wake of second-wave feminism, critical motherhood studies represent an important academic tradition. Since the 1976 publication of North American feminist thinker Adrienne Rich's *Of Woman Born: Motherhood as Experience and Institution,* scholars have sought to reveal the domestic construction of motherhood that Nari discusses as a tool of modern capitalist state patriarchy. In *Inventing Motherhood: The Consequences of an Ideal*, British psychologist Ann Dally notes that "there have always been mothers, but motherhood was invented" as part of the cultural, political, and economic ascendancy of the Victorian middle classes. For a concise history of the construction of motherhood in the United States, see Hays, 19–50. For a history of motherhood in Latin America, see O'Connor. For specific family legislation in Argentina, see Nari. For Cuba, see Domínguez Navarro and Stoner. For a classic study of motherhood legislation in early twentieth-century Britain, see Davin.

14. Throughout this book, I use "liberal" not in the sense that it has acquired in contemporary US politics, as one in favor of increased government intervention in the economy and a particular model of social pluralism, but in the nineteenth-century meaning of the term: capitalist and (moderate) democratic reform, as opposed to the maintenance of certain feudal economic and political structures.

15. "Gratitud y reconocimiento de los hijos de los nietos de aquellas que debieron la instrucción á sus desvelos."

16. Catherine Beecher conceived of the idea of female teachers before Horace Mann did and proved instrumental to the feminization of the US teaching force. I have chosen to focus on Mann because of the projection that he and his wife Mary had in Argentina and Cuba. For more on Beecher and the feminization of the teaching profession in the United States, see Goldstein, 13–46.

17. "Sensibilidad privilegiada"; "especialmente aptas para la tarea educacional."

18. "Influencia civilizadora de las mujeres."

19. Leroux complicates the generally accepted notion of teaching as an extension of bourgeois domesticity, claiming that "teaching was not a voluntary adjunct of middle-class women's domesticity; rather, it was a form of paid labor that appealed to women who needed to earn their own support and valued the social and cultural benefits that respectably gendered work might afford" ("Money" 206).

20. "Al entregar a la mujer educada y moral la dirección de la infancia, el pueblo argentino podrá [decir] con razón que ha confiado a las madres la más augusta de los labores, la de formar el corazón y la inteligencia de las generaciones venideras." Frederick, for her part, argues that the maternal discourse of mid-nineteenth century Argentina is a response to the feminization of the opposition during the Rosas dictatorship ("Harriet Beecher Stowe" 105). She argues that US-inspired discourses of republican motherhood later were adopted by the Argentine feminist movement.

21. "Ningún instituto prepara . . . mejor á la madre que la Escuela Normal, que se propone formar maestros, porque toda madre, debe ser maestra, así como toda mujer debe tener las aptitudes de la madre, que es el eje del hogar." Gustavo E. Frischman critiques the feminization of the teaching profession in Argentina on feminist grounds, arguing that it served to justify low wages and limited institutional support. It seems that Horace Mann, too, was aware that "a woman could be hired for a fraction of a man's salary" (Luigi, 65 *Valiants* 6). Avellaneda, meanwhile, in addition to noting the cost-effectiveness of female teachers (50), argues that nineteenth-century Argentina's newly industrializing economy presents "tantas ocupaciones para solicitar la actividad del hombre, que será siempre muy reducido el número de los que quieran dedicarse al profesorado" (so many occupations to attract men's energy, that it will always be a small number of men who wish to dedicate themselves to teaching). On the other hand, "la mujer tendrá . . . en él una carrera lucrativa, de la que se halla desprovista, á la vez que se le ofrece á su tiempo y á sus facultades un noble ejemplo" (women will always have in teaching a lucrative career, which they have been lacking, and noble employment for their time and talents) (49). All that said, at the Escuela Normal del Paraná, at least, North American female teachers were compensated at a rate almost three times higher than were their Argentine male counterparts (Avellaneda and Leguizamón). On Sarmiento and women's education, see Garrels, "Sarmiento ante la cuestión" and Ana María García.

22. "Allí formó maestras, allí formó madres, allí formó mujeres."

23. "Madre escuela"; "ley madre de la cultura argentina."

24. Szurmuk also discusses maternal metaphor and education in nineteenth-century Argentina (*Women in Argentina* 79).

25. Rodríguez de la O also discusses Argentine-Cuban entanglements, focusing on the figure of José Martí.

26. In accordance with the convention in inter-American studies, I use "North American" as a demonym for the United States. The term is a calque of the Spanish adjective *norteamericano* and is not intended as a commentary on the geographical situations of Canada or Mexico. For a comparative history of race relations in Argentina and Cuba, see Helg, "Race." For histories of racial thinking in Latin America see, Graham and Branche, *Colonialism*.

27. See Hobsbawm, Zea, Mignolo, and Chasteen, among others for discussions of this critical commonplace. For a reevaluation of this paradigm, see Saunders. Puiggrós, for her part, notes the abundance of scholarly studies of European influence on Latin American education compared to the dearth of work on US-Latin American educational relations (*Imperialismo y educación*, 41n6).

28. Throughout this book, I use "neocolonialism" to refer to the aggressions of creole elites against peoples of color within individual nation-states after formal independence and "imperialism" to refer to the formal or informal extraterritorial reach of northern powers such as Europe and, particularly, the United States. For a theoretical discussion of empire, see Hardt and Negri.

29. The term "extended South" is a play on Marxist theorist Immanuel Wallerstein's notion of the "extended Caribbean." For a problematization of Wallerstein's three-tiered capitalist world system from a Latin Americanist perspective, see Stern.

30. The idea that the "extended South" attempts to name has gained traction in recent years in the work of American studies scholars such as Smith and Cohn and Guterl. In the Caribbean, theories connecting the US South culturally and racially to the Antilles have been elaborated by the Martinican Édouard Glissant and the Cuban Antonio Benítez Rojo, influencing the work of Trinidadian J. Michael Dash. Mexican novelist Carlos Fuentes, meanwhile, famously viewed the US South as the northern extremity of Latin America, a formulation that destabilizes the binary oppositions upon which hemispheric power relations frequently rest. Indeed, regional (re)mappings are central to Latin Americanist formulations of comparative literature. Chilean literary scholar Ana Pizarro, for example, proposes dividing the map into "cultural subregions" (such as the Caribbean, the Southern Cone, the Andes, or the Amazon) cutting across the borders of existing nation-states (69). Similarly, the Brazilian literary scholar Tânia Franco Carvalhal calls for a Latin American school of comparative literature based on shared regional—instead of national—geopolitical concerns, as reflected in intraregional parallels and borrowings. For a foundational treatment of the role of the region in the study of Latin American literature, see Rama, *Transculturación*.

31. Harold Peterson's 1964 history of Argentina's political relations with the United States represents a notable exception to this tendency.

32. The Israeli Latin Americanist Ori Pruess, meanwhile, has researched Argentina's entanglements within the Southern Cone region.

33. For an overview of the historiography on inter-American cultural relations, see Rosenberg.

34. For a historical overview of Hispanism, see Moraña. On the paradigm's enduring power in university Spanish programs, see Hoyos (45–46). For discussions of new multilingual paradigms for Iberian and Latin American studies, see Newcomb and Gordon.

35. The activities of the International American Studies Association offer an important corrective to this situation, as does the work of many of the scholars cited in the present study.

36. This focus on uneven hemispheric relations is not without complications. Writing from within the United States, cultural studies scholar María Josefina Saldaña-Portillo warns that "even as hemispheric literary studies decenter the United States, they recenter it as the object of critique" (207). German Americanist Johannes Voelz takes this paradox into account when he acknowledges that, "not only is [nineteenth-century US literature] ambiguously situated between imperialism and transnationalism; it calls into question the very distinction between these two terms" (103). *Imperial Educación* explores this paradox by recognizing the "asymmetry and interdependency of nation-state development throughout the Americas" and the "importance of doing literary and cultural history from the perspective of a polycentric American hemisphere with no dominant center" (Levander and Levine 6–7). For a discussion of the perils and possibilities of comparative methodology in the Americas, see Rocha Teixeira. For a discussion of comparison in relation to hemispheric relations and imperialism, see Hooker 11–17.

37. Also referred to by the French term *histoire croisée* (crossed history), "entanglement" was first popularized by Shalini Randeria, an Indian postcolonial social anthropologist based in Switzerland, to describe the impact of British colonial rule on contemporary Indian society.

38. Emphasis in original. "Entanglement" was introduced to hemispheric historical studies by works such as Gilbert M. Joseph, Catherine C. LeGrand, and Ricardo D. Salvatore's 1998 edited volume *Close Encounters of Empire: Writing the Cultural History of U.S.-Latin American Relations*. The essays included in this volume theorize the paradigm that would come to be known as "entanglement," though they do not use the term. For an early and explicit discussion of "entanglement" in New World historiography, see Jorge Cañizares-Esguerra's 2006 monograph *Puritan Conquistadors: Iberianizing the Atlantic, 1550–1700*. For entanglement as a paradigm in hemispheric literary studies, see the German-based *Forum for Inter-American Research: Journal of the International Association of Inter-American Studies*'s December 2014 special issue "Theorizing Hemispheric American Studies."

39. For important early work in hemispheric studies, see Luis Alberto Sánchez's 1973 *Historia comparada de las literaturas americanas*. The present incarnation of hemispheric literary studies can be dated to the publication of

edited volumes such as Gustavo Pérez Firmat's *Do the Americas Have a Common Literature?* in 1990 and Jeffery Belnap and Raúl Fernández's *José Martí's "Our America": From National to Hemispheric Studies* in 1998, as well as the appearances of the monographs *Rediscovering the New World: Inter-American Literature in a Comparative Context* by Earl E. Fitz and *The Dialectics of Our America: Genealogy, Cultural Critique, and Literary History* by José David Saldívar in 1991, Amy Kaplan and Donald Pease's edited 1993 *Cultures of United States Imperialism,* Anna Brickhouse's 2004 *Transamerican Literary Relations in the Nineteenth-Century Public Sphere,* Iván Jaksic's 2007 *The Hispanic World and American Intellectual Life: 1820–1880,* and Louis Parkinson Zamora and Silvia Spitta's 2009 "The Americas, Otherwise" (a guest-edited issue of *Comparative Literature*). Additional important contributions have been made by Bauer, Castillo, Gillman, Greene, Handley, Luis-Brown, Murphy, and Gruesz, among others. See also the earlier historical work of Herbert Eugene Bolton and Lewis Hanke, as well as David Weber's more recent contribution to inter-American history. Meanwhile, Sophia McClennen, Earl Fitz, Claudia Sardowski Smith, and Claire Fox have productively critiqued the hemispheric project from the standpoint of Latin American studies. Though not framed as hemispheric studies, Cynthia Steele's *Narrativa indigenista en los Estados Unidos y México,* Alfred MacAdam's *Textual Confrontations,* Sibylle Fischer's *Modernity Disavowed,* Lois Parkinson Zamora's *Useable Past,* Lisa Voight's *Writing Captivity in the Early Modern Atlantic,* and the work of Robert McKee Irwin are all admirable examples of comparative American literary studies thought out of a Latin Americanist paradigm. Similarly, Wai Chee Dimock's appeal to read US literature across "deep time," though not written under the lens of hemispheric studies, furthers the field's project. Juliet Hooker, meanwhile, recently has made valuable contributions to the field from the perspective of political theory. Outside of the US academy (and frequently participating in different networks of scholarly circulation), in addition to the authors cited in this book, important contributions to hemispheric studies have been made in the Brazilian university system by the likes of Zilá Bernd, Antonio Cândido, and Viviana Gelado and María Verónica Secreto, Elena Palmero González, Livia Reis, Roberto Schwartz, Stelamaris Coser, and Miriam Gárate and in Canada by Marie Couillard and Patrick Imbert. Equally important inter-American work has been done by the German-Mexican Entreespacios research collaborative.

40. "Comparam e, por assim dizer, confrontam entre si de maneira estática as políticas, sociedades, economias ou produções simbólicas de diferentes países"; "orienta[m]-se em direção à mobilidade, ao intercâmbio e aos processos reciprocamente transformadores. Aos Estudos de Transárea interessam menos os espaços do que os caminhos, menos as demarcações de fronteiras do que os deslocamentos de fronteiras, menos os territórios do que relações e comunicações."

41. It is tempting to claim that "creole" is a calque of the Spanish *criollo.* Derived from the verb *criar,* which means "to raise" in Spanish and Portuguese, the

term refers to people and cultural phenomena born in the Hispanic Americas. The most common meaning of the word refers to a white person born in the Spanish colonies, but the term varies considerably in meaning from country to country (in Cuba, for example, it can refer to blacks born on the island and is used to distinguish the group from enslaved people kidnapped in Africa), and almost no one we call a "creole" today would have used that word to refer to him- or herself. The word's cognates in English, French, and Portuguese also vary substantially in meaning. It is probably safest simply to say that "creole" is the term used in English-language hemispheric studies to refer to whites born in the Americas and descended from European colonizers.

42. For more on "local histories and global designs," see Mignolo, *Local Histories*.

43. On "Americanity," see Quijano and Wallerstein.

1. Republican Motherhood and Citizen Educación

1. "Se podría decir que Adan al principio de la creación tuvo por naturaleza el primado y consiguiente el imperio sobre todos los hombres, y así que pudo derivar de él, o por el origen natural de los primogénitos o por la voluntad del mismo Adan. Así, pues, . . . que de un solo Adan todos los hombres han sido formados y procreados, para significar la subordinación a un príncipe."

2. "De acuerdo con el derecho natural, . . . la autoridad pasaba de Dios al padre de familia, quien reproduciría 'los vínculos de la misma naturaleza' y daba origen a pueblos y reinos. . . . El poder real, [fue] traspasado por Dios al primero hombre, del primer hombre al padre de familia y del padre de familia a los pueblos." On the Enlightenment in Spanish America, see Aldridge and Whitaker.

3. "Una gran familia que tiene al rey como padre y múltiples hijos, diferentes, pero igualados en el mismo deber de defenderlo y asistirlo."

4. On the nation-as-family allegory and the political reality underlying it specifically from the point of view of nineteenth-century Argentina, see Masiello 17–9. For a treatment of family metaphor in the British imperial context, see McClintock 45.

5. The particular danger from which the monarch has "failed" to protect his American children in this passage is attack from indigenous groups. In this way, the family metaphor constructs the future US nation as exclusively white, a subject to which I will return below.

6. For more on the transition from dynastic paternal allegory to republican family metaphor in the Enlightenment-era Americas, see Genova, "'La patria.'" For an explanation of metaphor as gestalt, see Lakoff and Johnson.

7. Sommer's theorization draws on Ernest Gellner's work on the development of national "literate high culture," Benedict Anderson's discussion of the role of the novel in nation building, and Frederic Jameson's notion of national allegory ("Third World Literature").

8. The focus on national origins and genealogies that the foundational romance genre implies reflects what Foucault in *Les Mots et les choses* (*The Order of Things*) identifies as the nineteenth-century Western intelligentsia's faith in history as a master discourse. Unzueta and Ianes Vera argue that, in Latin America, this interest in the past took the form of historical fiction focused on the nation's foundation, or its prehistory. For commentary on and reconsiderations of the foundational paradigm, see Chasteen and Castro-Klarén; Gerassi-Navarro; Achugar; and González-Stephan, "Forms." O'Brien, for her part, suggests that interracial romance may have functioned as an alternative to rebellion in the creole imaginary. For general discussions of the importance of lettered culture to nation-state formation in Latin America, see Rama and Klahn and Corral.

9. "Inalienable binomio 'natural' madre-niño."

10. For a broad critique of the absence of gender analysis in traditional theorizations of nationalism, see Yuval-Davis.

11. "Disciplinar las prácticas sociales de las mujeres y familiares, y que aportaba una esperanza de *regeneración* a la 'raza', la sociedad, la nación." Emphasis in original. For more on motherhood legislation in nineteenth-century Argentina, in addition to Nari, see Paz Trueba.

12. For a Latin Americanist critique of the maternalist discourses that I have been discussing in this subsection, see Palomar Vera.

13. "Dios ha dado al niño una madre en cada mujer."

14. "Preguntemos á la mujer mas vulgar por qué quiere á los niños, y nos contestará, si acierta á traducir sus sentimientos:—Quiero á los niños porque busco ángeles en la tierra y solo los encuentro en ellos."

15. "Muestran un interés sostenido en la dignificación de la mujer como madre de familia y compañera del hombre."

16. On *La Aljaba*, see Masiello 55–58. Though the Marianist cult to self-sacrificing motherhood is a fundamental feature of Hispanic traditionalism, the republican emphasis on domestic educación for citizenship represented a threat to the colonial values of the Argentine Federal Party; perhaps not surprisingly, conservative dictator Rosas ordered *La Aljaba* to suspend publication (Frederick, *Wily Modesty* 18). At the same time, as Batticuore points out, liberal interest in women's education was focused almost exclusively on the domestic and maternal spheres, and did not entail wider calls for emancipation (39–49).

17. "El cetro"; "en sus manos simbolizado en la moral y la religión."

18. For a transhistorical overview of women's education around the world, see Paulk, *Dominant Culture*.

19. See particularly "Carta remitida."

20. "La necesidad de libertar al bello sexo . . . , fijando en su imaginacion las buenas ideas, antes de que entren en el mundo su felicidad propia, la felicidad de las personas sobre las cuales han de ejercer mas inmediatamente [*sic*] su influencia, y hasta cierto punto el tono moral de la sociedad dependen de la educacion de las mujeres."

21. "La educación de las mujeres es mas importante que la de los hombres, pues la de estos es obra de aquellas." Albín, for her part, suggests that the women's educational project presented in *La ilustración* goes beyond training for motherhood to include preparation for full citizenship (72). For a discussion of women's education for domesticity, see Childs.

22. "Quisiéramos que no hubiese ni una sola [mujer] ignorante; pues de ese modo se vería la república convertida en un paraíso terrenal."

23. "Sábias y religiosas madres," "nuestros sentimientos serían mas arreglados, mas dóciles á la razón; y todos sabriamos por costumbre ser menos ambiciosos, menos exâltados [sic], y mas generosos para hacernos concesiones mutuamente [sic], y siempre marchariamos al tempo de la razon y de la concordia."

24. "Todos nos amariamos tambien á nuestra patria, no la ultrajariamos tomándola por asunto de nuestros odios, de nuestras venganzas, de nuestros resentimientos, y de nuestra abominable ambicion; todos la respetariamos."

25. For more on gender discourse in nineteenth-century Argentine liberalism, see Masiello 19–27. Guerrero Guerrero explores possible French influences on nineteenth-century Argentine views regarding women and education, paying particular attention to the Abbé Fénelon's 1687 *Traité de l'éducation des filles* in relation to the thinking of Domingo Faustino Sarmiento. Scholars also have pointed to Louis-Aimé Martin's 1834 *De l'éducation des mères de famille, ou, De la civilisation du genre humain par les femmes* as the source of many of Sarmiento's ideas on gender and education. While, like Martin, Sarmiento sees education as a means to control the social instability that the Age of Revolution wrought, he differs from his French predecessor in his insistence on teachers as potential mothers of the nation. On French influence on Argentine educational philosophy and institutions beyond Sarmiento, see Hodge 51–53.

26. Mann was influenced in his thinking by the Swiss pedagogue Johann Heinrich Pestalozzi.

27. For a critique of how national-maternalist discourse "reduces women to their motherhood," see Eisenstein (41).

28. Provencio Garrigós, for her part, offers a slightly different interpretation, viewing the elite biases of nineteenth-century discourses of republican motherhood more as expressing an ideal than as registering a social fact or referring to real women of a particular racial or class background (59).

29. "Como de raza híbrida, no hay que fiar mucho en su virtud." The image of the sensual mulata in nineteenth-century Cuban visual culture has been studied by Kutzinski, *Sugar's Secrets* and Fraunhar. On popular associations of mulatas with sex work in nineteenth-century Cuba, see Fraunhar (81–87).

30. This book's analysis of discourses surrounding the maternity of Afro-descended women is indebted to critical legal scholar Kimberlé Crenshaw's theoretical paradigm of "intersectionality." Historian Peter Wade's articulation of intersectionality as a space in and around which particular social phenomena

develop also has proven helpful to my analysis. For an early articulation of intersectionality in the context of Afro-Hispanic women's writing, see Feal. For more on structural barriers to domesticity for women of color, see Collins. On mothering practices in enslaved communities in the antebellum US South, see Shaw. Chang, for her part, comments on the irony that women of color historically have been deemed lacking in domesticity and unfit mothers at the same time that they have been recruited into low-paying domestic and childcare labor.

31. The *Narrative of Sojourner Truth* was written down by the subject's friend Olive Gilbert and first published in 1850. The 1878 reedition included an addendum called the "Book of Life," a collection of shorter texts on Truth by various authors.

32. On the trope of mother-child separation in Latin American antislavery discourse, see Cowling 99–103.

33. Spillers's and Hartman's theorizations build on Jamaican American sociologist Orlando Patterson's notion of "social death," or the denial of rights to the enslaved on account of their out-group status.

34. "No le permiten casarse con el hombre que le gusta o que quiere. Los amos le dan y le quitan el marido. Tampoco está segura de que podrá vivir siempre a su lado, ni de que criará a los hijos. Cuando menos lo espera, los amos la divorcian, le venden el marido, y a los hijos también, y separan la familia para no volver a juntarse en este mundo." In a recent article, Ivonne Pizarra de la Luz considers the limits and possibilities of understanding María de Regla's intervention as a subaltern *testimonio*. I will return to María de Regla and maternity in *Cecilia Valdés* in chapter 4.

35. Garner's story is probably best known to contemporary readers through Toni Morrison's 1987 novel *Beloved*. E. Franklin Frazier's 1939 *Negro Family in the United States* represents an early (now dated) effort to consider black kinship structures beyond the norms of the Anglo-American bourgeois family.

36. Prados-Torreira points out that "resources addressing the participation of poor, and often black, women are less common than the traces left by their middle-class counterparts" (7), although her own work proves a valuable exception to that rule (27–38). In addition to the studies cited here, important work on the lived experiences of Afro-descended women also has been carried out by Barbara Bush, among others. Classic firsthand accounts of the lives of Afro-descended mothers in the early-republican Americas include, in the United States, Harriet Jacobs's 1861 slave narrative *Incidents in the Life of a Slave Girl* (published under the pseudonym Linda Brent) and, in Cuba, the 1888–89 journal *Minerva: revista quincenal dedicada a la mujer de color* (discussed in chapter 5 of this book) and María de los Reyes Castillo Bueno's testimonial *Reyita sencillamente: testimonio de una negra cubana nonagenaria* (1996), cowritten with Daisy Rubiera Castillo (discussed in the conclusion of this book). Alejandro Solomianski has suggested that the popular poetry of the Argentine *payadoras* may shed similar light on the

thoughts of nineteenth-century Afro-Argentine women. For general studies of Afro-Latin(x) literature and culture, see Bueno; Coulthard; Feal; Richard Jackson; Shirley Jackson; Jiménez Román and Flores; Kutzinski, "Afro-Hispanic"; Lewis; Luis, *Voices;* and Smart. For an overview of Afro-Hispanic women's writing, see DeCosta-Willis, *Daughters of the Diaspora*. For a theoretical treatment of this body of literature, see DeCosta-Willis, "Afra-Hispanic." For a comparative study of maternity in Afro–North American and Afro-Cuban women's writing, see Sanmartín.

37. In addition to the sources discussed here, see Finch. On the entanglements of race and sexuality in Latin America, see Wade. On the sexuality of enslaved women and the maintenance of coloniality in British North America, see Hunter.

38. "Sumida por su raza en 'estado de ignorancia' permanente, lo que agudiza los peligros físicos para el niño, pues su incultura la entrega a toda clase de excesos contrarios a la salud."

39. "A los grandes inconvenientes que traen consigo el trato y la comunicación de los niños con los criados en general . . . , hay que agregar, cuando los sirvientes son esclavos, otros mil."

40. "Raza abyecta que . . . monopoliza el fiel comercio de la lactancia, y á la que con demasiado abandono encarga una madre la custodia de su hijo"; "en el tiempo de recibir las impresiones indelebles se ve de tal modo abandonado a la mercantil custodia de la nodriza sin mas modelo que sus toscos y descompuestos modales, sin oir mas lenguaje que el suyo destemplado."; "¿[Q]ué esperanza de porvenir inspirará? [Q]ué formas tomará una masa vaciada en tan grosero molde?"

41. I discuss Mann's and Villaverde's texts in chapter 4. For more on nineteenth-century Cuban creole concerns regarding "African wet nurses," see Camacho 83–112. For a cultural history of breastfeeding in the early modern Anglo-American world, see Salmon. For information on the shift away from wet nurses in the United States, see Golden.

42. "El trato familiar con los esclavos es el escollo mas peligroso que pondréis á vuestros hijos bajo el techo domestico; el ejemplo de las malas costumbres y de los vicios de esos seres degradados por su estado de servidumbre, tiene un influjo poderoso, y forman la desgracia de innumerables hijos de familias virtuosas, á quienes la confianza pone en un estado de ceguedad lamentable, contra sus mas caros intereses: las señoras madres fíjense bien en esto; pues á ellas toca velar, como responsables guardianes de sus hijos."

43. Provencio Garrigós, on the other hand, in her study of nineteenth-century Cuba, attributes the injunction against Afro-descended nursemaids to a creole fear of racial revenge for slavery (69).

44. On the "silencing" of the Haitian Revolution, see Trouillot. For the impact of the Haitian Revolution on other areas of the plantation zone, particularly Cuba, see Fischer, *Modernity Disavowed*, and Ferrer, *Freedom's Mirror*.

45. Some maintain that the novel was written by Bergeaud's wife (Daut 413n2).

46. "Rappelés à eux-mêmes par une voix amie, la voix de leur mère qui, du fond de la tombe, veillait encore sur leurs jours. Elle s'indigna de leur faiblesse, coupable, et leur montra son corps déchiré, sanglant. Un noble cri du cœur répondit à ce nouvel appel à la vengeance."

47. Emphasis in original.

48. "Remplacer à l'avenir tout l'amour de votre mère."

49. Duchesne argues that the two maternal figures meld into one, emblematizing a mulâtre republican spirit. I agree, though, for the purposes of this book, I am more interested in how whiteness predominates in that mixture.

50. Hoffman, for his part, claims that l'Africaine "can be considered another incarnation of Stella" (importantly, not the other way around) (154).

51. For a transhistorical study of the mother figure in Haitian literature, see Laroche.

52. "No es dudoso que en pueblos bien organizados, la accion de la familia se deja sentir en la escuela, justificando este influjo, desde el momento que aquella misma ha experimentado, el efecto provechoso de ésta, y que toda educacion sólidamente entendida, léjos de divorciada, debe ser á una manera de continuacion de la familia, en estrecha compenetracion con ella. Pero no puede sostenerse esta misma afirmacion en la hipótesis de una sociedad agena á ese organismo, donde es necesario, ante todo, empezar combatiendo los prejuicios del hogar doméstico. Bien pudiéramos comprobar nuestro aserto con multitud de referencias, hijas de la absoluta falta de *ciencia de las madres,* factor apenas si sospechado entre nosotros, juntamente con los errores del padre, produciéndose por este motivo el desacuerdo y el casi permanente estado de colision de la escuela con la familia." Emphasis in original.

53. "Obligación de educar al pueblo."

54. "Sin distinguir al hombre de la mujer, ni al chino, ni al mulato de los que se llaman nobles, ni al hijo legítimo del ilegítimo." In the Spanish American castas system of racial taxonomy, "chino" referred to someone with one mulato parent and one indigenous parent.

55. "Con el nuevo órden social se destruyeron los lazos que impedían los movimientos y el desarrollo de la multitud, dejándola, sin embargo, esclava de la ignorancia y subyugada al imperio de las pasiones.–'Sed libres, entrad en posesion de vuestros derechos,'–se decia á todos y no se pensaba en enseñarles en qué consiste la verdadera libertad, ni en prepararlos para que hicieran buen uso del poder que se depositaba en sus manos. Se les decia, sed libres, como pudiera habérseles dicho, sed ricos, sed dichosos, sin instruirles acerca de los medios legítimos de conseguirlo, y sin darles idea clara y exacta de los bienes que se les ofrecian en perspectiva. Palabras huecas y vacías de sentido, propias mas bien para exaltar el ánimo que para honrar y enaltecer las clases que se trataba de emancipar."

56. "Educacion conveniente á su estado y necesidades."

57. "El remedio de los males que nos amenazan."

58. Hitt notes that "the long tradition of Indian education in America" actually began in 1606, when "King James I urged the English settlers to educate, Christianize, and civilize the Indians in the First Charter of Virginia" (211).

59. Birthright citizenship finally was granted to Native Americans in 1924 by the Indian Citizenship Act.

60. "Una cruzada político-pedagógico"; "las transformaciones económicas, institucionales e ideológicas."

61. For a historical discussion of black teachers in the Reconstruction period, in addition to Butchart, see Goldstein 47–65.

62. For a discussion of education and domesticity in the work of Harper, see Novak.

2. Mothers, Moors, Mohicans, and Mulattas in Mansilla's *Miranda*

1. While I focus on blackness, Concha Meléndez and Cynthia Steele have studied Cooper in terms of hemispheric indigeneity. Other inter-American studies of *The Last of the Mohicans* can be found in Doris Sommer's *Foundational Fictions,* Anna Brickhouse's *Transamerican Literary Relations,* and Iván Jaksic's *Hispanic World and American Intellectual Life*—the latter two pairing the novel with the anonymous *Jicoténcal,* also from 1826. I differ from these studies in my interest in the role of racialized republican motherhood in the novel.

2. On economic trends in nineteenth-century Argentina, see Adelman. For a general history of the period, see Shumway.

3. "No se cuidó gran cosa que la nueva entidad constituyese un todo armónico: indios de diversas razas e idiomas, campos de agricultura, regiones mineras, montañas y llanuras, selvas y glaciares, todas las diferencias naturales y todos los climas comprendidos bajo 45 grados de latitud, fueron envueltos por la nueva frontera y sujetos a las decisiones del gobierno de Buenos Aires, que no se hallaba en el centro, sino en un extremo del territorio."

4. "Produjo una fractura de los pueblos del actual Noroeste Argentino y la unidad económica y cultural a la cual pertenecían desde hacía más de tres siglos."

5. "Alianza de clases y etnias: gauchos, afroargentinos (esclavos y emancipados) y aborígenes 'amigos'; pequeños propietarios rurales y grandes terratenientes criollos, a la vez que comerciantes y hacendados ingleses, coincidieron en apoyarlo, ya fuere por ver en el régimen una garantía de orden y prosperidad, o por considerarlo fuente de reivindicaciones materiales o simbólicas."

6. "La conexión forzada con el puerto de Buenos Aires, puerta del comercio exterior y el contrabando, cuna de una capital política y financiera renuente a hacerse cargo de su propio interior."

7. "Firme defensor de la soberanía nacional."

8. Members of the Generation of 1837 were in fact often less radical than the early Unitarios of the Rivadavia era. On the Generation of 1837, see Katra, *Argentine Generation*. For a discussion of Federal literature, see Lanctot.

9. Rock points out that foreign trade did, in fact, grow under Rosas, mostly through exports from cattle ranching (107).

10. "No hay tres jóvenes que sepan el inglés, ni cuatro que hablen francés."

11. "Razas americanas"; "en la ociosidad, y se muestran incapaces, aun por medio de la compulsión, para dedicarse a un trabajo duro y seguido"; "fatales resultados ha producido"; "la rezagada a la Europa"; "un todo homogéneo, que se distingue por su amor a la ociosidad e incapacidad industrial."

12. Sarmiento is at the heart of the nineteenth-century Argentine and Latin American literary canons. In addition to the works cited in this book, see, for example, Alonso, Altamirano and Sarlo, Jitrik, Katra, Leonard, Luna, Martínez Estrada, Palcos, Ramos, Sorensen Goodrich, Tacca, and Terán, to name just a handful of the thousands of studies on the author.

13. The novels are *The Pioneers: The Sources of the Susquehanna; A Descriptive Tale* (1823); *The Last of the Mohicans: A Narrative of 1757* (1826); *The Prairie: A Tale* (1827); *The Pathfinder: The Inland Sea* (1840); and *The Deerslayer: The First War Path* (1841).

14. An Iroquoian people from the Ontario–New York region, the Hurons (also known as the Wyandot) sided with the French in the French and Indian War, the North American iteration of the Seven Years' War lasting from 1754 to 1763. The Algonquin-speaking Mohicans of what is now the mid-Atlantic region of the United States, on the other hand, sided with the British during the conflict. Members of the Huron and Mohican groups continue to live in the United States and Canada.

15. Like Sarmiento, Cooper has generated an extensive bibliography over the years. In addition to the works cited directly in this chapter, my reading owes much to canonical studies of the author by Leslie A. Fielder and D. H. Lawrence. For a sample of Cooper studies, see the work of Axelrad, Wayne Franklin, Kelly, Lofren, B. Mann, McWilliams, Murray, Thorp, and J. Walker.

16. "Descripciones de usos y costumbres que parecen plagiadas de la pampa."

17. "Un fondo de poesía que nace de los accidentes naturales del país y de las costumbres excepcionales que engendra [*sic*]."

18. "Si un destello de literatura nacional puede brillar momentáneamente en las nuevas sociedades americanas, es el que resultará de la descripción de las grandiosas escenas naturales, y sobre todo de la lucha entre la civilización europea y la barbarie indígena, entre la inteligencia y la materia; la lucha imponente en América, y que da lugar a escenas tan peculiares, tan características y tan fuera de círculo de ideas en que se ha educado el espíritu europeo, porque los resortes dramáticos se vuelven desconocidos fuera del país donde se toman, los usos

sorprendentes y originales los caracteres." The passage reflects Sarmiento's notoriously ungrammatical Spanish, though the edition from which I cite modernizes and standardizes the author's original orthography, which was unconventional even in his era. On Sarmiento's style, see J. Ramos.

19. "El único romancista norteamericano que haya logrado hacerse un nombre europeo"; "la escena de sus descripciones fuera del círculo ocupado por los plantadores al límite entre la vida bárbara y la civilizada, al teatro de la guerra en que las razas indígenas y la raza sajona están combatiendo por la posesión del terreno." Cooper, for his part, in *The Travelling Bachelor; or, Notions of the Americans* (1828), argues (not without a certain irony) that North American society, free from the follies of feudalism, does not provide adequate fodder for the novelist (2:469–70).

20. For a classic study of Jacksonian Democracy, see Schlesinger.

21. Cooper, for his part, takes up this theme in *The Prairie* (1827), in which social leveling results from the relationship between the upper-class Ellen Wade and the frontiersman Paul Hoover, whose marriage at the end of the novel is made possible by the seeming irrelevance of birth in the newly acquired territory.

22. "Estos yankees tienen el derecho de ser impertinentes. Cien habitantes por milla, cuatrocientos pesos de capital por persona, una escuela o colejio para cada doscientos habitantes, cinco pesos de renta anual para cada niño, i ademas los colejios: esto para preparar el espíritu. Para la materia o la produccion tiene Boston una red de caminos de hierro, otra de canales, otra de rios, i una línea de costas; para el pensamiento tiene la cátedra del evanjelio i cuarenta i cinco diarios, periódicos i revistas; i para el buen órden de todo, la educacion" (447). In 1846, Sarmiento was sent by the government of Chile, where he was living in exile from the Rosas regime, on a tour of Europe, North Africa, and the United States, ostensibly to study public education in those regions, but possibly also in order to avoid the strain that his acerbic critiques of Rosas regime were putting on Chile's relations with the neighboring Argentina (Stavans xxv; González Echevarría, *Facundo* 8). I will return to Sarmiento's travels to the United States in chapter 3.

23. "Imprime su forma civilizada sobre el territorio e impone un orden frente al medio natural y los pueblos primitivos que amenazan con degradar el estatus racional del sujeto moderno"; "se caracteriza por confundirse y mezclarse con el medio natural."

24. "Como modelo para la Argentina."

25. Although Sarmiento's and Alberdi's ideas are often grouped together (as they are here), the two were, in fact, bitter political opponents. Though not the main point of conflict, among the important differences in their thinking is the fact that Alberdi did not share Sarmiento's faith in the power of public education to form republican citizens (Tedesco 10). On the rivalry between Sarmiento and Alberdi, see Shumway and Katra, *1837*. For primary sources, see Alberdi, *Grandes y pequeños hombres del Plata* and Sarmiento, *Las ciento y una*.

26. For an overview of Latin American positivism, see Zea. On the Argentine eugenics movement, see Stepan.

27. "Gobernar es poblar en el sentido que poblar es educar, mejorar, civilizar, enriquecer y engrandecer espontáneamente y rápidamente."

28. "Es instruir, educar, moralizar, mejorar la raza."

29. "La inteligencia y la costumbre de su propio gobierno y los medios de ejercerlo."

30. "Con gente inteligente en la industria y habituada al trabajo que produce y enriquece."

31. "Poblar es civilizar"; "se puebla con gente civilizada"; "con pobladores de la Europa civilizada."

32. While Sarmiento, Alberdi, and others of their generation hoped to attract northern European immigrants, the bulk of newcomers arrived from Italy and, ironically, Spain, the source of much of the "backwardness" that the *aluvión inmigratorio* was supposed to wash away.

33. Overshadowed in American studies by de Tocqueville, Beaumont accompanied his compatriot to the United States during his famous 1831 trip to study the prison system and also published an account of the journey: the didactic novel *Marie, ou l'esclavage aux Etats-Unis* (1835). Sarmiento clearly was aware of the now largely forgotten author, and cites him in his "Sobre la educacion" (243).

34. "Después de dos o tres años de *flirtear*, este es el verbo norteamericano, bailes, paseos, viajes i coqueterías, la niña de la historia, en el almuerzo i como quien no quiere la cosa, pregunta a sus padres si conocen a un jóven alto, rubio, maquinista de profesion, que suele venir a verla, de vez en cuando, todos los dias. Hacia un año que estaban esperando esta introduccion. El desenlace es que hai en la familia un enlace convenido, de que se da parte a los padres la víspera, los cuales ya lo sabian por todas las comadres de la vecindad. Celebrado el desposorio, los novios toman en el acto el próximo camino de hierro, i salen a ostentar su felicidad por bosques, villas, ciudades i hoteles" (348–49).

35. For a discussion of flirtation in Argentine travel writing about the United States, see Bramen.

36. "En los wagones se les ve siempre a estas encantadoras parejas de jóvenes de veinte años, abrazados, reposándose el uno en el seno del otro, i prodigándose caricias tan espresivas que edifican a todos los circunstantes, haciéndoles formar el propósito de casarse inmediatamente, aun a los mas contumaces solterones. No puede hacerse en términos mas insinuantes que esta esposicion al aire libre de las embriagueces matrimoniales, la propaganda del casamiento."

37. "Debido a esto es que el yankee no llega nunca a la edad de veinte i cinco años sin tener ya una familia numerosa; i yo no me esplico de otro modo la asombrosa propagacion de la especie en aquel suelo afortunado. En 1790 la poblacion constaba de cerca de 4000000; 1800, 5000000; 1810, 7000000; 1820, 9000000; 1830, 12000000; 1840, 17000000; 1850, contará 23000000."

38. On the "emplotment," or ideological construction of historical narrative, see White.

39. On the "possessive investment in whiteness," see Lipsitz. "Whiteness has a cash value: it accounts for advantage that comes to individuals through profits made from housing secured in discriminatory markets, through the unequal education allotted to children of different races, through insider networks that channel employment opportunities to the relatives and friends of those who have profited most from past discrimination, and especially through intergenerational transfers of inherited wealth that pass on the spoils of discrimination to succeeding generations. . . . Whiteness is . . . a social fact, an identity created and continued with all-too-real consequences for the distribution of wealth, prestige, and opportunity. . . . Whiteness is invested in, like property, but it is also a means of accumulating property, and keeping it from others" (vii–viii).

40. Though the aim of the war was ostensibly the removal of the Seminole nation from central Florida, an area that had recently been acquired by the United States from Spain, marronage was a key issue in the conflict, as the Amerindians were providing refuge to enslaved Afro-descendants who had escaped from plantations in Georgia. On the Black Seminoles, see Mulroy and Landers.

41. In addition to the phallic symbolism of the knife, the unusual use of "sheath" as a verb seems inspired by the fact that the English word "vagina" is derived from the Latin for "sheath."

42. On contact zones, or "social spaces where disparate cultures meet, clash, and grapple with each other, often in highly asymmetrical relations of domination and subordination—like colonialism, slavery, or their aftermaths as they are lived out across the globe today," see Pratt (4).

43. For a historical discussion of the economic effects of interracial relationships in the newly acquired territories, see Meacham-Gould.

44. Writing about eugenic maternity in early-twentieth-century Britain, Anna Davin observes that "it is assumed that all babies are male. . . . 'Future citizens,' in those days when women did not vote, were men of course. . . . Mothers thus become responsible to the nation above all for the production and rearing of healthy sons" (26).

45. Kaplan's theorization draws on the work of McClintock and Stoler.

46. As per traditional Hispanic naming practices, "Mansilla" was her father's surname and "García" was the name of her husband's paternal family. Over the course of her lifetime, the author variously signed her work as "Daniel," "Eduarda Mansilla de García," and "Eduarda." The author's name appears as "Eduarda Mansilla de García" on the title page of the 1879 edition of *Lucía Miranda*. "Es entonces cuando se pone en juego el otro 'efecto' buscado por ella, porque la aparición del nombre sirve ahora, entre otras cosas, para recordar que en el momento de su debut literario la escritora había elegido un seudónimo que evocaba otra faceta de su vida ligada con la maternidad: Daniel es el nombre del primer hijo de Mansilla. Sumado a esto, hay que señalar también que cuando

Eduarda decide revelar su nombre de autora firma con dos apellidos (el de soltera y el de casada), ofreciendo a los desconocidos la información más completa posible sobre su identidad civil y recordando a los conocidos cuál es su procedencia familiar y su inscripción social y con qué atributos prefiere ser reconocida en el escenario de las letras nacionales y americanas" (That is when the other "effect" that she sought comes into play, because the appearance of the name now serves, among other things, as a reminder that, at the moment of her literary debut, the writer had chosen a pseudonym that evoked another facet of her life, one related to motherhood. Daniel was the name of Mansilla's oldest son. Moreover, it must be noted that, when Eduarda decides to reveal her name, the author signs with both surnames [her maiden name and her married name], offering strangers the most complete information possible regarding her marital status and reminding acquaintances of her family origins and social standing, as well as by which attributes she preferred to be recognized on the national and New World literary scenes) (Batticuore 233). On the author's various names and pseudonyms, see Batticuore 229–34.

47. While Mansilla does not spell her protagonist's first name with an accent on the "i," most contemporary scholars do. Because my chapter is in conversation with recent scholarship on the text, I will follow twenty-first-century convention and write "Lucía" except when quoting directly from Mansilla's novel.

48. A "morisco" in early modern Spain was a Muslim who had converted to Christianity or the descendent of a converted Muslim. An "Old Christian" was the descendent of a family that ostensibly had always been Christian.

49. I will discuss popular responses to this movement in the next chapter.

50. I recognize that the term "Western Civilization" is fraught with uncomfortable racial and geopolitical connotations. It is, however, the category that Mansilla—however problematically—interpellates in her text even without naming it. For a critique of "Western Civilization" as a construct, see Appiah.

51. "Las raíces coloniales criollas de las Provincias Unidas del Río de la Plata."

52. Though in this study I frame the Lucía Miranda tradition in the context of New World literature, it is important to remember that the captivity genre had a long history in the Mediterranean world antedating the European conquest of the Americas. In these texts, Christians are kidnapped and often fall in love with Arabs and Ottoman Turks, and the genre is deployed to negotiate the frontiers of religious—rather than racial—identity. For a comparative study of captivity narratives in Iberia and the Americas, see Voigt.

53. In fact, 1860 saw the publication of two novelized versions of the tale, the other by Rosa Guerra. For a summary of adaptations of the Lucía Miranda myth, see Lojo, Introduction, and Langa Pizarro 110–12. Importantly, as Susan Rotker points out, "No one has proven that the characters of the tragedy of Lucía Miranda existed historically" (104). Diana Marre, on the other hand, suggests that there is a documentary basis to the myth of Lucía Miranda (349–51).

54. For theoretical discussions of war rape and nationalism, see Eisenstein 46–49 and V. Peterson 68–69.

55. Although I will not deal with the subject here, the novel also dedicates considerable space to the cultural achievements of Spanish Italy under Habsburg rule, yet another of the Hispanic world's historical contact zones.

56. Rosas changed the traditional spelling of his family name.

57. For a discussion of how this family political history influences Mansilla's novel, see Masiello 40 and Chikiar Bauer, *Entre ellos* chapter 1.

58. For a discussion of Sarmiento's views on Eduarda Mansilla, see Lojo, "Sarmiento," and Jagoe. Natalia Crespo suggests that participation in the arts and engagement in political discourse may have been considered acceptable conduct for female members of the nineteenth-century Argentine oligarchy. She points out that several women in Mansilla's family, such as her aunt by marriage Encarnación Ezcurra and her cousin Manuelita Rosas, had played active public roles during the Rosas dictatorship (21). Lojo makes similar observations, arguing that the creole-aristocratic tradition of female participation in the public sphere that Mansilla's family followed would become less acceptable toward the end of the nineteenth century as bourgeois cultural norms grew increasingly hegemonic in Argentina ("La importancia").

59. Long overshadowed in the Argentine literary canon by her more famous brother Lucio V. Mansilla, author of *Una excursión a los indios ranqueles* (*A Visit to the Ranquel Indians*) (1870), Eduarda Mansilla and her works have enjoyed a revival in the wake of pioneering studies by Francine Masiello and María Rosa Lojo. These studies form part of a larger upsurge in interest in nineteenth-century South American female reform writers such as the Argentines Juana Manso, Juana Manuela Gorriti, and Rosa Guerra and the Peruvians Clorinda Matto de Turner and Mercedes Cabello de Carbonera, among others. Contemporary scholars such as Lojo have suggested that these writers "seem to be able to see the positions of subaltern and marginal peoples from a different angle, from that of the 'other' and the savage, particularly, of the native peoples, who had been displaced from the nation's foundational imaginary" and incorporate marginalized populations (parecen ser capaces de mirar desde un ángulo distinto la posición del subalterno y marginal, del 'otro' y del salvaje, muy en particular, de los pueblos originarios, desplazados del imaginario fundacional de la nación) (Lojo, "Novela histórica" 45). For the history of scholarly neglect of Mansilla's work, see chapter 1 of Chikiar Bauer's *Entre ellos*. For a discussion of Mansilla's *Lucía Miranda* in the context of nineteenth-century Latin American women's literature, see Mataix. For discussions of nineteenth-century Argentine women's literature, see Fletcher, Masiello, Frederick, *Wily Modesty,* and Batticuore. For a comparative reading of representations of the other in the work of Eduarda and Lucio Mansilla, see Pérez Gras and Lojo, "Fronteras."

60. On uterine-nationalism, or biotechnological efforts to reproduce citizens of particular racial and class backgrounds, see Heng and Devan.

61. "¡La Pampa entera les brinda su inmensidad!"

62. Luis Alberto Sánchez, for his part, claims that *Cumandá* and *Tabaré* were inspired by the Lucía Miranda legend (144). On nineteenth-century Spanish translations of *The Last of the Mohicans*, see Ferguson; Viñuela Angulo; and Genova, "*Mohicans* in Spanish." On the influence of Cooper's canonical text on nineteenth-century Latin American letters, see Meléndez; Sommer, *Foundational Fictions;* and Genova, "Family Entanglements."

63. Auguste Defauconpret, Cooper's first French translator, rendered "Leatherstocking" as "Bas-de-Cuir" throughout *Le dernier des Mohicans* (1826).

64. "Unos veinte ó treinta indios, [con] los cuerpos casi desnudos, con las cabezas cubiertas de plumas y en la más completa inmovilidad, [que] semejaban estatuas de barro."

65. "Rebelde naturaleza"; "hijo del desierto."

66. "Una de las cosas á que más las exhortaba la virtuosa Española [a las mujeres indígenas], era á que inspirasen respeto á sus hijos, educándoles desde pequeños, respetuosos y sumisos, porque las indias, á ese respecto, tenían las más equivocadas creencias; juzgando que el amor maternal consistia en permitirles hasta los más descompuestos y chocantes actos." For a discussion of the role of women in the conquest of Río de la Plata, see Langa Pizarro.

67. "Un mestizaje donde el elemento masculino dominante (el padre) es blanco y Cristiano, y por lo tanto puede dar *forma* a la 'materia bárbara.' Pensar lo contrario (que Lucía tuviera descendencia de Siripó) subvertiría las relaciones de dominio y humillaría a la cultura del conquistador, al transformarla, como a una mujer, en objeto/cuerpo penetrable." Emphasis in the original.

68. "Lucia, que veía el naciente amor de los dos jóvenes, tomaba especial esmero, en preparar el corazón de la india, al goce íntimo y delicado de los dulces afectos, templando por medio de prédicas, la ardiente fogosidad de su alma de salvaje. Y a medida que el tiempo pasaba, el corazon de la Española trasmitia á la joven india una porcion de su delicado perfume."

69. "Sopla de improviso el viento, resuena en lontananza el eco de su voz quejumbrosa; la llama, próxima á extinguirse revive con mayor fuerza, enciéndese de nuevo la hoguera, que incendia, que consume cuanto halla á su alcance. Arden los árboles vecinos, ya el tronco que suspende el desfigurado cadáver, oscila, cae; un momento más, y las cenizas de Lucia y Sebastian se confunden en un último abrazo!"

70. "El bosque se convirtió en cenizas; hoy no quedan de él ni vestigios, los timbúes, mudaron su campamento el siguiente día."

71. For other readings of the chapters occurring before the novel's characters arrive in the Americas, see Lojo, introduction; Hanway; Moody; and Chikiar Bauer, "Lucía Miranda."

72. "Beduinos americanos"; "la misma lucha de civilización y barbarie [que] existe en África."

73. "Esta extensión de las llanuras imprime, por otra parte, a la vida del interior cierta tintura asiática. . . . Alguna analogía encuentra el espíritu entre la pampa y las llanuras que median entre el Tigris y el Eufrates. . . .

"Es el capataz un caudillo, como en Asia el jefe de la caravana. . . . A la menor señal de insubordinación, el capataz enarbola su chicote de hierro, y descarga sobre el insolente golpes que causan contusiones y heridas; si la resistencia se prolonga, . . . salta del caballo con el formidable cuchillo en mano y reivindica bien pronto su autoridad por la superior destreza con que sabe manejarlo.

"El que muere en estas ejecuciones del capataz no deja derecho a ningún reclamo, considerándose legítima la autoridad que lo ha asesinado.

"Así es como en la vida argentina empieza a establecerse por estas peculiaridades el predominio de la fuerza brutal, la preponderancia del más fuerte, la autoridad sin límites y sin responsabilidades de los que mandan, la justicia administrada sin formas y sin debate."

74. On the conflict between rule of law and anarchy in Sarmiento, see Bunkley.

75. For a discussion of Sarmiento's Orientalism, in addition to Beckman, "Bedouins," see de Sena. For more on the racialization of the Moor, see below.

76. For a theoretical study of nineteenth-century Orientalism, see Said.

77. "Lineamientos de los románticos argentinos, quienes, como Sarmiento y Echeverría, renegaron de lo español."

78. "Un sello de cultura, extraño hasta entonces, á aquellas remotas tierras."

79. The colonial Latin American counterpart to the sixteenth- and seventeenth-century Golden Age of Spanish culture, the *barroco de Indias* is regarded by some as the maximum aesthetic expression of Latin American cultural mestizaje.

80. While the castas system was significantly less complex in Argentina than in other areas of Spanish America, the region had belonged to the Viceroyalty of Peru—where a nuanced hierarchy based on blood fractions was a palpable feature of daily life—until 1776. Significantly, Sarmiento continues to use castas designations such as "zambos" and "chinos" in his 1838 periodical *El zonda* and Mansilla's brother Lucio also uses castas terminology in his *Excursión a los indios ranqueles,* suggesting that the colonial categories continued to circulate in Argentina during the 1800s. Moving in the same intellectual milieu as her brother and, to a certain extent, Sarmiento, Mansilla de García clearly had access to this racial vocabulary.

81. For a discussion of motherhood in *La Aljaba,* see chapter 1. For a different reading of Lucía's Moorishness, see Chikiar Bauer's *Entre ellos,* which discusses Mansilla's intertextual references to the *Cantar del mío Cid* and the Reconquista in the context of the conquest-era story recounted in *Lucía Miranda.*

82. Interestingly, Bernardino Rivadavia, the first president of the United Provinces of Río de la Plata, while known for his Europeanizing cultural policies, was of mixed race and, during his lifetime, was referred to by the somewhat

demeaning moniker of "Doctor Chocolate." This points to the not strictly sanguineous notion of whiteness that traditionally has prevailed in Latin America. As this book shows, the Latin American construction of whiteness would come into conflict with northern cultural notions as the nineteenth century progressed.

83. "La peculiar relación entre Rosas y los afroargentinos fue . . . uno de los rasgos caracterizadores fundamentales de su acción de gobierno."

84. "Los negros . . . ponían en manos de Rosas, un celoso espionaje en el seno de cada familia, por los sirvientes y esclavos, proporcionándole, además, excelentes e incorruptibles soldados."

85. "Un sistema de asesinatos y crueldades, tolerables tan sólo en Ashanti y Dahomai, en el interior de África."

86. For readings of race in these two works see Solomianski. See also Aponte-Ramos on the figure of the Afro-descendant in nineteenth-century Argentine literature.

87. To this day, Afro-descendants remain largely unacknowledged members of the Argentine imagined community. For more on race in contemporary Argentina, see Alberto and Elena.

88. "Tu padre, por ser español, no está exento de la sospecha de tener sangre mezclada, pues supongo que es andaluz, y de Sevilla vinieron a América los primeros esclavos negros. Tampoco los árabes, que dominaron en Andalucía más que en otras partes de España, fueron de raza pura caucásica, sino africana."

89. "Tomó Lucia por suya la piadosa tarea de instruir á las sencillas habitantes del desierto, en las sublimes verdades del Cristianismo. Todos los días, con incansable perseverancia, su celo la llevó á las chozas de los Timbúes. Veíasele allí, rodeada de las indias, sentadas sobre la yerba, con sus hijos en brazos las unas, las otras con las manos cruzadas sobre las rodillas, en atenta actitud, sueltos los cabellos sobre la espalda, y fijos los grandes ojos en el semblante de la joven, escuchar las palabras de amor y caridad, que despertaban en sus almas adormidos ecos; semejantes al niño que repite la oracion primera, enseñada por su madre y que sin darse cuenta, siente en el fondo del alma, mística revelacion, que sube del corazon hasta el semblante, iluminado con celestial reflejo."

90. "Blanca Española"; "mujer europea."

91. "Luz de la pampa, astro del día."

92. In addition to *The Last of the Mohicans,* see, for example, New Englander Mary Rowlandson's 1682 *Sovereignty and Goodness of God* and Echeverría's 1837 *Cautiva.*

93. "Reivindica y pone en valor a esa tradición." On Hispanics as "off-white," see M. de Guzmán.

94. Sarmiento, for his part, includes an anecdote in *Facundo* about the "negro Barcala," who distinguished himself fighting on the Unitario side in the Argentine civil wars, suggesting that, for the statesman, Afro-Argentines, though associated with Federal barbarism, were assimilable to the cause of liberal civilization. However, while Sarmiento feels that Barcala has been "redeemed" by his contact with

his enlightened masters, Mansilla presents the hybrid Lucía as taking charge of her own educación in order to function as a civilizing force in and of herself. For more on the negro Barcala episode, see Garrels, "Sobre los indios," and chapter 3 of this book.

95. As Chikiar Bauer explains in *Entre ellos,* the author was accompanying her husband on a diplomatic mission to study the US legal system.

96. "Yo era sudista.

"A pesar de los esclavos? se me dirá. Á pesar, respondo humildemente, que ese Sud, donde reinaba la esclavatura, era hasta entónces el monopolizador de la elegancia, del refinamiento, y de la cultura en la Union; verdad, que el Norte reconocia y proclamaba á cada paso en sus aspiraciones sociales."

As Beatriz Ferrús Antón explains, Mansilla considers that "el sur ha perdido porque defendía una causa injusta: la esclavitud, pero representa . . . el espacio de una clase social educada como ella, a modo de una aristocracia norteamericana que se verá abatida. Su historia familiar no está tan alejada de esta derrota" (the South lost because it defended an unjust cause: slavery, but it represented . . . the space of a social class that had been raised as she had, a sort of North American aristocracy that would be knocked down. Her family history was not far from that defeat) (108). Mansilla de García would later retract her pro-Confederate position. For more on *Recuerdos de viaje,* and on Argentine travel writing about the United States in general, see Viñas. For a comparison of Mansilla de García's travel narrative with that of Sarmiento, see Urraca. For a discussion of Mansilla de García's *Recuerdos* in relation to domesticity, see Lojo, "En las fronteras."

97. "Esta es la aristocracia de las balas de algodon i de las bolsas de azúcar, fruto del sudor de los esclavos. ¡Ah! ¡la esclavatura, la llaga profunda i la fístula incurable que amenaza gangrenar el cuerpo robusto de la Union! ¡Qué fatal error fué el de Washington i de los grandes filósofos que hicieron la declaracion de los derechos del hombre, el dejar a los plantadores del sud sus esclavos; ¿i por qué rara fatalidad los Estados Unidos, que en la práctica han realizado los últimos progresos del sentimiento de igualdad i de caridad, están condenados a dar las postreras batallas contra la injusticia antigua de hombre a hombre, vencida ya en todo el resto de la tierra?"

98. "Los estados libres son superiores en número i riqueza a los estados de esclavos."

99. For other discussions of Mansilla de García's southern sympathies, see Bramen and Szurmuk, *Women in Argentina*: 61–63. For a discussion of *Recuerdos* in the context of women's travel narratives, in addition to Szurmuk, see Miseres.

100. "É realidade e metáfora. Realidade geo-política, que acaba por reproduzir, no Novo Continente uma oposição Norte/Sul, originalmente européia, com a inflexão particular que ganha na segunda metade do século XIX, quando ali o Sul, além de aludir a uma oposição de riqueza e pobreza de regiões, liga-se as noções de latinidade, catolicismo, decadência. No paradígma construido, esse Sul opõe-se ao Norte anglo-saxão, ao protestantismo, ao progresso." See also

Szurmuk, "Géometries," on the articulation of an aristocratic Latin identity in Mansilla's *Recuerdos*.

101. For a discussion of *Recuerdos* as a critique of settler colonialism in both the United States and Argentina, see Szurmuk, *Women in Argentina* 61.

3. Una Maestra Norteamericana in the "South"

1. Luigi reports that the program ended in 1916 (*65 Valiants* 17), Chavarria in 1920 (386). Tristán Guevara, for his part, claims that the last North American teachers arrived in Argentina in 1898; they presumably served until several years later (16).

2. I have explored Sarmiento's relationship with Mary Mann in my article "Sarmiento's *Vida de Horacio Mann*: Translation, Importation and Entanglement," which, though it mentions the US teachers project in the context of the extended South, focuses mainly on the correspondence between the two reformers and the translations that they prepared of one another's work. Having already discussed this fascinating story in my article, I will not dedicate much attention to it here. Instead, the present chapter considers how the hemispheric trope of racialized republican motherhood influenced the US teachers program. For other hemispheric studies of Sarmiento's work, see Faust, Velleman, Jaksic, Leroux, Hooker, and Rothera, "Our South American Cousin." For a general overview of Sarmiento, education, and the United States, see Dorn. For more on white northern teachers in the Reconstruction-era South, see chapter 1 of this book.

3. On *The Last of the Mohicans* and *Lucía Miranda*, see Chapter 2 of this book.

4. On Sarmiento's negative views concerning the Rosas regime, see chapter 2 of this book.

5. The North American chapters are also, to the best of my knowledge, the only section of *Viajes* that has been translated into English. See Rockland for more information.

6. For a (somewhat embellished) firsthand account of Sarmiento's relation to the European lettered elite, see his 1850 intellectual autobiography *Recuerdos de provincia*.

7. "Triste mezcla de grandeza i de abyeccion, de saber i de embrutecimiento a la vez, sublime i sucio receptáculo de todo lo que al hombre eleva o le tiene degradado, ¡reyes i lacayos, monumentos i lazaretos, opulencia i vida salvaje!"

8. "Capacidad, voluntad e influencia suficiente para obrar tamaño bien, ilustrando la opinion pública i del gobierno, concentrando e impulsando la accion de los animosos amigos del progreso, señalando los obstáculos i guiando por el buen sendero que sus largos estudios, sus viajes y su diaria consagración le indican."

9. Harold Peterson reports that, during the same period, Rosas sent delegations to the United States with the intention of generating support for his regime (172–73).

10. "Me he vuelto a otro sol que no eclipsa, que ninguna nube oculta: Estados Unidos. Como teoría, como hecho, como poder, como influencia, como porvenir..., la democracia allí la encuentro fuerte, consistente consigo misma."

11. "Reencontró la ilusión."

12. Presumably, this is Patton's translation. According to biographer Allison Bunkley, Argentine president Bartolomé Mitre sent Sarmiento to the United States in the aftermath of an essay he had written criticizing the Federal caudillo Chacho Peñaloza (412). Mitre also may have wished to eliminate Sarmiento as a political rival by sending him abroad (González Echevarría, *Facundo* 9).

13. Sarmiento was not the only Argentine liberal to see public education as the "base" of the United States' "prosperity." Writing from exile in Brazil in 1854, educationalist Juana Manso would claim that the founding fathers of the United States, in their efforts to create "un pueblo sobrio, religioso e industrial" (a somber, religious, and industrious people), had turned to public education in order to lay "los cimientos seguros sobre los que levantaron el monumento eterno de la civilización y de prosperidad de su país" (the steady foundation upon which they raised the eternal monument of the civilization and prosperity of their country) ("Organización" 17–18). As a result, "Haya un presidente de la Unión Americana que diga:/'La ley soy yo. El estado soy yo.'/El pueblo lo despedazará!" (If ever there should be a president of the American Union who says/'I am the law. I am the state.'/The people will rip him to pieces!) (Manso, "Educación popular" 47).

14. "En materia de Informes de Educacion, de Escuelas Comunes, *common schools,* Superintendentes, etc. etc. nuestra Jurisprudencia [nuestros] antecedentes está[n] en los Estados Unidos, de donde nos vino la ley... y el sistema de Educacion Comun."

15. "Optó por el modelo napoleónico consistente en una pirámide en cuya cúspide está la universidad, que funciona como rectora de todos los establecimientos educativos."

16. "No era estatista en el sentido de la moderna educación pública democrática, sino con el carácter absolutista."

17. "Prefirieron promover Juntas Protectoras de la Educación, provinciales y locales, en las que los vecinos tuvieron activa participación y defendieran la autonomía de los sistemas educativos de sus provincias."

18. "Vinculaba la educación de los provincianos con la integración nacional; Rivadavia aspiraba formar una minoría esclarecida y privilegiada."

19. "Más ligado al orden que al trabajo, a la ritualización del régimen que a la formación de productores."

20. For more on Rosas's assault on public education in Buenos Aires, see Solari 89–91.

21. For more on schooling in Argentina before the 1860s, see Szuchman.

22. Across Latin America, only about 12 percent of children attended school in 1860. In 1870, the world literacy rate was only 18.74 percent (Roser and Ortiz-Ospina n.p.).

23. "La paz, el trabajo, las garantías constitucionales, el bienestar de la familia, las riquezas y las virtudes son imposibles."

24. "Como medio político en el afianzamiento de las instituciones, como medio económico en la riqueza púbica que se aumenta bajo el dominio del pensamiento metodizado aplicado á los objetos de la naturaleza que el hombre transforma y aprovecha, y como medio moral en la formación del criterio público que hace posible y asegura el bienestar de las agrupaciones humanas." For more details on the economic considerations of Sarmiento's educational reform, see his *Educación común en el estado de Buenos-Aires* (1855). Puiggrós, for her part, condemns the Sarmientine educational reforms as a method of social control (*Sujetos* 115–17) and claims that Sarmiento hoped to use public education to incorporate the children of ex-Federal families into the liberal project (87). Tosso similarly suggests that Sarmiento's educational reform, by making education public and consequently reducing the Catholic clergy's access to the county's children, may have been part of an effort to limit ecclesiastical influence in Argentina and thus undermine one of the bulwarks of Federal rule.

25. "Introducir nuevas ideas, nuevas prácticas"; "esto no se conseguirá sino trasplantando con los hombres mismos que han de hacerlas efectivas, las ideas, formas é instituciones que tan asombrosos resultados han producido donde son la base de todo el sistema político y social."

26. For an explanation of "gobernar es poblar," see chapter 2 of this book.

27. Roitenburd suggests that Argentine educationalist Juana Manso may have influenced Sarmiento in his decision to invite the North American teachers to the South American country (46–47).

28. Luigi claims that "sixty-five teachers were a small fraction of the number Sarmiento projected. He talked of a thousand" (*65 Valiants* 17). Tristán Guevara, for his part, estimates that close to one hundred US teachers went to Argentina between 1870 and 1898, but he admits that the exact number is impossible to determine (16). Rothera, meanwhile, notes that the US teachers originally were destined for elementary classrooms and that Sarmiento later decided to place them in normal schools instead (211).

29. Published in 1868, Mary's *Life in the Argentine Republic in the Days of Tyrants* was the only version of *Facundo* available in English until Kathleen Ross published her own translation in 2003. Throughout this book, I occasionally will break with convention and refer to Mary and Horace Mann by their first names in order to distinguish them from one another.

30. "Although Mrs. Horace Mann's counsel and encouragement to Sarmiento cannot be overestimated, no teacher procured directly through her efforts actually taught in Argentine normal schools" (Luigi, *65 Valiants* 48). In his bias toward upper-class educators, Sarmiento follows Horace Mann, who favored teachers from the privileged sectors of society, hoping that they would transfer their bourgeois values and comport to students from more humble origins (H. Mann, *Report* 91). However, Leroux has demonstrated that, despite Sarmiento's plans, most of

the US teachers in Argentina were in fact from lower-middle-class backgrounds ("Money").

31. For more on *Juanita* and the extended South, see chapter 4 of this book.

32. The third one was translated literally as "Social War."

33. "Los hombres de color de los Estados Unidos no se encuentran más faltos de educación que los habitantes blancos de nuestras campañas."

34. "Militan para continuar el atraso en los estados donde hubo esclavos, las mismas razones, aunque en menor escala que en los nuestros. El pueblo llano, ó lo que se llama aquí *blancos pobres,* no se afana mucho por educarse." Emphasis in original.

35. For biographical information on the maestras de Sarmiento, see Luigi, *65 Valiants.* Leroux, too, explores the US teachers' social origins. She suggests that the North American educators' motives in traveling to Argentina were chiefly economic, problematizing earlier ideas about the extent to which Reconstruction-era reformism prompted their migration ("Money" 195).

36. "Parecía un *colored school* americano."

37. On "guiding fictions," or national mythologies, in Argentina, see Shumway. For more on the racial composition of nineteenth-century Argentina, see chapter 2 of this book.

38. Indeed, the earliest mention that I have found in the *Memorias* of the schools being used to assimilate immigrant masses (through the teaching of the Spanish language) is in 1884 (V. Ferrer 172–73). At the pilot Escuela Normal de Paraná, the first Italian last name appears in the list of 1880 graduates (Torres "Escuela Normal del Paraná," 1881, 827). Meanwhile, in 1881, the model school at the Escuela Normal de Maestros de la Capital was almost evenly divided between students from traditional Argentine families and the children of European immigrants (94 versus 107, respectively, with 8 or 9 additional students of Paraguayan, Uruguayan, and Brazilian backgrounds) (Larsen and Levingston 353). In the same year, traditional Hispanic surnames significantly outnumber foreign ones on the rosters of graduates from the normal schools of Mendoza (Salcedo, "Informe anual" 457), Corrientes (Roca and Pizarro, "Decreto Corrientes" 482), Santiago del Estero (Roca and Pizarro, "Decreto Santiago" 483), and San Luis (Roca and Pizarro, "Decreto San Luis" 483). In Tucumán, meanwhile, all the 1881 graduates had traditional Hispanic surnames (Roca and Pizarro, "Decreto Tucumán" 437). In general, foreign surnames became more common on student rosters after 1882, though this change is largely concentrated in Buenos Aires. There are no foreign names on the list of normal school graduates in Mendoza for 1882 and 1883, for example (Salcedo, "Escuela Normal," 861). While this method is admittedly unscientific (and misses immigrants from Spain), it does suggest that the majority of students served by these institutions during the period were from traditional Argentine backgrounds. As E. N. de Caprile would write in her report on the Escuela Normal de Maestras de la Capital, in 1883, out of 112 students, "the majority were Argentine, as there were only six foreigners,

of whom three were Italian, two Spanish, and one French" (la mayoria eran argentinas, pues solo habia 6 estrangeras, de las que tres eran italianas, 2 españolas y 1 francesa) (Caprile 890). Even if the normal students were not typical of the national student body in general, the lack of European immigrants suggests that much of the teaching force was of mixed race and would be working with mixed-race students. While Sarmiento did suggest that it would be necessary to incorporate the children of European immigrants into the public education system ("El Editor" 5), the data that I am discussing here appear to confirm Puiggrós's assertion that it is only after the consolidation of the agro-export model under the *Generación del 1880* that immigrants becomes the loci of serious educational efforts in Argentina (*Sujetos* 99). For a primary source on immigrant education in the Argentine schools during the period, see *L'Educatore,* an Italian-language newspaper published in Buenos Aires in 1880. For more on the social origins of the normal students, see McMeley.

39. Even under Rivadavia, the charitable Sociedad de Beneficencia operated a school for Afro-Argentine girls in Buenos Aires, though it was underresourced and emphasized preparation in domestic arts, possibly to train servants (Szuchman 134).

40. This interest in the country's black population dates from Sarmiento's experiences commanding Afro-Argentine militia men during the civil wars between Unitarios and Federales (Bunkley 85).

41. "Un obstáculo, empero, se oponía a [la ambición de Quiroga]. Un vecino de Mendoza habia criado un negrito criollo esclavo, que desde temprano habia manifestado el talento i despejo que no es raro ver en los descendientes de raza africana; leia i escribia, i criado al lado de los amos, en contacto con ellos i oyéndoles sus conversaciones, habia completado una educacion suficiente para que el jénio de que la naturaleza le habia dotado se revelase en la primera oportunidad. Principió por ser asistente de su amo, i siguiendo una escala de ascensos vino a ser al fin comandante de un batallon de cívicos; lo que le ponia en contacto con las notabilidades políticas de la época. El negro Barcala es una de las figuras mas distinguidas de la revolucion arjentina, i una de las reputaciones mas intachables que han cruzado esta época tan borrascosa, en que tan pocos son los que no quisieron arrancar una pajina del libro de sus acciones. Elevado por su mérito, nunca olvidó su color i oríjen: era un hombre eminentemente civilizado en sus maneras, gustos e ideas, i en Haití hubiera podido figurar al lado de Petion y sus hombres mas notables. Pero lo que ha hecho de Barcala un personaje histórico, es su raro talento para la organizacion de cuerpos, i la habilidad con la que hacia descender a las masas las ideas civilizadoras. Los pardos y los hombres de la plebe transformaban en sus manos: la moral mas pura, el vestir y los habitos de los hombres decentes, el amor a la libertad i a las luces, distinguian a los oficiales y soldados de su escuela. En Mendoza ha costado muchos años i diezmar a los patricios, para borrar las profundas huellas que Barcala dejó en los ánimos, i en Córdova la revolucion de 1840 contra Rosas reunió un batallón de infantería numeroso i

decidido hasta el martirio, a merced de un farol de retreta que tenia escrita esta palabra: ¡*Barcala!*" (9–10). "Batallón" is spelled two different ways in the edition that I consulted.

42. Sarmiento's comments should not be taken as a statement of racial egalitarianism, however. Garrels suggests that, though he refers to Barcala as a "negro" in this passage, Sarmiento considered the historical figure to be of mixed race ("Sobre los indios" 106). In this way, the anecdote fits into the Argentine statesman's well-known belief that his country can only be improved through a whitening of the population as, according to Garrels, Sarmiento sees the mulato Barcala as redeemed and uplifted by his white ancestry. For more on the image of Haiti in the nineteenth-century Americas, see Fischer, *Modernity Disavowed*.

43. "El tipo Benjamin Franklin proyectado al discurso de la raza." On the influence of Benjamin Franklin's 1791 *Autobiography* on Sarmiento, see Molloy.

44. For more on Mendizábal, see Lewis and Solomianski.

45. "La escuela primaria tiene por único objetivo favorecer y dirigir simultáneamente el desarrollo moral, intelectual y físico de todo niño de seis a catorce años de edad."

46. For a theoretical discussion of "discipline" and the rise of the bourgeois-republican state, see Foucault, *Surveiller et punir*. Following Foucault, I use "discipline" to refer to the bourgeois emphasis on the self-monitoring of personal comport in modern society and the ways in which this cultural development has been encouraged and exploited by economic and political power.

47. "El Litoral é Interior de la República, destinadas á la preparacion industrial y reforma moral de la niñez ó juventud desvalida y callejera, cuya holgazaneria y hábitos viciosos, son una amenaza en el presente, y constituyen un verdadero peligro social en el porvenir."

48. "Falta de aplicacion en un alumno maestro, será considerada como causa de mala conducta, para motivar su espulsion de la Escuela."

49. See chapter 2 for more on this political-economic history.

50. For more on this attitude in Sarmiento, see Guerrero Guerrero.

51. "Nuestra querida madre, la España, fue conquistada por los Moros, que la retuvieron en su poder por más de 700 años, y si no la dejaron su religión e idioma, absolutamente, la dejaron por lo menos sus costumbres orientales."

52. "Completa degradación"; "angélicas formas"; "no [ve] sino un incentivo a las pasiones animales." In an 1875 appeal for the establishment of women's normal schools, Leguizamón claimed that, outside of Buenos Aires, even upper-class women typically were illiterate (xci).

53. "Los demás pueblos de Europa que no han sido dominados por los árabes o los moros."

54. "Le da las primeras ideas [a su hijo], instrúyala, para que lo haga feliz con una educación sabia; enséñele las bases de la moral, para que guíe su propia conducta, y aleccione a sus hijas, para que formen costumbres análogas a sus estados de civilización." Sarmiento would return to this topic in "De la educacion de

la mujer," an 1841 article that he published while he was living in exile in Chile. For an analysis of this article, see Garrels, "Sarmiento ante la cuestión." For more on images of women in the work of Sarmiento, see Masiello 25–27.

55. For a biography of Gorman, see Peard, *American Teacher.*
56. On "manifest domesticity," see chapter 2 of this book.
57. "Un ejército de doce mil maestros."
58. Armstrong later would travel to New Paltz, New York, in order to found a normal school for Cuban women during the first US occupation of the island. See chapter 5 for more information.
59. For more on the cultural legacy of the Good Neighbor Policy in Latin America, see Franco, *Decline and Fall* 21–38.
60. Ambassador Bliss would fund a chair in Latin American History and Economics at Harvard, an activity that Salvatore understands as part of a growing US "soft" imperialism in South America during the first half of the twentieth century (*Disciplinary* 106).
61. For a discussion of this agricultural metaphor in Sarmientine educational writing, see Szurmuk, *Women in Argentina* 79–80.
62. The respect that Washington had shown for Spanish American racial categories in the 1848 Treaty of Guadalupe Hidalgo—which guaranteed North American citizenship to "white" Mexican creoles in the newly conquered US Southwest—gradually had given way to the segregation of Mexican Americans in the ceded territory and, in times of economic crisis, to the deportation of native-born citizens of Mexican ancestry. Similarly, while mid-nineteenth-century Cuban creole slavocrats, according to historian Mathew Guterl, were considered the peers of US southern planters, the North American occupation of Cuba following the 1898 Spanish-Cuban-American War would be justified on the grounds that the country—now cast as a territory populated by recently liberated slaves—lacked a white political class capable of self-government. For a theoretical study of the racialization of the Hispanic in US imperial and cultural discourse, see M. de Guzmán. For a literary treatment of the racialization of the *californio* upper class, see Ruiz de Burton. For more on the racialization of Cubans in the US imaginary, see Pérez, *Cuba between Empires* and *Cuba in the American Imagination,* as well as chapters 4 and 5 of this book.
63. On the imbrication of discourses of Moorishness, Africanity, and "barbarism" in Argentina during the long nineteenth century, see chapter 2.
64. While the text concludes with an index of the "Names of the American Teachers in Argentina" (133–36), no students are identified by name anywhere in the book, including in the opening biographical sketch of Howard written by an anonymous former student.
65. "Las muchachas correntinas, mezcla de españolas con guaraníes, carecían de remilgos para gozar de la vida afectiva y sexual. Circulaban airosas, ataviadas de blanco, con los pies descalzos . . . ; bromeaban con los hombres, procuraban agradarles sin recato alguno y eran astutas para citarse discretamente con

sus enamorados en parajes solitarios. La virginidad de las novias no era objeto de preocupación: las jóvenes podían contraer matrimonio teniendo uno o más hijos de distintos padres, sin que nadie se molestase."

66. On the representation of late-nineteenth- and early-twentieth-century boom-and-bust economics in Latin American literature, see Beckman, *Capital Fictions*.

67. "En ciertos puntos de la Provincia, la clase indígena ó no conoce o habla muy imperfectamente el idioma pátrio, haciéndose allí necesario que el maestro posea la lengua quíchua."

68. On uneven modernity in Latin America and the African diaspora, see Mignolo, *Local Histories* and Gilroy, respectively. On hybridity, race, and modernity, see Cornejo Polar and García Canclini.

69. On "vasallaje cultural," see Uslar Pietri. For an interpretation of Sarmiento as a cultural vassal of the North, see Piglia. For theorizations of the sort of cultural cannibalization (to borrow Brazilian *modernista* Oswaldo de Andrade's metaphor for cultural reappropriation in the Global South) with which I am opposing Uslar Pietri's critical paradigm, see Silviano and Pérez Firmat.

70. "Nada provee sobre la educación del pueblo, y . . . los poderes federales se habían mostrado durante una dilatada serie de años, insensibles o indiferentes ante esta suprema necesidad de la Nación"; "Salta á la vista que la Constitución Argentina se ha mostrado á este respecto más previsora que la Constitución Americana, cuyo texto casi siempre adopta como modelo visible."

71. "La Constitución Argentina, reflejando un movimiento de ideas, cuya huella podría señalarse con honra para nuestro nombre, se desvía felizmente en este punto grave de su acreditado modelo; y cobra el fomento de la educación pública entre los deberes y funciones del Gobierno que organiza, para realizar los fines que ostenta en su preámbulo como el programa de nuestros futuros destinos. Así, la Constitución ha establecido entre los ramos de la administración ejecutiva, un Departamento de Instrucción Pública."

72. "La proporcion de Escuelas Normales con respecto á la poblacion total"; "superior á . . . la de los Estados Unidos."

73. I am indebted to William Katra for pushing me (in conversation) to consider this seriously.

74. Kate Dogett, the socialite wife of the Turkish consul in Chicago, and Sarmiento's North American mistress Ida Wickersham also proved instrumental to the recruitment of US teachers for Argentina (Museo Histórico Sarmiento).

75. Moreover, these Argentine teachers were often men, as changes in school legislation skewed admission to the normal schools in favor of male applicants (McMeley 108–9).

76. Sarmiento said that the school had been in operation for almost a century; it in fact had been founded fifty-seven years prior to the writing of the article in which he mentions it. Rothera, for his part, contends that, prior to

his encounter with the Manns, "Sarmiento had clearly been interested in female education, but he thought more about educating women . . . than hiring women as teachers" (210).

77. Peard, however, suggests that Manso's notions on domesticity were influenced by her contacts with the United States ("Enchanted Edens" 455).

78. "Admirable propósito de emancipar de las costumbres funestas de la vieja metrópoli, a esa parte del pueblo en cuyo seno toman esencialmente su raíz, la transformación de la sociedad, su progreso y su bienestar." For more on Sarmiento's early activities in the field of women's education, see Garrels, "Sarmiento ante la cuestión."

79. For primary sources, see Sarmiento, "Creación de la escuela normal de preceptores"; "Resultados del primer curso de la Escuela Normal"; and "Sobre la educacion popular, carta al intendente de Valparaíso."

80. The first normal school in the United States was founded in Concord, Vermont, in 1823. The first public normal school in the country was founded in Lexington, Massachusetts, by Horace Mann in 1839.

81. Somewhat paradoxically, in elaborating his educational philosophy independently of Mann, Sarmiento appears to have drawn on the very Hispanic tradition that he wished to use public education to overcome. The title of his treatise *Las escuelas: base de la prosperidad en los Estados Unidos,* for example, paraphrases Spanish Enlightenment philosopher Gaspar Melchor de Jovellanos's 1802 statement that public instruction is "el primer origen de la prosperidad social" (Jovellanos 230). Jovellanos's notion of "educación doméstica" (84), too, represents an early articulation of what for Sarmiento would become the explicit linking of republican motherhood and public education. For a summary of Sarmiento's educational activities and philosophy, see Solari 147–58.

82. "Cultura ostentatoria y de segunda mano."

83. On capital in nineteenth-century Latin American literature, see Beckman, *Capital.*

84. For a slightly different variation on the same idea, see Leroux, "Self-Strengthening." My study differs from Leroux's excellent article principally in its focus on race and the allegory of the republican teacher-mother.

85. "Los Estados Unidos necesitan decir que son país que media entre dos océanos i dos tratados."

86. "La *anexion,* la *absorcion* de vecindad, es la conquista sorda de que están amenazadas." Emphasis in original.

87. "Una de las plagas nocivas que nos dejó Sarmiento."

88. "Que las Escuelas Normales en general no llenan debidamente su fin, que los resultados que producen no corresponden á los sacrificios que su sustentamiento demanda, no solo porque la cantidad de graduados cada año es exigua, especialmente en las escuelas de varones, sinó también porque suelen egresar con una deficiente preparación profesional."

89. "Una oligarquía que se había decidido por un modelo de reproducción basado en la renta de la tierra, que requería baja densidad de mano de obra y excelentes relaciones con los compradores europeos."

90. "Más que una continuidad lo que en realidad existió fue una ruptura entre el pensamiento educacional elaborado por los emigrantes durante el período rosista (Alberdi y Sarmiento) y la acción educativa posterior a 1880."

91. On Argentine relations within the Americas during this period, see Preuss.

92. "La actitud de Monroe fue creada hace noventa y un años, cuando la América del Sur era inorgánica, cuando sus países, inclusive el nuestro, eran republiquetas gauchi-políticas, expuestas a ver humillada su bandera y sus intereses por la frecuente aparición de buques de guerra extranjeros."

93. "Este es un pueblo europeo, porque la masa ha hecho la absorción del indio y del negro; y los mestizos, por el desarrollo sucesivo de las generaciones, son hoy tan blancos y tan puros como fueron negros e indios en su origen! Hoy en cualquier parte del país . . . encontraréis esta misma palpitación europea de vida que admiráis en Buenos Aires, porque nuestro progreso en este sentido es uniforme: será menos rico en algunas partes; pero en todas tiene las mismas características europeas!"

94. "Con la actitud de Monroe protegieron nuestra infancia y después transformaron nuestros sistemas de educación."

4. Foundational Frustrations in Cirilo Villaverde, Mary Mann, and Martín Morúa Delgado

1. Earlier versions of some of the material in this chapter previously were published in *Decimonónica* 13.1 (Winter 2016). On North American influence on nineteenth-century Argentine modernization projects, see chapters 2 and 3 of this book.

2. In May 1945, the Cuban congress officially changed the name of the war to "La Guerra Hispano-Cubanoamericana" (Foner 1:140n). For inter-American studies of the 1898 conflict, in addition to the works cited here, see particularly José Saldívar, *The Dialectics of Our America: Genealogy, Cultural Critique, and Literary History*, and Amy Kaplan, *The Anarchy of Empire in the Making of US Culture*. See also Louis Pérez Jr., *The War of 1898* and *Cuba in the American Imagination*.

3. "¡Estos nacidos en América, que se avergüenzan porque lleva delantal indio, de la madre que los crió, y reniegan ¡bribones! de la madre enferma, y la dejan sola en el lecho de las enfermedades!" On the allegory of the national family in *The Last of the Mohicans* and *Lucía Miranda*, see chapter 2 of this book. On *In Distant Climes and Other Years*, see chapter 3.

4. "El genio hubiera estado en hermanar, con la caridad del corazón y el atrevimiento de los fundadores, la vincha y la toga."

5. "No hay odio de razas porque no hay razas."

6. "El Indio, mudo, nos daba vueltas alrededor"; "cantaba entre las olas y las fieras." For examples of the sharply divergent readings that Martí's text continues to inspire, see Roberto Fernández Retamar, José Saldívar (*The Dialectics*), Susan Gillman, and Anne Fountain on Martí's racial inclusivity; and Lourdes Martínez-Echazábal ("Mestizaje") and Luis Duno Gottberg on the exclusive undertones of Martí's racial-nationalist project. For more recent discussion of Martí, cultural pluralism, and race, see Camacho 139–62 and 221–45 and Ette, *TransArea* 118–68.

7. Villaverde served as López's personal secretary for three years in the United States (Álvarez-Amell 118). Álvarez-Amell recently has provided evidence that complicates the traditional view of López and Villaverde as annexationists (118).

8. On the Aponte Conspiracy, see Palmié; Fischer, *Modernity Disavowed* (41–56); and Franco, *Las conspiraciones*. On La Escalera (also known as the Ladder Conspiracy in English), see Paquette.

9. On Sarmiento, see chapters 2 and 3 of this book.

10. "La prensa había enmudecido desde 1824, no existía la milicia ciudadana, los ayuntamientos habían dejado de ser cuerpos populares, y no quedaba ni la sombra de libertad, pues por decreto de 1825 se declaró el país en estado de sitio, instituyéndose la Comisión Militar permanente."

11. "La conclusión de este proceso político fue que la metrópoli era incapaz de darle a Cuba ninguno de los derechos fundamentales: en lo económico, la libertad comercial; en lo social, la igualdad del criollo blanco con el español peninsular; en lo político, la representación del país en las estructuras de poderes del Estado español."

12. For a recent and thorough study of this history, see Aching.

13. "El sufragio universal que asegura la soberanía del pueblo"; "la emancipación, gradual y bajo indemnización, de la esclavitud." Ironically, precisely because Cuba was revolting against Spain at the time, it did not become subject to the 1873 law that abolished slavery in Puerto Rico.

14. For more on the political positions discussed here, see Pérez, *Cuba between Empires*.

15. "Medida que detenía el crecimiento de la población negra y suponía una abolición gradual de la esclavitud"; "obtener de la Corona el cese del *status* colonial en favor de un régimen autonómico, reorganizar y organizar la agricultura de la caña de azúcar, renovar el trasporte y las comunicaciones, erradicar la vagancia y los vicios, promover los estudios científicos y reformar el sistema educativo."

16. According to William Luis, the character of Cecilia Valdés was inspired by a woman courted by one of Villaverde's schoolmates (*Literary Bondage*,

104). Enrique Sosa Rodríguez, meanwhile, suggests that the character of Leonardo Gamboa (called Leocadio in the 1839 short story) was based on the figure of Cándido Rubio y Lima, a real-life student at the Universidad de La Habana (400–401). Lamore, meanwhile, states that the character of Cecilia was inspired by the protagonist of Cervantes's *Gitanilla* (15).

17. "La Virgencita de bronce."

18. On Villaverde's earlier fiction, see Sosa Cabanas.

19. Domínguez argues that the *costumbrista* genre represents a technology to inscribe the other into discourse while containing social heterogeneity.

20. "Y le estuvo hablando gran pieza de la noche con calor; aunque sin fruto . . . porque como hombre de letras menudas . . . no era tan facil se diese por convencido, dado que Gamboa le alegára su vanidad, y le pintára castillos de filigrana, que se desmoronaban ante la dialéctica positiva y ruda de un cursante de leyes. En esta batalla, el sueño se apoderó de entrambos mancebos por sorpresa, cual un esbirro de policía, que le echa el guante á los distraídos bebedores, teniéndolos en cama, medio desnudos, y atravesándoles las últimas palabras en la garganta: motivo para que quedasen con la boca abierta."

21. "La nobleza comprada con la sangre de los negros que tú y los demás españoles robaban en África para condenarlos a eterna esclavitud, no era nobleza, sino infamia, y que miraba el título como el mayor baldón."

22. "¡Vaya que le hierve la sangre criolla en las venas! Todavía sería capaz el muy trompeta de principiar por su padre la degollina como se armara en esta Isla el desbarajuste de la Tierra Firme.'"

23. "Muy independiente y no consentiré jamás que nadie me gobierne, mucho menos un extraño."

24. "Dans nombre de récits fondateurs, l'histoire commence par une transgression."

25. "Torcidos deseos."

26. "L'inceste dans *Cecilia Valdés* donne à cette oeuvre une dimension de roman fondateur, représentatif d'une société en pleine construction."

27. As both Helg (*Our Rightful Share*) and A. Ferrer (*Insurgent Cuba*) demonstrate, rather than a forgone conclusion, the question of whether the white minority would conserve political supremacy in an independent Cuba was intensely debated in the years leading up to independence. I will discuss this point further below.

28. "Alguna vez nos ha de tocar a nosotros."

29. "Camino formal."

30. "A diferencia de otras novelas decimonónicas que tan bien ha estudiado Doris Sommer, en la novela de Villaverde no hay una historia de amor que represente de manera alegórica la unificación nacional. Hay, en cambio, una historia de amor que termina en una especie de disolución nacional."

31. "Marca . . . al personaje que, al no amoldarse a la ley o norma lingüística del español cubano del siglo XIX, delata su condición de bastardo, que en este caso vendría a ser el que no es 'hijo legítimo' de la patria cubana."

32. While scholars such as Richard Jackson (*Black Image*) and Carl Degler have argued convincingly for the existence of a trinomial racial taxonomy in many Latin American countries (white, black/indigenous, and mulato/mestizo), Helg postulates that nineteenth-century Cuba had a binomial system in which *pardos* and *morenos* were often referred to as *negros* and subsumed under the *raza de color* (*Our Rightful Share*, 3). For a study of the figure of the mulato in Latin American literature, see Martínez-Echazábal, *Para una semiótica de la mulatez*. For a history of abolition in Cuba, see Scott.

33. For more on race and marriage laws in colonial Cuba, see Martinez-Alier. For a brief summary, see Camacho 136–37. For a history of interracial families in nineteenth-century Cuba, see Morrison, "Slave Mothers." For a historiographic critique of the racial paradigms presented in Villaverde's novel, see Morrison, *Cuba's Racial Crucible* 106–30.

34. "¡Ay hijo!¿Echarías tú tanto lujo, ni gozarías de tantas comodidades si tu padre dejase de trabajar?"

35. "Aquella alma había perdido el sentimiento; aquel brazo sólo parecía animado, de hierro, no se cansaba de descargar golpes."

36. "Del presupuesto familiar salieron múltiples recursos para ambas expediciones . . . , para socorrer a los emigrados recién llegados, o para ayudar a las familias desvalidas en Cuba. También compró armas para obsequiar a connotados jefes militares como Máximo Gómez."

37. Albín, Corbin, and Marrero-Fente, who maintain that Villaverde always harbored abolitionist views (100–102), suggest that the writer may have supported the activities of the American Colonization Society (97).

38. For more on race mixture in New World literature, see Kaup and Rosenthal.

39. "No era su esposa, mucho menos su igual."

40. For another reading of the metaphorical relationship between mulatos/mulattoes and mules in New World literature, see Eduardo González. For a discussion of the etymology of "mulato," see Forbes 131–90 and chapter 2 of this book.

41. "Como crecían juntas, como en realidad mamaran una misma leche, no obstante su opuesta condición y raza"; "se amaron con amor de hermanas."

42. "Verdadera madre."

43. L. Williams also argues that María de Regla is associated with both Yemayá and Ochún. For more on María de Regla and Yemayá, see also Méndez Rodenas.

44. "Obtener el completo perdón de sus pecados."

45. "Vengativa mulata."

46. On nineteenth-century US Latino writing, see Gruesz and Lazo and Alemán. On Spanish-language publishing in the US during the 1800s, see Kanellos, Gruesz, and Castillo.

47. Del Monte comments on Cooper in at least two essays: "Sobre la novela histórica" and "Bosquejo intelectual de los Estados Unidos en 1840." For more on the impact of Villaverde's time in the United States on his work, see Lazo, *Writing*.

48. For more on nineteenth-century Argentine history, see chapter 2.

49. The plot of Gorriti's 1861 short story is uncannily similar to that of Villaverde's 1882 novel. Set in colonial Peru, the text tells the story of a light-skinned mestiza named Cecilia who unwittingly begins a relationship with her creole half brother. Like Villaverde's Cecilia and Amalia, Gorriti's Cecilia bears a striking resemblance to her creole half sister Amelia. John Maddox recently has translated *La cuarterona* into English as *Juliet of the Tropics*.

50. The sexual union of siblings appears in several of Villaverde's earlier works. "El ave muerta" (1837), for example, tells the same tale of accidental incest as *Cecilia Valdés* but replaces the interracial aspect with a class difference between Vicenta and Leandro (an obvious literary cousin of *Cecilia Valdés*'s Leonardo), the tale's star-crossed white lovers. Similarly, though not fully developed in the earlier versions of *Cecilia Valdés,* the possibility of incest hovers in the background of the 1839 texts; the episode in which Cecilia encounters a very uncomfortable Cándido Gamboa and his family, including Adela, the legitimate daughter who bears a striking resemblance to Cecilia, made famous in the definitive 1882 text (75–77), is included in both 1839 versions ("Cecilia Valdés" 188–92; *Cecilia Valdés Tomo Primero* 24–26).

51. For a hemispheric reading of the interracial incest theme in the Andean region, see Deborah J. Rosenthal's "Race Mixture and the Representation of Indians" and my "Family Entanglements." On interracial incest in the twentieth-century United States, see Sheffer. For a general overview of interracial romance in New World literature, see Fitz, *Rediscovering the New World*.

52. On the Gothic and the incompatibility of nineteenth-century Cuba with northern paradigms of modernity, see Alonso.

53. "La posesión de ciertas comodidades, y el pertenecer á la clase social que, generalmente hablando, no brilla por su ternura materna, no han sido parte á impedirle que amamantase á sus tres hijos durante la infancia, ni á que les sirviese de celosa niñera y de aya inteligente hasta entrar en el uso de la razón."

54. "Señor desconocido"; "ayudaba á la causa de la patria del modo que me es dado servirla desde aquí, como mujer y con familia."

55. "En nombre de las madres cubanas, la intervención del gobierno americano en favor de los jóvenes estudiantes de medicina, á quienes habían condenado a presidio en la Habana."

56. "Nuestro sacrificio será útil si logramos estimular á los hombres hasta el heroísmo y si la fama de nuestros hechos llena de gloria la patria adorada."

57. The novel's posthumous publication was arranged by Elizabeth Peabody, founder of the US kindergarten movement and Mary Mann's older sister, who states that Mann did not publish *Juanita* in the 1830s in order to avoid embarrassment to the Morell family on whose plantation she stayed during her Cuban sojourn. Rick Rodriguez suggests that this decision to bow to social graces and delay publication is symptomatic of post–Civil War politics in the United States (161). For biographic information on the Peabodys, see Tharp and Marshall. A

talented painter, Sophia Peabody later would marry writer Nathaniel Hawthorne, who theorized the romance genre for North American letters. On Mary Mann's collaboration with Sarmiento, see chapter 3 of this book.

58. A reading of *The Cuba Journal,* the collected set of Sophia's and Mary's letters home from Matanzas, reveals that many of the people and events recounted in the novel had a factual basis. Several of the "fictional" characters, for example, share their names with real people that Mary met during her stay in Matanzas: the insouciant child Carlito, the creole Carolina Fernandez, the enslaved man named Pope Urban. Meanwhile, other characters, such as the North American nanny Mrs. Watson and the US-born black Fachon, have their real-life parallels in the *Journal* in the figures of Mrs. Batson and Escalinette, respectively. Mann also seems to have drawn on her memories of Matanzas for her depictions of a Christmas ball held in a warehouse and the traumatic repossession of slaves who had been on loan from a neighboring plantation, two memorable incidents in the novel. Yet, while the *Journal* does reveal that Mann was in contact with an enslaved young woman named Juanita, there is no indication that the real-life Juanita was involved romantically with her master. The inspiration for the novel's interracial relationship—a common literary trope at the time—then, must have come from other fictional works, such as the Cuban antislavery texts that I have been analyzing in this chapter.

59. For an alternate interpretation of the novel, see Havard, *Hispanicism*. Havard's analysis differs from mine in that he suggests that Mann takes an indulgent view toward race mixture while expressing misgivings concerning Cuban annexation and the United States' ability to bring liberal democracy to the island. I agree that these are important points, though I have chosen to focus my study on the inter-American dimensions of the novel's central maternal-pedagogical metaphor. Meanwhile, though Ivonne M. García also studies the role of US education in the novel, she considers the work primarily as "the first example of an extracontinental colonial gothic, in which an overseas contact zone becomes the space where individual and national anxieties are mediated through a particularly U.S. dimension of the gothic." García feels that, "in addressing the consequences of interracial (and cross-cultural) relationships, Mary also suggests that extracontinental colonialism will eventually destroy the national family and home" (89).

60. On the slippage between the US South and Cuba in Mann's novel, see Havard, *Hispanicism,* and Paulk, "Visions."

61. While scholars sometimes speak of the *Journal* as though it consisted entirely of Sophia's writing, texts by Mary (both her postscripts to Sophia's letters and her own missives to their mother) are also included. Ivonne García compares the attitudes expressed by Sophia and Mary in their letters and suggests that their mother may have written some of Sophia's letters (93–94).

62. The incident appears to be entirely fictional. Lott makes it clear that, while working as a governess in Cuba, Mann felt constrained by social convention and unable to voice her moral opposition to the plantation culture surrounding her.

63. Michael A. Cooper, on the other hand, takes a different stance toward the relationship between Isabella, Helen, and the slaves, arguing that "Mann tells a story that comes undone under the pressures of slavery and, in the process, offers a critique of the cult of domesticity, with its oppressive limitations for both white and black women" (146). Rather than suggesting that Cuban slavery interferes with woman's "natural" role as familial and national domesticator, "creating a female character who performs the dual roles of true woman and slave mistress—both victim and oppressor—Mann invites the reader to examine how these categories interact and conflict" (153).

64. See Pérez, *On Becoming Cuban* and *Cuba between Empires*.

65. For biographies of Morúa Delgado, see Horrego Estuch, *Martín Morúa Delgado,* and Pérez Landa and Rosell Pérez.

66. "El pueblo no está educado para la independencia"; "nuestra salvación está en la anexión a los Estados Unidos."

67. "Salir de una dependencia para caer en otra dependencia"; "la conveniencia particular en perjuicio de la colectiva."

68. "Cuba es muy capaz de establecer las mismas libertades que han establecido los Estados de Norte América."

69. "Hemos de envidiar hoy lo que podemos inaugurar mañana nosotros mismos?"; "¿y cuando esté ya educada qué haremos? Volvérsenosla a llevar?"; "¿Cuánto tiempo durará su educación, corriendo, como correría, por cuenta nuestra su pupilaje? ¿Cuánto habría de costarnos?"

70. "La raza de color no es refractaria a la libertad"; "las infinitas veces que se ha resistido a sufrir las imposiciones que sólo con el derecho del más fuerte le han sido administradas. Holanda, Inglaterra, Francia, España misma, son otros tantos testigos que no harán otra cosa que afirmar lo que decimos."

71. For more examples of Morúa Delgado's interest in Haiti, see his 1892 Spanish translation of John R. Beard's *Toussaint L'Ouverture: A Biography and Autobiography.*

72. "Todos, aunque algunos tratan de ocultarlo, saben perfectamente que los negros una vez puestos en las condiciones de los demás hombres, no han de atentar contra las vidas de [los blancos]"; "todos saben perfectamente, por más que afecten lo contrario, que los negros de Cuba no sienten odio alguno hacia los blancos"; "la cadena horripilante que lo [sic] retiene en la servidumbre; detestan esa degradante dominación que todos los pueblos han sufrido y detestado; y, como todos los pueblos la sacudirán una y otra vez, hasta destruir la soberbia de los opresores, ya sean éstos más blancos que el armiño, o sean ya más negros que la calumnia de que son objeto."

73. "Cuba o será española o será africana": "se equivoca[n] tristemente"; "Cuba no será feliz si no es esclava de España."

74. On slavery as a metaphor for Spanish colonialism, see D. Davis, L. Williams, Luis-Brown, and Sartorius.

75. "La ilustrada Inglaterra"; "crudísimos debates"; "definir al negro como hombre"; "desde 1814 andan resolviendo la misma."

76. "¡Tal parece que sólo España oyó cuando dijo el político florentino, 'Divide y reinarás'!"

77. "El amor del negro"; "la sinceridad del blanco"; "esta franca exposición y práctica de ambos sentimientos, nos traerá la independencia de la isla, que no se hará esperar, no obteniendo otros resultados que el renacimiento de las riqueza pública [sic], y la efectividad del progreso general."

78. "No reconocerá diferencias entre sus ciudadanos, que gozarán de los mismos derechos, libres todos, todos iguales y hermanos como hijos de la misma madre, la patria, Cuba." Kornweibel traces Morúa's integrationist views to his mixed family origins (100–101).

79. "Completamente inútil"; "ridículamente pretensiosa"; "el absurdo principio de la división popular"; "los negros con su cuerpo diplomático peticionario y su organización autonómica dentro de la actual administración colonial"; "los blancos, *negando* más o menos declaradamente los derechos *suplicados*, o bien *concediéndolos* con tal cual ostensible grado de protectora generosidad [sic], no como se *reconoce* un derecho, sino como se *dispensa* un honor más o menos merecido, a una colectividad determinada. Y éso, precisamente, es lo que hay que combatir." Emphasis in original.

80. "Todo lo que sea agruparse en Cuba individuos de una clase cualquiera entre sí para mejorar su condición, constituye una parcialidad que ha de resultar altamente perjudicial al país en general; porque agruparse por fracciones no sería más que acentuar la barrera divisoria que nos degrada a todos y perpetuar la línea de razas que mata el progreso de la sociedad cubana." For a discussion of Morúa's essays, see Kornweibel.

81. "No se considerará, en ningún caso, como partido político o grupo independiente, ninguna agrupación constituida exclusivamente por individuos de una sola raza o color, ni por individuos de una clase con motivo de nacimiento, la riqueza o el título profesional."

82. "Los africanos que fueron esclavos"; "condición de cubanos." For a discussion of the Morúa Law, see Guillén 260–63.

83. For a detailed description of events, see Helg, *Our Rightful Share*, and Branche, *Colonialism* 223–26.

84. On Morúa's coerced vote in favor of the Platt Amendment, see Guillén 258–60 and Horrego Estuch, *Martín Morúa Delgado* 169.

85. Morúa would return to his earlier separatist beliefs by the beginning of the war in 1895 (Guillén 257).

86. "En toda la obra se nota el censurable y deliberado empeño de justificar las líneas divisorias trazadas y conservadas por el exclusivismo colonial"; "el autor acepta el orden establecido, y sigue rutinariamente la desgraciada argumentación de los que aspiran a subir, reteniendo bajo su planta a los infortunados que allí colocara el régimen autoritario que combaten a juro de aniquilamiento."

87. "No hay que dar nunca entero crédito a lo que dicen los negros."

88. Zettl, for her part, studies narrative authority in Morúa's novel, explicating the various levels of narration that exist in the text.

89. In this way, Morúa's novel is not unlike the Afro–North American Martin Delany's *Blake* (1859), which rewrites Harriet Beecher Stowe's canonical *Uncle Tom's Cabin* with an eye to restoring the black agency that the white abolitionist text denies. On *Sofía* as a critical adaptation of *Cecilia Valdés*, see Luis, *Literary Bondage* 145–46 and L. Williams 159–200.

90. North American William Faulkner's *Absalom! Absalom!* (1936) is notable in reversing the gender dynamic of this trope. The Brazilian author Aluíso Azevedo's 1881 *O mulato*, on the other hand, features a light-skinned man who is unaware of his mixed-race background knowingly engaged in relations with his white cousin. Meanwhile, while they do not deal with incest, the Cuban Francisco Calcagno's *Romualdo, uno de tantos* (1891) and North American Mark Twain's *Pudd'nhead Wilson* (1894) use male protagonists to discuss the topic of mistaken identity and wrongful enslavement.

91. "Teniendo mujer é hijos, y dándose mucho tonelete de altas personalidades"; "casa y caprichos á mulatas callejeras"; "con su nombre' á los 'hijos de adulterio"; "casi se emparejaban." "Callejera" (which I have translated as "stray") is a particularly offensive term. Literally "pertaining to the street," it also is used to refer to stray dogs. When applied to a woman, it is doubly derogatory, combining the traditional taboo against women appearing alone in public spaces (i.e., the street and the connotations of sex work that it entails) with insulting language likening women to dogs.

92. Horrego Estuch, on the other hand, suggests that the main character was inspired by a former romantic interest of Morúa's (*Martín Morúa Delgado*). Even if that is true, it does not mean that *Sofía* does not also inscribe itself into the tragic mulatta tradition. For discussions of the mulata in nineteenth-century Cuban literature, see Kutzinski, *Sugar's Secrets;* Camacho (21–24, 113–38); and Fraunhar. On the transatlantic topos of the tragic mulatta outside of the Hispanic and Lusophone worlds, see Manganelli.

93. Many critics have pointed out that Morúa rejects the inclusion of mulatos together with *negros* in la raza de color, a nineteenth-century Cuban category for all Afro-descendants. Rather, he argues that mulatos constitute a new race. For Helg, this suggests a notion of racial evolution toward whiteness that contradicts the egalitarianism that Morúa professed at other moments in his work (*Our Rightful Share* 55). While this is true, it is important to recognize that, as he explains in "Factores sociales," Morúa does not see the differences that he draws between negros and mulatos as biologically determined but, rather, the result of comparative distance from slavery and access to cultural capital (212–16). The result of oppressive social structures, the differentiations upon which he insists in "Factores sociales" in no way contradict Morúa's reflections on the constructedness of racial categories in *Sofía*.

94. "Cabeza ostentadora de una cabellera negra, reluciente, ondeada, magnífica"; "de finísimas facciones"; "iluminado por dos rasgados ojos de negras pupilas." Literally "wheat-colored," in the Caribbean and elsewhere, "trigueño" denotes a light-skinned, racially ambiguous person of color.

95. "Bien sabes tú que la que más y la que menos, tóas tenemos la noblesa en la cosina del amo."

96. "Demócratas de mugre."

97. "¿Qué moralidad intenta establecer el Sr. Villaverde con sentencia tan desmoralizadora? ¿Dónde está la justica de este juicio? ¿Para quién escribe? ¿Qué pretende establecer o consolidar el autor?"

98. "Estos modernos librepensadores no se dan cuenta de su contradicción, como no se la daba Esladislao al tutear á Sofía"; "¿habríala tuteado si ignorase su pobre estado social?" In Spanish, the informal second person singular pronoun *tú* is used with its corresponding verb forms to address someone with whom the speaker is familiar, or someone of equal or lower status than the speaker. The formal pronoun *usted* is used with its corresponding verb forms to indicate a polite regard for social differences.

99. "Con motivo de Sofía, que había asistido en el servicio de la mesa, se habló de la esclavitud y de las reformas que se operaban, lamentando algunos que 'aquella mulatica tan buena fuera esclava.'"

100. "¿Luego Sofía no era mulata, no era esclava? Y se le había tenido como tal, y había sido enviada a un ingenio para que la castigasen, y había sido azotada, y sus hermanas lo habían consentido."

101. For a discussion of differences between the antislavery sentiments of nineteenth-century creole reformers and the desires of the enslaved, see Aching.

102. For more on the place of "Americanized criollos" in Morúa's thinking, see Lamas.

103. Morúa originally "offered" *La familia Unzúazu* to Tomás Estrada Palma to aid the war effort (Morúa, August 4, 1896, letter to Tomás Estrada Palma, in *Obras*, vol. 3, *Integración cubana* 176). This plan was not realized, and the novel had to wait until after the war to be published. For a different interpretation of Morúa's vote for the Platt Amendment, see Luis, *Literary Bondage* 158.

104. "—Repito—decía Eladislao,—que ese collar es preciosísimo, y que la belleza de usted realza en sumo grado su valor artístico. ¿Es de manufactura extranjera?

—No,—respondió Magdalena, cojiendo entre sus diminutos dedos la estrella colgante;—es hecho todo en Cuba, y yo misma hice el dibujo de la obra, que ha sido interpretado á mi gusto.

—Verdaderamente, señorita, es una obra de arte . . . pero ése es el símbolo americano . . .

—Según,—contestó vivamente la joven.—No he querido colgarle un águila en la punta vacante para no completar la idea norteamericana."

105. For an alternative reading of this passage, see Kornweibel 125.

5. "La Dignidad de la Mujer Cubana"

1. "Pobre hija mía sacrificada en la flor de su juventud, por mi mismo en el ara de la patria. Por dilatada que llegue á ser mi vida, moriré antes de que pueda consolarme de tu muerte; mas por grande y desoladora que sea ésta, pena mía nunca podrá igualarse á la que me sobrecoje cuando pienso que pueda morir también en la conciencia del pueblo cubano el sentimiento de la solidaridad moral, que debe ser el punto de apoyo del *fulcro* de la palanca de su conciencia política, si esta conciencia es capaz de constituirse, al cabo, en nosotros. Mutilados, si cualquier accidente nos mutila (y creo que todos sabrán entender lo que digo) debemos pugnar por reintegrar nuestra alma." Emphasis in original.

2. "Si por cualesquiera causas no persiste para un pueblo, en la paz, el sentimiento de solidaridad social que determinó é hizo posible la guerra única, todo, todo se habría perdido para todos como se malogra el fruto de la concepción por el aborto."

3. "Sobre el trasfondo del vacío simbólico provocado por el cese de los más de cuatrocientos años de dominación colonial española emergen, a la par, exaltadas corrientes de patriotismo nacionalista y contradictorios procesos de americanización de las instituciones y las costumbres."

4. For an overview of race relations in the early Cuban Republic, see de la Fuente 1–95. On public educación and national regeneration in Argentina, see chapter 3 of this book.

5. On the discourse of Anglo-Saxonness at this time, see Horsman.

6. For a study of race in *The Rough Riders,* see Kaplan, "Black and Blue." For a discussion of gender in Roosevelt, see Bederman.

7. On nineteenth-century Latin American formulations of masculinity, see Peluffo and Prado.

8. David Sartorius has recently problematized this racialization of the separatist forces as black, arguing that a substantial number of Afro-Cubans remained loyal to Spain until relatively late in the independence process.

9. For more on women during the independence period, see Prados-Torreira and Curnow.

10. "Reforma de la enseñanza pública, y sobre todo de la educación primaria, afectará a miles de escolares de cualquier clase, sexo o raza, a lo largo y ancho de todo el país."

11. This period in the history of Cuban education is a central theme of the recent ICAIC feature film *Cuba Libre* (2016), directed by Jorge Luis Sánchez.

12. "La instrucción pública es casi nula en nuestros campos, pudiendo considerarse la fundación de una escuela en ellos como un servicio de mayor importancia al Estado."

13. "Las clases más humildes"; "viejos libertos de color."

14. "El aprendizaje imperfecta de estas *amigas;* ordinariamente dirigidas por mujeres de color, ó tan crasamente ignorantes, inciviles y totalmente ineptas para

el encargo que pretendían desempeñar, que al fin ningún otro provecho se sacaba de ellos." Emphasis in original.

15. "Más escuelas . . . servidas por maestros de color que por blancos."

16. For a thorough overview of education during the period, see Huerta Martínez, *Enseñanza*.

17. "Restrictivo sistema de educación"; "tan ignorantes que no conozcamos nuestros sagrados derechos."

18. Previously, education had been administered by the Secretaría de Justicia.

19. Frye's numbers are somewhat lower than those of Varona, cited above. The North American superintendent would blame this failure on the Wood administration.

20. For a concise history of education in Cuba during the colonial period and opening years of the twentieth century, see Gonzalo de Quesada 267–70.

21. "La reconstrucción material del país y la reforma de la educación popular. Sin riqueza pública estable, no tendremos independencias; sin verdadera educación popular, no tendremos democracia."

22. "Resulta materialmente imposible que se rija democráticamente un pueblo, donde el setenta y cinco por ciento de la población ignora los rudimentos de las letras y cuyo *standard of life* apenas se alza á pasarse con lo estrictamente necesario. Un país, así compuesto, entrega masas al impulso de los demagogos; no congrega ciudadanos en los comicios, para escoger entre programas políticos ó decidir con acierto quienes hayan de aplicarlos." For a discussion of Varona's views regarding blackness and morality, see Camacho 185–86. On race and the suffrage debate in occupied Cuba, see de la Fuente 56–60.

23. On the slipperiness of "slavery" in the eighteenth and nineteenth centuries, see D. Davis and Buck-Morss.

24. "Las tinieblas que oscure[cen] la conciencia moral y artística del país"; "la oscura existencia moral de las capas sociales más bajas de la colonia": "en aquel grupo más numeroso no dignificado por una aspiración política elevada y contaminado de toda suerte de concupiscencia, no es muy sano nuestro bagaje histórico. En lo bueno y en lo malo, obra es de la raza nuestra alma."

25. "El triste estado de oscuridad y esclavitud en que se encuentra y vislumbrar lo que está destinado á ser."

26. "Niños y niñas de color con objeto de que reciban la primera enseñanza elemental"; "la parte moral y religiosa."

27. For more on laws governing Afro-Cuban education and their application during the 1870s and '80s, see Scott 273.

28. "Si, venida abajo la esclavitud, fuente rica de nuestras desgracias, han de seguir nuestras clases populares víctimas de la esclavitud moral de la ignorancia, fuerza será convenir que el país, á modo de factoría ambulante, habrá de arrastrar una existencia algo semejante á la de los pueblos primitivos."

29. "En error muy grande está ... aquel que piense que para ser libre basta á un pueblo cualquiera, (por superiores que sean sus aptitudes intelectuales) hacerse independiente."

30. "Es forzoso antes y junto con ello y siempre y en todas ocasiones *educarse*: preparar el espíritu por una cultura moral depurada; la inteligencia por la selección de las nociones que acopie para la vida mejor que le espera: es necesario ser capaces de recibir digna y fructuosamente al huésped: no está todo en inutilizar al enemigo exterior: es forzoso combatir al par y arrojar de nosotros al peor enemigo: al de la casa, al que llevamos con nosotros mismos: el hábito vicioso, á la ignorancia bajo cualquiera de sus repugnantes aspectos: al vicio y á la ignorancia que son sin duda las cadenas más pesadas con que quiso sujetar y sujetó nuestro espíritu en su obra de corrupcion secular, el gobierno torpe, desatento é impío que nos hizo su víctima."

31. On the del Monte group, see chapter 4.

32. "La Sociedad cubana que se constituyó sobre base muy [¿deleznable?] en lo moral como que descansaba en el trabajo esclavo, flaquea hoy y vacila ante [el] golpe que en ella produjo la irrupción de una idea política, infecunda, por desdichada, aunque generosa y parece disolverse ante el conflicto social que la desposeyó de su esclavo y, como aquel que ha perdido todo rumbo toma á ciegas por el primero camino que, se abre á sus ojos atónitos, aquí mudamos así, á ciegas."

33. "Hibridismo social y político de la Intervención nos somete á pruebas tremendas, cuya gravedad y peligros se abultan en este conflicto por el estado de penuria, de miseria, (y aun diría *de hambre*) en que ha quedado, desvalido, un pueblo, nuestro pueblo, que así y todo y entre las sombras de su enflaquecida mente acaricia la hermosa y conmovedora ilusión de su soberanía política." Emphasis in original.

34. Ironically, North American opponents of Cuban annexation often would make the same argument of racial incapacity for democracy in order to argue for US withdrawal from the island. Steel magnate Andrew Carnegie, who was "a leading figure in the [Anti-Imperialist] League," for example, "opposed annexation of Cuba on the grounds that it would mean the addition of a large Negro population to the American Union" (Foner 2:416).

35. Opposition to full Cuban sovereignty also existed within the island. "In August 1898, the *New York Times* reported on the Cuban upper classes made up of Spanish merchants and landowners who were afraid that independence of the island would result in 'a long reign of terror,' and were 'in favor of American annexation, or at least of a permanent American protectorate.' In Havana, several hundred planters signed a petition to President McKinley appealing for the annexation of Cuba to the United States" (Lorini 207).

36. "La cultura de una elite que abogaba por una Cuba 'civilizada' (a imagen y semejanza de las naciones de Occidente) y la comprensión popular de las expresiones de identidad cultural"; "los cubanos se encuentran compulsados a tratar

de 'aprobar' una suerte de 'examen' de civilidad, ante el 'tribunal' autoerigido por los interventores norteamericanos."

37. "Los participantes de la fiesta de *ñáñigos* pagaron caro el error de confundir el cese de la soberanía de España con el advenimiento de una era de plena libertad"; "asociación ilícita." For more on the repression of Afro-Cuban cultural practices during the occupation and early-republican periods, see Bronfman.

38. On the Morúa Law and its consequences, see chapter 4 of this book.

39. "La cubana posee condiciones excelentes para desempeñar como educadora"; "ella, como nosotros, adolece los defectos y de los vicios propios de la infame tutela colonial á que hemos estado sometidos." For a discussion of women's education in nineteenth-century Cuba, see Prados-Torreira 9–11.

40. "La educación para la vida pública ha de tener por base la educación, ésa que han de comenzar los padres desde que el hijo despierte á la razón: el ciudadano ha de salir ya bosquejado del hogar. Y aquí, ante el espectáculo que entreveo de nuestra futura agitación en la patria libre, aquí es donde aparece de repente á mis ojos nuestra educación actual con toda su deformidad y deficiencia. El régimen de la brutal España, á que hemos estado sometidos, no nos ha preparado, no ha podido prepararnos para el ejercicio de la libertad y del derecho, ni nos permitió adquirir siquiera grandes virtudes domésticas." Simón Bolívar deploys the same anticolonial metaphor of Spain as a bad mother, a "desnaturalizada madrastra" ("unnatural or wicked stepmother") in his 1815 "Jamaican Letter."

41. "El estado de decadencia moral en que vivimos por la falta de ilustración"; "más que para los deleites de la danza"; "sacrosantos deberes del hogar"; "necesidad más grande que . . . tiene hoy la raza á que pertenezco."

42. "*Asociación para la enseñanza de la mujer* de nuestra raza; en donde podamos aprender todas, tanto la niña como la mujer ya hecha, todo lo necesario é indispensable para el cumplimiento de nuestros deberes, una Asociación que responda á todas nuestras necesidades morales." Emphasis in original.

43. "Podrá ser la maestra de su prole"; "intelectualidad y cultura"; "poderosísimos elementos de que ha de disponer la mujer para dirigir á sus hijos por el camino del bien"; "salir de la esclavitud de la ignorancia"; "para ser libre [se] debe ser instruida; pues donde no hay instrucción no hay libertad."

44. For more on *Minerva*, see Mirabal 118–22. For more on the turn-of-the-century debate on the sexual morality of Afro-Cuban women, see de la Fuente 155–56.

45. For more on the Harvard program, see Iglesias Utset 130–44, Minichino 211–20, and González Lucena.

46. Afro-Cuban students were welcome at Booker T. Washington's Hampton and Tuskegee Institutes, however (MacDonald 95).

47. Minichino suggests that the secondary-school curriculum may have been drafted by Varona (172) and notes that the introduction of civics instruction during the occupation marked a break with the Spanish colonial system of education, in which students received religiously based lessons on morality (291).

48. Gill was acquainted personally with Wood, as well as presidents Cleveland, Harrison, McKinley, and Roosevelt through the Patriot's League, of which they all were members (Minichino 307). On school cities in Cuba, see Minichino 307–13. Similar postwar efforts existed to implement US-style education in Puerto Rico and the Philippines (Luigi, *65 Valiants* 196; Tosso). Of particular interest are maestra de Sarmiento Edith Howe's labors in (also US-occupied) Puerto Rico. "When, after the Spanish-American War, the United States took over the island of Puerto Rico and immediately began to set up common schools, Edith Howe's knowledge of the Spanish language and Latin customs made her invaluable there. For eleven more years she pioneered: in the model school of San Juan, 1899–1900; in the grammar school from 1900 to 1905; and in the high school five years more" (Luigi, *65 Valiants* 152).

49. See also Foner 2:463n. Foner gives the number as 30; the webpage of the SUNY New Paltz school archive as 50; Luigi as 77 (*65 Valiants*).

50. "Su industria florece asombrosamente: cuenta con grandes fábricas de paño, cristales, fundición de metales y construcción de máquinas; la industria del papel, de la loza, de la tipografía, de la destilación de aguardiente y licores; curtiembres, saladerías é imprentas; siendo este país uno de los que más periódicos publican con relación a su población. Buenos Aires es una pieza eminentemente mercantil, las letras se desarrollan en ella ventajosamente, su Universidad y Escuela de Medicina son muy frecuentadas, Sus [*sic*] Escuelas Normales son las mejores de la América española. Su Ley de Educación una de las más completas. Cuenta con numerosas casas de beneficencia, varios teatros, líneas férreas y tranvías, bibliotecas públicas, museo, bolsa, bancos, magníficas plazas y un espléndido hipódromo."

51. "Han carecido de un Sarmiento que les haya hecho ver la urgente y primordial necesidad de difundir en todas direcciones los beneficios de la educación popular."

52. For additional biographical information on Armstrong, see Chavarria 369–71.

53. New Paltz had a history of involvement in North American imperial ventures. Mary Deyo, an 1887 graduate, for example, had gone to newly "opened" Japan to do missionary work and later returned to the United States to teach (Lang 38). More recently, "several New Paltz graduates had arrived in the Philippines to teach under the newly formed American Department of Public Instruction for the islands. Their overseas mission was part of America's first technical assistance program, set up at this time under Governor General William H. Taft, to develop a modern system of education where none had existed before" (57). Similarly, the February 1902 edition of the school newspaper, the *Normal Review*, details a former student's trip to the Philippines via Hawaii and Guam to teach English for the newly installed US military government. These projects generated much interest in the New Paltz community and, during the first decade of the twentieth century, several lectures were given on campus on life in the Philippines (62).

54. "La bella Srta. Peligero, Redactora Jefe de la Sección Cubana de esta Revista, me impone la dura pena de escribir esta nota, pena que yo juzgo inaplicable á mi delito de ser el único cubano que ha dejado gustoso las gratas sensaciones de su modesto hogar, por venir á contemplar como se desarrolla la pre coz [sic] y fecunda inteligencia de la mujer cubana, en esta tierra de grandezas llena y donde tanto culto se rinde á la instruccion. Pero yo, obsecuente a los mandatos de la belleza, obedezco con placer aunque me sea imposible pintar el cuadro que se me pide, con los verdaderos tintes de su natural coloracion."

55. Though this passage in many ways raises the question, the term *eyaculación precoz* was not yet in common parlance in 1901.

56. In more contemporary, colloquial Spanish, the sentence might read "esta tierra llena de grandezas." Later in the twentieth century, Latin American critics would reevaluate the baroque in positive, cultural-nationalist terms.

57. "Como padre de aquellas . . . futuras maestras de su patria; reconocimiento que, aun siendo pobre, era, sin embargo, reflejo fiel del que Cuba siente por la Nación Americana, que tan valiosa ayuda le ha dado para alcanzar su independencia que, á su sombra benéfica, espera ver consolidada para siempre."

58. For more on the de la Rionda family, see McGillivray.

59. "La confrontación de los valores y las costumbres coloniales con las representaciones políticas y culturales patrocinadas por las autoridades interventoras"; "toda la simbología de la existencia cotidiana."

60. "Esforzarnos por sacar el mayor provecho posible del corto tiempo de que disponemos para nuestra instrucción aquí, tratar de indagar, observar y aprovechar todos los adelantos y ventajas con que cuenta la instrucción aquí, para después poderlos poner en práctica con toda perfección en nuestro país; y á la vez instruirnos y prepararnos para la ardua empresa que se encomienda al magisterio. Debemos poner todas nuestras miras en nuestra conducta de tal manera, que con justicia no se nos pueda tachar, pues aquí representamos, primero, la dignidad de nosotras mismas; segundo, la de nuestros apellidos y la de nuestros padres, y tercero, amigas mías, la de nuestras compatriotas, la de la mujer cubana, la del magisterio de Cuba, en una palabra, la del pueblo cubano.

"Hemos de demostrar á este país que sabemos llevar la representación de todas estas dignidades. Este es mi anhelo y creo debe ser el de toda la que por verdadera cubana se tenga."

61. "Hierarquias socias do Antigo Regime, . . . implicando, consequèntemente, na desigualdade e na exclusão, já que a condição necessária de sua existência é que nem todos tinham acesso a ela"; "universalista e igualitaria, própia das sociedades democráticas que, ao contrario, inclui a todos."

62. "Um outro fator vai dotar a noção de reconhecimento que emerge com a democracia de uma nova dimensão: trata-se de uma certa concepção de identidade que surge no fim do século XVIII, como a de uma identidade individualizada, particular."

63. "Objeto del capricho, el entretenimiento, el juguete del hombre . . . fementido y cruel"; "indignadas nuestra frente y hagamos titánicos esfuerzos para reconquistar la dignidad que plugo al cielo concederle á *todas* nuestras congéneras." Emphasis in original.

64. In this way, Cuban antislavery writing repurposes an age-old trope in Hispanic literature in which sexual violence is figured as a metonymy for abuse of political power. Lope de Vega's 1619 play *Fuenteovejuna* is a canonical example.

65. On the class and racial origin of early US Latino writers, see Gruesz.

66. Pérez has shown that allegorizations of the island as a black child became common in US political cartoons during the occupation (*Cuba in the American Imagination*, 95–174).

67. "Señoras y señoritas emancipadas"; "trabajaban 'en la calle' como *typewriters* en oficinas o *nurses* en hospitales."

68. For a discussion of similar gendered-metaphorical reactions to US imperialism in the work of Martí, see Pita 137–39.

69. The term "to-be-conquered-ness" is a play on feminist film scholar Laura Mulvey's notion of the "to-be-looked-at-ness" of female cinematic personages.

Conclusion

1. On the "white legend" of Argentine racial identity, see Alberto.

2. For a more recent treatment of black maternity in the Brazilian cultural context, see Ana María Gonçalves's novel *Um defeito de cor*.

3. Martha Stewart (*née* Kostyra) is, in fact, of Polish descent, and the more English-sounding "Stewart" is her former husband's last name. I am arguing that her image has been mobilized as a symbol of traditional, Anglo–New England domestic and gender values ("Martha Stewart").

4. The statistic is widely known and available. For a list of sources on the subject, see Malave.

5. The most recent iteration may be the trope of the "anchor baby," or the child of a racialized woman who allegedly seeks to smuggle her nonwhite progeny into the citizen body and burden the nation's coffers.

6. For more on the 1805 Haitian constitution, see Fischer, *Modernity Disavowed* 227–44.

7. For more on education under the Federal caudillos, see Solari 94–97.

8. For theoretical studies of black diasporan literature, see Edwards and Branche, *Poetics*.

Bibliography

Archives

Biblioteca Nacional José Martí, Sala Cubana Antonio Bachiller y Morales, Havana, Cuba

Manuscripts collection

PERIODICALS

La enseñanza
La escuela moderna

Biblioteca Nacional de Maestros, Sala Americana, Buenos Aires, Argentina—Government Publications

Avellaneda, Nicolás. *Memoria presentada al Congreso de 1873 por el Ministro de Justicia, Culto é Instrucción Pública.* Buenos Aires: Imprenta de la Unión, 1873.

Beláustegi, Luis. *Memoria presentada al Congreso Nacional de 1898, por el Ministro de Justicia, Culto é Instrucción Pública.* Vol. 2. Buenos Aires: Penitencia Nacional, 1898.

Lastra, Bonifacio. *Memoria del Departamento de Justicia, Culto é Instrucción Pública correspondiente al año de 1878 presentada al Honorable Congreso de la Nación en sus sesiones del año 1879.* Buenos Aires: El Nacional, 1879.

Leguizamón, Onésimo. *Memoria presentada al Congreso Nacional de 1875 por el Ministro de Justica, Culto é Instrucción Pública.* Buenos Aires: Imprenta Americana, 1875.

———. *Memoria presentada al Congreso Nacional de 1877 al Ministro de Justicia, Culto é Instrucción Pública.* Buenos Aires: Courrier de la Plata, 1877.

Magnasco, Osvaldo. *Memoria presentada al Congreso Nacional de 1899, por el Ministro de Justica, Culto é Instrucción Pública.* Buenos Aires: Penitencia Nacional, 1898.

Memoria de Justicia e Instrucción Pública. Buenos Aires: Taller Tipográfico de la Penitencia Nacional, 1867.

Memoria de Justicia, Culto e Instrucción Pública, 1868. Buenos Aires: Taller Tipográfico de la Penitencia Nacional, 1868.

Memoria del Consejo Nacional de Educación. Vol. 2, Anexos correspondientes a 1884. Buenos Aires: La Tribuna, 1886.

Memoria del Ministerio de Justicia, Culto é Instrucción Pública. Buenos Aires: Imprenta Argentina de El Nacional, 1871.

Memoria del Ministerio de Justicia, Culto é Instrucción Pública, 1872. Buenos Aires: Imprenta de la Unión, 1872.

Memoria presentada por el Ministro de Estado en el Departamento de Justicia, Culto é Instrucción Pública al Congreso Nacional de 1869. Reimpresión oficial. Buenos Aires: Taller Tipográfico de la Penitenciaria Nacional, 1900.

Pizarro, Dr. Manuel D. *Memoria presentada al Congreso Nacional de 1881 por el Ministro de Justicia, Culto é Instrucción Pública.* Buenos Aires: Imprenta de la Penitenciaria, 1881.

Wilde, Eduardo. *Memoria presentada al Congreso Nacional de 1882 por el Ministro de Justicia, Culto é Instrucción Pública.* Imprenta de la Penitenciaria: Buenos Aires, 1882.

Wilde, Eduardo. *Memoria presentada al Congreso Nacional de 1884 por el Ministro de Justicia, Culto é Instrucción Pública.* 2 vols. Buenos Aires: Tribuna Nacional, 1884.

Cuban Heritage Collection, University of Miami

La moda, o, recreo semanal del bello sexo. 3 vols. Havana, 1829–31.

Instituto de Literatura y Lingüística José Antonio Portuondo Valdor

Minerva: revista quincenal dedicada a la mujer de color (1888–89).

Museo Histórico Sarmiento, Buenos Aires, Argentina—Correspondence

Carpeta 1
Carpeta 41
Carpeta 42
Armario 1
Armario 3

Sojourner Truth Library, Special Collections—College History Collection, State University of New York at New Paltz

"Sección cubana" of the *Normal Review* (student newspaper), 1901–2.

Other Sources

Aching, Gerard. *Freedom from Liberation: Slavery, Sentiment, and Literature in Cuba.* Bloomington: Indiana UP, 2015.

Achugar, Hugo. "Foundational Images of the Nation in Latin America." In Acree and González Espitia, 11–31.
Acree, William, and Juan Carlos González Espitia, eds. *Building Nineteenth-Century Latin America*. Nashville: Vanderbilt UP, 2010.
Adams, David Wallace. *Educating for Extinction: American Indians and the Boarding School Experience, 1875–1928*. Lawrence: U of Kansas P, 1995.
Adelman, Jeremy. *Republic of Capital: Buenos Aires and the Legal Transformation of the Atlantic World*. Stanford, CA: Stanford UP, 1999.
Alberdi, Juan Bautista. *Bases y puntos de partida para la organización política de la República argentina*, edited by Raúl García Orza. 1852. Buenos Aires: Centro Editor de América Latina, 1984.
———. *Grandes y pequeños hombres del Plata*. 1864. Buenos Aires: Plus Ultra, 1975.
Alberto, Paulina L. "Indias blancas, negros febriles: Racial Stories and History-Making in Contemporary Argentine Fiction." In *Rethinking Race in Modern Argentina*, edited by Paulina Alberto and Eduardo Elena. Cambridge: Cambridge UP, 2018, 289–317.
Alberto, Paulina L., and Eduardo Elena, eds. *Rethinking Race in Modern Argentina*. New York: Cambridge UP, 2016.
Albín, María C. "Fronteras de género, nación y ciudadanía: la Ilustración. *Álbum de las damas* (1845) de Gertrudis Gómez de Avellaneda." In *Actas del XIII Congreso de la Asociación Internacional de Hispanistas, Madrid, 6–11 de julio de 1998*, edited by Florencio Sevilla Arroyo and Carlos Alvar. Madrid: Castalia-Asociación Internacional de Hispanistas-Fundación Duques de Soria, 2000, 67–75.
Albín, María C., Megan Corbin, and Raúl Marrero-Fente. "A Transnational Figure: Gertrudis Gómez de Avellaneda and the American Press." *Gender and the Politics of Literature: Hispanic Issues Online* 18 (2017): 1–67.
Álbum cubano de lo bello y lo bueno. 1860.
Álbum de la expedición de los maestros cubanos a la Universidad de Harvard. Cambridge: Geo. O. Griffith, 1900.
Alcott, Louisa May. *Little Women*. 1868. New York: Pocket Books, 1994.
Aldridge, Alfred Owen. *The Ibero-American Enlightenment*. Urbana: U of Illinois P, 1971.
Alencar, José de. *O guarany*. Rio de Janeiro: Antundes, 1857.
Alegría, Fernando. *Historia de la novela hispanoamericana*. Mexico City: Ediciones de Andrea, 1966.
Alier, Manuel S. Prólogo. In Chavarria, *La escuela normal y la cultura argentina*, vii–xi.
Alonso, Carlos J. *The Burden of Modernity: The Rhetoric of Cultural Discourse in Spanish America*. Oxford UP: New York, 1998.
Altamirano, Carlos, and Beatriz Sarlo. "The Autodidact and the Learning Machine." In Halperín Donghi et al., *Sarmiento, Author of a Nation*, 19–30.
Álvarez, Juan. *Las guerras civiles argentinas*. 1912.

Álvarez-Amell, Diana. "The Strange Case of Narciso: Villaverde's Politics." *Camino real* 9.12 (2017): 115–32.
Álvarez García, Imeldo, ed. *Acerca de Cirilo Villaverde.* Havana: Letras Cubanas, 1982.
"Amor a la patria." *La Aljaba: Dedicada al bello sêxo Argentino.* 6 (December 3, 1830): 3.
Anderson, Benedict. *Imagined Communities: Reflections on the Origin and Spread of Nationalism.* London: Verso, 1983.
Andioc, Sophie. *Centón epistolario.* 4 vols. Domingo del Monte. Havana: Imagen Contemporánea, 2002.
Andrade, Oswaldo de. "Manifesto Antropófago." Universidade Federal de Rio Grande do Sul. 1928.
Andrews, George Reid. *The Afro-Argentines of Buenos Aires, 1800–1900.* Madison: U of Wisconsin P, 1980.
———. *Afro-Latin America, 1800–2000.* Oxford: Oxford UP, 2004.
Ángelis, Pedro de, ed. *Colección de obras y documentos relativos a la historia Antigua moderna de las provincias de Río de la Plata; ilustrados con notas y disertaciones.* Buenos Aires: Imprenta del Estado, 1836.
Apes, William. *A Son of the Forrest: The Experiences of William Apes, a Native of the Forrest, Comprising a Notice of the Pequod Tribe of Indians. Written by Himself.* New York, 1829.
Appiah, Kwame Anthony. "There Is No Such Thing as Western Civilisation." *Guardian,* November 9, 2016.
Aponte-Ramos, Dolores. "Cuando la Pampa se colorea: Los negros en la Argentina decimonónica." *Revista Iberoamericana* 45.188–89 (July–December 1999): 733–39.
Apple, Rima D., and Janet Golden, eds. *Mothers and Motherhood: Readings in American History.* Columbus: Ohio State UP, 1997.
Arbery, Glenn Cannon. "Victims of Likeness: Quadroons and Octoroons in Southern Fiction." In *Interracialism: Black-White Intermarriage in American History, Literature, and Law,* edited by Werner Sollors. Oxford: Oxford UP, 2000, 393–407.
Ard, Patricia. M. "Seeds of Reform: The Letters of Mary Peabody Mann and Domingo Faustino Sarmiento." PhD diss., Rutgers University, 1996.
Arnold, Albert James, Julio Rodriguez-Luis, and J. Michael Dash, eds. *A History of Literature in the Caribbean.* Vol. 1, *Hispanic and Francophone Regions.* Amsterdam: John Benjamins, 1994.
Avellaneda, Nicolás, and Onésimo Leguizamón. *Decreto organizando el personal docente de la Escuela Normal del Paraná.* February 7, 1875. In Leguizamón, *Memoria 1875,* 275–76.
Axelrad, Allan M. "Cooper, Aristocracy, and Capitalism." Conference of the American Literature Association, San Diego, June 1996.
Azevedo, Aluísio. *O mulato.* São Paulo: Universidade de São Paulo, 1881.

Balderston, Daniel, ed. *The Historical Novel in Latin America*. Gaithersburg, MD: Ediciones Hispamérica, 1986.
Balibar, Étienne. "The Nation Form: History and Ideology." In *Race, Nation, Class: Ambiguous Identities*, by Étienne Balibar and Immanuel Wallerstein, translated by Chris Turner. London: Verso, 1988, 86–106.
Baralt, Luis A. "¿Qué es la educación?" *La escuela moderna* 2.8 (May 30, 1900): 89.
Barcia Zequiera, María del Carmen. *La otra familia: parientes, redes y descendencia de los esclavos en Cuba*. Havana: Casa de las Américas, 2003.
Barrondo, A. I. "Informe del Inspector Nacional de Escuelas de la Provincia de San Luis." In *Memoria del Consejo*, 437–508.
Batticuore, Graciela. *La mujer romántica: Lectoras, autoras y escritores en la Argentina, 1830–1870*. Buenos Aires: Edhasa, 2005.
Bauer, Ralph. "Hemispheric Studies." *PMLA* 124 (2009): 234–50.
Beaumont, Gustave de. 1835. *Marie, ou l'esclavage aux Etats-Unis: Tableau de mœurs américaines*. Paris: Gosselin, 1840.
Beckman, Erika. "Bedouins and Troubadours on the Pampa: Orientalism and Medievalism in Sarmiento's *Facundo*." *Chasqui* 38.2 (2009): 37–46.
———. *Capital Fictions: The Literature of Latin America's Export Age*. Minneapolis: U of Minnesota P, 2013.
Bederman, Gail. *Manliness and Civilization: A Cultural History of Gender and Race in the United States, 1880–1917*. Chicago: U of Chicago P, 1995.
Belnap, Jeffry, and Raúl Fernandez, eds. *José Martí's "Our America": From National to Hemispheric Studies*. Durham, NC: Duke UP, 1998.
Benítez Rojo, Antonio. *La isla que se repite: El Caribe y la perspectiva posmoderna*. Hannover, NH: Ediciones del Norte, 1988.
Benjamin, Walter. *The Origin of German Tragic Drama*. Translated by John Osborn. 1925. London: Verso, 1998.
Bergeaud, Éméric. *Stella*. 1859. Paris: Dentu, 1887.
Bernd, Zilá, ed. *Brasil/Canadá: mobilidades (trans)culturais*. Porto Alegre, Brazil: Nova Prova e Abecan, 2008.
Bhabha, Homi. *Nation and Narration*. New York: Routledge, 1990.
Blackwell, Marilyn S. "The Republican Vision of Mary Palmer Tyler." In Apple Golden, *Mothers and Motherhood*, 31–51.
Bolívar, Simón. "Carta de Jamaica." 1815.
Bolt, Jutta, Robert Inklaar, Herman de Jong, and Jan Luiten van Zanden. "Rebasing 'Maddison': New Income Comparisons and the Shape of Long-Run Economic Development." Maddison Project Working Paper 10, Maddison Project Database.
Bolton, Herbert Eugene. *The Spanish Borderlands: A Chronicle of Old Florida and the Spanish Southwest*. New Haven, CT: Yale UP, 1921.
Bone, Martyn. "The (Extended) South of Black Folk: Intraregional and Transnational Migrant Labor in *Jonah's Gourd Vine* and *Their Eyes Were Watching God*." *American Literature* 79.4 (2007): 753–79.

Borrero Echeverría, Esteban. "Apuntes sobre la mujer." Manuscript, n.d.
———. "Asuntos escolares." *Patria,* January 15, 1901.
———. "Borradores acerca de la escuela pública y los maestros." Manuscript. N.p.
———. "Una carta de doctor Borrero Echeverría (a Varona)." *Diario de la Marina.* February 3, 1905.
———. *El ciervo encantado.* 1905. Havana: Editorial Cubana, 1935.
———. "Cuestionario pedagógico." *Revista de Instrucción Pública.* November 10, 1900, 70–72.
———. "Los cursos pedagógicos de verano." *El Fígaro* 16.34 (September 9, 1900).
———. "La Instrucción Pública en la República Cubana." *El Fígaro.* May 18, 1903.
———. Letter to don Nicolás Heredia. March 25, 1900. In *Alma cubana,* n.d.
———. "Los niños." *La escuela moderna,* February 28, 1899, 4–6.
———. "San Carlos." *El Yara,* February 15, 1897.
Borucki, Alex. *From Shipmates to Soldiers: Emerging Black Identities in the Rio de la Plata.* Albuquerque: U of New Mexico P, 2015.
Bouciacault, Dion. *The Octoroon; or, Life in Louisiana.* In *Interracial Literature: Black-White Contacts in the Old World and the New,* edited by Werner Sollars. 1859. New York: New York UP, 2004, 300–36.
Bramen, Carrie Tirado. "Flirting in Yankeeland: Rethinking American Exceptionalism through Argentine Travel Writing." In *The Latino Nineteenth Century,* edited by Rodrigo Lazo and Jesse Alemán. New York: New York UP, 2016, 210–29.
Branche, Jerome. *Colonialism and Race in Luso-Hispanic Literature.* Columbia: U of Missouri P, 2006.
———. *The Poetics and Politics of Diaspora: Transnational Musings.* New York: Routledge, 2015.
Brent, Linda [Harriet Jacobs]. *Incidents in the Life of a Slave Girl.* Edited by Lydia Maria Child. Boston: 1861.
Brickhouse, Anna. *Transamerican Literary Relations in the Nineteenth-Century Public Sphere.* Cambridge: Cambridge UP, 2004.
Bronfman, Alejandra. *Measures of Equality: Social Science, Citizenship and Race in Cuba, 1902–1940.* U of North Carolina P, 2004.
Brown, William Wells. *Clotel; or, The President's Daughter: A Narrative of Slave Life in the United States.* Edited by Robert Levine. 1853. Boston: Bedford, 2000.
Brunson, Takkara. "'Writing Black Womanhood in the Early Cuban Republic, 1904–16." *Gender & History* 28.2 (August 2016): 480–500.
Brushwood, John S. *Genteel Barbarism: Experiments in Analysis of Nineteenth-Century Spanish-American Novels.* Lincoln: U of Nebraska P, 1981.

Buck-Morss, Susan. *Hegel, Haiti, and Universal History.* Pittsburgh: U of Pittsburgh P, 2009.
Bueno, Salvador. *El negro en la novela hispanoamericana.* Havana: Letras cubanas, 1983.
Bueno Castillo, María de los Reyes, and Daisy Rubiera Castillo. *Reyita sencillamente: testimonio de una negra cubana nonagenaria.* Havana: Instituto del Libro Cubano, 1996.
Bullock, Penelope. "The Mulatto in American Fiction." In *Interracialism: Black-White Intermarriage in American History, Literature, and Law,* edited by Werner Sollars. Oxford: Oxford UP, 2000, 280–83.
Bunkley, Allison Williams. *The Life of Sarmiento.* 1952. New York: Greenwood, 1969.
Buscaglia-Salgado, José F. *Undoing Empire: Race and Nation in the Mulatto Caribbean.* Minneapolis: U of Minnesota P, 2003.
Bush, Barbara. "African Caribbean Slave Mothers and Children: Traumas of Dislocation and Enslavement across the Atlantic World." *Caribbean Quarterly* 56.1/2 (March–June 2010): 69–94.
———. *Slave Women in Caribbean Society, 1650–1832.* Bloomington: U of Indiana P, 1990.
Butchart, Ronald E. *Schooling the Freed People: Teaching, Learning, and the Struggle for Black Freedom, 1861–1876.* Chapel Hill: U of North Carolina P, 2010.
Byron, George Gordon, Lord. 1824. *Don Juan.* Halifax: Milnee and Sowerby, 1837.
Cable, George Washington. "Salomé Müller, The White Slave, 1818–1845." In *Strange True Stories of Louisiana.* New York: C. Scribner's Sons, 1889, 145–91.
Cairo, Ana. "Emilia Casanova y la dignidad de la mujer cubana." In Campuzano, *Mujeres latinoamericanas,* 231–41.
Calcagno, Francisco. *Romualdo, uno de tantos: Novela cubana.* Havana: M. de Armas, 1891.
Camacho, Jorge. *Miedo negro, poder blanco en la Cuba colonial.* Madrid: Iberoamérica, 2015.
Cambaceres, Eugenio. *Sin rumbo.* 1885.
Campuzano, Luisa, ed. *Mujeres latinoamericanas: Historia y cultura, Siglos XVI al XIX.* Havana: Casa de las Américas, 1997.
Cândido, Antonio. "Os brasileiros e a nossa América." In *Recortes.* Rio de Janeiro: Ouro sobre Azul, 2004, 143–55.
Cañizares-Esguerra, Jorge. "Entangled Histories: Borderland Historiographies in New Clothes?" *American Historical Review* 112 (2007): 787–99.
———. *Puritan Conquistadors: Iberianizing the Atlantic, 1550–1700.* Stanford, CA: Stanford UP, 2006.

Caprile, E. N. de. "Escuela Normal de Maestras de la Capital." In Wilde, *Memoria 1884*, II. 888–903.

———. "Informe de la Directora de la Escuela Normal de Maestras de la Capital." In Pizarro, *Memoria 1881*, 489–520.

Cardero, Mariano. "Del carácter y trascendencia de la educación popular en las sociedades modernas." *Álbum cubano de lo bello y lo bueno*, 1860, 289–93.

Carpentier, Alejo. 1978. *La consagración de la primavera*. Madrid: Alianza Editorial, 2004.

"Carta remitida." *La moda, o, recreo semanal del bello sexo* 2 (July 3, 1830): 106–9.

Carvalhal, Tânia Franco. "Fronteras de la crítica y la crítica de fronteras." In *Literatura comparada en América latina: ensayos*, edited by Eduardo F. Coutinho. Cali: Universidad del Valle, 2003, 129–53.

———. "Limiares Culturais: As Complexas Relações do Sul/Sur." *Revista Iberoamericana* 44.182–83 (January–June 1998): 97–106.

Casanova, Pascale. *République mondiale des lettres*. Paris: Seuil, 1997.

Castañeda Fuertes, Digna. "Demandas judiciales de las esclavas en el siglo XIX cubano." In Campuzano, *Mujeres latinoamericanas*, 221–30.

Castillo, Debra. *Redreaming America: Towards a Bilingual American Culture*. Albany: SUNY P, 2005.

Cecilia. "A la señora doña Pastora Ramírez de Calvo." *Minerva: Revista quincenal dedicada a la mujer de color* 1.5 (December 15, 1888): 3–4.

Céspedes, Carlos Manuel. "Manifiesto de la junta revolucionaria de la Isla de Cuba, dirigido a sus compatriotas, y a todas las naciones." 1868.

Chang, Grace. "Undocumented Latinas: The New 'Employable Mothers.'" In Glen, Chang, and Forcey, *Mothering*, 259–85.

Chasteen, John Charles. *Americanos: Latin America's Struggle for Independence*. Oxford: Oxford UP, 2008.

Chasteen, John Charles, and Sandra Castro-Klarén, eds. *Beyond Imagined Communities: Reading and Writing the Nation in Nineteenth-Century Latin America*. Baltimore: Johns Hopkins UP, 2003.

Chavarria, Juan Manuel. *La escuela normal y la cultura argentina*. Buenos Aires: Atenec, 1947.

Chevigny, Bell Gale. Introduction to *Reinventing the Americas: Comparative Studies of Literature of the United States and Spanish America*, edited by Chevigny and Gari Laguardia. London: Cambridge UP, 2009, 139–57.

Chikiar Bauer, Irene. *Eduarda Mansilla. Entre ellos: una escritora argentina en el siglo XIX*. Buenos Aires: Biblos, 2013.

———. "Lucía Miranda: o el camino de la extrañeza a la absorción." *Olivar* 12.15 (June 2011): 37–57.

Childers, William. "The Moriscos and 'Race': Exploring the Roots of Modern Racism in Sixteenth-Century Spain." Hispanic Studies Lecture Series, Concordia College, November 24, 2011.

Childs, Matt D. "Sewing Civilization: Cuban Female Education in the Context of Africanization, 1800–1860." *Americas* 54.1 (July 1997): 83–107.

Chodorow, Nancy. *The Reproduction of Mothering: Psychoanalysis and the Social Production of Gender.* Berkeley: U of California P, 1978.

Clymer, Jeffory. *Family Money: Property, Race, and Literature in the Nineteenth Century.* New York: Oxford UP, 2012.

Collins, Patricia Hill. "Shifting the Center: Race, Class, and Feminist Theorizing about Motherhood." In Glenn, Chang, and Forcey, *Mothering*, 45–65.

Conant, Ernest. Letter to Charles Elliot. February 6, 1900. In *Álbum de la expedición*, n.p.

Condé, Maryse. *Moi, Tituba sorcière . . . noire de Salem.* Paris: Mercure de France, 1986.

Conrad, Sebastian. *What Is Global History?* Princeton, NJ: Princeton UP, 2016.

Cooper, Frederick, Thomas Holt, and Rebecca Scott. *Beyond Slavery: Explorations of Race, Labor, and Citizenship in Postcolonial Societies.* Chapel Hill: U of North Carolina P, 2000.

Cooper, James Fenimore. *The American Democrat; Or, Hints on the Social and Civic Relations in the United States of America.* Cooperstown, NY: H. and E. Phinney, 1838.

———. *The Deerslayer: The First War Path.* In *The Leatherstocking Tales*, 2 vols., edited by Blake Nevius. 1841. New York: Literary Classics of the United States, 1985.

———. *The Last of the Mohicans.* 1826. Edited by Blake Nevius.

———. *Mercedes of Castile; Or, the Voyage to Cathay.* 1840. New York: Hurd and Houghton, 1867. Making of America Books.

———. *The Pathfinder: The Inland Sea.* 1840. Edited by Blake Nevius.

———. *The Pioneers, or the Sources of the Susquehanna: A Descriptive Tale.* 1823. Ed. Blake Nevius.

———. *The Prairie: A Tale.* 1827. London: Richard Bentley, 1836.

———. *The Travelling Bachelor; or, Notions of the Americans.* 2 vols. 1828. New York: Stringer and Townsend, 1852.

Cooper, Michael A. "Should Not These Things Be Known? Mary Mann's *Juanita* and the Limits of Domesticity." In Elbert, Hall, and Rodier, *Reinventing the Peabody Sisters*, 146–62.

Coopiner, Cornelio C. "Memoria sobre el estado de la Instrucción primaria en 1881."

Cornejo Polar, Antonio. "Mestizaje, transculturación, heterogeneidad." *Revista de crítica literaria* 22.40 (1994): 368–71.

Coronado, Raúl. *A World Not to Come: A History of Latino Writing and Print Culture.* Cambridge, MA: Harvard UP, 2013.

Correas, Edmundo. *Sarmiento and the United States.* Gainesville: U of Florida P, 1961. Rpt. in *Nineteenth-Century Latin Americans in the United States*, edited by Carlos E. Cortés. New York: Arno, 1980, 1–45.

Coser, Stelamaris. *Bridging the Americas: The Literature of Paule Marshall, Toni Morrison, and Gayle Jones*. Philadelphia: Temple UP, 1994.

Couillard, Marie, and Patrick Imbert, eds. *Les Discours du Nouveau Monde au XIXe siècle au Canada et en Amérique latine*. New York: Legas, 1995.

Coulthard, G. R. *Raza y color en la literatura antillana*. Sevilla: Escuela de Estudios Hispanoamericanos, 1958.

Cowling, Camillia. *Conceiving Freedom: Women of Color, Gender, and the Abolition of Slavery in Havana and Rio de Janeiro*. Chapel Hill: U of North Carolina P, 2013.

Crenshaw, Kimberlé. "Mapping the Margins: Intersectionality, Identity Politics, and Violence against Women of Color." *Stanford Law Review* 43.6 (July 1991): 1241–99.

Crespo, Julio. *Las maestras de Sarmiento*. Buenos Aires: Grupo Abierto Comunicaciones, 2007.

Crespo, Natalia. "'Señor y amigo': Persuasión y política en nueve cartas inéditas de Eduarda Mansilla." *Decimonónica: Revista de producción cultural hispánica decimonónica* 13.1 (Winter 2016): 18–37.

Crèvecoeur, J. Hector St. John de. *Letters from an American Farmer*. Edited by Susan Manning. 1782. Oxford: Oxford UP, 1997.

Croguennec-Massol, Gabriel. "Cecilia Valdés ou les deux versions de la colline de l'ange." In *Unité et fragmentation, Production et réception, Généalogies d'une œuvre*, edited by Milagros Ezquerro and Julien Roger. *Les Ateliers du Séminaire Amérique Latine, Université Paris-Sorbonne* 3 (2009): 1–6.

Cruz, sor Juana Inés de la. *Respuesta de la poetisa a la muy ilustre sor Filotea de la Cruz*. José Luis Gómez Martínez. 1691. Proyecto Ensayo Hispánico.

Cubena. *Chombo*. Miami: Ediciones Universal, 1981.

———. *Los nietos de Felicidad Dolores*. Miami: Ediciones Universal, 1991.

Curnow, Ena. "La mujer en la era colonial." In *La mujer cubana: historia e infrahistoria*, edited by Instituto Jacques Maritain de Cuba. Miami: Universal, 2000, 15–37.

Curtis, Lesley S., and Christen Mucher. Editors' introduction to *Stella: A Novel of the Haitian Revolution*, by Émeric Bergeaud, translated by Leslie S. Curtis and Christen Mucher, ix–xxxviii. 1859. New York: New York UP, 2015.

Daly, Brenda O., and Maureen T. Reddy, eds. *Narrating Mothers: Theorizing Maternal Subjectivities*. Knoxville: U of Tennessee P, 1991.

Dally, Ann. *Inventing Motherhood: The Consequences of an Ideal*. New York: Schocken, 1983.

Dash, J. Michael. *The Other America: Caribbean Literature in a New World Context*. Charlottesville: UP of Virginia, 1998.

Daut, Marlene. *Tropics of Haiti: Race and the Literary History of the Haitian Revolution in the Atlantic World, 1789–1865*. Liverpool: Liverpool UP, 2015.

Davin, Anna. "Imperialism and Motherhood." *History Workshop*. 5 (Spring 1978): 9–65.

Davis, Angela Y. *Women, Race, and Class*. New York: Vintage, 1983.
Davis, Darién J., ed. *Beyond Slavery: The Multi-Layered Legacy of Africans in Latin America and the Caribbean*. Lanham, MD: Rowman and Littlefield, 2007.
Davis, David Brion. *The Problem of Slavery in Western Culture*. Ithaca, NY: Cornell UP, 1966.
DeCosta-Willis, Miriam, ed. "Afra-Hispanic Writers and Feminist Discourse." *NWSA Journal* 5.2 (Summer 1993): 204–17.
———. *Daughters of the Diaspora: Afra-Hispanic Writers*. Kingston: Ian Randle, 2003.
Defauconpret, Auguste Jean-Baptiste, trans. *Le dernier des Mohicans: Histoire de 1757*. Translation of *The Last of the Mohicans*, by James Fenimore Cooper. Paris: Charles Gosselin, 1826.
Dekker, George. *James Fenimore Cooper: The American Scott*. New York: Barnes and Noble, 1967.
"De la influencia del bello sexo." *La moda, o, recreo semanal del bello sexo*, October 9, 1830, 325–30.
Delany, Martin R. *Blake, or, the Huts of America*. Edited by Floyd J. Miller. 1859. Boston: Beacon, 1970.
Degler, Carl. *Neither White nor Black: Slavery and Race Relations in Brazil and the United States*. Madison: U of Wisconsin P, 1971.
Departamento de Instruccion Pública. (Nicolás Avellaneda and Bonifacio Lastra.) "Resolucion dictada en consulta hecha por el Director de la Escuela Normal de Tucuman, sobre exclusion de alumnos del Establecimiento." March 18, 1879. In Lastra, *Memoria 1878*, 135–36.
Díaz de Guzmán, Ruy. *La Argentina manuscrita*. 1612.
Dillion, Susana. *Las locas del camino*. Río Cuarto, Argentina: Universidad Nacional de Río Cuarto, 1995.
Dimock, Wai Chee. *Through Other Continents: American Literature across Deep Time*. Princeton, NJ: Princeton UP, 2009.
"Documento 5." ("Agasajos a Mr. Roosevelt . . . Recepción en la Facultad de Medicina.") In Satas, *Una política exterior argentina*, 227–32.
"Documento importante." *La escuela moderna* 1.4 (March 30, 1899): 6–7.
Domínguez, Daylet. "Cuadros de costumbres en Cuba y Puerto Rico: de la historia natural y la literatura de viajes a las ciencias sociales." *Revista hispánica moderna* 29.2 (2016): 133–49.
Domínguez Navarro, Ofelia. "The First Wave of Cuban Feminism." In *The Cuba Reader: History, Culture, Politics*, edited by Aviva Chompsky, Barry Carr, and Pamela Maria Smorkaoff. Durham, NC: Duke UP, 2003, 19–25.
Dore, Elizabeth. "One Step Forward, Two Steps Back: Gender and the State in the Long Nineteenth Century." In Dore and Molyneux, *Hidden Histories of Gender*, 3–32.

Dore, Elizabeth, and Maxine Molyneux, eds. *Hidden Histories of Gender and the State in Latin America.* Durham, NC: Duke UP, 2000.

Dorn, Georgette Magassy. "Sarmiento, the United States, and Public Education." In *Sarmiento and His Argentina,* edited by Joseph T. Crescenti. Boulder, CO: Lynne Rienner, 1993.

Douglas, Susan J., and Meredith W. Michaels. *The Mommy Myth: The Idealization of Motherhood and How It Has Undermined All Women.* New York: Simon and Schuster, 2005.

Dubois, Laurent. *Avengers of the New World: The Story of the Haitian Revolution.* Cambridge, MA: Harvard UP, 2004.

Du Bois, W. E. B. *Black Reconstruction.* 1935. Edited by Herbert Aptheker. Millwood, NY: Kraus-Thomson, 1976.

Duchesne, Dafne. "Two Contending Mothers: Discrepant Allegories in Émeric Bergeaud's *Stella.*" *Research in African Literatures* 46.2 (Summer 2015): 104–18.

Duno Gottberg, Luis. *Solventando las diferencias: La ideología del mestizaje en Cuba.* Madrid: Iberoamericana, 2003.

Echeverría, Esteban. "La cautiva." In *Obras completas de D. Esteban Echeverría.* Vol. 1. Buenos Aires: Imprenta y Librería de Mayo, 1870, 35–138.

———. "El matadero." In *Revista del Río de la Plata: Periódico mensual de Historia y Literatura de América.* 1838. Buenos Aires: Imprenta y Librería de Mayo, 1871.

"Educación." *La Aljaba: Dedicada al bello sêxo Argentino* 7 (December 7, 1830): 3–4.

"Educación." *La Aljaba: Dedicada al bello sêxo Argentino* 11 (December 21, 1830): 1–2.

"Educación de las hijas." *La Aljaba: Dedicada al bello sêxo Argentino* 6 (December 3, 1830): 1–2.

L'Educatore. 1–9 (April 6, 1880–May 30, 1880).

Edwards, Brent Hayes. *The Practice of Diaspora: Literature, Translation, and the Rise of Black Internationalism.* Cambridge, MA: Harvard UP, 2003.

Einsentein, Zillah. "Writing Bodies on the Nation for the Globe." In Ranchod-Nilson and Tetreault, *Women, States and Nationalism,* 35–53.

Elbert, Monika M., Julie E. Hall, and Katherine Rodier, eds. *Reinventing the Peabody Sisters.* Iowa City: U of Iowa P, 2006.

"Emigration to Washington Territory of Four Hundred Women on the Steamer 'Continental.'" *Harper's Weekly Magazine,* January 6, 1866, 8–9.

Errázuriz, Rebeca. "Sarmiento y Martí en los EE.UU: imaginarios de la modernidad." *Revista Universum* 23.1 (2008): 44–65.

Erkkila, Betsy. *Mixed Blood and Other Crosses: Rethinking American Literature from the Revolution to the Culture Wars.* Philadelphia: U of Pennsylvania P, 2005.

Escobar, Roberto. "Alejandro Carbó." In Figueroa, *Escuela Normal de Paraná*, 195–99.
Ette, Ottmar. "Pensar o futuro: a poética do movimento nos Estudos de Transárea." *Alea: Estudos Neolatinos* 18.2 (May–August, 2016): 192–209.
———. *TransArea: A Literary History of Globalization*. Translated by Mark W. Person. Berlin: de Gruyter, 2016.
"Exámen de niñas." *La moda, o, recreo semanal del bello sexo* 2 (November 6, 1830): 402–6.
Faulkner, William. *Absalom! Absalom!* 1936. New York: Modern Library, 1964.
Faust, A. F. "The Influence of the United States upon the Developing Argentine Normal School." *History of Education Journal* 2.2 (Winter 1951): 62–64.
Feal, Rosemary Geisdorfer. "Feminist Interventions in the Race for Theory: Neither Black nor White." *Afro-Hispanic Review* 10.3 (September 1991): 11–20.
Feijóo, Benito Jerónimo. "Defensa de las mujeres." In *Teatro crítico universal, o Discursos varios en todo género de materias para desengaño de errores comunes*, vol. 1, *Discurso XVI* 1726.
Felstiner, Mary Lowenthal. "Family Metaphors: The Language of an Independent Revolution." *Comparative Study of Society and History* 25.1 (1983): 154–80.
Fénelon, Abbé François de. *Traité de l'éducation des filles*. 1681. Paris: Hachette, 1909.
Ferguson, John De Lancey. *American Literature in Spain*. New York: Columbia UP, 1916.
Fernández de Lizardi, José Joaquín. *La educación de las mujeres; o, la Quijotita y su prima: historia muy cierta con apariencias de novela*. 1819. Mexico City: Ballescá, 1897.
———. *El periquillo sarniento*. Edited by Carmen Ruiz Barrionuevo. 1816. Cátedra: Madrid, 1997.
Fernández Retamar, Roberto. *Calibán y otros ensayos: Nuestra América y el mundo*. Havana: Editorial Arte y Literatura, 1979.
Ferrer, Ada. *Freedom's Mirror: Cuba and Haiti in the Age of Revolution*. New York: Cambridge UP, 2014.
———. *Insurgent Cuba: Race, Nation, and Revolution, 1868–1898*. Chapel Hill: U of North Carolina P, 1999.
Ferrer, Vicente R. "Sección Escolar de la Capital. Informe de Inspección." In *Memoria del Consejo*, 172–73.
Ferrús Antón, Beatriz. *Mujer y literatura de viajes en el siglo XIX: Entre España y las Américas*. Valencia: Universitat de València, 2011.
Fielder, Leslie A. *Love and Death in the American Novel*. New York: Criterion Books, 1960.
Figueiredo, Eurídice. "Identidade nacional e identidade cultural." In *Conceitos de Literatura e Cultura*, edited by Figueiredo. Rio de Janeiro: Editora UFRJ, 2012, 189–205.

Figueroa, Sara. *Escuela Normal de Paraná: datos históricos, 1871–1895.* Buenos Aires: Pressadi Impresores, 1934.
Figueras, Francisco. *Cuba y su evolución colonial.* Havana: Avisador Comercial, 1907.
Finch, Aisha K. "Scandalous Scarcities: Black Slave Women, Plantation Domesticity, and Travel Writing in Nineteenth-Century Cuba." *Journal of Historical Sociology* 23.1 (2010): 101–43.
Fiol-Matta, Licia. *A Queer Mother for the Nation: The State and Gabriela Mistral.* Minneapolis: U of Minnesota P, 2002.
Fischer, Sibylle. Introduction to *Cecilia Valdés,* by Cirilo Villaverde. Translated by Helen Lane. New York: Oxford UP, 2005.
———. *Modernity Disavowed: Haiti and the Cultures of Slavery in the Age of Revolution.* Durham, NC: Duke UP, 2004.
Fitz, Earl. "Inter-American Studies as an Emerging Field: The Future of a Discipline." *Vanderbilt e-Journal of Luso-Hispanic Studies* 1 (2004).
———. *Rediscovering the New World: Inter-American Literature in a Comparative Context.* Iowa City: U of Iowa P, 1991.
Fletcher, Lea, ed. *Mujeres y cultura en la Argentina del siglo XIX.* Buenos Aires: Feminaria Editora, 1994.
Foner, Phillip S. *The Spanish-Cuban-American War and the Birth of American Imperialism.* 2 vols. New York: Monthly Review Press, 1972.
Font, América. "Mis opinions." *Minerva: revista quincenal dedicada a la mujer de color* 1.4 (November 30, 1888): 1–3.
Forbes, Jack D. *Africans and Native Americans: The Language of Race and the Evolution of Red-Black Peoples.* Urbana: U of Illinois P, 1993.
Foucault, Michel. *The History of Sexuality.* Vol. 1, *An Introduction,* translated by Robert Hurley. New York: Vintage, 1976.
———. *Les Mots et les choses: Une archéologie des sciences humaines.* Paris: Gallimard, 1966.
———. *Surveiller et punir : Naissance de la prison.* Paris: Gallimard, 1975.
Fountain, Anne. *José Martí, the United States, and Race.* Gainesville: UP of Florida, 2014.
Fox, Claire, ed. "Critical Perspectives and Emerging Models of Inter-American Studies." Special issue, *Comparative American Studies: An International Journal* 3.4 (2005).
Franco, Jean. *The Decline and Fall of the Lettered City: Latin America and the Cold War.* Cambridge, MA: Harvard UP, 2008.
———. *A Literary History of Spain: Spanish American Literature since Independence.* London: Ernest Benn Limited, 1973.
Franco, José Luciano, ed. *Las conspiraciones de 1810 y 1812.* Caracas: Ayacucho 2010.
Franklin, Benjamin. *The Autobiography of Benjamin Franklin.* 1791. Carlisle, MA: Applewood, 2008.

Franklin, Wayne. "Introduction: Becoming James Fenimore Cooper." In *James Fenimore Cooper: The Birth of American Maritime Experience*, edited by Robert Foulke. Originally published in *The American Neptune: A Quarterly Journal of Maritime History and Arts* 57.4 (Fall 1997): 299–314.
———. *James Fenimore Cooper*. Vol. 1, *The Early Years*. New Haven, CT: Yale UP, 2007.
Fraunhar, Alison. *Mulata Nation: Visualizing Race and Gender in Cuba*. Jackson: UP of Mississippi, 2018.
Frazier, E. Franklin. *The Negro Family in the United States*. 1939. Chicago: U of Chicago P, 1966.
Frederick, Bonnie. "Harriet Beecher Stowe and the Virtuous Mother: Argentina, 1852–1910." *Journal of Women's History* 18.1 (2006): 101–20.
———. *Wily Modesty: Argentine Women Writers, 1896–1910*. Tempe: Arizona State UP, 1998.
Freixa, Omer. "Los primeros africanos en el Nuevo Mundo: más de tres siglos de trata de esclavos." *Todo es historia* 524 (March 2011): 6–18.
Freud, Sigmund. *Totem and Taboo: Some Points of Agreement between the Mental Lives of Savages and Neurotics*. 1913. Translated by James Strachey. New York: Norton, 1962.
Frischman, Gustavo E. "Persistence and Ruptures: The Feminization of Teaching and Teacher Education in Argentina." *Gender and Education* 19.3 (April 2007): 353–68.
Fuchs, Barbara. *Exotic Nation: Maurophilia and the Construction of Early Modern Spain*. Philadelphia: U of Pennsylvania P, 2009.
Fuente, Alejandro de la. *A Nation for All: Race, Inequality, and Politics in Twentieth-Century Cuba*. Chapel Hill: U of North Carolina P, 2001.
Fuentes, Carlos. *El espejo enterrado*. Mexico City: Fondo de Cultura Económica, 1992.
Gálvez, Manuel. 1914. *La maestra normal*. Buenos Aires: Patria, 1921.
Gárate, Miriam V. *Civilização e barbárie n'os Sertões: entre Domingo Faustino Sarmiento e Euclides da Cunha*. São Paulo: Fapesp; Campinas, SP: Mercado de Letras, 2001.
García, Ana María. "Sarmiento y la educación de la mujer." *Revista la Universidad* 8.54 (2011): n.p.
García, Ivonne M. "Anticipating 1898: Writings of U.S. Empire on Puerto Rico, Cuba, the Philippines, and Hawai'i." PhD diss., Ohio State University, 2008.
García Canclini, Néstor. *Culturas híbridas: Estrategias para entrar y salir de la modernidad*. Mexico: Grijalbo, 1989.
García Orza, Raúl. Introduction to *Bases y puntos de partida*, by Juan Bautista Alberdi.
García Pons, César. "Momentos aurales de la cultura en Cuba." In Otero, *Libro de Cuba*, 554–64.

Garrels, Elizabeth. "Sarmiento ante la cuestión de la mujer: desde 1839 hasta el 'Facundo.'" In *La imaginación histórica en el siglo XIX*, edited by Lelia Area and Mabel Moraña. Rosario, Argentina: UNR Editoria, 215–42.

———. "Sobre los indios, afroamericanos y los racismos de Sarmiento." *Revista Iberoamericana* 63 (January–June 1997): 99–113.

Geiger, Shirley M. "African-American Single Mothers: Public Perceptions and Public Policies." In Vaz, *Black Women in America*, 244–57.

Gelado, Viviana, and María Verónica Secreto, eds. *Afrolatinoamérica: Estudos Comparados*. Rio de Janeiro: Mauad, 2016.

Gelpí, Juan G. "El discurso jerárquico en *Cecilia Valdés*." *Revista de crítica literaria latinoamericana* 17.34 (1991): 47–61.

Gellner, Ernest. *Nations and Nationalism*. Ithaca, NY: Cornell UP, 1983.

Genova, Thomas. "Family Entanglements: Cooper in Nineteenth-Century South America." *James Fenimore Cooper Society Miscellaneous Papers* 31 (May 2015): 17–19.

———. "Foundational Frustrations: Incest and Incompletion in Cirilo Villaverde's *Cecilia Valdés*." *Decimonónica: Revista de Producción Cultural Hispánica Decimonónica* 13.1 (Winter 2016): 66–86.

———. "*The Last of the Mohicans* in Spanish: A Racialized Dialogue." *Latin Americanist (SECOLAS Annals)* 59.1 (March 2015): 35–46.

———. "'La patria es nuestra madre': Family Metaphor and Race in the La Guaira Conspiracy." *Alea: Estudos neolatinos* 19.2 (May/August, 2017).

———. "Sarmiento's *Vida de Horacio Mann*: Translation, Importation and Entanglement." *Hispanic Review* 82.1 (Winter 2014): 21–41.

Gerassi-Navarro, Nina. *Pirate Novels: Metaphors of Nation Building in Spanish America*. Durham, NC: Duke UP, 1999.

Gerbi, Antonello. *La disputa del Nuevo Mundo: Historia de una polémica, 1750–1900*. Spanish translation by Antonio Alatorre. 1960. Mexico City: Fondo de Cultura Económica, 1993.

Gilbert, Olive. *Narrative of Sojourner Truth*. 1878. New York: Arno, 1968.

Giles, Paul. "Commentary: Hemispheric Partiality." *American Literary History* 18 (2006): 648–56.

Gill, Wilson L. *The Gill system of moral and civic training as exemplified in the school cities and school state at the State normal school, New Paltz, New York. A symposium by the faculty and students of the school, the author of the system and other educators*. New Paltz, NY: Patriot League, 1901.

———. "The School City." *Journal of the Franklin Institute* 156.1 (1903): 19–31.

———. *The School City: A New System of Moral and Civic Training*. Philadelphia: National School City League, 1901.

———. *A Social and Political Necessity: Moral, Civic, and Industrial Training; Experiences, Reports, and Proposed Legislation*. New Paltz, NY: Patriot League, 1902.

Gilliam, Franklin D., Jr. "The 'Welfare Queen' Experiment: How Viewers React to Images of African-American Women on Welfare." *Nieman Reports* 53.2 (Summer 1999).
Gillman, Susan. "*Ramona* in 'Our America.'" In Belnap and Fernandez, *José Martí's "Our America,"* 91–112.
Gilroy, Paul. *The Black Atlantic: Modernity and Double Consciousness.* London: Verso, 1993.
Glenn, Evelyn Nakano. "Social Constructions of Mothering: A Thematic Overview." In Glenn, Chang, and Forcey, *Mothering*, 1–29.
Glenn, Evelyn Nakano, Grace Chang, Linda Rennie Forcey, eds. *Mothering: Ideology, Experience, and Agency.* New York: Routledge, 1994.
Glissant, Édouard. *Le Discours antillais* . Paris: Éditions du Seuil, 1983.
Golden, Janet. "The New Motherhood and the New View of Wet Nurses, 1780–1865." In Apple and Golden, *Mothers and Motherhood*, 72–89.
Goldgel Carballo, Víctor. "Spectral Realism: *Cecilia Valdés* as Gothic Novel." *Journal of Latin American Cultural Studies* 27.3 (2018): 313–29.
Goldstein, Dana. *The Teacher Wars: A History of America's Most Embattled Profession.* New York: Doubleday, 2014.
Gómez de Avellaneda, Gertrudis. *Sab.* 1841. Edited by José Servera. Madrid: Cátedra, 2003.
Gonçalves, Ana María. *Um defeito de cor.* 2006. Rio de Janeiro: Record, 2009.
González, Eduardo. "American Theriomorphia: The Presence of *Mulatez* in Cirilo Villaverde and Beyond." In *Interracialism: Black-White Intermarriage in American History, Literature, and Law,* edited by Werner Sollors. Oxford: Oxford UP, 2000, 437–60.
González Echevarría, Roberto. "A Lost World Rediscovered: Sarmiento's *Facundo.*" In Halperín Donghi et al., *Sarmiento, Author of a Nation*, 220–56.
———. "*Facundo:* An Introduction." In *Facundo: Civilization and Barbarism*, by Domingo Faustino Sarmiento, translated by Kathleen Ross, First Complete English Translation. Berkeley: U of California P, 2003: 1–16.
González Lucena, Danny, dir. *Los cubanos de Harvard, 1900.* Cambridge, MA: Cuban Studies Program at Harvard University, 2017.
González-Stephan, Beatriz. "Forms of Historic Imagination: Visual Culture, Historiography, and the Tropes of War in Nineteenth-Century Venezuela." In Acree and González Espitia, 101–32.
Gorriti, Juana Manuela. "Si haces mal, no esperes bien." In *Obras completas de Juana Manuela Gorriti,* vol. 4. 1861. Salta: Fundación del Banco del Noroeste, 1982: 224–35.
Goyal, Yogita. "Chronology." In *Transnational American Literature.* New York: Cambridge UP, 2017, xiii–xxxv.
Graham, Richard, ed. *The Idea of Race in Latin America, 1870–1940.* Austin: U of Texas P, 1990.

Grandin, Greg. *Empire of Necessity: Slavery, Freedom, and Deception in the New World*. New York: Metropolitan Books, 2014.
Greene, Roland. "New World Studies and the Limits of National Literatures." *Stanford Humanities Review* 6 (1998): 88–110.
———. "Wanted: A New World Studies." *American Literary History* 12.1/2 (Spring–Summer 2000): 337–47.
Groussac, Paul. "Informe del Director de la Escuela Normal de Tucuman." In Pizarro, *Memoria 1881*, 437–49.
Gruesz, Kirsten Silva. *Ambassadors of Culture: The Transamerican Origins of Latino Writing*. Princeton, NJ: Princeton UP, 2002.
Guerrero Guerrero, Eva. "La educación de la mujer en el proyecto civilizador de Domingo Faustino Sarmiento." *Monteagudo* 3.16 (2011): 109–25.
Guerra, François Xavier. "Lógicas y ritmos de las revoluciones hispánicas." In *Las revoluciones hispánicas: independencias americanas y liberalismo español*, ed. Guerra. Madrid: Editorial Complutense, 1995, 13–46.
Guerra, Rosa. "Lucía Miranda." 1860. Buenos Aires: Facultad de Filolosofía y Letras, Instituto de Literatura Argentina, 1956.
Guevara, Ernesto (Che). *El socialismo y el hombre en Cuba*. Havana: Ediciones Revolución, 1965.
Guevara, Tristán Enrique. *Las maestras que trajo Sarmiento*. Córdoba: Servicio Cultural e Informativo de los Estados Unidos de América, 1954.
Guillén, Nicolás. "Martín Morúa Delgado." In *La familia Unzúazu*, by Martín Morúa Delgado. 1949. Havana: Instituto Cubano del Libro, 1975, 245–65.
Guimarães, Bernardo. *A escrava Isaura*. 1875. São Paolo: FTD Editora, 2011.
Guterl, Mathew. *American Mediterranean: Southern Slaveholders in the Age of Emancipation*. Cambridge, MA: Harvard UP, 2008.
Gutman, Herbert G. *The Black Family in Slavery and Freedom, 1750–1925*. New York: Pantheon, 1976.
Guy, Donna J. ''Parents before the Tribunals: The Legal Construction of Patriarchy in Argentina.'' In Dore and Molyneux, 172–93.
Guzmán, Florencia. "María Remdios del Valle: 'La Capitana,' 'Madre de la Patria,' y 'Niña de Ayohuma.' Historiografía, memoria y representaciones en torno a esta figura singular." *Nuevo mundo/Mundos nuevos*, 16 December 2016.
Guzmán, María de. *Spain's Long Shadow: The Black Legend, Off-Whiteness, and Anglo American Empire*. Minneapolis: U of Minnesota P, 2005.
Halperín Donghi, Tulio. "Sarmiento's Place in Postrevolutionary Argentina." In Halperín Donghi et al., *Sarmiento, Author of a Nation*, 19–30.
Halperín Donghi, Tulio, Iván Jaksić, Gwen Kirkpatrick, and Francine Masiello, eds. *Sarmiento, Author of a Nation*. Berkeley: U of California P, 1994.
Handley, George B. "A New World Poetics of Oblivion." In Smith and Cohn, *Look Away!*, 25–51.
Hanke, Lewis, ed. *Do the Americas Have a Common History? A Critique of the Bolton Theory*. New York: Knopf, 1968.

Hanway, Nancy. *Embodying Argentina: Body, Space, and Nation in 19th Century Narrative*. Jefferson, NC: McFarland, 2003.
Hardt, Michael, and Antonio Negri. *Empire*. Cambridge, MA: Harvard UP, 2000.
Harney, Lucy D. "The Enlightenment Origins of Cuba's Iconic *Mulata*." In *La Ilustración de Eva: Enlightenment and Women's Experience in Spain and Latin America*, edited by Cristina Sánchez-Conejero. New Castle: Cambridge Scholars' Publishing, 2007, 33–42.
Harper, Frances Watkins. *Iola Leroy, or, Shadows Uplifted*. Edited by Hazel V. Carby. 1892. Boston: Beacon, 1987.
———. "The Slave Mother." 1854.
Hartman, Saidiya. *Lose Your Mother: A Journey along the Atlantic Slave Route*. New York: Farrar, Straus, and Giroux, 2007.
Havard, John C. *Hispanicism and Early US Literature*. Tuscaloosa: U of Alabama P, 2018.
———. "Mary Mann's *Juanita*: Cuba and US National Identity." *Studies in the Novel* 44.2 (Summer 2012): 144–63.
Hawthorne, Nathaniel. *The House of the Seven Gables*. Edited by Robert S. Levine. 1851. New York: Norton, 2005.
Hawthorne, Sophia Peabody. *The Cuba Journal, 1833–1835*. Edited by Claire Badaracco. University Microfilms International, 1985. Berg Collection. University of Michigan, Ann Arbor.
Hays, Sharon. *The Cultural Construction of Motherhood*. New Haven, CT: Yale UP, 1996.
Helg, Aline. *Our Rightful Share: The Afro-Cuban Struggle for Equality, 1886–1912*. Chapel Hill: U of North Carolina P, 1995.
———. "Race in Argentina and Cuba, 1880–1930: Theory, Policies, and Popular Reaction." In Graham, *The Idea of Race in Latin America*. 37–71.
Heng, Geraldine, and Janadas Devan. "State Fatherhood: The Politics of Nationalism, Sexuality, and Race in Singapore." In Parker et al., *Nationalisms and Sexualities*, 343–64.
Henríquez Ureña, Pedro. 1945. *Las corrientes literarias en la América hispánica*. Mexico City: Fondo de Cultura Económica, 1949.
Heredia, José María. *Niágara y otros textos (poesía y prosa selecta)*. Edited by Ángel Augier. Caracas: Ayacucho, 1990.
Hernández, José. 1872. *El gaucho Martín Fierro y la vuelta de Martín Fierro*. Buenos Aires: Sopena, 1956.
Hernández González, Manuel. "Emilia Casanova, heroína de la independencia de Cuba." *Dossiers Feministes: Mujeres en la historia; Heroínas, damas y escritoras (siglos xvi–xix)* 15 (2011): 48–62.
Hernández-Miyares, Julio E. "El tema negro en las novelas naturalistas de Martín Morúa Delgado." In *Homenaje a Lydia Cabrera*, edited by Reinaldo Sánchez et al. Miami: Ediciones Universales, 1977, 211–19.

Hitt, Sarah Jayne. "Work among the People: How Susan La Flesche Picotte and Zitkala Sa Used Boarding School Education for the Benefit of Their Tribes." In Paulk, *Dominant Culture and the Education of Women*, 209–20.
Hobsbawm, E. J. *The Age of Revolution, 1789–1848*. Cleveland: World Publishing, 1962.
———. *Nations and Nationalism: Programme, Myth, Reality*. New York: Cambridge UP, 1990.
Hodge, John E. "The Formation of the Argentine Public Primary and Secondary School System." *Americas* 44.1 (July 1987): 45–65.
Hoffman, Léon-François. "En marge du premier roman haïtien: *Stella*, d'Émeric Bergeaud." In *Haïti : Lettres et l'être*. Toronto: FREF, 1992, 146–65.
Hoganson, Kristin L. *Fighting for American Manhood: How Gender Politics Provoked the Spanish-American and Philippine-American Wars*. New Haven, CT: Yale UP, 1998.
Hooker, Juliet. *Theorizing Race in the Americas: Douglas, Sarmiento, Du Bois, and Vasconcelos*. New York: Oxford UP, 2017.
Hopkins, Pauline. *Hagar's Daughter*. In *The Magazine Novels of Pauline Hopkins*, edited by Hazel V. Carby. 1901–2. New York: Oxford UP, 1988, 1–284.
Horrego Estuch, Leopoldo. *Emilia Casanova: la vehemencia del separatismo*. Havana: Academia de la Historia Cubana, 1951.
———. *Martín Morúa Delgado*. Havana: Universidad Central Las Villas, 1957.
Horsman, Reginald. *Race and Manifest Destiny: The Origins of American Racial Anglo-Saxonism*. Cambridge, MA: Harvard UP, 1981.
Howard, Jennie E. *In Distant Climes and Other Years*. Buenos Aires: American Press, 1931.
Howe, Daniel Walker. *What Hath God Wrought: The Transformation of America, 1815–1848*. New York: Oxford UP, 2007.
Hoyos, Héctor. "The Case for Ad Hoc Transnationalism." In Newcomb and Gordon, 37–53.
Huerta Martínez, Ángela. *La enseñanza primaria en Cuba en el siglo XIX (1812–1866)*. Seville: Diputación Provincial de Sevilla, 1992.
———. "Escuelas normales en Cuba (1890–1898): Un profesorado de ida y vuelta." In *Culture et éducation dans les mondes hispaniques. Essais en hommage à Eve-Marie Fell*, edited by Jean-Luis Guereña and Mónica Zapata. Tours : Presses Universitaires François Rabelais, 2005, 195–208.
Hunt, Nancy Rose. "Domesticity and Colonialism in Belgian Africa: Usumbura's Foyer Social, 1946–1960." *Signs* 15.3 (Spring 1990): 447–74.
Hunter, Tera W. *Bound in Wedlock: Slave and Free Black Marriage in the Nineteenth Century*. Cambridge, MA: Harvard UP, 2017.
Ianes Vera, Raúl. *De Cortés a la huérfana enclaustrada: La novela histórica del romanticismo hispanoamericano*. New York: Peter Lang, 1999.
Iglesias Utset, Marial. *Las metáforas del cambio en la vida cotidiana: Cuba, 1898–1902*. Havana: Unión, 2003.

Imbernó, José. "Primeros consejos á las madres." Translated by M. Thiéry. *La Enseñanza* 2.2 (September 18, 1876): 4–6.
Irving, Washington. 1819. *Rip Van Winkle: A Posthumous Tale of Diedrich Knickerbocker.* New York: Dover, 2014.
———1820. *Tales of the Alhambra.* Boston: Houghton Mifflin, 1910.
Irwin, Robert McKee. "¿Qué han hecho los nuevos americanistas? The New American Studies, Ten Years Later." In Raussert, *Routledge Companion to Inter-American Studies,* 68–76.
Jackson, Holly. *American Blood: The Ends of the Family in American Literature, 1850–1900.* Oxford: Oxford UP, 2014.
Jackson, Richard. *The Black Image in Latin American Literature.* Albuquerque: U of New Mexico P, 1976.
———. *Black Writers and the Hispanic Canon.* London: Prentice Hall, 1997.
———. "The Emergence of Afro-Hispanic Literature." *Afro-Hispanic Review* 21.1/2 (Spring–Fall 2002): 23–29.
Jackson, Shirley. *La novela negrista en Hispanoamérica.* Madrid: Pliegos, 1986.
Jagoe, Eva-Lynn Alicia. "Family Triangles: Eduarda Mansilla, Domingo Sarmiento, and Lucio Mansilla." *Revista canadiense de estudios hispánicos* 29.3 (Spring 2005): 507–524.
Jaksic, Iván. *The Hispanic World and American Intellectual Life, 1820–1880.* Hampshire: Palgrave Macmillan, 2007.
Jameson, Frederic. *The Political Unconscious: Narrative as a Socially Symbolic Act.* Ithaca, NY: Cornell UP, 1981.
———. "Third World Literature in the Era of Multinational Capitalism." *Social Text* 15 (1986): 65–88.
Jefferson, Thomas. Letter to John Adams. October 28, 1813. In *The Adams-Jefferson Letters: The Complete Correspondence between Thomas Jefferson and Abigail and John Adams,* edited by Lester J. Cappon. Chapel Hill: U of North Carolina P, 1959.
Jiménez Román, Miriam, and Juan Flores, eds. *The Afro-Latin@ Reader: History and Culture in the United States.* Durham, NC: Duke UP, 2010.
Jitrik, Noé. "De la historia a la escritura: predominios, disimetrías, acuerdos en la novela histórica latinoamericana." In Balderston, *The Historical Novel in Latin America,* 13–29.
———. *Muerte y resurrección de Facundo.* Buenos Aires: Centro Editor de América Latina, 1983.
Jones, Gayle. *Corregidora.* 1975. Boston: Beacon, 1987.
Joseph, Gilbert M. "Close Encounters: Towards a New Cultural History of U.S.–Latin American Cultural Relations." In Joseph, LeGrand, and Salvatore, *Close Encounters of Empire,* 3–46.
Joseph, Gilbert M., Catherine C. LeGrand, Ricardo D. Salvatore, eds. *Close Encounters of Empire: Writing the Cultural History of U.S.-Latin American Relations.* Durham, NC: Duke UP, 1998.

Jovellanos, Gaspar Melchor de. "Memoria sobre educación pública, tratado de enseñanza con aplicación á las escuelas y colegios de niños." In *Obras publicadas é inéditas de D. Gaspar Melchor de Jovellanos*. 1802. Madrid: Rivadeneyra, 1858, 230–67.

Kanellos, Nicolás, ed. *Herencia: The Anthology of Hispanic Literature of the United States*. New York: Oxford UP, 2002.

Kaplan, Amy. *The Anarchy of Empire in the Making of U.S. Culture*. Cambridge, MA: Harvard UP, 2005.

———. "Black and Blue on San Juan Hill." In Kaplan and Pease, *Cultures of United States Imperialism*, 219–36.

Kaplan, Amy, and Donald E. Pease, eds. *Cultures of United States Imperialism*. Durham, NC: Duke, UP, 1993.

Katra, William. *The Argentine Generation of 1837: Echeverría, Alberdi, Sarmiento, Mitre*. Madison, NJ: Associated University Presses, 1996.

———. *Domingo F. Sarmiento: Public Writer (between 1839 and 1852)*. Tempe: Arizona State University, 1985.

———. "Reading *Facundo* as Historical Novel." In Balderston, *The Historical Novel in Latin America*, 31–46.

———. "Sarmiento en los Estados Unidos." In *Viajes por Europa, África y América, 1845–1847*, by Domingo Faustino Sarmiento, edited by Javier Fernández. Madrid: Archivos, 1996, 853–911.

Kaup, Monika, and Deborah Rosenthal. *Mixing Race, Mixing Culture: Inter-American Literary Dialogues*. Austin: U of Texas P, 2002.

Kelly, William P. *Plotting America's Past: Fenimore Cooper and the Leatherstocking Tales*. Carbondale: Southern Illinois UP, 1983.

Kendi, Ibram X. *Stamped from the Beginning: The Definitive History of Racist Ideas in America*. New York: Nation Books, 2016.

Kerber, Linda K. *Women of the Republic: Intellect and Ideology in Revolutionary America*. Chapel Hill: U of North Carolina P, 1980.

Kipling, Rudyard. "The White Man's Burden." *McClure's Magazine*. 12.4 (February 1899):1–2.

Klahn, Norma, and Wilfredo H. Corral, eds. *Los novelistas como críticos*. 2 vols. Mexico City: Ediciones del Norte, Fondo de Cultura Económica, 1991.

Klotzberger, Edward Lewis. *The Growth and Development of State Teachers College, New Paltz, State University of New York*. New Paltz: University Microfilms, 1968.

Kocka, Jürgen. "Comparison and Beyond." *History and Theory* 42 (February 2003): 39–44.

Kornweibel, Karen Ruth. *Writing for Inclusion: Literature, Race, and Identity in Nineteenth-Century Cuba and the United States*. Teaneck, NJ: Fairleigh Dickinson UP, 2018.

Kristal, Efraín. "The Incest Motif in Narratives of the United States and Spanish America." In *Internationalität Nationaler Literaturen*, edited by Udo Schöning. Göttingen: Wallestein Verlag, 2000, 390–403.

Kutzinski, Vera. "Afro-Hispanic American Literature." In *The Cambridge History of Latin American Literature*, vol. 2, ed. Roberto González Echeverría and Enrique Pulpo-Walker. New York: Cambridge UP, 1996, 164–94.

———. *Sugar's Secrets: Race and the Erotics of Cuban Nationalism*. Charlottesville: UP of Virginia, 1993.

Lacerda, João Batista de. *Sur les métis au Brésil*. Paris: Devouge, 1911.

Lakoff, George, and Mark Johnson. *Metaphors We Live By*. Chicago: U of Chicago P, 1980.

Lamore, Jean. Introducción to *Cecilia Valdés, o la loma del Ángel*, by Cirilo Villaverde. Madrid: Cátedra, 1992, 9–56.

Lanctot, Brendan. *Beyond Civilization and Barbarism: Culture and Politics in Postrevolutionary Argentina*. Lewisburg, PA: Bucknell UP, 2014.

Landers, Jane. "Slave Resistance on the Southeastern Frontier: Fugitives, Maroons, and Banditti in the Age of Revolution." In Smith and Cohn, *Look Away!*, 80–93.

Laney, Lucy Craft. "The Burden of the Educated Colored Woman." In *Lift Every Voice: African American Oratory, 1787–1900*, edited by Philip Sheldon Foner and Robert J. Branham. U of Alabama P, 1998, 885–90.

Lang, Elizabeth, and Robert Lang. *In a Valley Fair: A History of the State University College of Education at New Paltz*. New Paltz, NY: State University College of Education, 1960.

Langa Pizarro, Mar. "La gran figura silenciada: la mujer en el primer siglo de la conquista rioplatense." *América sin nombre* 9–10 (2007): 109–22.

Langley, Lester D. *The Americas in the Age of Revolution, 1750–1850*. New Haven, CT: Yale UP, 1998.

Laroche, Maximilien. "La Longue marche des femmes haïtiennes : De la soeur à la mère." *Alea: Estudos Neolatinos* 18.3 (2016): 454–69.

Larroque, Alberto M. Telegram to Benjamín Zorrilla. In *Memoria del Consejo*, 678–88.

Larsen, J. M., and Roberto Levingston. "Informe de la Escuela Normal de Maestros de la Capital." March 15, 1881. In Pizarro, *Memoria 1881*, 333–68.

Larsen, Neil. "A Note on Lukács *The Historical Novel* and the Latin American Tradition." In Balderston, *The Historical Novel in Latin America*, 121–28.

Lasso, Marixa. *Myths of Harmony: Race and Republicanism in the Age of Revolution, Colombia, 1795–1831*. Pittsburgh: U of Pittsburgh P, 2007.

Lawrence, D. H. *Studies in Classic American Literature*. New York: Doubleday, 1922.

Lazo, Raimundo. "*Cecilia Valdés*: Estudio crítico." In Álvarez García, *Acerca de Cirilo Villaverde*, 233–73.

Lazo, Rodrigo. "Against the Cuba Guide: The 'Cuba Journal,' *Juanita*, and Travel Writing." In Elbert, Hall, and Rodier, *Reinventing the Peabody Sisters*, 189–95.

——. *Writing to Cuba: Filibustering and Cuban Exiles in the United States*. Chapel Hill: U of North Carolina P, 2005.

Leante, César. "*Cecilia Valdés*, espejo de la esclavitud." *Casa de las Américas* 89 (1975): 19–25.

Leguizamón, Onésimo. "Circular a los Gobernadores de Provincias sobre el establecimiento de Escuelas Normales para maestras en la capital de cada Provincia que lo solicite. 14 de octubre de 1875." In Leguizamón, *Memoria 1875*, 208.

León, Fray Luis de. *La perfecta casada*. Zaragoza: Domingo Portonoarijs y Ursino, 1584.

Leroux, Karen. "'Money Is the Only Advantage': Reconsidering the History of Gender, Labor, and Emigration among US Teachers in the Late Nineteenth Century." *International Labor and Working-Class History* 87 (Spring 2015): 184–212.

——. "Sarmiento's Self-Strengthening Experiment: Americanizing Schools for Argentine Nation-Building." In *Teaching America to the World and the World to America: Education and Foreign Relations since 1870*, edited by Richard Garlitz and Lisa Jarvinen. New York: Palgrave Macmillan, 2012, 51–72.

Levander, Caroline F., and Robert S. Levine. "Introduction: Hemispheric American Literary History." *American Literary History* 18 (2006): 397–407.

Levin, Josh. *The Queen: The Forgotten Life behind an American Myth*. New York: Little, Brown, 2019.

——. "The Welfare Queen." *Slate*, December 19, 2013.

Lewis, Marvin. *Afro-Argentine Literature: Another Dimension of the Black Diaspora*. Columbia: U of Missouri P, 1996.

——. *Afro-Hispanic Poetry, 1840–1980: From Slavery to Negritude in South American Verse*. Columbia: U of Missouri P, 1983.

——. *Afro-Uruguayan Literature: Post-Colonial Perspectives*. Lewisburg, PA: Bucknell UP, 2003.

Ley de Educación. July 8, 1884. In *Memoria del Consejo*, 174–94.

Limerick, Patricia Nelson. *The Legacy of Conquest: The Unbroken Past of the American West*. New York: Norton, 1988.

Lindstrom, Naomi. *Early Spanish American Narrative*. Austin: U of Texas P, 2004.

Lipsitz, George. *The Possessive Investment in Whiteness: How White People Profit from Identity Politics*. Philadelphia: Temple UP, 2009.

Lamas, Carmen. "Americanized Criollos: Latino/a Figures in Late Nineteenth-Century Cuban Literature." *Revista Hispánica Moderna* 61.1(2008): 69–87.

——. "The Black *Lector* and Martín Morúa Delgado's *Sofía* (1891) and *La familia Unzúazu* (1901)." *Latino Studies* 13.1 (2015): 113–30.

Lofgren, Hans Borje. "Democratic Skepticism: Literary-Historical Point of View in Cooper, Hawthorne, and Melville." PhD diss. University of California Santa Cruz, 1977.

Lojo, María Rosa. "En las fronteras de la nación: usos de la memoria y el olvido." *Revista de literatura hispánica* 77/78 (2013): 347–70.

———. Introduction to *Lucía Miranda*. By Eduarda Mansilla de García. Frankfurt: Vervuert, 2007.

———. "La importancia de llamarse Eduarda Mansilla." December 11, 2017. Eduardamansilla.com.

———. "*Lucía Miranda* (1860) de Eduarda Mansilla y sus genealogías italianas." *Gramma* 27 (2016): 13–37.

———. "La novela histórica en la Argentina, del romanticismo a la posmodernidad." *Cuadernos del CILHA* 14.2 (2013): 38–66.

———. "Sarmiento crítico literario y promotor de mujeres escritoras: Su lectura de Eduarda Mansilla." In *Jornadas Visiones de Sarmiento, 24 y 25 de septiembre de 2009*, edited by Miguel Ángel de Marco and Javier Roberto González. Buenos Aires: Facultad de Filosofía y Letras, Universidad Católica Argentina, 2010, 121–31.

Lope de Vega, Félix. *Fuenteovejuna*. 1619. Madrid: Espasa-Calpe, 1995.

López, Alejandra María. "Examen de Maestros." *Revista de Instrucción Pública*, November 10, 1900, 1.5 and 1.6, 93–95.

López Condeal, Julián. "Educación é instrucción: Diferencias entre una y otra." *La enseñanza* 1.6 (December 16, 1875): 61–63.

Lorini, Alessandra. "Cuba Libre and American Imperial Nationalism: Conflicting Views of Racial Democracy in the Post-Reconstruction United States." In *Contested Democracy: Freedom, Race, and Power in American History*, edited by Marisha Sinha and Penny Marie Von Eschen. New York: Columbia UP, 2007, 191–214.

Lott, Deshae A. "Like One Happy Family: Mary Peabody Mann's Method for Influencing Reform." In Elbert, Hall, and Rodier, *Reinventing the Peabody Sisters*, 91–107.

Luigi, Alice Houston. *65 Valiants*. Gainesville: UP of Florida, 1965.

———. "Some Letters of Sarmiento and Mary Mann, 1865–1876, Part I." *Hispanic American Historical Review* 32 (1952): 187–211.

———. "Some Letters of Sarmiento and Mary Mann, 1865–1876, Part II." *Hispanic American Historical Review* 32 (1952): 347–75.

Luis, William. *Literary Bondage: Slavery in Cuban Narrative*. Austin: U of Texas P, 1990.

———, ed. *Voices from Under: Black Narrative in Latin America and the Caribbean*. Westport, CT: Greenwood, 1984.

Luis-Brown, David. "An 1848 for the Americas: The Black Atlantic, 'El negro mártir,' and Cuban Exile Anticolonialism in New York City." *American Literary History* 21.3 (2009): 431–63.

Lukács, Georg. *The Historical Novel*. Translated by Hannah Mitchell and Stanley Mitchell. 1937. London: Merlin, 1962.

Luna, Félix. *Historia integral de la Argentina*. Vol. 4, *La Independencia y sus conflictos*. Buenos Aires: Planeta, 1994.
———. *Historia integral de la Argentina*. Vol. 5, *Discordia y dictadura*. Buenos Aires: Planeta, 1994.
———. *Historia integral de la Argentina*. Vol. 6, *La nación argentina*. Buenos Aires: Planeta, 1994.
———. *Historia integral de la Argentina*. Vol. 7, *El país y el mundo*. Buenos Aires: Planeta, 1994.
Lynch, John. *The Spanish American Revolutions, 1808–1826*. London: Weinfield and Nicolson, 1973.
MacAdam, Alfred J. *Textual Confrontations: Comparative Readings in Latin American Literature*. Chicago: U of Chicago P, 1987.
MacDonald, Victoria-María, ed. *Latino Education in the United States: A Narrated History from 1513–2000*. New York: Palgrave Macmillan, 2004.
Malave, Louis de. "Sterilization of Puerto Rican Women: A Selected, Partially Annotated Bibliography." University of Wisconsin-Madison Libraries.
Manganelli, Kimberly Snyder. *Transatlantic Spectacles of Race: The Tragic Mulatta and the Tragic Muse*. New Brunswick, NJ: Rutgers UP, 2012.
Mann, Barbara Alice. "Fancy Girls: The Creole and the Quadroon in Cooper's *Leatherstocking Tales*." In Walker, *Reading Cooper, Teaching Cooper*, 222–43.
———. "Sex and the Single Mixed Blood." In Walker, *Leather-Stocking Redux*, 57–85.
Mann, Horace. *A Few Thoughts on the Powers and Duties of Woman: Two Lectures*. Syracuse, NY: Hall Mills, 1853.
———. *Annual Reports of the Secretary of the Board of Education of Massachusetts for the years 1839–1844*. Boston: Lee and Shepard, 1891.
———. *Report of an Educational Tour in Germany, and Parts of Great Britain and Ireland: Being Part of the Seventh Annual Report of Horace Mann, Esq., Secretary of the Board of Education, Mass., U.S., 1844, with Preface and Notes, by W. B. Hodgson*. London: Simpkin, Marshall, 1846.
Mann, Mary Peabody. *Juanita: A Romance of Real Life in Cuba Fifty Years Ago*. Edited by Patricia M. Ard. 1887. Charlottesville: U of Virginia P, 2000.
———. *Life in the Argentine Republic in the Days of Tyrants*. 1868. New York: Hafner, 1960.
Mansilla, Lucio V. *Una excursión a los indios ranqueles*. Edited by Saul Sosnowski. 1870 Miami: Stockero, 2007.
Mansilla de García, Eduarda. *Cuentos*. Buenos Aires: Imprenta de la República, 1880.
———. *El médico de San Luis*. Edited by Rafael Pombo. 1860. Buenos Aires: Biblioteca Popular de Buenos Aires, 1879.
———. *Lucía Miranda*. Edited by María Rosa Lojo de Beurter. Frankfurt: Vervuert, 2007.
———. *Pablo, ou la vie dans les pampas*. Paris: E. Lachaud, 1869.

———. *Recuerdos de viaje*. Edited by J. P. Spicer-Escalante. 1882. Buenos Aires: Stockcero, 2006.

Manso, Juana. "Educación popular." *Álbum de señoritas: periódico de literatura, modas, bellas artes y teatro* 1.4 (1854): 46–50.

———. "Organización de las escuelas." *Álbum de señoritas: periódico de literatura, modas, bellas artes y teatro*. 1.2: 16–19.

Mataix, Remedios. "Romanticismo, feminidad e imaginarios nacionales: Las *Lucía Miranda* de Rosa Guerra y Eduarda Mansilla." *Río de la Plata* 29–30 (2006): 209–29.

Martin, Louis Aimé. *De l'éducation des mères de famille, ou, De la Civilisation du genre humain par les femmes*. 1834. Paris: Auguste Desrez, 1838.

Martinez-Alier, Verena. *Marriage, Class, and Colour in Nineteenth-Century Cuba: A Study of Racial Attitudes and Sexual Values in a Slave Society*. Cambridge: Cambridge UP, 1974.

Martínez-Echazábal, Lourdes. "Mestizaje and the Discourse of National/Cultural Identity in Latin America, 1845–1959." *Latin American Perspectives* 25.3 (1998): 21–42.

———. *Para una semiótica de la mulatez*. Madrid: J. Porrúa Turanzas, 1990.

Mármol, José. *Amalia*. Edited by Teodosio Fernández. 1855. Madrid: Cátedra, 2000.

Marr, Carolyn J. "Assimilation through Education: Indian Boarding Schools in the Pacific Northwest." University of Washington Libraries: 2000.

Marre, Diana. "Género y etnicidad: Relatos fundacionales y omisiones en la construcción de la nación argentina." *Revista de historia contemporánea* 21 (2000): 333–62.

Marshall, Megan. *The Peabody Sisters: Three Women Who Ignited American Romanticism*. Boston: Mariner, 2006.

"Martha Stewart." *Reference for Business*.

Martí, José. *La edad de oro*. 1889. Havana: Ediciones Universal, 1959.

———. *Nuestra América*. Edited by Pedro Henríquez Ureña. 1891. Buenos Aires: Losada, 1980.

Martínez Estrada, Ezequiel. *Radiografía de la pampa*. Buenos Aires: Babel, 1933.

Masiello, Francine. *Between Civilization and Barbarism: Women, Nation, and Literary Culture in Modern Argentina*. Lincoln: U of Nebraska P, 1992.

Matto de Turner, Clorinda. *Aves sin nido*. 1889. Buenos Aires: Solar, 1968.

McClennen, Sophia. "Comparative Literature and Latin American Studies: From Disarticulation to Dialogue." *CLCWeb: Comparative Literature and Culture* 4 (2002).

———. "Inter-American Studies or Imperial American Studies?" *Comparative American Studies: An International Journal* 3 (2005): 393–413.

McClintock, Anne. *Imperial Leather: Race, Gender and Sexuality in the Colonial Contest*. New York: Routledge, 1995.

McGillivray, Gillian. *Blazing Cane: Sugar Communities, Class, and State Formation in Cuba, 1868–1959*. Durham, NC: Duke UP, 2009.

McMeley, Mark. "Teacher Training and the Promise of Social Ascent: The Case of Argentina's Normal Schools, 1871–1881." *Latin Americanist* 50.1 (2006): 103–39.

McWilliams, John P., Jr. *Political Justice in a Republic: James Fenimore Cooper's America*. Berkeley: U of California P, 1972.

Meacham-Gould, Virginia. "Slave and Free Women of Color in the Spanish Ports of New Orleans, Mobile, and Pensacola." In Flores and Roman, *The Afro-Latin@ Reader*, 38–50.

Meléndez, Concha. *Obras Completas*. Vol. 1, *La novela indianista en Hispanoamérica (1832–1889)*. 1934. San Juan: Instituto de Cultura Puertorriqueña, 1970.

Méndez Rodenas, Adriana. "Incest and Identity in *Cecilia Valdés*: Villaverde and the Origin(s) of the Text." *Cuban Studies* 24 (1995): 83–104.

Mendizábal, Horacio. *Horas de meditación*. Buenos Aires, 1869.

Mera, Juan León. *Cumandá, o un drama entre salvajes*. Edited by Alfonso M. Escudero. 1877. Madrid: Austral, 1951.

Merimée, Prosper. *Carmen*. 1845. Paris: Michel Lévy Frères, 1846.

Meriño Fuentes, María de los Ángeles, and Aisnara Perera Díaz. *Matrimonio y familia en el ingenio: una utopía posible; La Habana (1825–1886)*. San Antonio de los Baños: Unicornio, 2007.

Mignolo, Walter. *The Idea of Latin America*. Malden, MA: Blackwell, 2005.

———. *Local Histories / Global Designs: Coloniality, Subaltern Knowledges, and Border Thinking*. Princeton, NJ: Princeton UP, 2000.

Minichino, Mario John. "In Our Image: The Attempted Reshaping of the Cuban Education System by the United States Government, 1898–1912." PhD diss., University of South Florida, 2014.

Mirabal, Nancy Raquel. *Suspect Freedoms: The Racial and Sexual Politics of Cubanidad in New York, 1823–1957*. New York: New York UP, 2017.

Miranda, Bruno V. "La educación popular" (pt. 2). *La Enseñanza* (Matanzas) 1.3 (November 20, 1887): 18–20.

Miseres, Vanesa. *Mujeres en tránsito: viaje, identidad y escritura en Sudamérica (1830–1910)*. Chapel Hill: U of North Carolina P, 2017.

Molloy, Sylvia. "The Unquiet Self: Mnemonic Strategies in Sarmiento's Autobiographies." In Halperín Donghi et al., *Sarmiento, Author of a Nation*, 156–68.

Monte, Domingo del. "Bosquejo intelectual de los Estados Unidos en 1840." In *Escritos de Domingo del Monte*, 2:245–54.

———. *Escritos de Domingo del Monte*. 2 vols. Edited by José A. Fernández de Castro, Havana: Cultura, 1929.

———. "Exposición de los trabajos en que se ha ocupado, el año 1831, la Sección de Educación de la Real Sociedad Patriótica." In *Escritos de Domingo del Monte*, 1:255–64.

———. "Informe sobre el estado actual de la Enseñanza Primaria en la Isla de Cuba en 1836, su costo y mejoras de que es susceptible." In *Escritos de Domingo del Monte,* 1:265–324.

———. "Informe sobre el estado actual de la Enseñanza Primaria en la Isla de Cuba en 1836, su costo y mejoras de que es susceptible" (pt. 2). In *Escritos de Domingo del Monte,* 2:7–66.

———. "Sobre la novela histórica." In *Escritos de Domingo del Monte,* 211–45.

Montejo, Esteban, and Miguel Barnet. *Biografía de un cimarrón* 1966. Barcelona: Ariel, 1968.

Moody, Sarah. "Eduarda Mansilla's Mestizo Argentina: Orphanhood, Transnationalism, and Race in *Lucía Miranda.*" *Decimonónica: Revista de Producción Cultural Hispánica Decimonónica* 12.2 (Summer 2015): 14–29.

Moraña, Mabel, ed. *Ideologies of Hispanism.* Nashville: Vanderbilt UP, 2005.

Moreno, Marisel C. *Family Matters: Puerto Rican Women Authors on the Island and the Mainland.* Charlottesville: U of Virginia P, 2012.

Morgade, Graciela. *El determinante de género en el trabajo docente de la Escuela Primaria.* Cuadernos de investigación 12. Buenos Aires: Miño y Dávila, 1992.

———. "¿Quiénes fueron las primeras maestras?" *Revista del Instituto de Investigación en Ciencias de Educación* 2 (1993): 52–60.

Morrison, Karen Y. *Cuba's Racial Crucible: The Sexual Economy of Social Identities, 1750–2000.* Bloomington: Indiana UP, 2015.

———. "Slave Mothers and White Fathers: Defining Family and Status in Late Colonial Cuba." *Slavery and Abolition: A Journal of Slave and Post-Slave Studies* 31.1 (March 2010): 29–55.

Morrison, Toni. *Beloved.* New York: Knopf, 1987.

Morúa Delgado, Martín. *Biografía del Libertador Toussaint L'Ouverture por John R. Beard: Vida de Toussaint L'Ouverture (Autobiografía).* In *Obras completas,* vol. 4, *Traducciones de Martín Morúa Delgado.*

———. "Enmienda adicional al artículo 17 de la Ley Electoral." In *Obras completas,* vol. 3, *Integración cubana,* 23–245.

———. "Ensayo político, o, Cuba y la raza de color." In *Obras completas,* vol. 3, *Integración cubana,* 45–108.

———. "Factores sociales." In *Obras completas* vol. 3, *Integración cubana,* 207–38.

———. *La familia Unzúazu. Novela cubana.* Havana: La Prosperidad, 1901.

———. "Las novelas del Sr. Villaverde." In *Obras completas,* vol. 5. Havana: Comisión Nacional del Centenario de Martín Morúa Delgado, 1957, 15–51.

———. Letter to Tomás Estrada Palma. In *Obras completas,* vol. 3, *Integración cubana,* 176.

———. *Obras completas de Martín Morúa Delgado.* Vol. 3, *Integración cubana.* Havana: Comisión Nacional del Centenario de Martín Morúa Delgado, 1957, 23–245.

———. *Sofía: Novela cubana.* Havana: Álvarez, 1891.

Moynihan, Daniel Patrick. *The Negro Family: The Case for National Action.* Washington, DC: Department of Labor, Office of Policy Planning and Research, 1965.

Mulroy, Kevin. *Freedom on the Border: The Seminole Maroons in Florida, the Indian Territory, Coahuila, and Texas.* Lubbock: Texas Tech UP, 1993.

Mulvey, Laura. "Visual Pleasure and Narrative Cinema." In *Film Theory and Criticism: Introductory Readings,* edited by Leo Braudy and Marshall Cohen. New York: Oxford UP, 1999, 833–44.

Murphy, Gretchen. "The Hemispheric Novel in the Post-Revolutionary Era." In *The Cambridge History of the American Novel,* edited by Leonard Cassuto, Claire Virginia Ebby, and Benjamin Reiss. Cambridge: Cambridge UP, 2011: 553–571.

Murray, Keat. "Indians and Dissembling Gentlemen in James Fenimore Cooper's *The Pioneers.*" Conference of the American Literature Association, San Francisco, 2008.

Nari, Marcela. *Políticas de la maternidad y maternalismo político: Buenos Aires, 1890–1940.* Buenos Aires: Biblos, 2004.

El negrito: Diario de la aurora. 1 (July 1833).

Nelsen, Vanessa. "Narrative Intervention and the Black Aesthetic in Cirilo Villaverde's *Cecilia Valdés* and Martín Morúa Delgado's *Sofía.*" *Decimonónica: Revista de Producción Cultural Hispánica Decimonónica* 8.1 (2011): 57–75.

Nelson, Dana. *National Manhood: Capitalist Citizenship and the Imagined Fraternity of White Men.* Durham, NC: Duke UP, 1998.

Newcomb, Robert Patrick, and Richard Gordon, eds. *Beyond Tordesillas: New Approaches to Comparative Luso-Hispanic Studies.* Columbus: Ohio State UP, 2017.

Nichols, Madeline W. *Sarmiento: A Chronicle of Inter-American Friendship.* Washington, DC, 1940.

Novak, Terry. "The Struggle for Independence and the Education of African American Women in the Works of Frances Ellen Watkins Harper." In Paulk, *Dominant Culture and the Education of Women,* 197–208.

"Nuestros deberes como futuras maestras de Cuba." *Normal Review,* October 1901.

Nwankwo, Ifeoma Kiddoe. *Black Cosmopolitanism: Racial Consciousness and Transnational Identity in the Nineteenth-Century Americas.* Philadelphia: U of Pennsylvania P, 2005.

O'Brien, Colleen C. *Romance and Rebellion: Literatures of the Americas in the Nineteenth Century.* Charlottesville: U of Virginia P, 2013.

Ocasio, Rafael. *Afro-Cuban Costumbrismos: From Plantation to Slum.* Gainesville: UP of Florida, 2012.

O'Connor, Erin E. *Mothers Making Latin America: Gender, Households, and Politics since 1825.* Oxford: John Wiley and Sons, 2014.

O'Gorman, Edmundo. *La invención de América*. 1958. Mexico City: Fondo de Cultura Económica, 2006.
Olds, Madelin Joan. "The Rape Complex in the Postbellum South." In Vaz, *Black Women in America*, 179–205.
Operé, Fernando. *Indian Captivity in Spanish America: Frontier Narratives*. Translated by Gustavo Pellón. Charlottesville: U of Virginia P, 2008.
O'Reilly, Andrea, ed. *From Motherhood to Mothering: The Legacy of Adrienne Rich's "Of Woman Born."* Albany: SUNY P, 2004.
Ortiz, Fernando. *Contrapunteo cubano del tabaco y de azúcar (Advertencias de sus contrastes agrarios, económicos, históricos y sociales, su etnografía y su transculturación)*. Edited by Enrico Mario Santí. 1940. Madrid: Cátedra, 2002.
Otero, Juan Joaquín, ed. *Libro de Cuba: Una enciclopedia ilustrada que abarca las Artes, las Letras, las Ciencias, la Economía, la Política, la Historia, la Docencia y el Progreso General de la Nación Cubana*. Havana: Publicaciones Unidas, 1954.
Padula, Francisco Eduardo. "A função narrativa em *Cecilia Valdés* de Cirilo Villaverde." *La Junta: Revista de Graduação em Espanhol* 1 (2017): 8–33.
Pagasartundua, Vicente, trans. *El último de los mohicanos. Historia de mil setecientos cincuenta y siete*. 2 vols. Translation of *The Last of the Mohicans*, by James Fenimore Cooper. Madrid: Tomás Jordán, 1832.
Palcos, Alberto, ed. *El "Facundo": rasgos de Sarmiento*. By Domingo Faustino Sarmiento. Segunda edición corregida y aumentada. Buenos Aires: Elevación, 1945.
Palermo González, Elena, and Stelamaris Coser, eds. *Entre Traços e Rasuras: Intervenções da memória na escrita da América*. Rio de Janeiro: FAPERJ, 2013.
Palmié, Stephan. *Wizards and Scientists: Explorations in Afro-Cuban Modernity and Religion*. Durham, NC: Duke UP, 2002.
Palomar Vera, Cristina. "'Malas madres': la construcción social de la maternidad." *Debate feminista: maternidades ¿quién cuida a quién?* 15.30 (2004): 12–34.
Parker, Andrew, Mary Russo, Doris Sommer, and Patricia Yaeger, eds. *Nationalisms and Sexualities*. New York: Routledge, 1991.
Patterson, Orlando. *Slavery and Social Death: A Comparative Study*. Cambridge, MA: Harvard UP, 1982.
Patton, Elda Clay. *Sarmiento in the United States*. Evansville, IN: U of Evansville P, 1976.
Paquette, Robert L. *Sugar Is Made with Blood: The Conspiracy of La Escalera and the Conflict between Empires over Slavery in Cuba*. Middletown, CT: Wesleyan UP, 1990.
Paulk, Julia C. "Beyond the American Home: The Contributions of Catherine Beecher and Clorinda Matto de Turner to Women's Education." In Paulk, *Dominant Culture and the Education of Women*, 184–96.

———, ed. *Dominant Culture and the Education of Women*. Newcastle: Cambridge Scholars, 2008.

———. "Visions of Cuba: Mary Peabody Mann's *Juanita: A Romance of Real Life in Cuba Fifty Years Ago*." *Studies in the Novel* 44.2 (Summer 2012): 144–63.

Paz, José María. "Decreto del gobernador de Córdoba, José María Paz, autorizando el ingreso de los pardos a las escuelas." 1829. In Solari, *Historia de la educación argentina*, 105–6.

Paz, Octavio. *El laberinto de la soledad*. 1950. Mexico City: Fondo de Cultura Económica, 2007.

Paz Trueba, Yolanda de. "El discurso de la maternidad moderna y la construcción de la feminidad a través de la prensa. El centro y sur bonaerenses a finales del siglo XIX y a principios del XX." *Quinto sol* 15.2 (2011): 1–20.

Peard, Julyan G. *An American Teacher in Argentina: Mary Gorman's Nineteenth-Century Odyssey from New Mexico to the Pampas*. Lewisburg, PA: Bucknell UP, 2016.

———. "Enchanted Edens and Nation-Making: Juana Manso, Education, Women, and TransAmerican Encounters in Nineteenth-Century Argentina." *Journal of Latin American Studies* 40.3 (2008): 453–82.

Peluffo, Ana, and Ignacio M. Sánchez Prado, eds. *Entre hombres: masculinidades del siglo XIX en América Latina*. Madrid: Iberoamericana, 2010.

Peña, Juana. "¡Viva la Patria!" *La negrita* 1 (July 21, 1833): 1–2.

Pérez, Louis A., Jr. *Cuba between Empires, 1878–1902*. Pittsburgh: U of Pittsburgh P, 1983.

———. *Cuba in the American Imagination: Metaphor and the Imperial Ethos*. Chapel Hill: U of North Carolina P, 2008.

———. "Imperial Design: Politics and Pedagogy in Occupied Cuba, 1899–1902." *Cuban Studies* 12.2 (1982): 1–20.

———. *On Becoming Cuban: Identity, Nationality and Culture*. Chapel Hill: U of North Carolina P, 1999.

———. *The War of 1898: The United States and Cuba in History and Historiography*. Chapel Hill: U of North Carolina P, 1998.

Pérez Firmat, Gustavo, ed. *The Cuban Condition: Translation and Identity in Modern Cuban Literature*. Cambridge: Cambridge UP, 1989.

———. *Do the Americas Have a Common Literature?* Durham, NC: Duke UP, 1990.

Pérez Gras, María Laura. "Ojos visionarios y voces transgresoras: La cuestión del *Otro* en los relatos de viajes de los hermanos Mansilla." *Anales de literatura hispanoamericana* 39 (2010): 281–304.

Pérez Landa, Rufino, and María Rosell Pérez. *Vida pública de Martín Morúa Delgado*. Havana: Academia de la Historia, 1957.

Pestalozzi, Johann Heinrich. *How Gertrude Teaches Her Children: An Attempt to Help Mothers to Teach Their Own Children and an Account of the Method*. Edited by Ebenezer Cooke. 1801. London: S. Sonnenschein, 1894.

Peterson, Harold F. *Argentina and the United States, 1810–1960*. 2 vols. New York: SUNY P, 1964. Translated as *La Argentina y los Estados Unidos* by Patricio Canto and Denise Rivero. Buenos Aires: Editorial Universitaria de Buenos Aires, 1970.
Peterson, V. Spike. "Sexing Political Identities/Nationalism as Heterosexism." In Ranchod-Nilson and Tétreault, *Women, States and Nationalism*, 143–63.
Piglia, Ricardo. "Notas sobre Facundo." *Puntos de vista*. 3.8 (March-June 1980): 15-18.
Pike, James Shepard. *The Prostrate State: South Carolina under Negro Government*. New York: Appleton, 1874.
Pita, Beatrice. "Engendering Critique: Race, Class, and Gender in Ruiz de Burton and Martí." In Belnap and Fernandez, *José Martí's "Our America,"* 129–44.
Pizarra de la Luz, Ivonne. "La voz 'testimonial' de la esclava María de Regla en *Cecilia Valdés* de Cirilo Villaverde." *Revista de estudios hispánicos* 30.1–2 (2008): 159–72.
Pizarro, Ana. *El sur y los trópicos: ensayos de cultura latinoamericana*. Alicante, Spain: Universidad de Alicante P, 2008.
Pizarro, M. D. "Nota al Gobierno de Santa Fé contestando la que dirijió sobre traslacion á la Capital de esa provincia, de la Escuela Normal que funciona en la Ciudad del Rosario." In Pizarro, *Memoria 1881*, 524–25.
Poblete, Juan. *Literatura chilena del siglo XIX: entre públicos lectores y figuras autoriales*. Santiago: Cuarto Propio, 2003.
Prado, Eduardo. *A Ilusão Americana*. Sao Paulo, 1893.
Prados-Torreira, Teresa. *Mambisas: Rebel Women in Nineteenth-Century Cuba*. Gainesville: UP of Florida, 2005.
Pratt, Mary Louise. *Imperial Eyes: Travel Writing and Transculturation*. London: Routledge, 1992.
"Programa general para las escuelas." *La escuela moderna* 1.6 (April 30, 1899): 7–9.
Provencio Garrigós, Lucía. "La *trampa* discursiva del elogio a la maternidad cubana del siglo XIX." *Americanía: revista de estudios latinoamericanos de la Universidad Pablo de Olavide de Sevilla* 1 (January 2011): 42–73.
Preuss, Ori. *Bridging the Island: Brazilians' Views of Spanish America and Themselves, 1865–1912*. Madrid: Iberoamericana, 2011.
———. *Transnational South America: Experiences, Ideas, and Identities, 1860s–1900s*. New York: Routledge, 2016.
Puiggrós, Adriana. *Imperialismo y educación en América latina*. Mexico City: Nueva Imagen, 1980.
———. *Qué pasó en la educación argentina: breve historia desde la conquista hasta el presente*. Buenos Aires: Galerna, 2002.
———. *Sujetos, disciplina y currículo en los orígenes del sistema educativo argentino (1885–1916)*. Buenos Aires: Galerna, 1990.
Quesada, Gonzalo de. *Cuba*. Washington, DC: Government Printing Office, 1905.

Quijano, Aníbal. 1994. "Colonialidad del poder, eurocentrismo y América latina." Buenos Aires: CLASCO, 2014.

Quijano, Aníbal, and Immanuel Wallerstein. "Americanity as a Concept, or the Americas in the Modern World System." *International Social Science Journal* 134 (1992): 549–57.

Rama, Ángel. *La ciudad letrada*. Hanover, NH: Ediciones del Norte, 1984.

———. 1982. *La transculturación narrativa en América latina*. Mexico City: Siglo XXI, 2004.

Ramos, Julio. *Divergent Modernities: Culture and Politics in Nineteenth-Century Latin America*. Durham, NC: Duke UP, 2001.

Ramos Mejía, T. P. "Extractos del Informe de la Inspección General." In Beláustegi, *Memoria presentada al Congreso Nacional de 1898*, 37–53.

Ranchod-Nilsson, Sita, and Mary Ann Tetreault, eds. *Women, States and Nationalism: At Home in the Nation?* London: Routledge, 2003.

Randeria, Shalini. "Entangled Histories of Uneven Modernities: Civil Society, Caste Solidarities and Legal Pluralism in Post-Colonial India." In *Unraveling Ties: From Social Cohesion to New Practices of Connectedness*, edited by Yehuda Elkana, Ivan Krastev, Elisio Macamo, and Randeria. Frankfurt: Campus, 284–311.

Raussert, Wilifried, ed. *The Routledge Companion to Inter-American Studies*. London: Routledge, 2017.

Raussert, Wilfried, and Yolanda Campos, eds. "Theorizing Hemispheric American Studies." Special issue, *Forum for Inter-American Research: Journal of the International Association of Inter-American Studies* 7.3 (December 2014).

Reis, Livia de Freitas. *Conversas ao sul: ensaios sobre literatura e cultura latinoamericana*. Niterói: Editora da Universidade Federal Fluminense, 2009.

Reglamento Orgánico de Instrucción Primaria en la Isla de Cuba. *La Enseñanza* (Havana) 1.1 (1875): 10–12.

Rem. July 25, 1900, letter to the journal. "Desde Harvard." *La escuela moderna* 2.11–12 (July 15 and 30, 1900): 148.

Rey, Juan Carlos. "El pensamiento político en España y sus provincias americanas durante el despotismo ilustrado (1759–1808)." In Elías Pino Iturrieta et al., eds. *Gual y España: la Independencia frustrada*. Caracas: Fundación Empresa Polar, 2007. 43–161.

Reyes y Galindo, Micaela de los. "Carta abierta." *La escuela moderna* 2.11–12 (July 15 and 30, 1900): 140–41.

Rich, Adrienne. *Of Woman Born: Motherhood as Experience and Institution*. New York: Norton, 1976.

Rionda, Bernardo de la. "El Lago Mohan." *Normal Review* 8.3 (November 1901): 27–30.

Roca, Julio Argentino, and Manuel D. Pizarro. "Decreto confiriendo el título de Maestro á cuatro alumnos de la Escuela Normal de Corrientes." December 20, 1880. In Pizarro, *Memoria 1881*, 482.

———. "Decreto confiriendo el título de Maestro á cuatro alumnos de la Escuela Normal de San Luis." March 18, 1881. In Pizarro, *Memoria 1881*, 483.
———. "Decreto confiriendo el título de Maestro á cuatro alumnos de la Escuela Normal de Santiago." December 21, 1880. In Pizarro, *Memoria 1881*, 483.
———. "Decreto confiriendo el título de Maestro á cuatro alumnos de la Escuela Normal de Tucuman." In Pizarro, *Memoria 1881*, 437.
Rock, David. *Argentina, 1516–1987: From Spanish Colonization to Alfonsín*. Berkeley: U of California P, 1987.
Rockland, Michael Aaron. Introduction to *Sarmiento's Travels in the U.S. in 1847* (partial translation of *Viajes*). Princeton, NJ: Princeton UP, 1970, 1–106.
Rodó, José Enrique. *Ariel*. 1900. Madrid: Espasa-Calpe, 1948.
Rodríguez, Ida Edelvira. *La flor de la montaña*. Buenos Aires: Sud-Americana, 1887.
Rodríguez, Manuel. "Educacion." *La Enseñanza*. 2.2 (September 18, 1876): 3–6.
Rodríguez, Mariela Eva, and Lea Geler. "Argentina." In *The Wiley Blackwell Encyclopedia of Race, Ethnicity, and Nationalism*, edited by John Stone, Rutledge M. Denis, Poly S. Rizova, Anthony D. Smith, and Xiaoshuo Hou. Malden, MA: Wiley, 2016, 1–4.
Rodriguez, Rick. "Between North and South: Cuba and the Ends of US Sovereignty." *Canadian Review of American Studies* 48.2 (2018): 146–70.
Rodríguez, Simón. "Consejos de amigo dado al Colegio Nacional de Latacunga." In *Sociedades americanas*, 260–77.
———. "Extracto de mi obra sobre educación republicana." In *Sociedades americanas*, 278–308.
———. *Luces y virtudes sociales*. In *Sociedades americanas*, 152–249.
———. *Sociedades americanas en 1828*. Edited by Óscar Rodríguez Ortiz. Caracas: Ayacucho, 1990.
Rodríguez de la O, Raúl. *La Argentina en Martí*. Havana: Abril, 2007.
Rodríguez de Tío, Lola. "A los niños cubanos." *La escuela moderna* 2.3 (March 15, 1900).
Rodríguez Herrera, Esteban. "Estudio crítico a *Cecilia Valdés*." In Álvarez García, *Acerca de Cirilo Villaverde*, 131–81.
Rodríguez Valdés, Manuel. *La educación popular en Cuba*. Havana: Álvarez, 1891.
———. "*El problema de la educación*": *Colección de artículos y trabajos publicados en "El País" y "La revista cubana."* Havana: Álvarez, 1891.
Roitenburd, Silvia N. "Sarmiento: entre Juana Manso y las maestras de los EE.UU. Recuperando mensajes olvidados." *Antítesis* 2.3 (2009): 39–66.
Rojas, Rafael. *Las repúblicas de aire: Utopía y desencanto en la revolución de Hispanoamérica*. Madrid: Taurus Historia, 2009.
Roosevelt, Theodore. *The Rough Riders*. New York: C. Scribner's and Sons, 1898.
Root, Elihu. Telegram to Alexis Frye. August 4, 1900. *Álbum*, n.p.

Roseberry, William. "Social Fields and Cultural Encounters." In Joseph, LeGrand, and Salvatore, *Close Encounters of Empire,* 515–24.

Rosenberg, Emily S. "Turning to Culture." In Joseph, LeGrand, and Salvatore, *Close Encounters of Empire,* 497–514.

Rosenthal, Deborah. "Race Mixture and the Representation of Indians in the U.S. and the Andes: *Cumandá, Aves sin nido, The Last of the Mohicans,* and *Ramona.*" In Kaup and Rosenthal, *Mixing Race, Mixing Culture,* 122–39.

Roser, Max, and Esteban Ortiz-Ospina. "Literacy." 2018.

Ross, Kathleen. Translator's introduction to *Facundo: Civilization and Barbarism,* by Domingo Faustino Sarmiento. First Complete English Translation. Berkeley: U of California P, 2003.

Rothera, Evan C. "Civil Wars and Reconstructions in America: The United States, Mexico, and Argentina, 1860–1880." PhD diss., Pennsylvania State University, 2017.

———. "Our South American Cousin: Domingo F. Sarmiento and Education in Argentina and the United States." In *Reconstruction in a Globalizing World,* edited by David Prior. New York: Fordham UP, 2018: 21–49.

Rotker, Susan. *Captive Women: Oblivion and Memory in Argentina.* Translated by Jennifer French. Minneapolis: U of Minnesota P, 1999.

Rousseau, Jean-Jacques. *Émile, ou, de l'éducation.* Amsterdam: Jean Néaulme, 1762.

Rowe, John Carlos. *Literary Culture and U.S. Imperialism: From the Revolution to World War II.* New York: Oxford UP, 2000.

Rowlandson, Mary. *The Sovereignty and Goodness of God, with Related Documents.* 1682. Boston: Bedford/St. Martin's, 2017.

Ruiz de Burton, María Amparo. *The Squatter and the Don.* 1885. Houston: Arte Público, 1997.

Sáenz de la Cámara, Sisto. "Educación." *La ilustración: Álbum de las damas* 29 (1846): 23.

Sagra, Ramón de la. "La mujer." *La ilustración: Álbum de las damas* 11 (1845): 1–2.

Said, Edward W. *Orientalism.* New York: Pantheon, 1979.

Salcedo, Lisandro J. "Escuela Normal de Profesores de Mendoza." In Wilde, *Memoria 1884* II. 859–87.

———. "Informe anual de la Escuela Normal de Maestros en Mendoza." March 1, 1881. In Pizarro, *Memoria 1881,* 450–82.

Saldaña-Portillo, Josefina. "Hemispheric Literature." In *Transnational American Literature,* edited by Yogita Goyal. New York: Cambridge UP, 2017, 203–18.

Saldívar, José David. *The Dialectics of Our America: Genealogy, Cultural Critique, and Literary History.* Durham, NC: Duke UP, 1991.

———. *Trans-Americanity: Subaltern Modernities, Global Coloniality, and the Cultures of Greater Mexico.* Durham, NC: Duke UP, 2012.

Salmon, Marylynn. "The Cultural Significance of Breast-Feeding and Infant Care in Early Modern England and America." In Apple and Golden, *Mothers and Motherhood*, 5–30.

Salvatore, Ricardo D. *Disciplinary Conquest: U.S. Scholars in South America, 1900–1945*. Durham, NC: Duke UP, 2016.

———. "The Enterprise of Knowledge: Representational Machines of Informal Empire." In Joseph, LeGrand, and Salvatore, *Close Encounters of Empire*, 69–104.

———. "Integral Outsiders: Afro-Argentines in the Era of Juan Manuel de Rosas and Beyond." In Davis, *Beyond Slavery*, 57–80.

Sánchez, Jorge Luis, dir. *Cuba Libre*. Cuba: Instituto Cubano de Arte e Industria Cinematográficas, 2016.

Sánchez, Luis Alberto. *Historia comparada de las literaturas americanas*. 4 vols. Buenos Aires: Losada, 1973.

Sanmartín, Paula. *Black Women as Custodians of History: Unsung Rebel (M) Others in African American and Afro-Cuban Women's Writing*. Amherst, NY: Cambria, 2014.

Sardowski-Smith, Claudia, and Claire Fox. "Theorizing the Hemisphere: Inter-Americas Work at the Intersection of American, Canadian, and Latin American Studies." *Comparative American Studies: An International Journal* 2 (2004): 5–38.

Sarmiento, Domingo Faustino, ed. *Ambas Américas: Revista de Educación, Bibliografía y Agricultura*. 3 vols. New York: Hallet and Breen, 1867–68.

———. "Apertura del Colegio de Pensionistas de Santa Rosa." *El zonda* 1.1 (2 July 1839): 5–10.

———. *Argirópolis, o, la capital de los Estados Confederados del Río de la Plata*. Santiago: Julio Belín, 1850.

———. *Cartas de Sarmiento a la señora Mary Mann*. Buenos Aires: Academia Argentina de las Letras, 1936.

———. "Chile." *El monitor de la educacion común* 1.3 (December 1881): 77–82.

———. *Las ciento y una*. Edited by Augusto Belín Sarmiento. In *Obras de D. F. Sarmiento: Las ciento y una (época preconstitucional)*. vol. 15. 1852. Buenos Aires: Mariano Moreno, 1867.

———. *Conflicto y armonías de razas en América*. Buenos Aires: Ostwald, 1883.

———. "Correspondencia: Contestación de los editores a una madre de familia." *Zonda* 1.5 (August 17, 1839): 54–57.

———. "Creación de la escuela normal de preceptores." In *Obras de D. F. Sarmiento*, vol. 44 245–68.

———. "De la educacion de la mujer." 1841. *Obras completas*, 4:180.

———. *De la educacion popular*. Santiago: Julio Belín i Compañía, 1849.

———. "El Editor." *Anales de la educación común* 1.1 (1858): 1–10.

———. *Educación común en el estado de Buenos-Aires*. 1855. Buenos Aires: El Censor, 1887.

---. *Las escuelas: base de la prosperidad i de la república en los Estados Unidos. 1867.* New York: Appleton, 1870.

---. "Estado de la educación primaria en Jujuy." *Monitor de la educación común* 1.1 (September 1881): 4–12.

---. *Facundo*. 1845. Ed. Raimundo Lazo. Mexico City: Porrúa, 1991.

---. "Informe del Exmo. Sr. Gobernador de Juyjuy." *Monitor de la educación común* 1.1 (September 1881): 2–12.

---. "Nota dando cuenta al Superintendente del Disentimiento que se ha suscitado en el seno del Congreso al interpretar el Art. 19 del Decreto de 28 de Enero. June 5, 1881." In Wilde, *Memoria 1882*, 10–14.

---. *Obras de D. F. Sarmiento*. Vol. 4, *Ortografía, Instruccion Pública, 1841–1854*. Santiago: Gutenberg 1886.

---. *Obras de D. F. Sarmiento*. Vol. 5, *Viajes por Europa, África y América: 1845–1847*. 1847. Santiago: Gutenero, 1886.

---. *Recuerdos de provincia*. 1850. Buenos Aires: Emecé, 1944.

---. "Resultados del primer curso de la Escuela Normal." In *Obras de D. F. Sarmiento*, vol. 4: 328–31.

---. *Revelations on the Paraguayan War and the Alliances of the Atlantic and the Pacific*. Translated by Mary Mann. New York: Hallet and Breen, 1866.

---. "El siglo." *El zonda* 1.6 (25 August 1839): 71–76.

---. "Sobre la educacion popular, carta al intendente de Valparaíso." In *Obras de D. F. Sarmiento*, 4:331–37.

---. *Vida de Aldao*. 1843. Proyecto Sarmiento.

---. *Vida de Lincoln, décimo sesto presidente de los Estados Unidos*. New York: Appleton, 1866.

Sarmiento, Domingo Faustino, and Nicolás Avellaneda "Al H. Congreso de la Nación." Buenos Aires, August 23, 1869. In *Memoria del Ministerio de Justicia, Culto é Instrucción Pública*, 1871.

Sartorius, David. *Ever Faithful: Race, Loyalty, and the Ends of Empire in Spanish Cuba*. Durham, NC: Duke UP, 2014.

Satas, Hugo Raúl. *Una política exterior argentina: comercio exterior e ideas en sus orígenes y consolidación (1862–1914)*. Buenos Aires: Hyspa, 1987.

Saunders, James E. *Vanguard of the Atlantic World: Creating Modernity, Nation, and Democracy in Nineteenth-Century Latin America*. Durham, NC: Duke UP, 2014.

Savarí, Guillermo. "A la Escuela Normal de Paraná." In Figueroa, *Escuela Normal de Paraná*, n.p.

Schlesinger, Arthur Meir. *The Age of Jackson*. Boston: Little, Brown, 1953.

Schwarz, Roberto. *Misplaced Ideas: Essays on Brazilian Culture*. London: Verso, 1992.

Scott, Rebecca J. *Slave Emancipation in Cuba: The Transition to Free Labor, 1860–1899*. Pittsburgh: U of Pittsburgh P, 1985.

Seigel, Micol. *Uneven Encounters: Making Race and Nation in Brazil and the United States.* Durham, NC: Duke UP, 2009.

Sena, Isabel de. "Beduinos en la Pampa: el espejo oriental de Sarmiento." *Palimpszest* 23 (April 2005).

Shaw, Stephanie J. "Mothering under Slavery in the Antebellum South." In Glenn, Change, and Forcey, *Mothering*, 237–58.

Sheehan, Susan. "A Welfare Mother." *New Yorker,* September 29, 1975, 42–99.

Sheffer, Jolie A. *The Romance of Race: Incest, Miscegenation, and Multiculturalism in the United States, 1880–1930.* New Brunswick, NJ: Rutgers UP, 2013.

Shukla, Sandhya, and Heidi Tinsman. *Imagining Our Americas: Toward a Transnational Frame.* Durham, NC: Duke UP, 2007.

Shulman, Iván. Prólogo. In *Cecilia Valdés, o La Loma del Ángel,* by Cirilo Villaverde. Caracas: Ayacucho, 1981, ix–xxvii.

Shumway, Nicolas. *The Invention of Argentina.* Berkeley: U of California P, 1991.

Silvestre de Feliu, Aurora. "A la niñez de Cuba." *Revista de Instrucción Pública,* November 10, 1900, 1.5 and 1.6, 87.

Silviano, Santiago. "O entre-lugar do discurso latino-americano." 1978. *Uma literatura nos trópicos: Ensaios sobre dependência cultural.* Rio de Janeiro: Rocco, 2000.

Skinner, Lee Joan. *History Lessons: Refiguring the Nineteenth-Century Historical Novel in Spanish America.* Newark: Juan de la Cuesta, 2006.

Smart, Ian. *Central American Writers of West Indian Origin: A New Hispanic Literature.* Washington, DC: Three Continents, 1984.

Smith, Henry Nash. *The Virgin Land: The American West as Symbol and Myth.* 1950. Cambridge, MA: Harvard UP, 1970.

Smith, Jon, and Deborah Cohn. *Look Away! The U.S. South in New World Studies.* Durham, NC: Duke UP, 2004.

"Sobre la educacion: Carta segunda." *La moda, o recreo semanal del bello sexo* 3 (April 16, 1831): 314–16.

Solari, Manuel Horacio. *Historia de la educación argentina.* 1972. Buenos Aires: Paidós, 1991.

Solás, Humberto, dir. *Lucía.* Cuba: ICAIC, 1968.

Sollors, Werner. *Neither Black nor White yet Both: Thematic Explorations of Interracial Literature.* New York: Oxford UP, 1997.

Solomianski, Alejandro. *Identidades secretas: la negritud argentina.* Buenos Aires: Beatriz Viterbo, 2003.

Sommer, Doris. *Foundational Fictions: The National Romances of Latin America.* Berkeley: U of California P, 1991.

———. "Who Can Tell? Villaverde's Blacks." In *Proceed with Caution When Engaged by Minority Writing in the Americas.* Cambridge, MA: Harvard UP, 1999, 187–210.

Sorensen Goodrich, Diana. *"Facundo" and the Construction of Argentine Culture.* Austin: U of Texas P, 1996.

Sosa Cabanas, Alberto. "Paisaje insular: mujer, nación y noche en Cirilo Villaverde." *Decimonónica: Revista de Producción Cultural Hispánica Decimonónica* 16.2 (Summer 2019): 34–50.

Sosa Rodríguez, Enrique. "Apreciaciones sobre el plan y el método de Cirilo Villaverde para la versión definitiva de *Cecilia Valdés:* su historicismo consciente." In Álvarez García, *Acerca de Cirilo Villaverde*, 381–410.

Spillers, Hortense. "'Mama's Baby Papa's Maybe': An American Grammar Book." In *Black, White, and in Color: Essays on American Literature and Culture*, edited by Spillers. Chicago: U of Chicago P, 2003, 203–29.

Spivak, Gayatri Chakravorty. *Death of a Discipline*. New York: Colombia UP, 2003.

Stavans, Ilan. Introduction to *Facundo: Or, Civilization and Barbarism*, by Domingo Faustino Sarmiento. Translated by Mary Mann. 1845. New York: Penguin, 1998.

Stepan, Nancy Leys. *"The Hour of Eugenics": Race, Gender, and Nation in Latin America*. Ithaca, NY: Cornell UP, 1991.

Stearns, John W. "Informe de la Escuela Normal de Tucuman." February 4, 1877. In Leguizamón, *Memoria presentada al Congreso Nacional de 1877*.

Steele, Cynthia. *Narrativa indigenista en los Estados Unidos y México*. Mexico City: Instituto Nacional Indigenista, 1985.

Stern, Steven J. "The Decentered Center and the Expansionist Periphery: The Paradoxes of Foreign-Local Encounter." In Joseph, LeGrand, and Salvatore, *Close Encounters of Empire*, 47–68.

Stoler, Laura Ann. *Race and the Education of Desire: Foucault's History of Sexuality and the Colonial Order of Things*. Durham, NC: Duke UP, 1995.

Stoner, K. Lynn. *From the House to the Streets: The Cuban Women's Movement for Legal Reform, 1898–1940*. Durham, NC: Duke UP, 1991.

Storni, María Angela. "Una carta." *Minerva: revista quincenal dedicada a la mujer de color* 1.4 (November 30, 1888): 3–5.

Stowe, Harriet Beecher. *Uncle Tom's Cabin, or Life among the Lowly*. Edited by Ann Douglas. 1852. New York: Penguin, 1986.

Suárez, Francisco, P. *Tratado de las leyes y de Dios legislador*. Vol. 3, *Tractatus de legibus ac Deo legislatore*. Translated by Jaime Torrubiano Ripoll. 1612.

Suárez y Romero, Anselmo. *Francisco: El ingenio, o las delicias del campo*. Ed. Mario Cabrera Caqui. 1880. Havana: Ministerio de Educación, Dirección de Cultura, 1947.

Szuchman, Mark D. "Childhood, Education, and Politics in Nineteenth-Century Argentina: The Case of Buenos Aires." *Hispanic American Historical Review* 70.1 (February 1990): 109–38.

Szurmuk, Mónica. "Géometries de la mémoire: Les Récits de voyge d'Eduarda Mansilla." *Sociocriticism* 29.1–2 (2014): 335–45.

———. *Women in Argentina*. Gainsville: UP of Florida, 2000.

Tacca, Óscar. *Los umbrales de "Facundo" y otros textos sarmientinos.* Buenos Aires: Academia Argentina de Letras, 2000.
Tanco y Bosmeniel, Félix M. *Petrona y Rosalía.* 1838. Havana: Letras Cubanas, 1980.
Tannenbaum, Frank. *Slave and Citizen: The Negro in the Americas.* New York: Knopf, 1947.
Tapia y Rivera, Alejandro. *Juliet of the Tropics.* Translated by John Maddox. Amherst, NY: Cambria, 2017.
———. *La cuarterona: Drama original en tres actos.* Madrid: Establecimiento Tipográfico de T. Fortanet, 1867.
Tedesco, Juan Carlos. *Educación y sociedad en la Argentina (1880–1900).* Buenos Aires: Pannedille, 1970.
Teixeira, Susana Rocha. "Introduction: Doing and Undoing Comparisons in the Americas from Colonial Times to the Present." *Forum for Inter-American Research* 12.1 (June 2019): 6–11.
Tejera, Diego Vicente. "La educación en las sociedades democráticas." Havana: El Fígaro, 1900.
———. *La mujer cubana.* Havana: El Fígaro, 1898.
Terán, Oscar. *Para leer el "Facundo": Civilización y barbarie; Cultura de fricción.* Buenos Aires: Capital Intelectual, 2007.
Tharp, Elizabeth Hall. *The Peabody Sisters of Salem.* Boston: Little, Brown, 1950.
Thorp, William. "Cooper beyond America." *New York History* 35.4 (October 1954): 522–39.
Thwaites, A. "Estadística Escolar." In *Memoria del Consejo,* 81–90.
Tocqueville, Alexis de. *Democracy in America.* 1835. Edited by Joseph Epstein, translated by Henry Reeve. Bantam: New York, 2000.
Torres, José M. "Escuela Normal del Paraná." In Wilde, *Memoria 1884,* 2:824–42.
———. Informe de la Escuela Normal del Paraná. Pizarro, *Memoria 1881,* 369–437.
———. Informe de la Escuela Normal del Paraná. Wilde *Memoria 1882,* 272–311.
Torriente, Loló de la. "Cirilo Villaverde y la novela cubana." In Álvarez García, *Acerca de Cirilo Villaverde,* 124–32.
Tosso, Raúl Alberto, dir. *1420: La aventura de educar.* Argentina: INCAA, 2005.
Trouillot, Michel-Rolph. *Silencing the Past: Power and the Production of History.* Boston: Beacon, 1995.
Trueba, Antonio de. "Las mujeres y los niños." *Álbum cubano de lo bello y lo bueno,* 1860: 216–17.
Turner, Frederick Jackson. *The Frontier in American History.* New York: H. Holt, 1921.
Twain, Mark. *The Tragedy of Pudd'nhead Wilson.* 1894. Edited by Susan L. Rattiner. Mineola, NY: Dover, 1999.
Unzueta, Fernando. *La imaginación histórica y el romance nacional en Hispanoamérica.* Lima: Latinoamérica Editores, 1996.

Urraca, Beatriz. "'Quien a Yankeeland se encamina . . .': The United States and the Nineteenth-Century Argentine Imagination." *Ciberletras* 1 (2000).

Uslar Pietri, Arturo. *En busca del nuevo mundo.* Mexico City: Fondo de Cultura Económica, 1969.

Valenti, Patricia Dunlavy. *Sophia Peabody Hawthorne: A Life.* Vol. 2, *1848–1871.* Columbia: U of Missouri P, 2015.

Varona, Enrique José. *La instrucción pública en Cuba: Su pasado—su presente.* Havana: Rambla y Baza, 1900.

———. "La segunda enseñanza." *La escuela moderna* 1.19 (November 15, 1899): 1–2.

Vasconcelos, José. *La raza cósmica.* Madrid: Agencia Mundial de Librería, 1925.

Vaz, Kim Marie, ed. *Black Women in America.* Thousand Oaks, CA: Sage, 1995.

Velleman, Barry, ed. *My Dear Sir: Mary Mann's Letters to Sarmiento, 1865–1881.* Buenos Aires: ICANA, 2001.

Vergara, C. N. "Provincia de Mendoza—Informes." In *Memoria del Consejo,* 529–80.

Villaverde, Cirilo. *Apuntes biográficos de Emilia Casanova de Villaverde. Escritos por un contemporáneo.* New York: 1874.

———. "El ave muerta." 1837. In *La joven de la flecha,* 27–51.

———. "Cecilia Valdés" ("La primitiva *Cecilia Valdés*"). 1839. In *Cuentos cubanos del siglo XIX: Antología,* edited by Salvador Bueno. Havana: Arte y Literatura, 1975. 182–207.

———. *Cecilia Valdés, o La Loma del Ángel. Tomo Primero.* 1839. Havana: Imprenta Literaria, 1975.

———. *Cecilia Valdés, o La Loma del Ángel.* Edited by Jean Lamore. 1882. Madrid: Cátedra, 1992.

———. *Cuentos de mi abuelo. El penitente: novela de costumbres cubanas.* Edited by Manuel M. Hernández. 1844. New York: El Avisador Hispanoamericano, 1889.

———. *La joven de la flecha de oro y otros relatos.* Edited by Imeldo Álvarez García. Havana: Letras Cubanas, 1984.

———. "La peña blanca." 1837. In *La joven de la flecha,* 50–72.

———. "La Revolución de Cuba vista desde Nueva York." In *Cuba en la UNESCO: Homenaje a Cirilo Villaverde.* 1874. Havana: Comisión Nacional Cubana de la Unesco, 1964, 25–49.

Viñas, David. *Viajeros argentinos a los Estados Unidos.* Buenos Aires: Sudamericana, 1998.

Viñuela Angulo, Urbano. "James Fenimore Cooper: entre la popularidad y la transformación texual." *Livius (Journal of Translation Studies)* 4 (April 1993): 267–79.

Voelz, Johannes. "Transnationalism in Nineteenth-Century Literature." In *Transnational American Literature,* edited by Yogita Goyal. New York: Cambridge UP, 2017, 91–106.

Voigt, Lisa. *Writing Captivity in the Early Modern Atlantic: Circulations of Knowledge and Authority in the Iberian and English Imperial Worlds.* Chapel Hill: U of North Carolina P, 2009.

Wade, Peter. *Race and Sex in Latin America.* New York: Palgrave Macmillan, 2009.

Walker, Jeffrey, ed. *Leather-Stocking Redux; Or, Old Tales, New Essays.* New York: AMS, 2011.

———, ed. *Reading Cooper, Teaching Cooper.* New York: AMS, 2007.

Wallerstein, Immanuel. *The Capitalist World Economy.* Cambridge: Cambridge UP, 1979.

Washington, Booker T. *Up from Slavery: An Autobiography.* 1901. Garden City, NY: Doubleday, 1963.

Weber, David J. *Spanish Frontier in North America.* New Haven, CT: Yale UP, 1992.

Weber, Eugene. *Peasants into Frenchmen: The Modernization of Rural France, 1870–1914.* Stanford, CA: Stanford UP, 1976.

Weber, Max. *The Protestant Ethic and the Spirit of Capitalism.* New York: Scribner, 1958.

Werner, Michael, and Bénédicte Zimmerman. "Beyond Comparison: *Histoire croisée* and the Challenge of Reflexivity." *History and Theory* 45 (2006): 30–50.

White, Hayden. *Metahistory: The Historical Imagination in Nineteenth-Century Europe.* Baltimore: Johns Hopkins UP, 1975.

Williams, Eric. *Capitalism and Slavery.* Chapel Hill: U of North Carolina P, 1944.

Williams, Lorna Valerie. *The Representation of Slavery in Cuban Fiction.* Columbia: U of Missouri P, 1994.

Windell, Maria A. "Moor, *Mulata,* Mulatta: Sentimentalism, Racialization, and Benevolent Imperialism in Mary Peabody Mann's *Juanita*." *J19: The Journal of Nineteenth-Century Americanists* 2.2 (Fall 2014): 301–29.

Whitaker, Arthur P. *Latin America and the Enlightenment.* Ithaca, NY: Cornell UP, 1961.

Whitten, Norman E., and Arlene Torres, eds. *Blackness in Latin America and the Caribbean.* Bloomington: Indiana UP, 1998.

Yee, Shirley J. "Organizing for Racial Justice: Black Women and the Dynamics of Race and Sex in Female Antislavery Societies, 1832–1860." In Vaz, *Black Women in America,* 38–53.

Yuval-Davis, Nira. *Gender and Nation.* New York: SAGE, 1997.

Zamora, Louis Parkinson. *The Useable Past: The Imagination of History in Recent Fiction of the Americas.* Cambridge: Cambridge UP, 1997.

Zamora, Louis Parkinson, and Silvia Spitta, eds. "The Americas, Otherwise." Special issue, *Comparative Literature* 61.3 (June 2009).

Zapata Olivella, Manuel. *Changó, the Biggest Badass.* Translated by Jonathan Tittler. Lubbock: Texas Tech UP, 2010.

———. *Changó, el gran putas.* Bogotá: Oveja Negra, 1983.

———. *Las claves mágicas de América.* Bogotá: Plaza y Janés, 1989.

Zea, Leopoldo, ed. *Pensamiento positivista latinoamericano*. 2 vols. Caracas: Ayacucho, 1980.
Zettl, Erika Katharina. "From Reflection to Deception: Martín Morúa Delgado's Narrative Series: *Sofía* and *La familia Unzúazu*." PhD diss., University of Texas at Austin, 2006.
Zorrilla de San Martín, Juan. *Tabaré*. 1886. Mexico City: Porúa, 1970.
Zubiar, J. B. "Colegio Nacional de Uruguay." In Magnasco, *Memoria 1899*, 48–95.

Index

abolition of slavery: advocacy for, 139, 148; in Cuba, 126, 128, 150; education following, 43–44, 46, 88; international pressure for, 126; in literary traditions, 12, 36, 131; republican influences on, 28; suppression of slave trade and, 128; women of color following, 33, 34. *See also* antislavery texts

Afro-Argentines of Buenos Aires, The (Andrews), 76

Afro-descended populations: annexationist views of, 160; at Argentine normal schools, 97; assimilation of, 99; biopolitical control of, 22; bourgeois republicanism and, 48, 182–91, 210; citizenship for, 18, 33, 44, 215, 218; colonial discrimination against, 162; creole elite views of, 190; economic and political hegemony over, 54; fears of political power in hands of, 159; Federales supported by, 77–78; marginalization of, 123–24, 137, 141; racial and gender dynamics between US and, 178–80; in Southern Cone, 51; in transnational mobilization model, 219; voting rights for in Cuba, 137, 187–88. *See also* slaves and slavery; women of color

"A la niñez de Cuba" (Silvestre de Feliu), 191

Albarracín, Paula, 100–101

Alberdi, Juan Bautista: on economic development, 63; on government through population, 57–60, 79, 94, 97, 108; racialized modernization projects of, 64; rivalry with Sarmiento, 238n25; on US threat to Latin American sovereignty, 119

Alcott, Louisa May, 29, 32

"A los niños cubanos" (Rodríguez de Tío), 184–86

Álvarez, Juan, 49–50

Álvarez García, Imeldo, 133

Amalia (Mármol), 78, 97, 144

Amerindians. *See* indigenous populations

Andrews, George Reid, 76

antislavery texts: by creoles, 128–29; in Gothic literary tradition, 147; recurring themes of, 136, 167. See also *Cecilia Valdés; Juanita; Sofía*

Apes, William, 62

Arango y Parreño, Francisco, 186

Argentina: blackness as conceptualized in, 76–80; child-rearing practices in, 38–39; civic motherhood in, 31–32; civil wars in, 49; economic and social progress in, 196; Europeanization of, 49, 76–77; in extended South paradigm, 9, 86, 96, 115; feminization of teachers in, 5–7, 226n21; genocide in, 49, 69, 118, 119, 221; history of, 49–50; immigrant populations in, 57–58, 239n32; imperial entanglements of education, 7–9, 177, 220–21; lack of representation in interAmerican studies, 9–10; public education and school reform in, 43, 91–94, 99–100, 116–17, 216; racial classification in, 76–85; regional politics in, 49, 51–53; US model for nation-state of, 55, 56; women's education in, 31–32, 101, 231n16, 232n21. *See also* Argentine normal schools; Federales; Unitarios; whitening of populations

318 Index

Argentine Generation of 1837, 52, 77, 218, 237n8
Argentine normal schools: code of conduct for, 100; criticisms of, 120; curriculum for, 113; establishment of, 8, 88, 94, 197; local teachers at, 116; per capita numbers of, 114; physical discipline at, 109; students at, 97, 250–51n38, 254n75. *See also* North American teachers
Armstrong, Clara, 102, 103, 197–99, 253n58
Artigas, José Gervasio, 216
Avellaneda, Nicolás, 93, 114
Aves sin nido (Matto de Turner), 47, 83, 145, 146

Balibar, Étienne, 27
Baralt, Luis A., 3, 186
Barbour, George M., 158
Barker, Walter, 158
Beaumont, Gustave de, 58, 239n33
Bederman, Gail, 178
Beecher, Catherine, 5, 225n16
Bergeaud, Émeric, 18, 39–42, 215
black cosmopolitanism, 219–20
Black Legend discourse, 73, 75, 81
Blacks. *See* Afro-descended populations
Blake (Delany), 157, 216–17, 264n89
blanqueamiento. See whitening of populations
Bolívar, Simón, 37
Bone, Martyn, 9
Borrero Echeverría, Esteban, 5, 174–76, 184, 186–90, 218
bourgeois republicanism: Afro-descendants and, 48, 182–91, 210; child-rearing and, 37, 39, 102; citizenship and, 4, 30; idealized forms of, 214–15; motherhood in, 63, 80, 86, 205, 213, 220; neocolonial, 206, 218; paradigms of, 9, 220; public education and, 42, 43, 47, 184, 186, 197; sociocultural patterns of, 113, 217–18; teacher-mothers and, 206; whiteness of, 215–16
Brazil, Mãe Preta movement in, 208
Bueno Castillo, María de los Reyes, 209
Bunkley, Allison, 248n12
Buscaglia-Salgado, José, 217, 219

Cádiz Constitution, 33, 42, 44, 78, 126, 218

Calvo, Nicolás, 186
Camaña, Raquel, 6
capitalism: core-periphery relations and, 113; education on values of, 19, 102, 184; exploitation of Global South and, 119; patriarchal, 63; racial, 56, 61, 63, 64, 68
captivity genre, 19, 62, 66, 69, 83, 241n52
Cardero, Mariano, 43–44
Caro Baroja, Julio, 201, 202
Carvalhal, Tânia Franco, 86
Casanova, Emilia, 131, 138–40, 147–49
Casanova, Pascale, 118
Catholic Church: education provided by, 216; efforts to limit power of, 52, 249n24; Hispano-Catholic traditions, 82, 112, 113; ideals of femininity in, 30; saint's day celebrations in, 110–12
Cautiva (Echeverría), 66, 68
Cecilia Valdés (Villaverde): Black Legend discourse in, 81; on child-rearing practices, 38, 142–43; comparative analysis with, 21; contradictions within, 140–41; criticisms of, 164–66, 169; early versions of, 129, 131–33; as foundational romance, 129–32, 134–36, 144–45; incest in, 130–31, 134–36, 140–41, 144–47; interracial relationships in, 20, 122, 124, 130–37, 140; *Lucía Miranda* as reversal of racial order in, 68; mulata stereotypes in, 33, 130; republican motherhood in, 131, 142–43, 149; on slave models of motherhood, 35, 142–44; *Sofía* as counterdiscourse to, 164, 166; on Spanish colonialism, 126, 183
Céspedes, Carlos Manuel, 126, 140, 148, 183
Changó, el gran putas (Zapata Olivella), 220
Chavarria, Juan Manuel, 6
child-rearing: bourgeois republicanism and, 37, 39, 102; institutionalized, 2; race and, 37–39, 142–43, 157–59, 208. *See also* motherhood
citizenship: for Afro-descendants, 18, 33, 44, 215, 218; bourgeois republicanism and, 4, 30; educational requirements for, 44–45; for indigenous populations, 44–45, 232n59; as manhood right, 178; race as element of, 62, 253n62
civic motherhood, 31–32, 78

Civil War, US (1861–65), 1, 8, 19, 45–47, 95–96, 146
colonialism: critiques of, 159–62; discriminatory policies of, 162; extracontinental, 261n59; internal, 11; racial and cultural legacies of, 121; rhetoric on indigenous populations and, 70; settler, 8, 63, 67, 71, 146, 220; transition to republicanism from, 176. *See also* neocolonialism; Spanish colonialism
Condé, Maryse, 220
Conflicto y armonías de razas (Sarmiento), 55
Cooper, James Fenimore: national family allegory and, 7–8; *The Prairie*, 238n21; Sarmiento influenced by, 7–8, 19, 54–55; *The Travelling Bachelor; or, Notions of the Americans*, 59, 62, 238n19. See also *Last of the Mohicans*
Cooper, Michael A., 262n63
Coopiner, Cornelio, 183, 187
Corregidora (Jones), 220
costumbrista genre, 130, 131, 258n19
Crenshaw, Kimberlé, 232n30
creole elites: Afro-descendants as viewed by, 190; child-rearing among, 37–38; colonial race hierarchies and, 9, 157; contradictions in actions of, 87; criticisms of, 131, 169–70; fears of racialized subjugation among, 187–88; female participation in public sphere among, 242n58; national-familial discourse of, 22, 171; in plantation economy, 137–38; public education mobilized by, 218; racial and gender dynamics between US and, 180; resistance to liberal reforms, 125–26
creoles: Anglo-American views of, 14, 122, 127; antislavery texts and, 128–29; in Black Legend discourse, 81; independence movements of, 26; *letrado* culture among, 114; nationalism among, 21, 146, 159, 172–73, 175, 217; neocolonialism and, 1, 9, 47–48, 65, 177, 207, 217; in patriarchal systems, 200, 204; public education for, 43–44, 186; use of term, 7, 16, 17, 229–30n41; whiteness of, 14, 190. *See also* creole elites
Crèvecoeur, J. Hector St. John de, 26–28
Croguennec-Massol, Gabriel, 134

Cuba: abolition of slavery in, 126, 128, 150; annexationist views of, 126–27, 140, 152, 157, 160, 181, 268n35; antislavery texts in, 21, 95, 128–29; binomial racial system in, 259n32; discursive assimilation to US, 151–52; in extended South paradigm, 9, 152; imperial entanglements of education, 7–9, 177, 220–21; independence movements in, 122–23, 125–27, 137; legal protections for slaves in, 36–37; normal schools in, 181, 194, 195; public education and school reform in, 43–44, 46, 176, 180–87, 196; revolution in (1959), 123, 136; US occupation of (1898–1902), 8, 127–28, 175, 180–84, 253n62; voting rights in, 137, 162, 187–89; women's education in, 31, 192–93. *See also* whitening of populations
Cuentos (Mansilla de García), 76
cult of domesticity, 5, 33, 101, 262n63
cultural imperialism, 10, 111, 181–82, 197
Cumandá (Mera), 68, 145, 146

Dally, Ann, 225n13
Daly, Brenda O., 63
Daut, Marlene, 40, 41
Davis, Angela, 33, 212
Dawes Act of 1887, 44
Degler, Carl, 259n32
Dekker, George, 63
De la educacion popular (Sarmiento), 88, 91, 93
Delany, Martin, 157, 216–17, 264n89
Democracy in America (Tocqueville), 27
Díaz de Guzmán, Ruy, 65, 68
divine motherhood, 142
domesticity, cult of, 5, 33, 101, 262n63
Domínguez, Daylet, 258n19
Dore, Elizabeth, 203
Douglas, Susan, 211
Dubois, Laurent, 39
Duchesne, Dafne, 41, 42

Echeverría, Esteban, 53, 66, 68, 78, 97
education (educación): as citizenship requirement, 44–45; definitions of, 2–3; imperial entanglements of, 7–9, 177, 220–21; for indigenous populations, 44–45, 236n58; instrucción vs., 3–4; moral purpose of, 38; polysemic

education (educación) *(continued)*
  nature of, 2; republican motherhood and, 191–93; social functions of, 3–4; during Spanish colonialism in Cuba, 186, 269n47; in whitening of populations, 99, 120, 121, 194–95; for women, 30–32, 101, 192–93, 231n16, 232n21. *See also* normal schools; public education; teachers
elites. *See* creole elites
entanglement paradigm, 13, 228nn37–38
Escobar, Roberto, 6
Escuela Normal de Paraná (Figueroa), 6–7, 97
escuelas, Las (Sarmiento), 55, 88, 93, 95–96, 119, 255n81
Estrada Palma, Tomás, 171, 176
eugenics, 57, 212
Eurocentrism, 18, 41, 114
extended South paradigm, 9, 86, 96, 115, 152, 227nn29–30

Facundo (Sarmiento): Barcala episode in, 97–98, 252n42; Cooper's influence on, 19, 54, 69; English-language translation of, 95, 96; hybridity of Hispanic society condemned by, 65; Orientalist discourse in, 73–75, 101; Rosas regime attacked in, 68, 77–78, 92
familia Unzúazu, La (Morúa Delgado), 170–71
family allegory. *See* national family allegory
Federales: Afro-descendants as, 77–78; conflict with Unitarios, 49, 52–53, 95, 98; education reform by, 91–92, 216; sectors of support for, 52
females. *See* women
Fernández de Lizardi, José Joaquín, 31, 37
Ferrer, Ada, 123, 125–26
Ferrús Antón, Beatriz, 246n96
Few Thoughts on the Powers and Duties of Woman, A (H. Mann), 32
Figueroa, Sara, 6–7, 97
Fischer, Sibylle, 39, 41
Foner, Phillip, 123
Font, América, 193
Forbes, Jack D., 80
Foucault, Michel, 201
foundational romances: gender role rescripting in, 206; incest in, 130–31, 134–36, 144–47; interracial, 130–32, 134, 150–51; national family allegory and, 7–8, 25–29, 231n8. *See also Cecilia Valdés; Juanita; Last of the Mohicans; Lucía Miranda*
Fountain, Anne, 144
Francisco (Suárez y Romero), 128, 150, 167, 203
Frederick, Bonnie, 99
freedmen's schools, 7, 8, 19, 45–47, 88
Freud, Sigmund, 134
Freyre, Gilberto, 54
Frischman, Gustavo E., 226n21
Frontier in American History (Turner), 55–56
Frye, Alexis Everett, 181, 184
Fuchs, Barbara, 81
Fuentes, Carlos, 11, 227n30

Gálvez, Manuel, 120
García, Ivonne M., 261n59
García Canclini, Néstor, 118
Garner, Margaret, 36, 233n35
Garrels, Elizabeth, 252n42
gauchesque literature, 52–53
Gelpí, Juan, 136
gender paradigms, 19, 177–80, 198–200, 205–6
genocide, 49, 69, 118, 119, 214, 221
George III (England), 26–27
Gill, Wilson, 195, 196, 270n48
Gilliam, Franklin D., Jr., 210
Global North: assimilation to standards of, 68, 99; exploitation of Global South, 118–19; Hispanic racialized difference from, 82; Latin America in relation to, 11, 65, 89; legitimization of Haiti to, 41; values sanctioned by, 16, 100
Global South: exploitation by Global North, 118–19; extended, 9, 86, 96, 115, 152, 227nn29–30; neocolonial and imperial mappings of, 9–13
Gómez, Juan Gualberto, 124, 136, 162, 163
Good Neighbor Policy, 88, 103, 110, 114
Gorriti, Juana Manuela, 145, 260n49
Gothic literary tradition, 36, 147, 203
government through population, 57–60, 79, 94, 97, 108
Grandin, Greg, 10
Groussac, Paul, 96, 106–7

Guadalupe Hidalgo, Treaty of (1848), 253n62
Gutman, Herbert G., 36
Guzmán, María de, 14, 81

Haiti: citizenship for Afro-descendants in, 215; republican motherhood in, 39–42; revolution in, 39–42, 125, 186, 219; in Spanish American nationalist discourse, 98
Hampton Institute, 45, 46, 269n46
Hanna, Matthew H., 181, 195
Hanway, Nancy, 78
Harper, Frances Watkins, 34–35, 46
Harvard, John C., 81, 261n59
Helg, Aline, 259n32, 264n93
Hemings, Sally, viii, 7, 9, 210, 214
Hitt, Sarah Jayne, 236n58
Hoganson, Kristin, 204–5
Howard, Jennie E.: background of, 103, 105; economic support from students, 110–12; racialization of moral failings by, 107; as republican mother, 20, 88, 104, 110. See also *In Distant Climes and Other Years*

Iglesias Utset, Marial, 175–76, 179
immigration, whitening of populations through, 57–58, 120, 128
imperialism: creole neocolonialism and, 1, 48; cultural, 10, 111, 181–82, 197; Global South in, 9–13; intersection with nation building, 23; psychological violence of, 219; race and gender paradigms of, 177–80, 198–200; in rescripting of national family allegory, 157; settler-colonialist model of, 63, 67; soft, 1, 10, 88, 197; in Southern Cone, 8, 10, 66, 114; use of term, 227n28
indigenous populations: at Argentine normal schools, 97; assimilation of, 47, 71, 99; citizenship for, 44–45, 232n59; colonialist rhetoric on, 70; creole intermixture with, 14; economic and political hegemony over, 54; education for, 44–45, 236n58; evangelization of, 82; genocide against, 49, 69, 118, 119, 214; land rights stripped from, 61; marginalization of, 123–24; in patriarchal systems, 67; Sarmiento on, 53–54
In Distant Climes and Other Years (Howard): on civilizational processes, 103–4; on culinary customs, 105; culturally hybrid maternal figure in, 20, 89, 102; ethnographic descriptions in, 106–8; on living conditions of teachers, 106; on physical discipline, 109; prologue to, 103, 104; on republican motherhood, 110; on saint's day celebrations, 110–12
interracial marriage: in *Lucía Miranda*, 67; prohibitions on, 15, 28, 29, 62; reinstatement of in Cuba, 137; social reform and, 63; of US-Cuban families, 152, 153; whitening of populations through, 15, 208
intersectionality, 232–33n30
Irving, Washington, 104

Jackson, Richard, 259n32
Jacksonian Democracy, 56, 61, 215
Jefferson, Thomas: expansionism of, 55; Hemings and, viii, 7, 9, 210, 214; on natural aristocracy, vii–ix, 7, 9; as polyglot, viii, 223n2
Jitrik, Noé, 28
Jones, Gayle, 220
Juanita (M. Mann): annexationist sentiment in, 152, 157, 160; on child-rearing practices, 38, 157–59; discursive assimilation of Cuba to US in, 151–52; factual basis for elements of, 261n58; interracial relationships in, 20, 122, 124, 150–51, 154; lack of scholarly recognition for, 21; Moorishness in, 80–81; motivations for writing, 121, 150; republican motherhood in, 153–57; tragic mulatta trope in, 151

Kaplan, Amy, 63–64, 66, 67, 71–72, 79, 102
Kerber, Linda K., 29–30
Kipling, Rudyard, 157
Kutzinski, Vera, 133

Lacerda, João Batista de, 15
Laney, Lucy Craft, 45
Larroque, Alberto M., 113
Last of the Mohicans (Cooper): creole nationalism in, 146; as foundational romance, 124, 130; *Lucía Miranda* as counterdiscourse to, 19, 69–70, 86; on racial exclusion, 19, 56, 60–63, 214–15; republican motherhood in, 48, 59–60, 63–64; Sarmiento on, 54–55

Latin America: child-rearing practices in, 37–39; Global North views of, 11, 65, 89; Good Neighbor Policy toward, 88, 103, 110, 114; *letrado* culture in, 54, 114, 190–91; moral motherhood in, 30; public education in, 42–44; racial categories in, 14–17, 76–85, 259n32; US threat to sovereignty of, 119. See also *specific countries*
Lazo, Rodrigo, 152, 155–56, 205
Leguizamón, Onésimo, 6, 252n52
Leroux, Karen, 115, 118, 249–50n30
Letters from an American Farmer (Crèvecoeur), 26–27
literary nationalism, 11, 12, 203, 209
Little Women (Alcott), 29, 32
Lojo, María Rosa, 68–69, 73, 242nn58–59
López, Narciso, 125, 139, 148, 257n7
López Condeal, Julián, 3–4
Louisiana Purchase (1803), 55, 56
Lucía Miranda (Mansilla de García): as counterdiscourse to *Last of the Mohicans*, 19, 69–70, 86; creole nationalism in, 146; as foundational romance, 66, 78, 124, 130; mestizaje promoted by, 68–72, 78, 83; Morisco heritage of main character, 64, 72–80, 82–85; myth associated with, 65–67, 72–73, 241n53; racially exclusive republicanism rejected by, 64; republican motherhood in, 68, 82; whitening critiqued by, 19, 48, 68, 70, 78
Ludlow, William, 189
Luna, Félix, 108, 109

maestra normal, La (Gálvez), 120
Mann, Horace: *A Few Thoughts on the Powers and Duties of Woman*, 32; intellectual influences on, 232n26; relationship with Sarmiento, 89–90, 116, 117; on teachers, 5, 32, 226n21, 249n30
Mann, Mary: collaboration with Sarmiento, 19, 88, 95, 115, 121; as republican mother, 110; translation of *Facundo* by, 95, 96. See also *Juanita*
Mansilla de García, Eduarda: contradictions in works of, 87; *Cuentos*, 76; family background, 49, 68, 84; *Médico de San Luis*, 69, 76; names and pseudonyms used by, 240–41n46; *Pablo, ou la vie dans les pampas*, 68, 69, 76; on racial-capitalist model, 64; *Recuerdos de viaje*, 76, 85, 86; on US South, 85, 86, 246n96. See also *Lucía Miranda*
Manso, Juana, 116, 248n13, 249n27
Mármol, José, 53, 78, 97, 144
Marre, Diana, 72–73, 241n53
marriage: civil marriage, legalization of in Argentina, 58; courtship rituals leading to, 58–59; among enslaved populations, 35–37. See also interracial marriage
Martí, José: as children's magazine editor, 176; disavowal of race politics, 127; exile from Cuba, 152, 159; intellectual decolonization proposed by, 188; on mestizaje in Latin American society, 15; national mother described by, 123, 162, 207, 209, 220; "Nuestra América," 123–25, 140, 166
"Matadero" (Echeverría), 78, 97
Matto de Turner, Clorinda, 47, 83, 145, 146
McKinley, Ida, 21, 197
Médico de San Luis (Mansilla de García), 69, 76
Mendizábal, Horacio, 99, 192
Mera, Juan León, 68, 145, 146
mestizaje: colonial legacy of, 11, 65, 84; *Lucía Miranda* on, 68–72, 78, 83; moral value attached to, 107–8; origins of term, 14; whitening of populations through, 15, 208, 209. See also interracial marriage
Michaels, Meredith, 211
Miranda, Bruno V., 196
miscarriage, use as metaphor, 125, 166, 170, 175
miscegenation: narrative anxiety concerning, 141, 154; origins of term, 14; prohibitions on, 62, 63, 70; US views on, 19. See also interracial marriage
Mitre, Bartolomé, 91, 248n12
mixed marriage. See interracial marriage
Moi, Tituba . . . sorcière noire de Salem (Condé), 220
Monte, Domingo del, 2, 38, 128, 138, 182–83, 194
Moorishness, 73–75, 80–85, 107
moral motherhood, 30, 143
Morúa Delgado, Martín: as antiannexationist, 159; background of, 159–60; on *Cecilia Valdés*, 164–66, 168–69; colonialism critiqued by, 159–62; exile from Cuba, 152, 159; familial language

used by, 8; *La familia Unzúazu*, 170–71; opposition to political organization around race, 163–64; on Platt Amendment, 163–64, 172–73. See also *Sofía* Morúa Law, 163, 190

motherhood: civic, 31–32, 78; divine, 142; moral, 30, 143; under patriarchal capitalism, 63; slave models of, 35, 142–44; social construction of, 33, 82, 225n13; spiritual, 143; traditionalist views of, 82; welfare mothers, 210–14; women of color and, 32–37, 40–42, 78, 142, 192, 213. *See also* republican motherhood

Moynihan, Daniel Patrick, 34

mujer cubana, La (Tejera), 191

mulatos/mulattoes and mulatas/mulattas: classification of, 264n93; Morisco heritage and, 75; origins of terms, 80; political rights for, 127; stereotypes regarding, 33, 130; tragic mulatta trope, 150, 151, 167–68; use of terms, 16; visual representations of, 78

national family allegory: creole independence movements and, 26; foundational romance and, 7–8, 25–29, 231n8; incest and, 134, 135, 166; intergenerational conflict and, 133; paternalist metaphor and, 25–27; race and, 20, 27–28, 32–33, 62, 122, 157, 162; republicanism and, 28, 29; rescripting of, 157, 166; transnationalization of, 174, 206; whitening of populations through, 20, 89

nationalism: creole, 21, 146, 159, 172–73, 175, 217; literary, 11, 12, 203, 209; mestizo, 123, 207; settler-colonialist, 8

nation building: creole-centric, 207; interracial, 130, 131, 209; intersection with imperialism, 23; maternal role in, 4, 31; republican, 31, 94, 182; tools of, 89

natural aristocracy, vii–ix, 7, 9, 218

Negro Family, The (Moynihan), 34

neocolonialism: bourgeois republicanism and, 206, 218; creole, 1, 9, 47–48, 65, 177, 207, 217; discriminatory policies of, 162; Global South in, 9–13; indigenous populations and, 61; racialized hierarchies in, 146; use of term, 227n28

New Paltz Normal School (New York): Cuban students at, 21–22, 196, 198–202; engagement with racialized and gendered imperial metaphors, 177, 204; imperial ventures involving, 270n53; school city model at, 21–22, 195–96; "Sección cubana" at, 22, 177, 198, 201–2; teachers at, 176, 196–98, 206

new traditionalist movement, 211–12

New Woman paradigm, 22, 177, 205

normal schools: in Cuba, 181, 194, 195; founded by North American teachers, 8, 88, 94, 197; in United States, 103, 255n80. *See also* Argentine normal schools; New Paltz Normal School

North American teachers: backgrounds of, 96, 250n30; Hispanicization of, 20, 89, 113; lack of institutional support for, 115; living conditions of, 106; normal schools founded by, 8, 88, 94, 197; physical discipline imposed by, 109; recruitment of, 8, 19, 88, 95; as republican mothers, 20, 88, 99, 102–4, 110

"Nuestra América" (Martí), 123–25, 140, 166

Nwankwo, Ifeoma Kiddoe, 219

Ortiz, Fernando, 54

Pablo, ou la vie dans les pampas (Mansilla de García), 68, 69, 76

paternalist metaphor, 25–27

patriarchal systems: capitalism in, 63; creoles in, 200, 204; indigenous populations in, 67; moral responsibilities of, 179; paternalist metaphor in, 25–27; republican motherhood in, 4; of slaveholders, 34; Spanish colonialism as, 133, 134, 176, 199, 203; teachers in, 4–5; whiteness in, 178

Paz, Octavio, 207, 220

Peake, Mary, 45, 46

Peña, Juana, 79

Peterson, V. Spike, 4

"Petrona y Rosalía" (Tanco y Bosmeniel), 128, 150, 167, 203

Pike, James Shepard, 44

Pizarro, M. D., 100

Platt, Orville, 158

Platt Amendment (1901), 158, 163–64, 172–73

positivism, 57, 119–20, 182

Prados-Torreira, Teresa, 35, 233n36

Prairie, The (Cooper), 238n21

324 *Index*

Protestant ethic, 85–86, 100, 112–13, 158, 185
public education: in Argentina, 43, 91–94, 99–100, 116–17, 216; bourgeois republicanism and, 42, 43, 47, 184, 186, 197; in Cuba, 43–44, 46, 176, 180–87, 196; purpose of, 2, 39, 43–44, 93, 180, 218; race and, 42–47, 97, 184–87; as soft imperialism, 1, 197; in United States, viii–ix, 44–46, 91, 248n13; in whitening of populations, 99, 121
Puiggrós, Adriana, 45

race: categories of, 14–17, 76–85; child-rearing and, 37–39, 142–43, 157–59, 208; citizenship as defined by, 62, 253n62; imperialist paradigms related to, 177–80, 200; Moorishness and, 73, 80–85; national family allegory and, 20, 27–28, 32–33, 62, 122, 157, 162; polysemic nature of, viii, 14; public education and, 42–47, 97, 184–87; republican motherhood and, 9, 23, 33–42, 78, 122, 142, 192, 213; teacher-mothers and, 7, 9, 193, 207
racial capitalism, 56, 61, 63, 64, 68
Ramos Mejía, T. P., 120
Raussert, Wilifried, 13
Recuerdos de provincia (Sarmiento), 100–101
Recuerdos de viaje (Mansilla de García), 76, 85, 86
Reddy, Maureen T., 63
Remedios del Valle, María, 78
republicanism: of annexationists, 159; national family allegory and, 28, 29; nation building and, 31, 94, 182; natural aristocracy and, vii–ix; school city model and, 195; transition from colonialism to, 176; use of term, 223n1. *See also* bourgeois republicanism
republican motherhood: bourgeois, 63, 80, 86, 205, 213, 220; in *Cecilia Valdés,* 131, 142–43, 149; characteristics of, 4, 29, 32; education and, 191–93; enslaved populations and, 34–35, 40–41; Eurocentric vision of, 18, 41; in *Juanita,* 153–57; in *Last of the Mohicans,* 48, 59–60, 63–64; in *Lucía Miranda,* 68, 82; in national narratives, 207–8; North American teachers and, 20, 88, 99, 102–4, 110; political influence through, 29–30; possessive investment in whiteness and, 60–64; race and, 9, 23, 33–42, 78, 122, 142, 192, 213. *See also* teacher-mothers
Río de la Plata. *See* Argentina
Rionda, Bernardo de la, 198–200, 204
Rivadavia, Bernardino, 5, 43, 49, 52, 92, 244–45n82
Rodríguez, Ida Edelvira, 99, 192
Rodríguez, Simón, 2
Rodríguez de Tío, Lola, 184–86
Rodríguez Valdés, Manuel, 42–43, 187–88
Roitenburd, Silvia, 116, 117, 249n27
Roman Catholic Church. *See* Catholic Church
romances, foundational. *See* foundational romances
Roosevelt, Theodore, 177–81, 185–86, 188–89, 199–200, 204–6
Rosas, Juan Manuel de, 49, 52, 53, 65, 71, 77–78, 92–93
Rough Riders, The (Roosevelt), 177–80, 198–200
Rowe, John Carlos, 10, 11

Sáenz de la Cámara, Sisto, 38, 142
Sagra, Ramón de la, 31
saint's day celebrations, 110–12
Sánchez de Thompson, Mariquita, 4
Saraví, Guillermo, 6–7
Sarmiento, Domingo Faustino: on Argentina–US South comparison, 95–96; collaboration with Mary Mann, 19, 88, 95, 115, 121; *Conflicto y armonías de razas,* 55; on courtship rituals in US, 58–59; *De la educacion popular,* 88, 91, 93; *Las escuelas,* 55, 88, 93, 95–96, 119, 255n81; on indigenous populations, 53–54; intellectual influences on, 7–8, 19, 54–55, 89–90, 117; on mestizaje in Latin American society, 15; on public education, 43, 46–47, 93, 97–98, 116–17; racialized modernization projects of, 64, 117–18; *Recuerdos de provincia,* 100–101; rivalry with Alberdi, 238n25; *Viajes por Europa, África y América,* 10, 55–56, 59, 85–86, 89; whitening policies exposed by, 48. *See also* Argentine normal schools; *Facundo*
school city model, 21–22, 195–96

"Sección cubana" (*Normal Review*), 22, 177, 198, 201–2
Seigel, Micol, 208
self-strengthening, 115, 118, 119, 121
settler colonialism, 8, 63, 67, 71, 146, 220
Sheehan, Susan, 212–14, 217
Shukla, Sandhya, 12
Silvestre de Feliu, Aurora, 191
slaves and slavery: child-rearing by, 37–39; critiques of, 76, 85–86, 138, 155; economic importance of, 51; free-born children of, 187, 193; kinship structures of, 34–37; marriage among, 35–37; psychological violence of, 219; purchase of freedom for, 33; republican motherhood and, 34–35, 40–41; trade in, 34, 77, 126, 128, 138. *See also* abolition of slavery; Afro-descended populations; antislavery texts
Small, Samuel, 190
Smith, Henry Nash, 11
Sofía (Morúa Delgado): as counterdiscourse to *Cecilia Valdés*, 164, 166; creoles criticized in, 169–70; incest in, 165–68; interracial relationships in, 20, 122, 124, 166–68; lack of scholarly recognition for, 21; miscarriage as metaphor in, 125, 166, 170, 175; national family allegory in, 162, 166; tragic mulatta trope in, 167–68
soft imperialism, 1, 10, 88, 197
Sommer, Doris, 28, 40, 133–35, 165, 230–31n7
Son of the Forrest, A (Apes), 62
Southern Cone: Afro-descendants in, 51; education reform in, 116; federative system of, 216; foreign investment in, 115; imperialism and, 8, 10, 66, 114; North American teachers in, 89; Spanish conquest of, 66, 72; Western civilization in, 82–84. *See also* Argentina
Spanish colonialism: critiques of, 126, 159–62, 183; education during, 186, 269n47; familial language in efforts to break from, 8, 191; immorality of, 128–29, 192; initiation of in Argentina, 49; mestizaje as legacy of, 11, 65, 84; as patriarchal system, 133, 134, 176, 199, 203; positive portrayals of, 65, 84
Spanish-Cuban-American War (1898), 20–21, 122–23, 174

Spillers, Hortense, 34
spiritual motherhood, 143
Stearns, John, 4
Stella (Bergeaud), 18, 39–42, 215
Stewart, Martha, 211, 272n3
Stoner, K. Lynn, 136
Storni, María Angela, 192–93
Stowe, Harriet Beecher, 216–17
Suárez, Francisco, 25
Suárez y Romero, Anselmo, 128, 150, 167, 203
suffrage. *See* voting rights

Taft, William H., 157, 270n53
Tanco y Bosmeniel, Félix M., 128, 150, 167, 203
Taylor, Linda, 211
teacher-mothers: bourgeois republican, 206; emergence of, 4–7, 32, 100, 176; at freedmen's schools, 7, 8, 19, 45–47, 88; race and, 7, 9, 193, 207; recruitment and development of, 95, 198
teachers: compensation for, 226n21; feminization of, 5–7, 198, 225n16, 226n21; at New Paltz Normal School, 176, 196–98, 206; in patriarchal systems, 4–5; student–teacher ratios, 93–94; women of color as, 45–46, 182–83, 193, 209. *See also* education; normal schools; North American teachers; teacher-mothers
Tejera, Diego Vicente, 191–92
Tinsman, Heidi, 12
Tocqueville, Alexis de, 27, 58, 59
Tosso, Raúl Alberto, 249n24
Totem and Taboo (Freud), 134
tragic mulatta trope, 150, 151, 167–68
transnational mobilization model, 219
Travelling Bachelor, The; or, Notions of the Americans (Cooper), 59, 62, 238n19
Trueba, Antonio de, 30
Truth, Sojourner, 34, 36
Turner, Frederick Jackson, 55–56
Tuskegee Institute, 46, 269n46

Uncle Tom's Cabin (Stowe), 216–17
Unitarios: Afro-descendants as viewed by, 77–78; conflict with Federales, 49, 52–53, 95, 98; education reform by, 91–92; sectors of support for, 51–52

United States: child-rearing practices in, 38; citizenship rights in, 62, 178; Civil War in, 1, 8, 19, 45–47, 95–96, 146; courtship rituals in, 58–59; discursive assimilation of Cuba to, 151–52; expansionism of, 55, 119; exploitation of Global South by, 118; feminization of teachers in, 5, 225n16; freedmen's schools in, 7, 8, 19, 45–47, 88; Good Neighbor Policy, 88, 103, 110, 114; imperial entanglements of education, 7–9, 177, 220–21; Jacksonian Democracy in, 56, 61, 215; as model for Argentine nation-state, 55, 56; new traditionalist movement in, 211–12; normal schools in, 103, 255n80; occupation of Cuba (1898–1902), 8, 127–28, 175, 180–84, 253n62; public education in, viii–ix, 44–46, 91, 248n13; republican motherhood in, 29–30, 32–34; as threat to Latin American sovereignty, 119; voting rights in, 56; welfare mothers in, 210–14
Ureña, Pedro Henríquez, 11
Urquiza, José Justo, 216

Varona, Enrique José, 184, 192
Vasconcelos, José, 15, 54, 207
Vera, Raúl Ianes, 60
Vergara, C. N., 113
Viajes por Europa, África y América (Sarmiento), 10, 55–56, 59, 85–86, 89
Villaverde, Cirilo: annexation, views on, 139, 149; exile from Cuba, 125, 145, 152, 176; familial language used by, 8; revolutionary activities of, 125, 138, 139; slavery, views on, 139–40, 259n37; wife of, 131, 138–40, 147–49. See also *Cecilia Valdés*
"¡Viva la Patria!" (Peña), 79
voting rights, 29, 56, 137, 162, 187–89

Wade, Peter, 203, 232–33n30
Washington, Booker T., 46, 269n46

Weber, Max, 202
welfare mothers, 210–14
whiteness: of bourgeois republicanism, 215–16; in *Cecilia Valdés*, 141; of creole populations, 14, 190; cultural traits associated with, 15; in *Lucía Miranda*, 83, 87; of New Paltz students, 204; in patriarchal systems, 178; possessive investment in, 60–64, 240n39; racial classification and, 76, 81, 264n93; republican motherhood and, 142; in *Sofía*, 168–69
whitening of populations: education in, 99, 120, 121, 194–95; genocide in, 49, 119; immigration as method of, 57–58, 120, 128; *Lucía Miranda* as critique of, 19, 48, 68, 70, 78; mestizaje in, 15, 208, 209; in modernizing projects, 49, 207; national family allegory and, 20, 89
Wilde, Eduardo, 4, 114, 120
women: in cult of domesticity, 5, 33, 101, 262n63; education for, 30–32, 101, 192–93, 231n16, 232n21; New Woman paradigm, 22, 177, 205; voting right restrictions on, 29. See also motherhood; republican motherhood; teacher-mothers; women of color
women of color: child-rearing by, 37–39, 208; national family allegory and, 32, 33, 157; republican motherhood and, 33–35, 40–42, 78, 142, 192, 213; stereotypes regarding, 33, 210, 211; sterilization among, 212; as teachers, 45–46, 182–83, 193, 209; welfare mothers and, 210–14; white men's monopoly over, 135. See also Afro-descended populations
Wood, Leonard, 180–81, 186, 188, 189, 195–96

Zapata Olivella, Manuel, 219–20
Zea, Leopoldo, 15
Zubiar, J. B., 6

RECENT BOOKS IN THE SERIES
New World Studies

The Quebec Connection: A Poetics of Solidarity in Global Francophone Literatures
Julie-Françoise Tolliver

Comrade Sister: Caribbean Feminist Revisions of the Grenada Revolution
Laurie R. Lambert

Cultural Entanglements: Langston Hughes and the Rise of African and Caribbean Literature
Shane Graham

Water Graves: The Art of the Unritual in the Greater Caribbean
Valérie Loichot

The Sacred Act of Reading: Spirituality, Performance, and Power in Afro-Diasporic Literature
Anne Margaret Castro

Caribbean Jewish Crossings: Literary History and Creative Practice
Sarah Phillips Casteel and Heidi Kaufman, editors

Mapping Hispaniola: Third Space in Dominican and Haitian Literature
Megan Jeanette Myers

Mourning El Dorado: Literature and Extractivism in the Contemporary American Tropics
Charlotte Rogers

Edwidge Danticat: The Haitian Diasporic Imaginary
Nadège T. Clitandre

Idle Talk, Deadly Talk: The Uses of Gossip in Caribbean Literature
Ana Rodríguez Navas

Crossing the Line: Early Creole Novels and Anglophone Caribbean Culture in the Age of Emancipation
Candace Ward

Staging Creolization: Women's Theater and Performance from the French Caribbean
Emily Sahakian

www.ingramcontent.com/pod-product-compliance
Lightning Source LLC
Chambersburg PA
CBHW021342300426
44114CB00012B/1052